Wild Ones
アラクレ

Vol. 1

Story & Art by
Kiyo Fujiwara

AH.

Wild Ones
アラクレ

Volume 1

CONTENTS

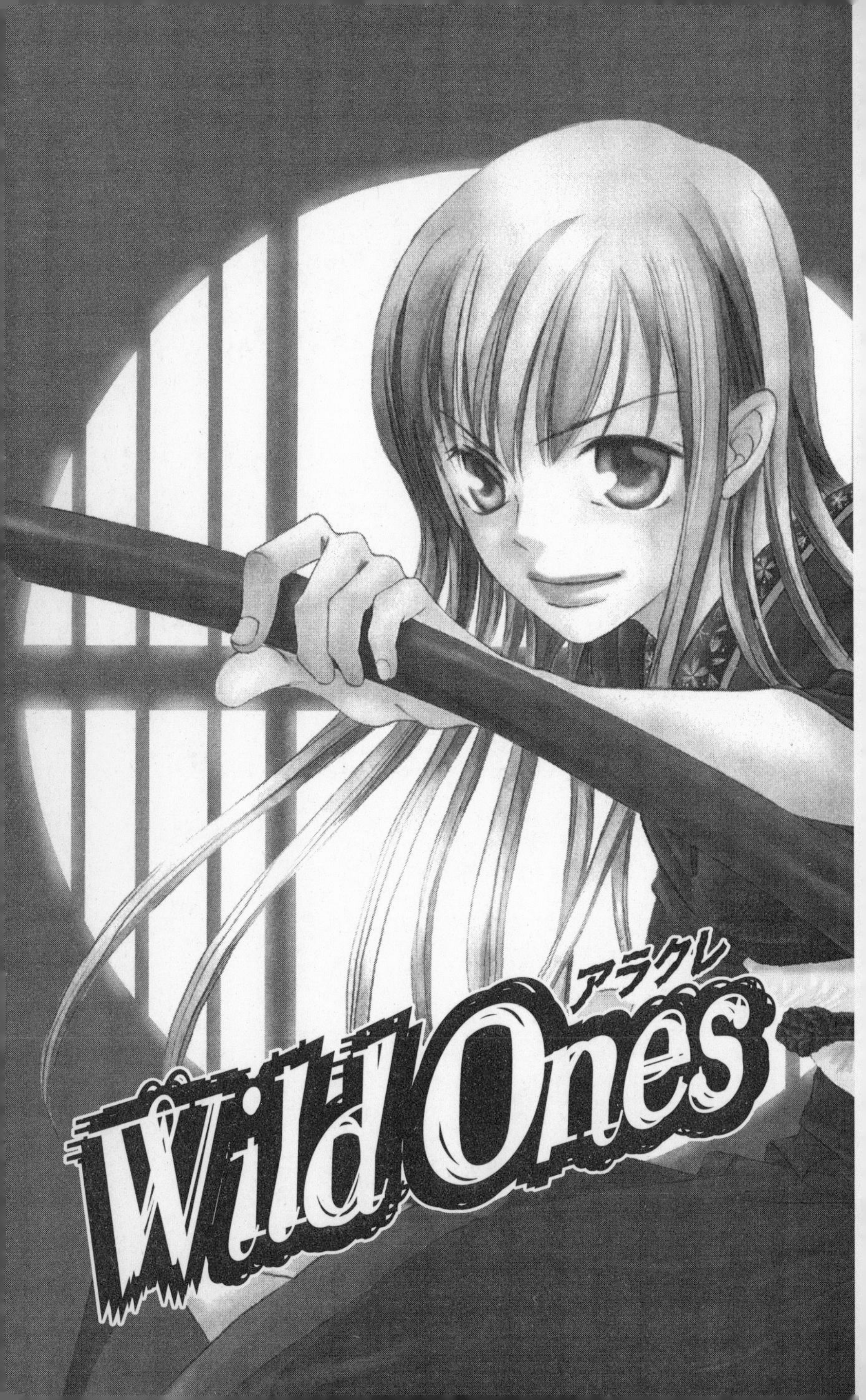
アラクレ
Wild Ones

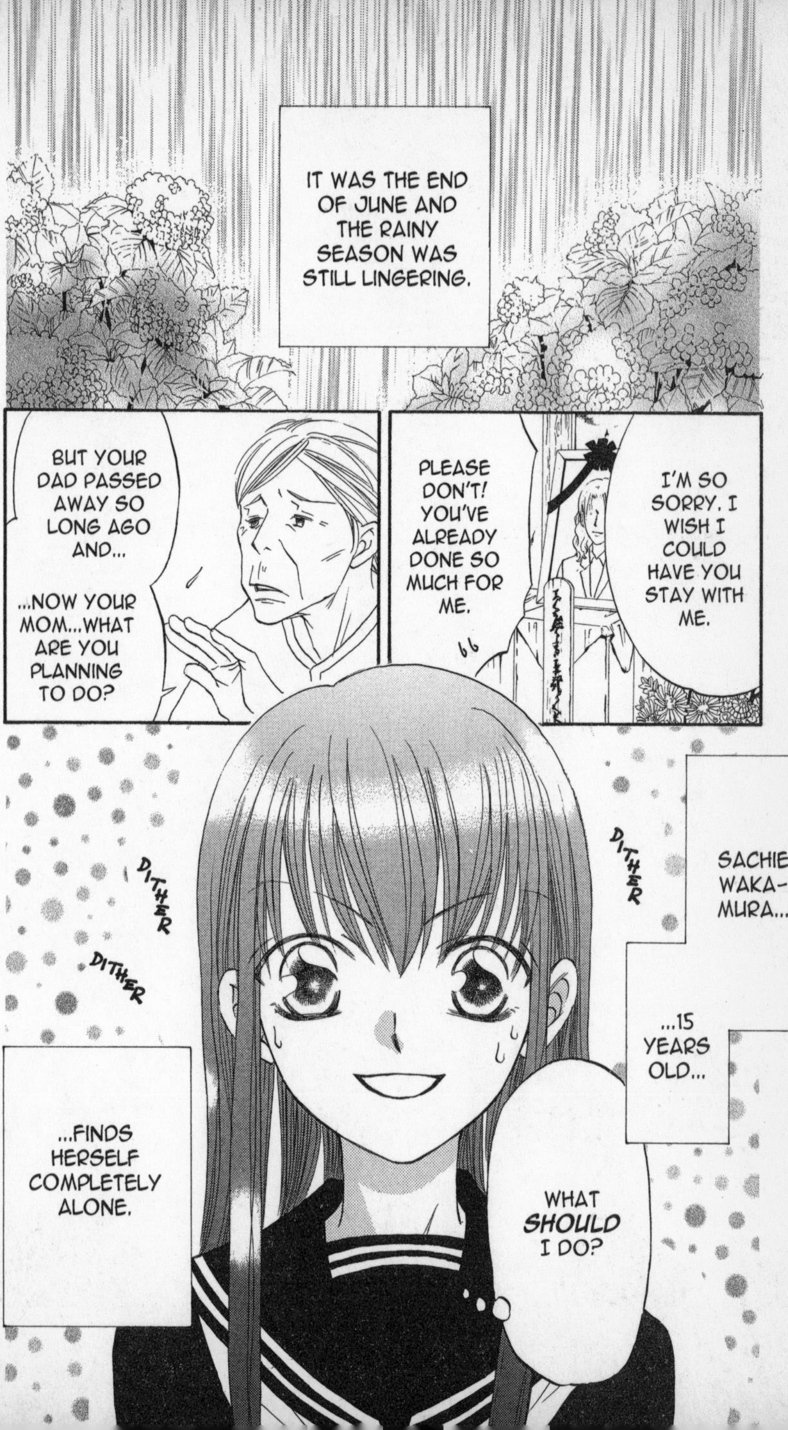

IT WAS THE END OF JUNE AND THE RAINY SEASON WAS STILL LINGERING.
I'M SO SORRY. I WISH I COULD HAVE YOU STAY WITH ME.
PLEASE DON'T! YOU'VE ALREADY DONE SO MUCH FOR ME.
BUT YOUR DAD PASSED AWAY SO LONG AGO AND...
...NOW YOUR MOM...WHAT ARE YOU PLANNING TO DO?
SACHIE WAKA-MURA...
DITHER
DITHER
DITHER
...15 YEARS OLD...
WHAT SHOULD I DO?
...FINDS HERSELF COMPLETELY ALONE.

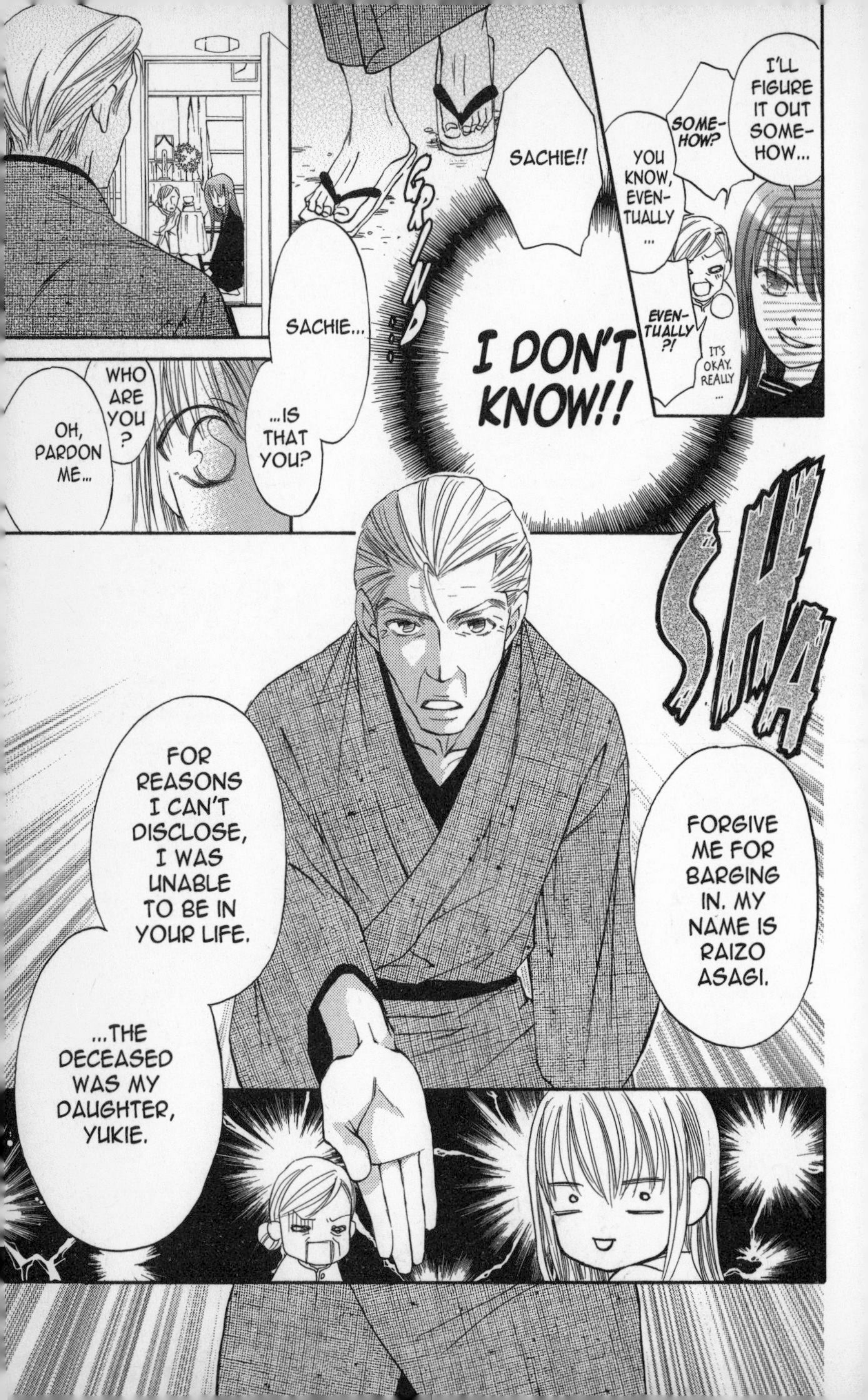
I'LL FIGURE IT OUT SOME-HOW...
SOME-HOW?
YOU KNOW, EVEN-TUALLY...
EVEN-TUALLY?!
IT'S OKAY. REALLY...
I DON'T KNOW!!
SACHIE!!
GRIND
SACHIE...
...IS THAT YOU?
WHO ARE YOU?
OH, PARDON ME...
SHA
FORGIVE ME FOR BARGING IN. MY NAME IS RAIZO ASAGI.
FOR REASONS I CAN'T DISCLOSE, I WAS UNABLE TO BE IN YOUR LIFE.
...THE DECEASED WAS MY DAUGHTER, YUKIE.

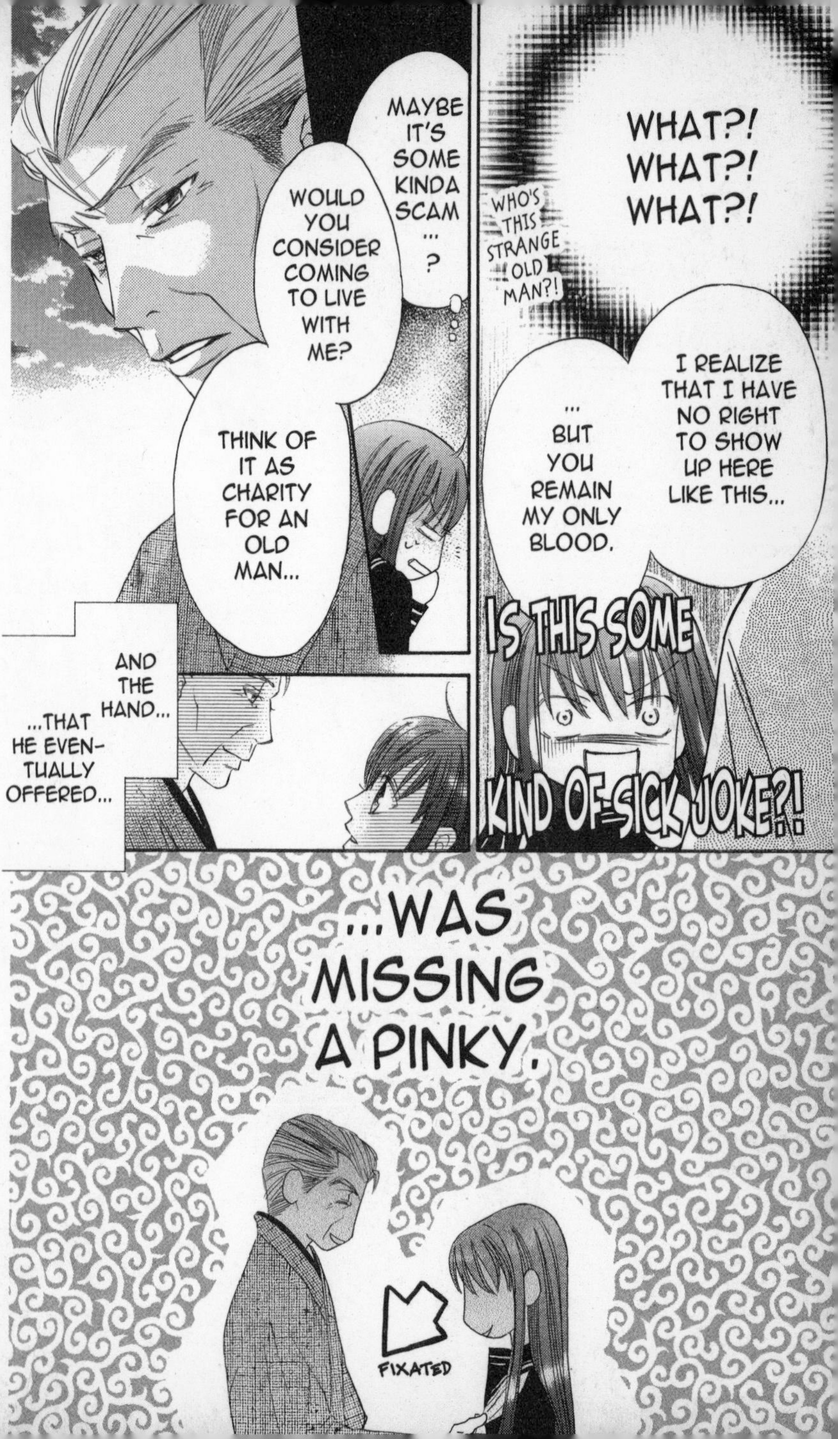
WHAT?! WHAT?! WHAT?!
WHO'S THIS STRANGE OLD MAN?!
I REALIZE THAT I HAVE NO RIGHT TO SHOW UP HERE LIKE THIS...
...BUT YOU REMAIN MY ONLY BLOOD.
IS THIS SOME KIND OF SICK JOKE?!
WOULD YOU CONSIDER COMING TO LIVE WITH ME?
MAYBE IT'S SOME KINDA SCAM...?
THINK OF IT AS CHARITY FOR AN OLD MAN...
AND THE HAND...
...THAT HE EVENTUALLY OFFERED...
...WAS MISSING A PINKY.
FIXATED

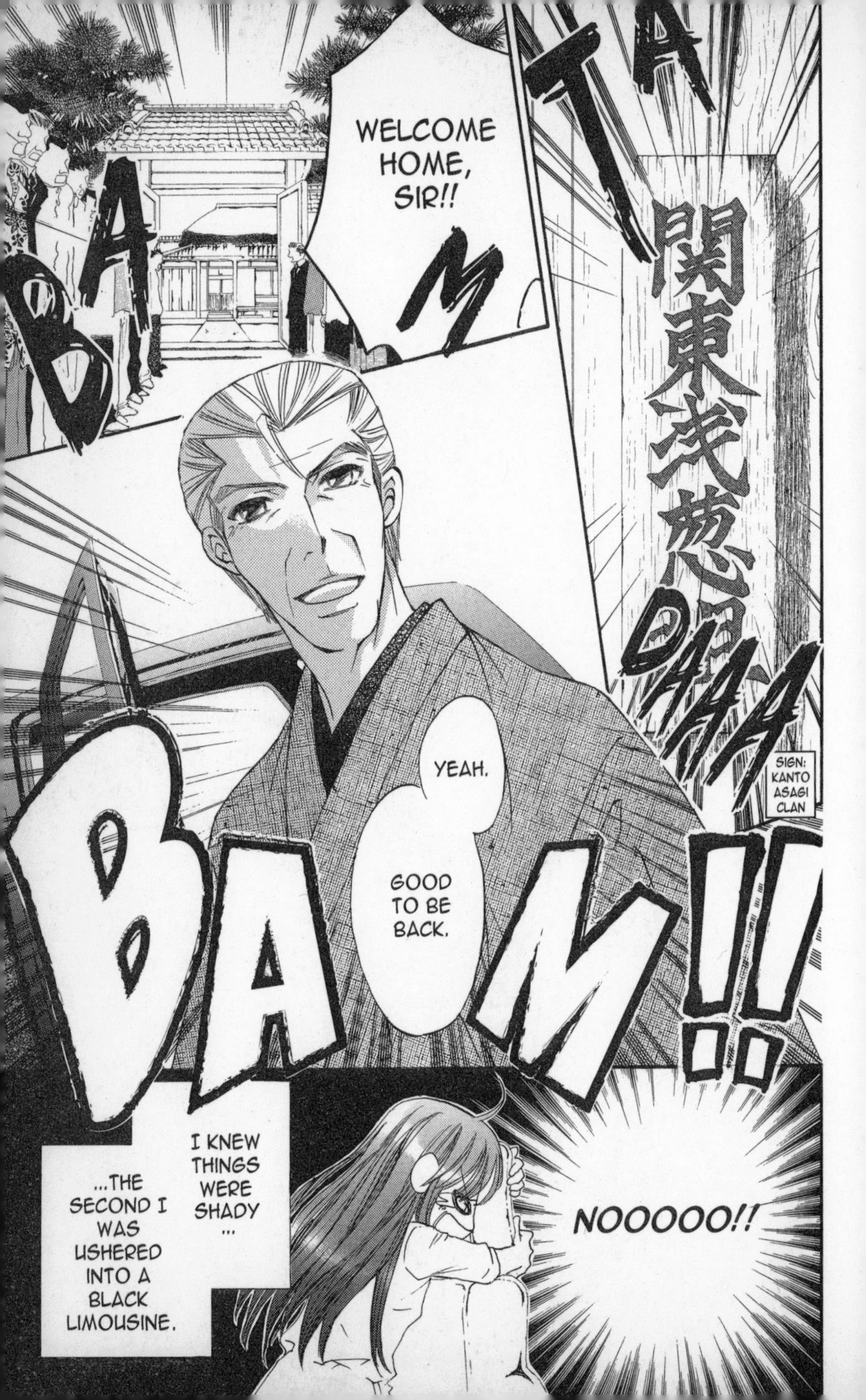
SIGN: KANTO ASAGI CLAN
WELCOME HOME, SIR!!
YEAH.
GOOD TO BE BACK.
BAM!!
NOOOOO!!
I KNEW THINGS WERE SHADY ...
...THE SECOND I WAS USHERED INTO A BLACK LIMOUSINE.

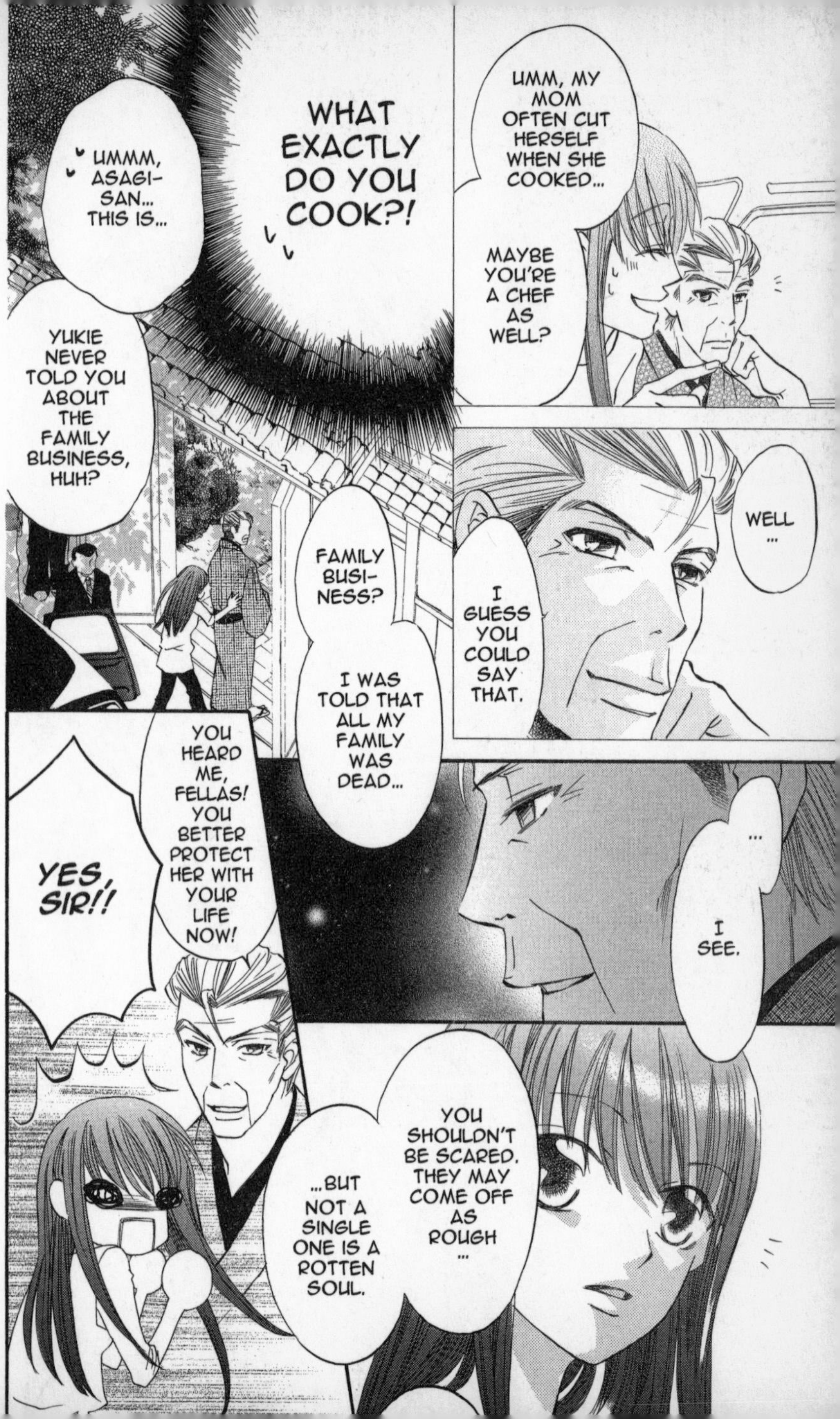

UMM, MY MOM OFTEN CUT HERSELF WHEN SHE COOKED...
MAYBE YOU'RE A CHEF AS WELL?
WELL...
I GUESS YOU COULD SAY THAT.
WHAT EXACTLY DO YOU COOK?!
UMMM, ASAGI-SAN... THIS IS...
YUKIE NEVER TOLD YOU ABOUT THE FAMILY BUSINESS, HUH?
FAMILY BUSINESS?
I WAS TOLD THAT ALL MY FAMILY WAS DEAD...
...
I SEE.
YOU HEARD ME, FELLAS! YOU BETTER PROTECT HER WITH YOUR LIFE NOW!
YES, SIR!!
YOU SHOULDN'T BE SCARED. THEY MAY COME OFF AS ROUGH...
...BUT NOT A SINGLE ONE IS A ROTTEN SOUL.

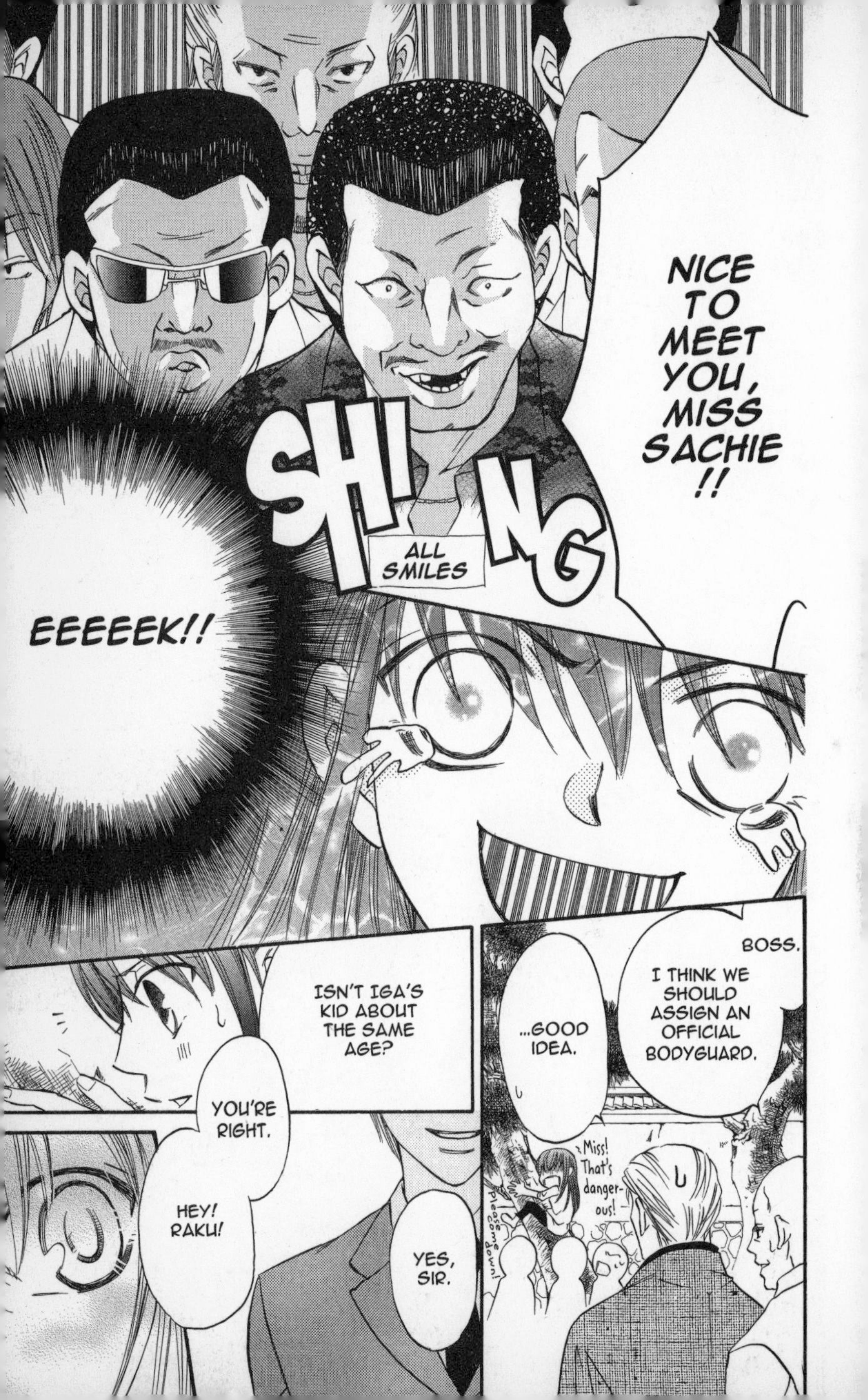
NICE TO MEET YOU, MISS SACHIE!!
SHING
ALL SMILES
EEEEEK!!
BOSS.
I THINK WE SHOULD ASSIGN AN OFFICIAL BODYGUARD.
...GOOD IDEA.
Miss! That's danger-ous!
Please come down!
ISN'T IGA'S KID ABOUT THE SAME AGE?
YOU'RE RIGHT.
HEY! RAKU!
YES, SIR.

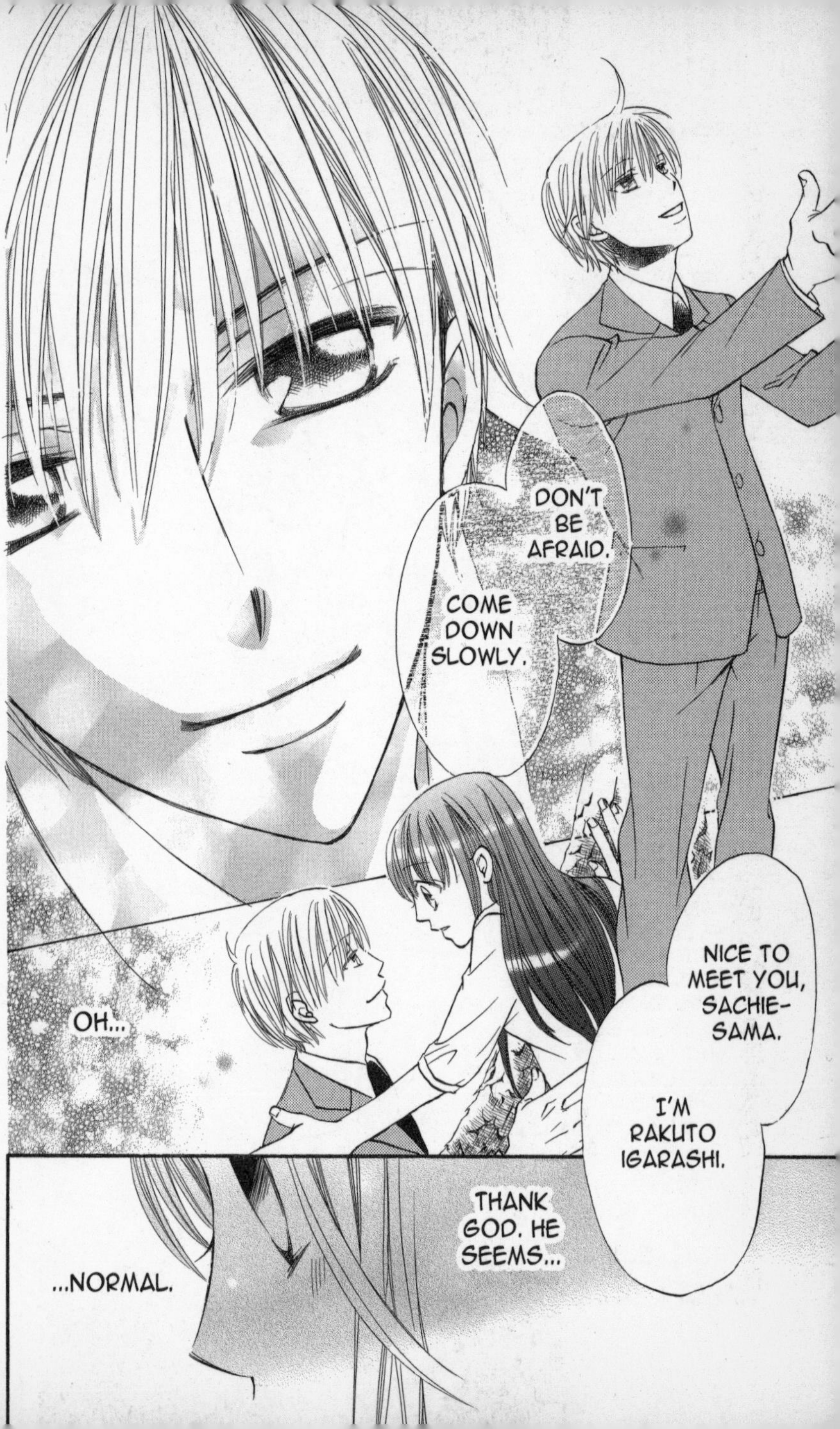
DON'T BE AFRAID.
COME DOWN SLOWLY.
NICE TO MEET YOU, SACHIE-SAMA.
I'M RAKUTO IGARASHI.
OH...
THANK GOD. HE SEEMS...
...NORMAL.

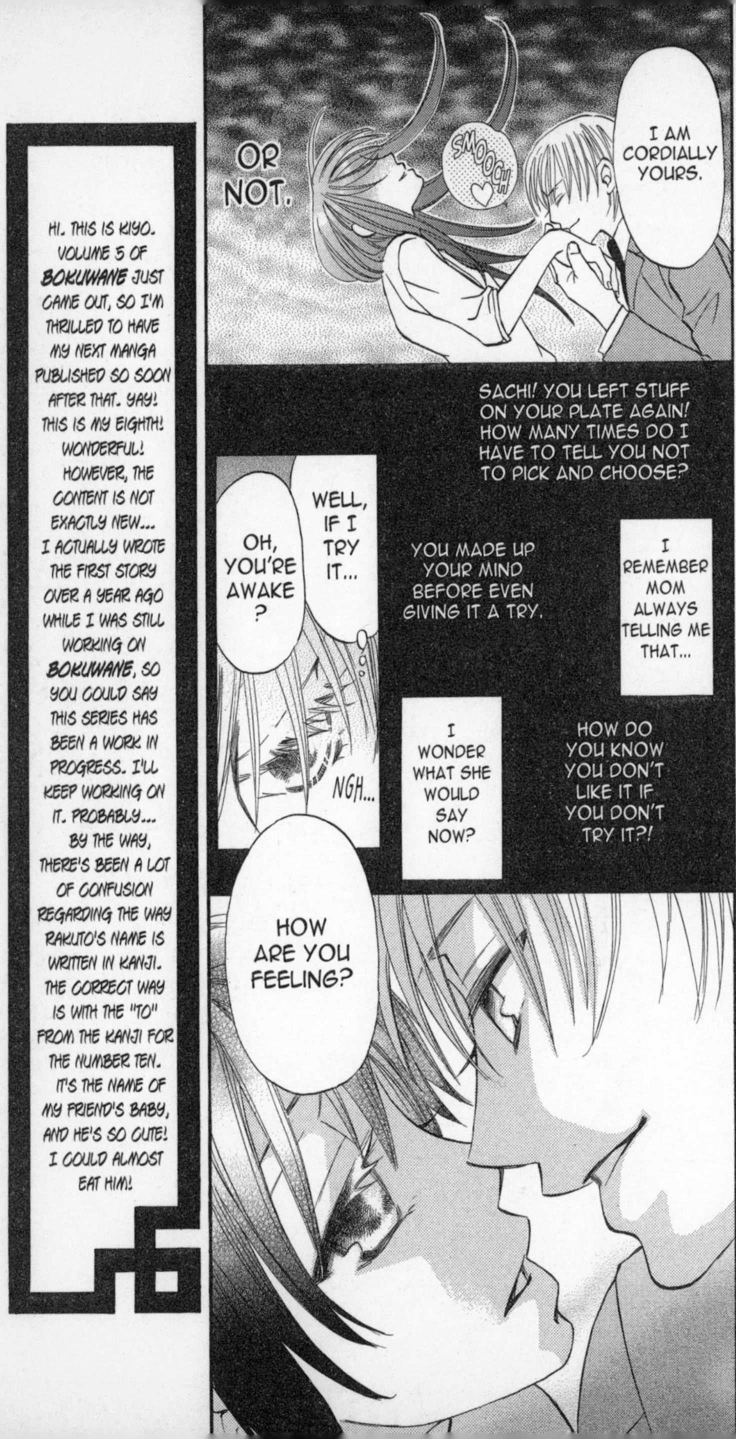
I AM CORDIALLY YOURS.
SMOOCH
OR NOT.
SACHI! YOU LEFT STUFF ON YOUR PLATE AGAIN! HOW MANY TIMES DO I HAVE TO TELL YOU NOT TO PICK AND CHOOSE?
I REMEMBER MOM ALWAYS TELLING ME THAT...
YOU MADE UP YOUR MIND BEFORE EVEN GIVING IT A TRY.
HOW DO YOU KNOW YOU DON'T LIKE IT IF YOU DON'T TRY IT?!
I WONDER WHAT SHE WOULD SAY NOW?
WELL, IF I TRY IT...
OH, YOU'RE AWAKE?
NGH...
HOW ARE YOU FEELING?

HI. THIS IS KIYO. VOLUME 5 OF ***BOKUWANE*** JUST CAME OUT, SO I'M THRILLED TO HAVE MY NEXT MANGA PUBLISHED SO SOON AFTER THAT. YAY! THIS IS MY EIGHTH! WONDERFUL!

HOWEVER, THE CONTENT IS NOT EXACTLY NEW... I ACTUALLY WROTE THE FIRST STORY OVER A YEAR AGO WHILE I WAS STILL WORKING ON ***BOKUWANE***, SO YOU COULD SAY THIS SERIES HAS BEEN A WORK IN PROGRESS. I'LL KEEP WORKING ON IT. PROBABLY...

BY THE WAY, THERE'S BEEN A LOT OF CONFUSION REGARDING THE WAY RAKUTO'S NAME IS WRITTEN IN KANJI. THE CORRECT WAY IS WITH THE "TO" FROM THE KANJI FOR THE NUMBER TEN.

IT'S THE NAME OF MY FRIEND'S BABY, AND HE'S SO CUTE! I COULD ALMOST EAT HIM!

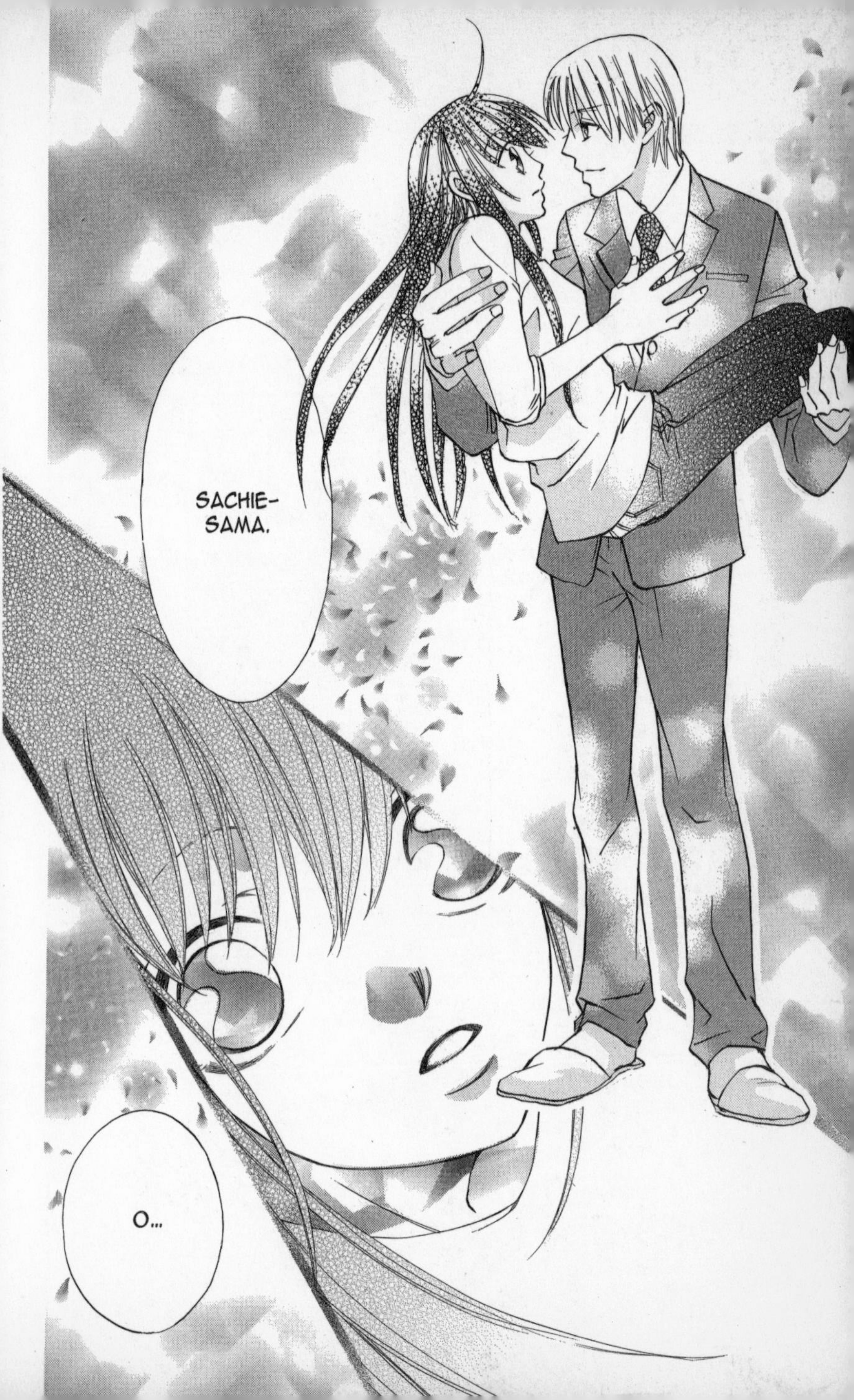
SACHIE-SAMA.
O...

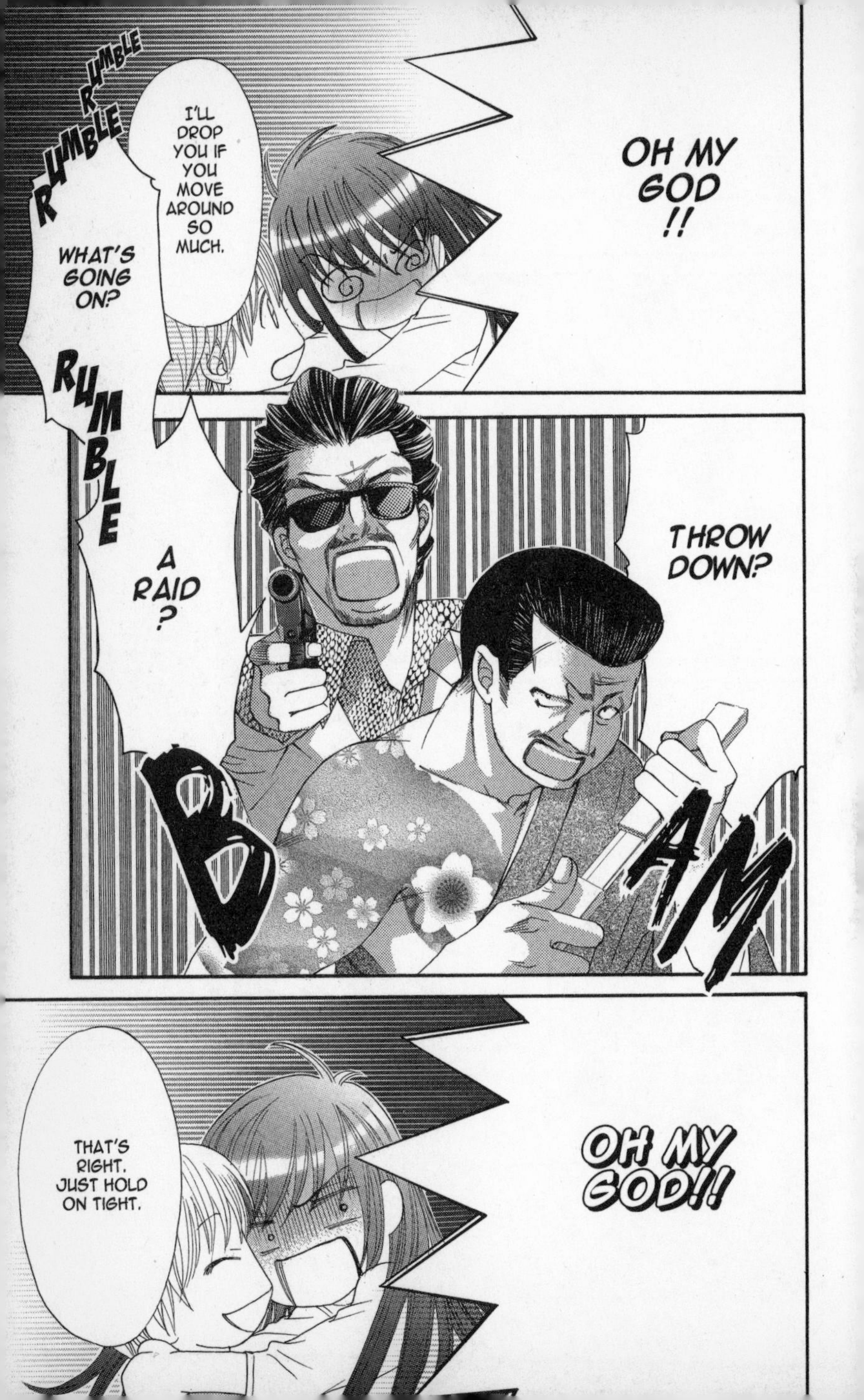
OH MY GOD !!
I'LL DROP YOU IF YOU MOVE AROUND SO MUCH.
RUMBLE RUMBLE
WHAT'S GOING ON?
RUMBLE
THROW DOWN?
A RAID ?
BAM
OH MY GOD!!
THAT'S RIGHT. JUST HOLD ON TIGHT.

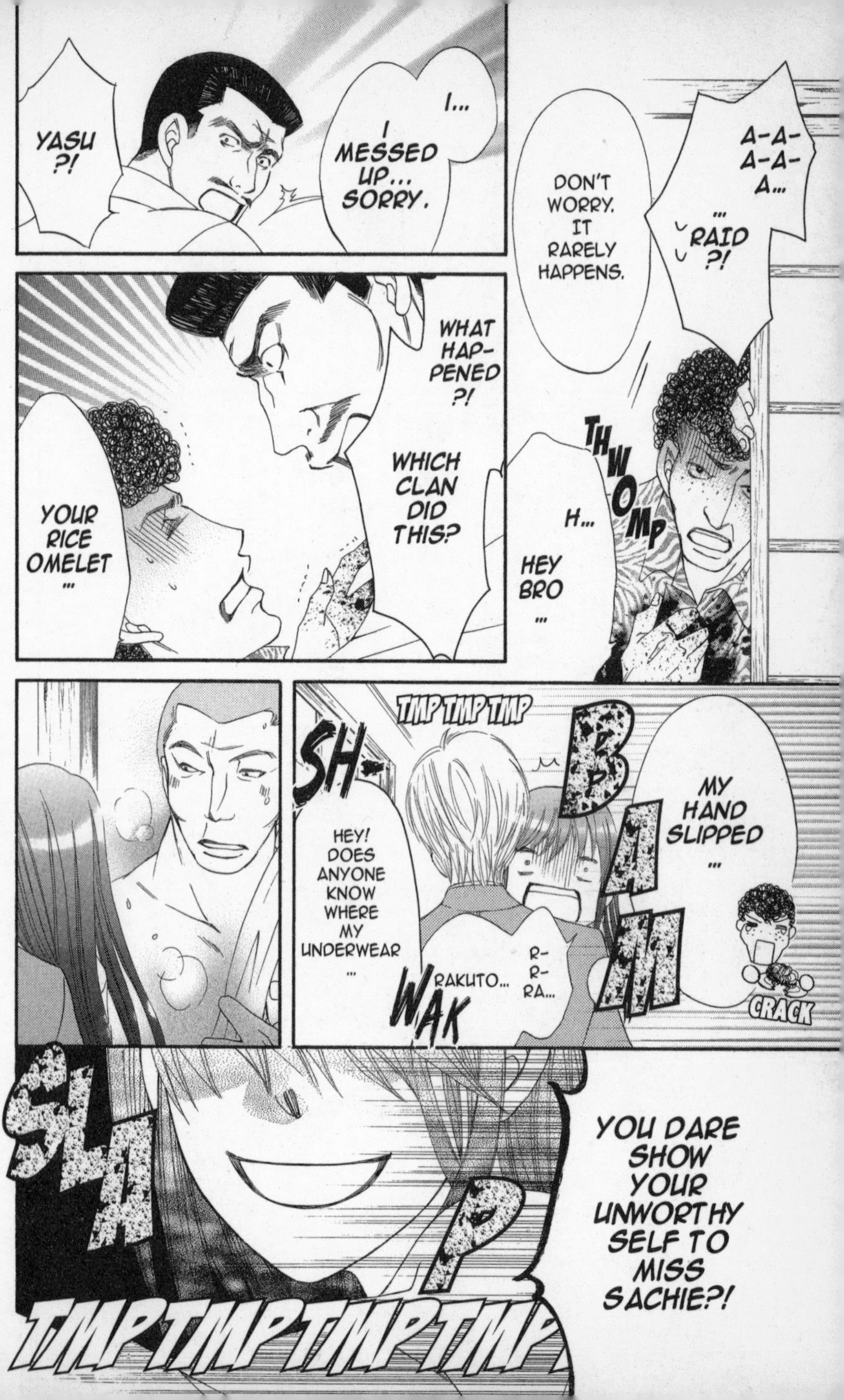
A-A-A-A-A...
... RAID ?!
DON'T WORRY. IT RARELY HAPPENS.
THWOMP
H... HEY BRO ...
I... I MESSED UP... SORRY.
YASU ?!
WHAT HAP-PENED ?!
WHICH CLAN DID THIS?
YOUR RICE OMELET ...
TMP TMP TMP
BAM
MY HAND SLIPPED ...
CRACK
SH-
HEY! DOES ANYONE KNOW WHERE MY UNDERWEAR ...
R-R-RA...
RAKUTO...
WAK
YOU DARE SHOW YOUR UNWORTHY SELF TO MISS SACHIE?!
SLAP
TMPTMPTMPTMP

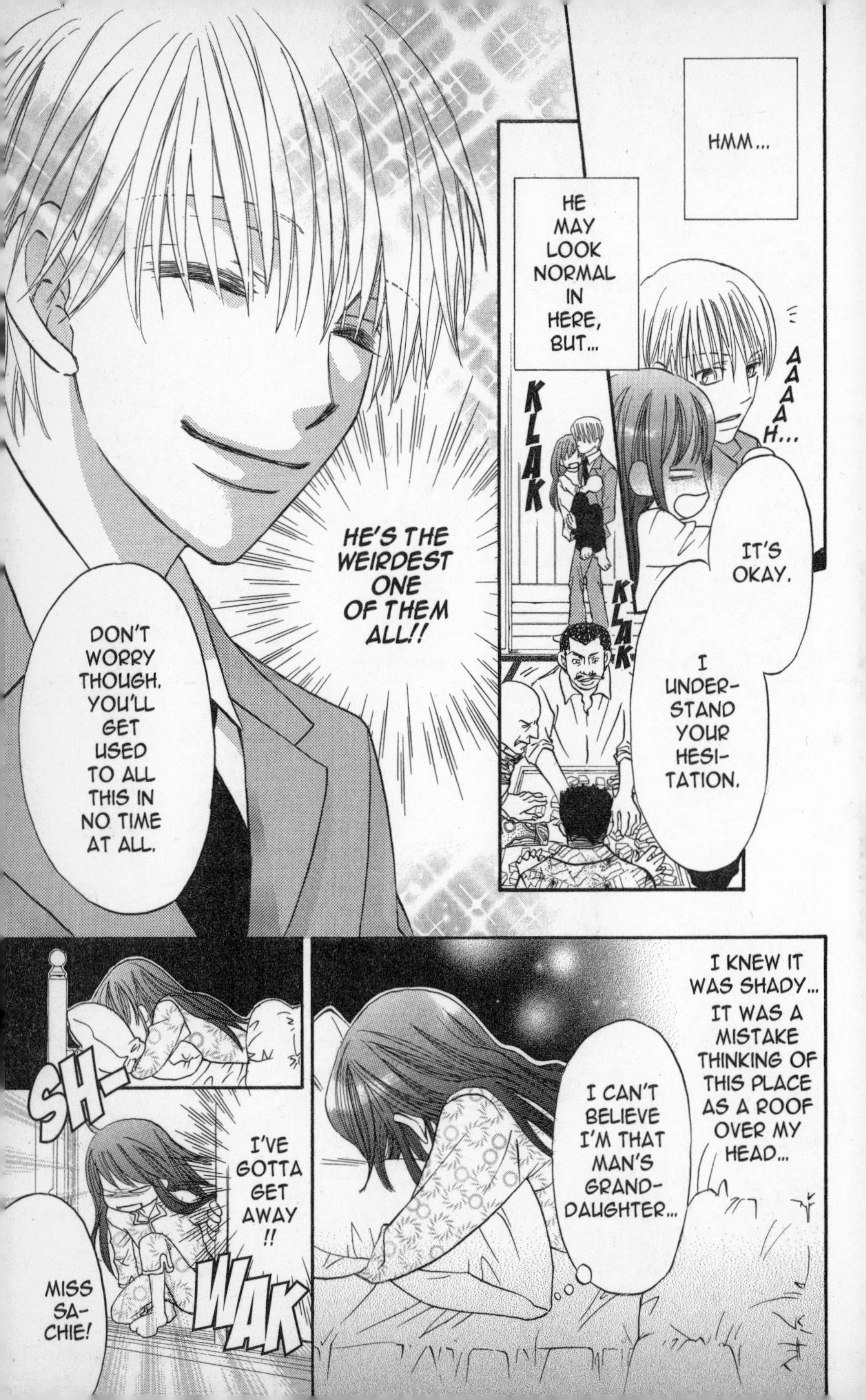
HMM...
HE MAY LOOK NORMAL IN HERE, BUT...
AAAAH...
IT'S OKAY.
I UNDERSTAND YOUR HESITATION.
KLAK
KLAK
HE'S THE WEIRDEST ONE OF THEM ALL!!
DON'T WORRY THOUGH. YOU'LL GET USED TO ALL THIS IN NO TIME AT ALL.
I KNEW IT WAS SHADY... IT WAS A MISTAKE THINKING OF THIS PLACE AS A ROOF OVER MY HEAD...
I CAN'T BELIEVE I'M THAT MAN'S GRAND-DAUGHTER...
SH-
I'VE GOTTA GET AWAY!!
MISS SA-CHIE!
WAK

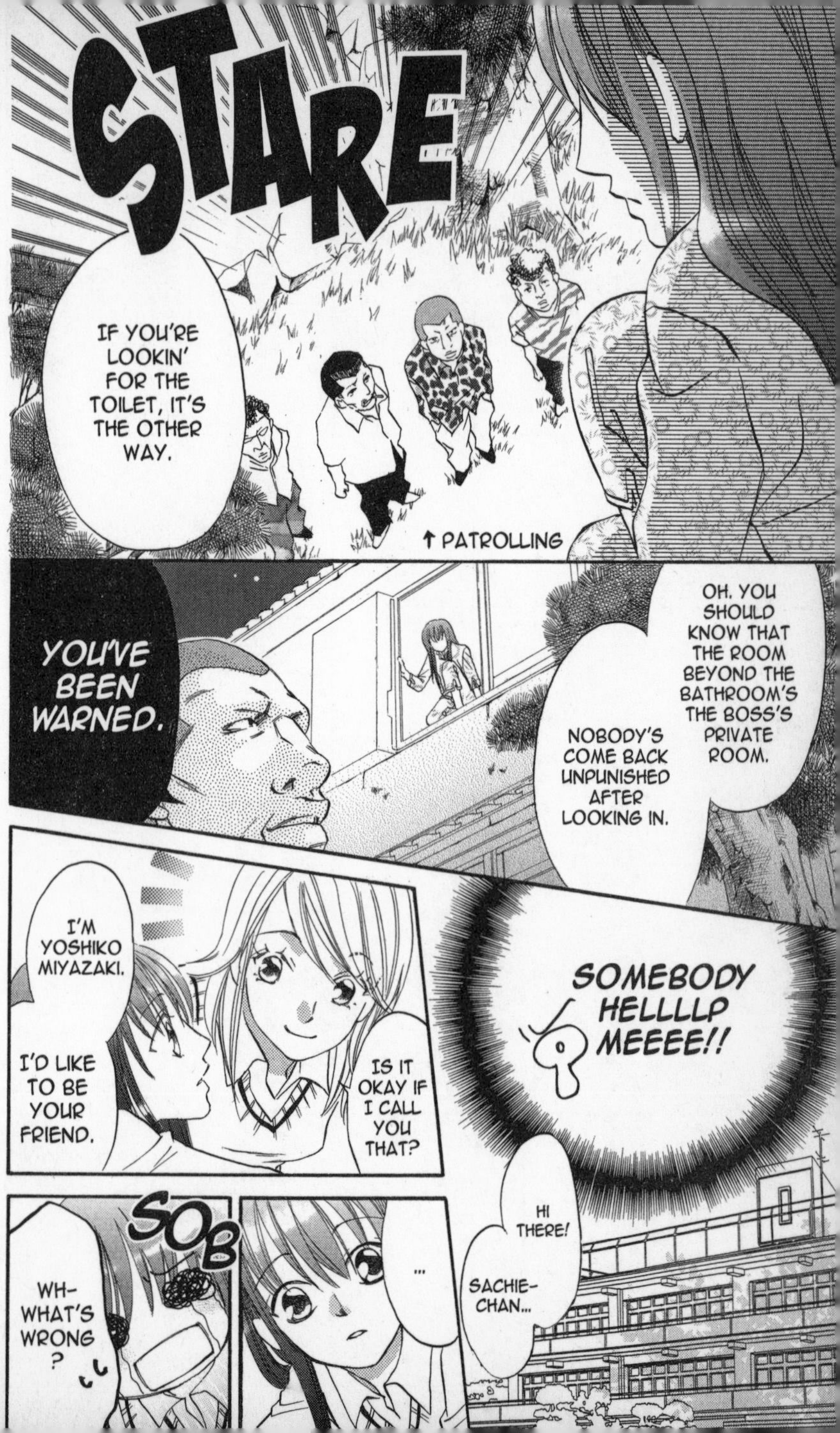
STARE
IF YOU'RE LOOKIN' FOR THE TOILET, IT'S THE OTHER WAY.
↑ PATROLLING
OH. YOU SHOULD KNOW THAT THE ROOM BEYOND THE BATHROOM'S THE BOSS'S PRIVATE ROOM.
NOBODY'S COME BACK UNPUNISHED AFTER LOOKING IN.
YOU'VE BEEN WARNED.
SOMEBODY HELLLLP MEEEE!!
HI THERE!
SACHIE-CHAN...
I'M YOSHIKO MIYAZAKI.
I'D LIKE TO BE YOUR FRIEND.
IS IT OKAY IF I CALL YOU THAT?
...
SOB
WH- WHAT'S WRONG ?

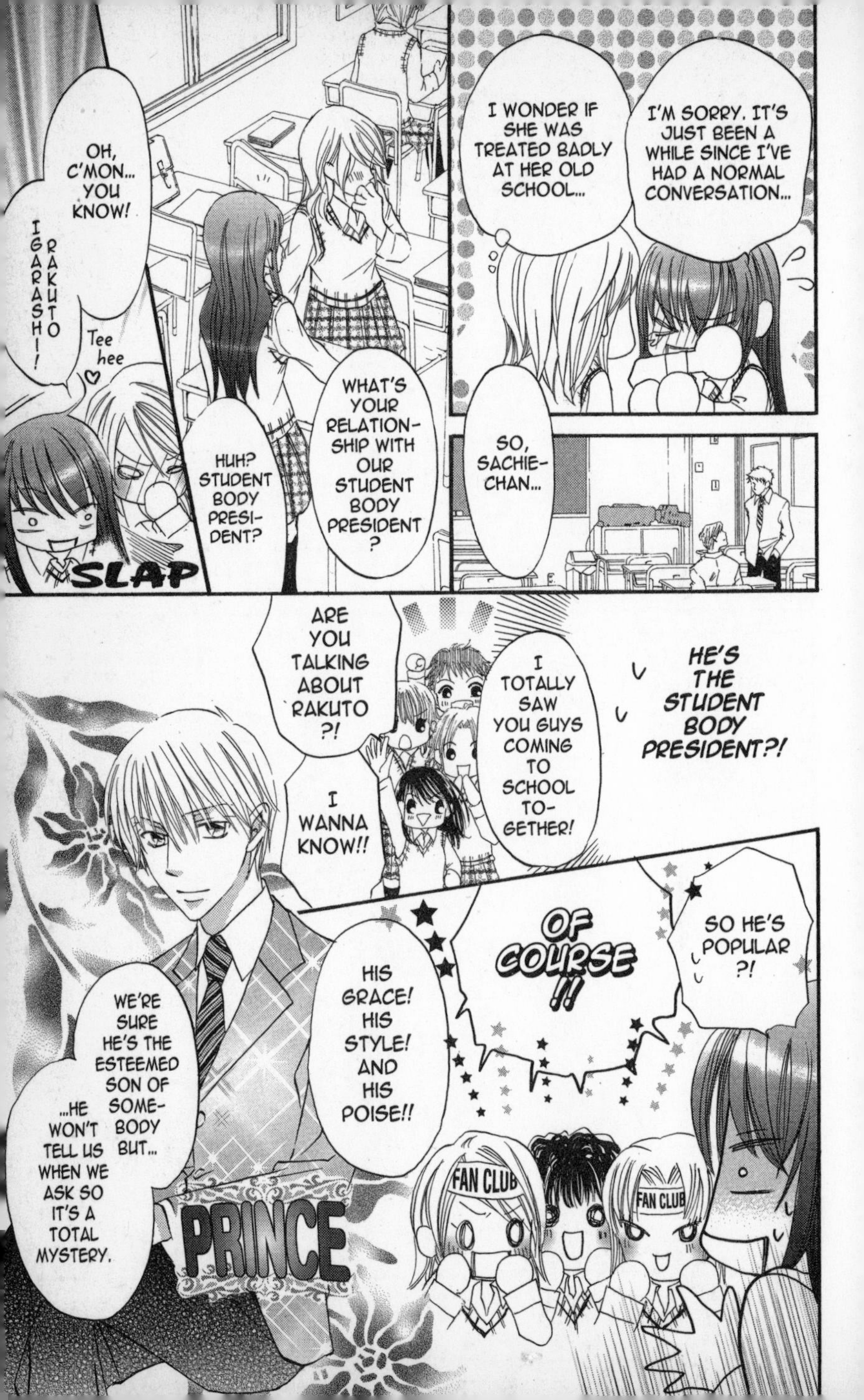
I'M SORRY. IT'S JUST BEEN A WHILE SINCE I'VE HAD A NORMAL CONVERSATION...
I WONDER IF SHE WAS TREATED BADLY AT HER OLD SCHOOL...
SO, SACHIE-CHAN...
WHAT'S YOUR RELATIONSHIP WITH OUR STUDENT BODY PRESIDENT?
HUH? STUDENT BODY PRESIDENT?
OH, C'MON... YOU KNOW!
RAKUTO IGARASHI!
Tee hee
SLAP
HE'S THE STUDENT BODY PRESIDENT?!
I TOTALLY SAW YOU GUYS COMING TO SCHOOL TO-GETHER!
ARE YOU TALKING ABOUT RAKUTO?!
I WANNA KNOW!!
SO HE'S POPULAR?!
OF COURSE!!
HIS GRACE! HIS STYLE! AND HIS POISE!!
WE'RE SURE HE'S THE ESTEEMED SON OF SOME-BODY BUT...
...HE WON'T TELL US WHEN WE ASK SO IT'S A TOTAL MYSTERY.
PRINCE
FAN CLUB
FAN CLUB

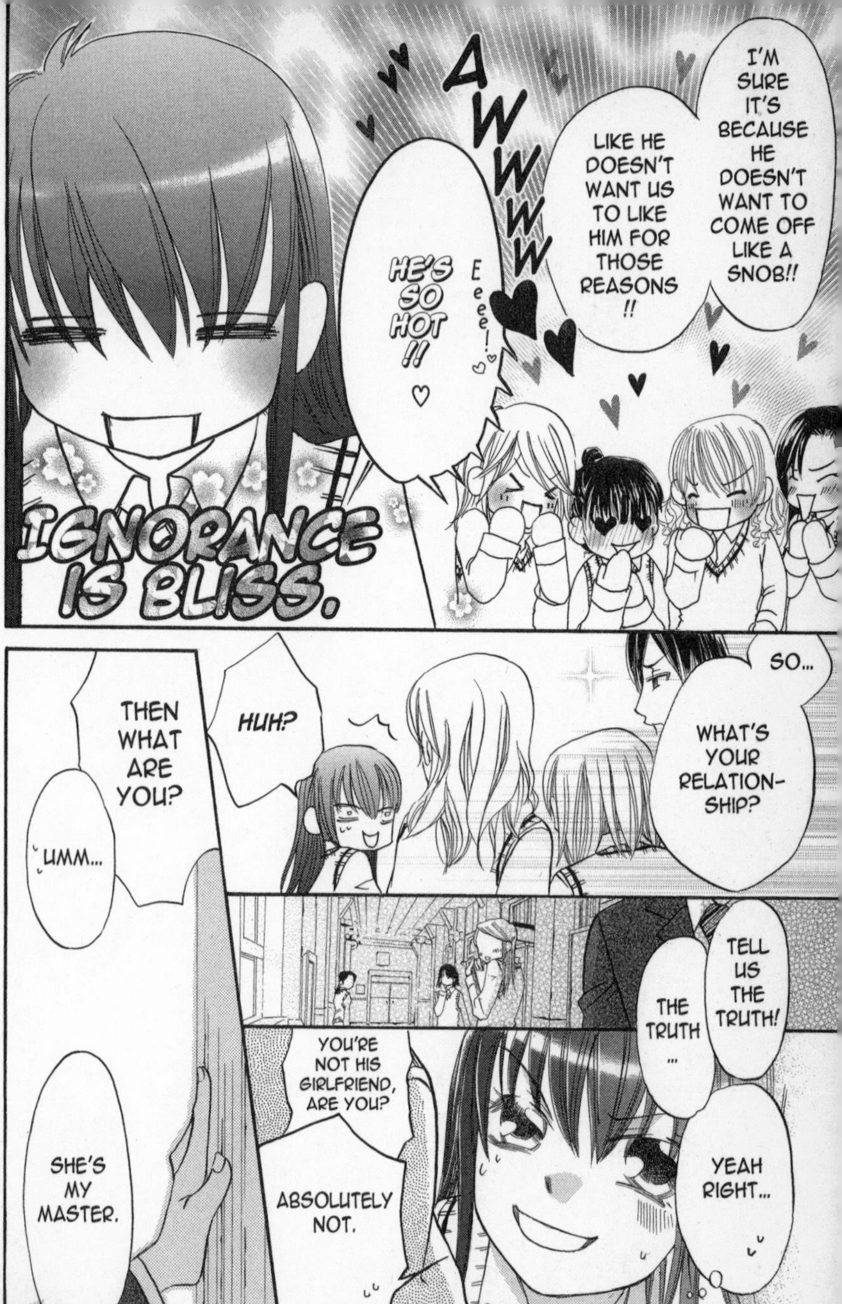
I'M SURE IT'S BECAUSE HE DOESN'T WANT TO COME OFF LIKE A SNOB!!
LIKE HE DOESN'T WANT US TO LIKE HIM FOR THOSE REASONS!!
AWWWWW
Eeee!
HE'S SO HOT!!
IGNORANCE IS BLISS.
SO...
WHAT'S YOUR RELATIONSHIP?
HUH?
TELL US THE TRUTH!
THE TRUTH...
YOU'RE NOT HIS GIRLFRIEND, ARE YOU?
ABSOLUTELY NOT.
YEAH RIGHT...
THEN WHAT ARE YOU?
UMM...
SHE'S MY MASTER.

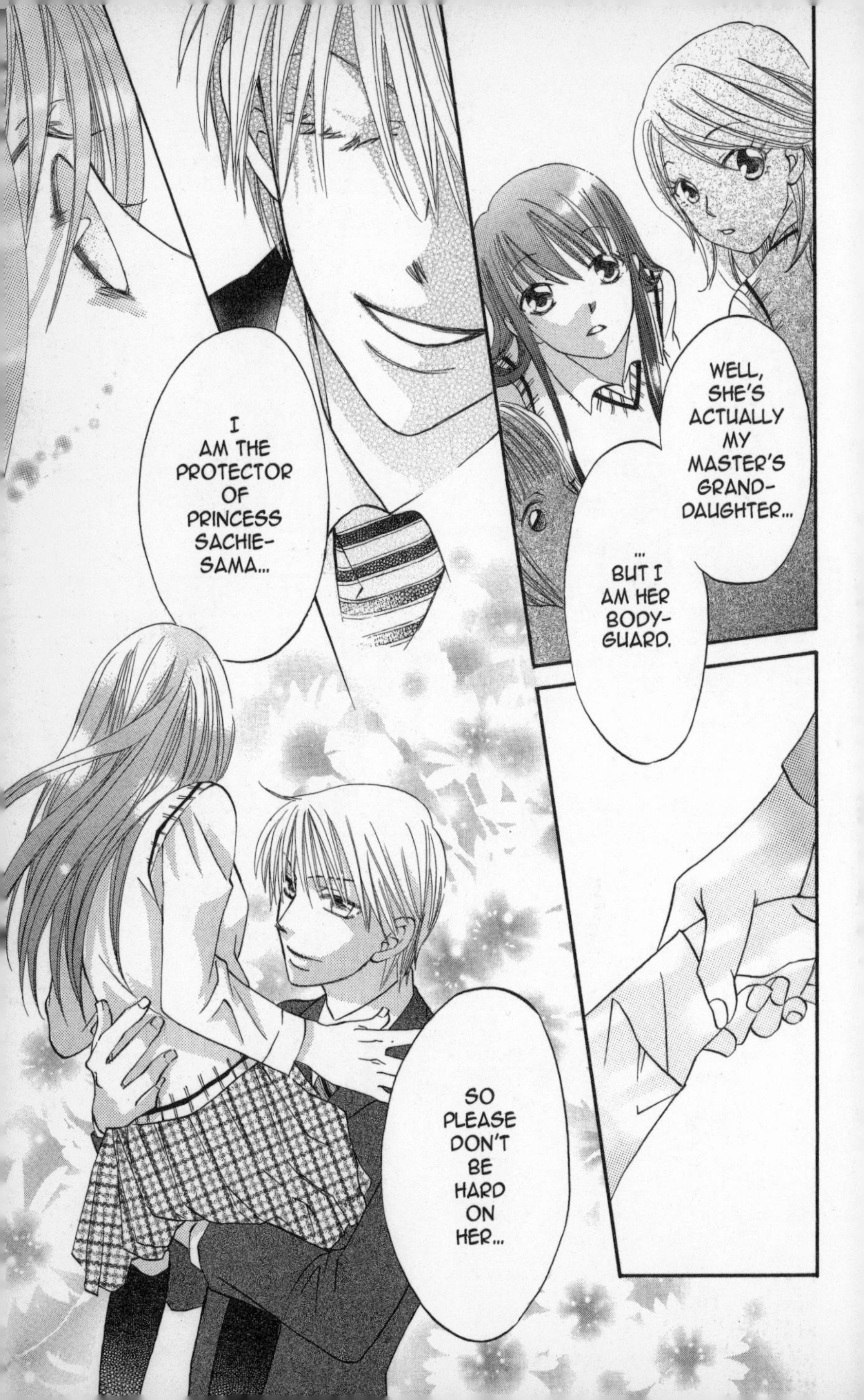
WELL, SHE'S ACTUALLY MY MASTER'S GRAND-DAUGHTER...
... BUT I AM HER BODY-GUARD.
I AM THE PROTECTOR OF PRINCESS SACHIE-SAMA...
SO PLEASE DON'T BE HARD ON HER...

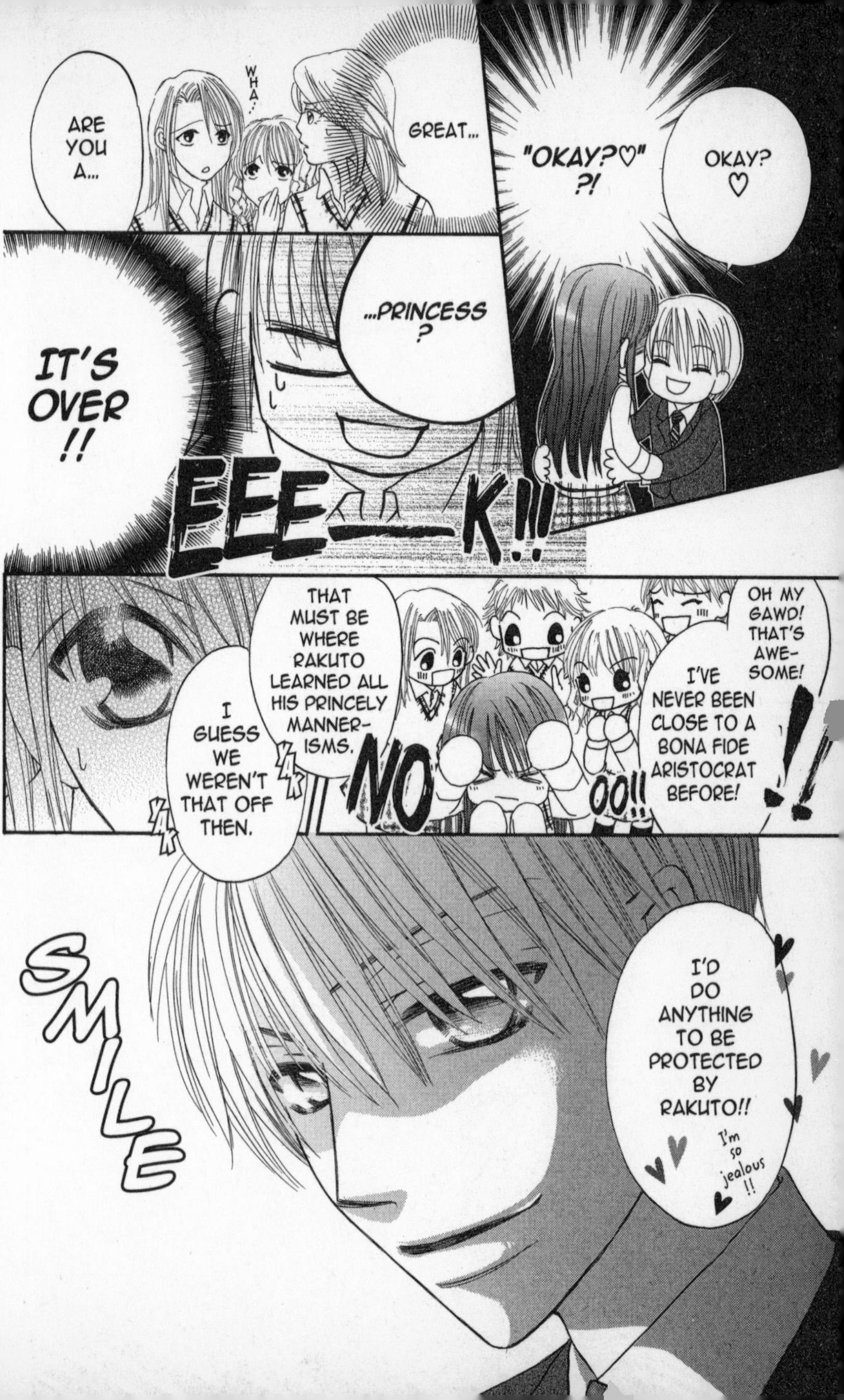
OKAY? ♡
"OKAY?♡" ?!
GREAT...
WHA...
ARE YOU A...
...PRINCESS?
IT'S OVER!!
EEE—K!!!
OH MY GAWD! THAT'S AWE-SOME!
I'VE NEVER BEEN CLOSE TO A BONA FIDE ARISTOCRAT BEFORE!
NO
OO!!
THAT MUST BE WHERE RAKUTO LEARNED ALL HIS PRINCELY MANNER-ISMS.
YAK
I GUESS WE WEREN'T THAT OFF THEN.
YAK
I'D DO ANYTHING TO BE PROTECTED BY RAKUTO!!
I'm so jealous!!
SMILE

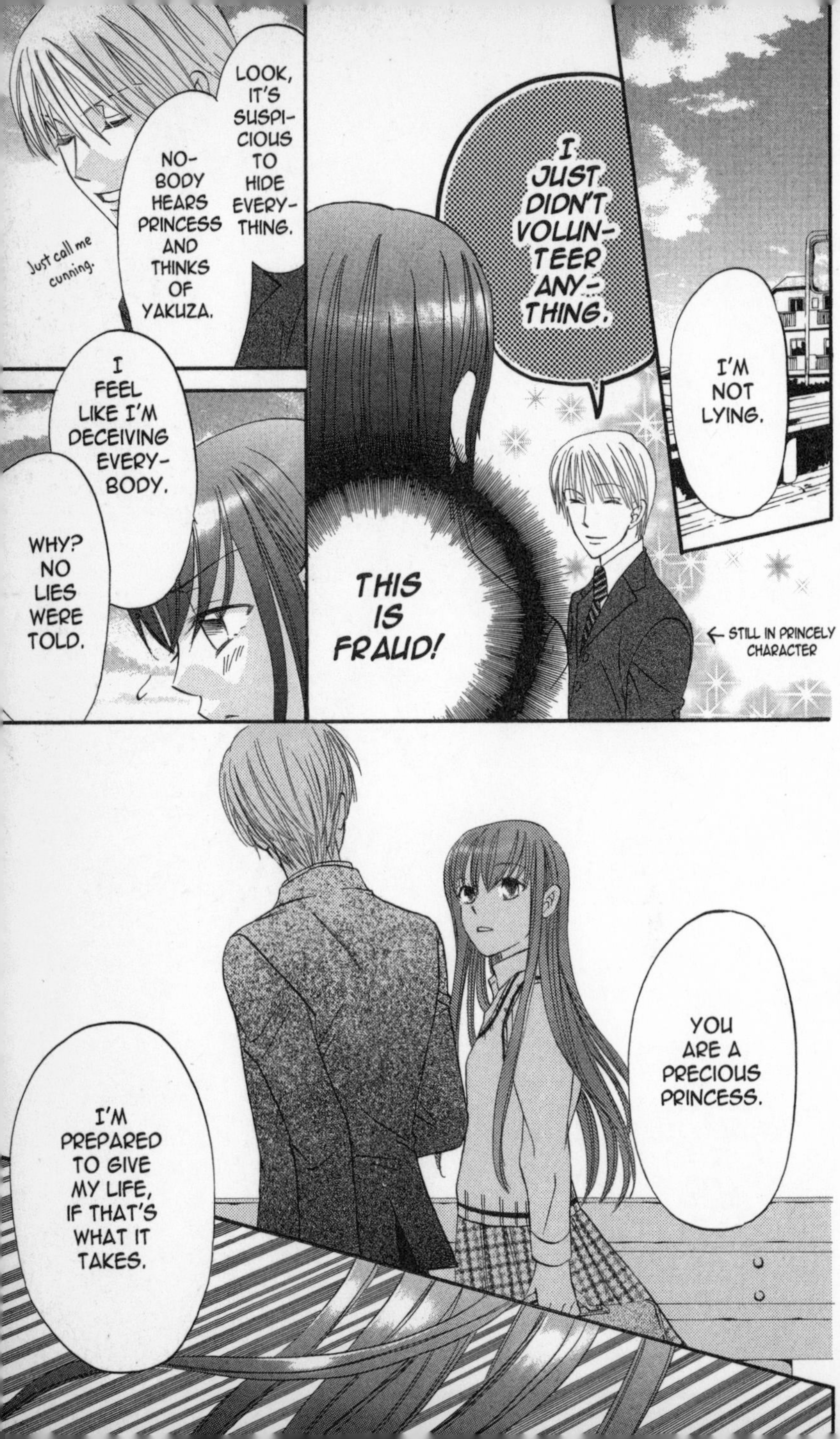
I'M NOT LYING.
I JUST DIDN'T VOLUNTEER ANYTHING.
← STILL IN PRINCELY CHARACTER
THIS IS FRAUD!
LOOK, IT'S SUSPICIOUS TO HIDE EVERYTHING.
NOBODY HEARS PRINCESS AND THINKS OF YAKUZA.
Just call me cunning.
I FEEL LIKE I'M DECEIVING EVERYBODY.
WHY? NO LIES WERE TOLD.
YOU ARE A PRECIOUS PRINCESS.
I'M PREPARED TO GIVE MY LIFE, IF THAT'S WHAT IT TAKES.

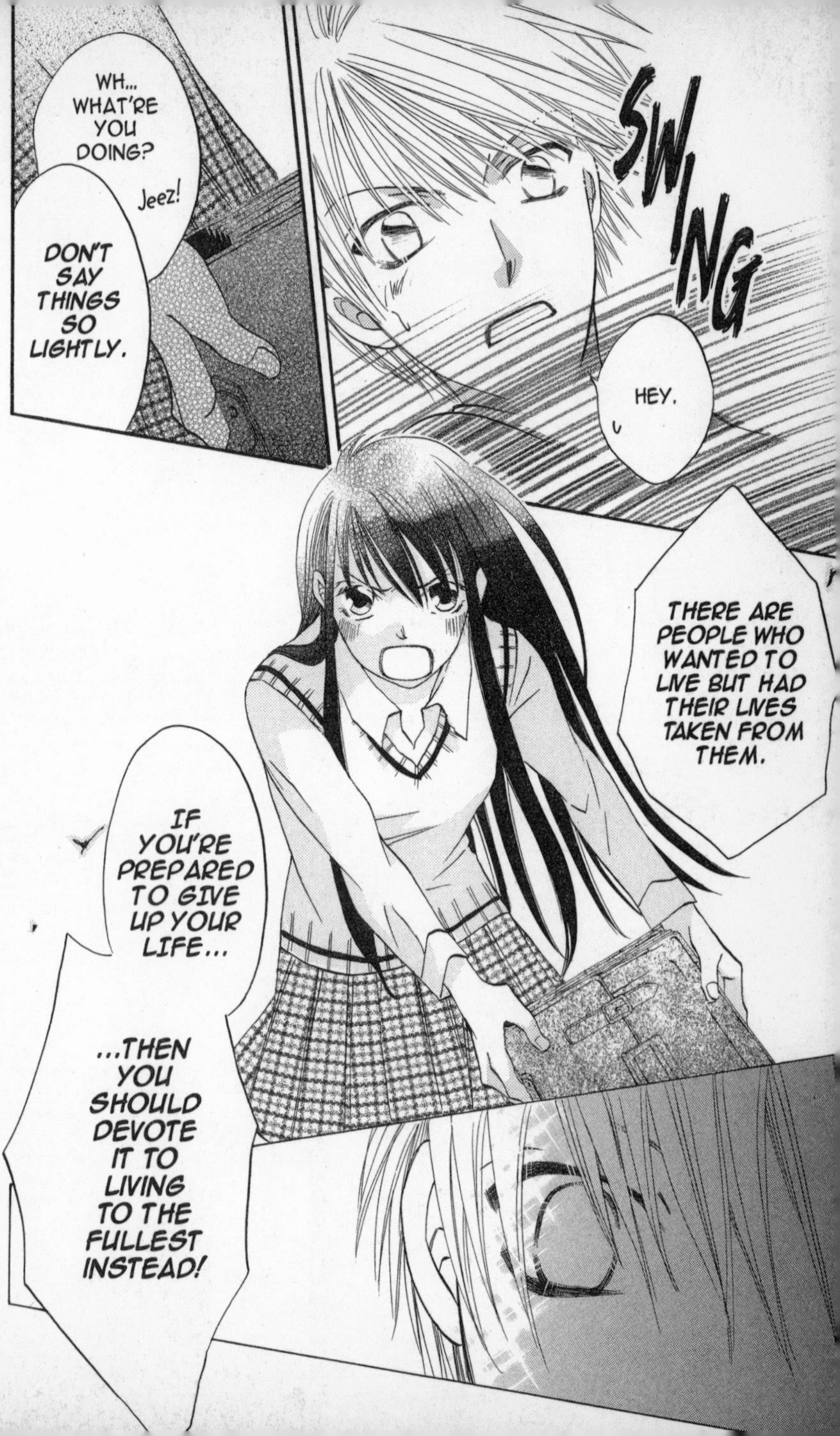
SWING
HEY.
WH... WHAT'RE YOU DOING?
Jeez!
DON'T SAY THINGS SO LIGHTLY.
THERE ARE PEOPLE WHO WANTED TO LIVE BUT HAD THEIR LIVES TAKEN FROM THEM.
IF YOU'RE PREPARED TO GIVE UP YOUR LIFE...
...THEN YOU SHOULD DEVOTE IT TO LIVING TO THE FULLEST INSTEAD!

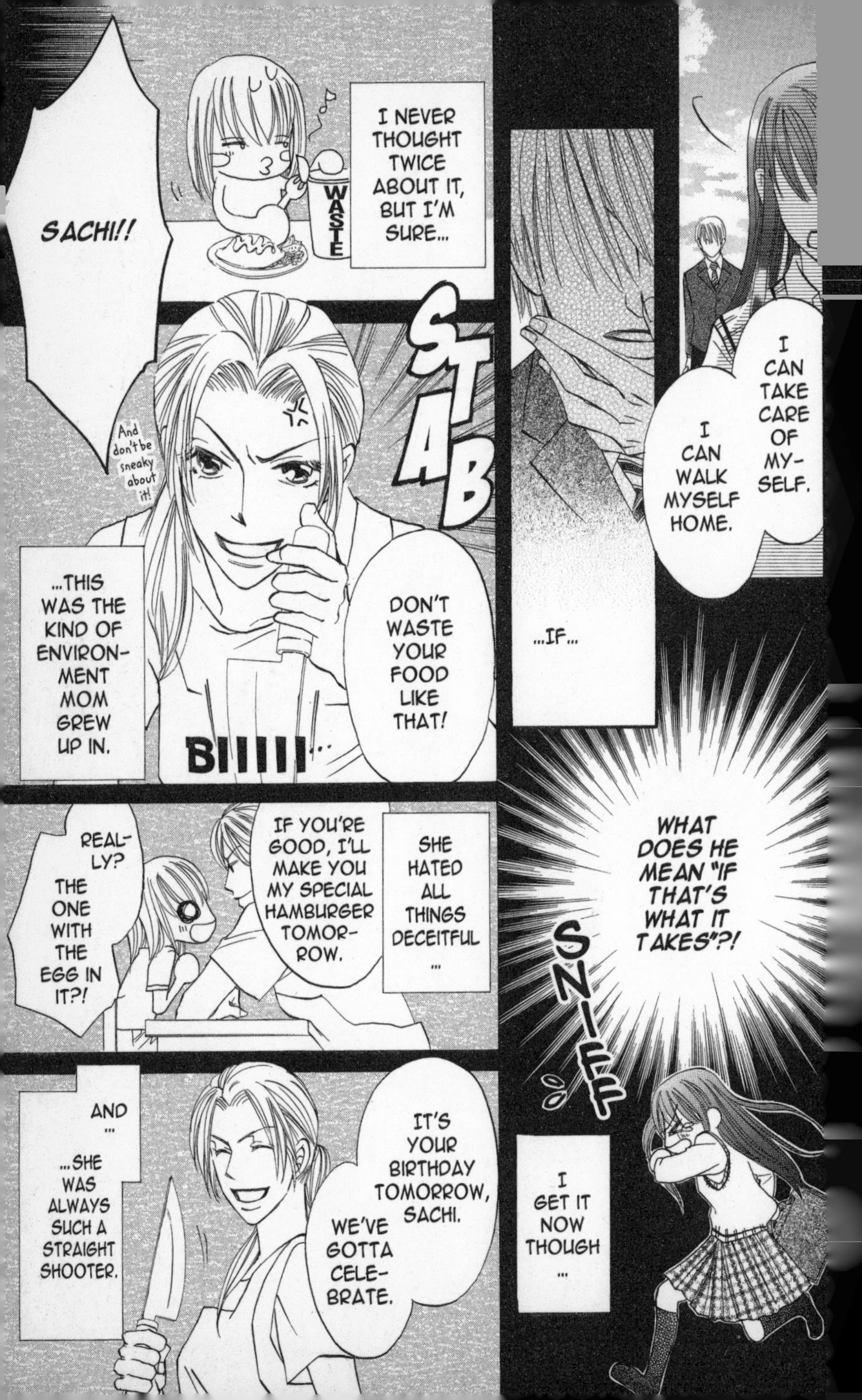

I CAN TAKE CARE OF MYSELF.
I CAN WALK MYSELF HOME.
...IF...
WHAT DOES HE MEAN "IF THAT'S WHAT IT TAKES"?!
SNIFF
I GET IT NOW THOUGH...
I NEVER THOUGHT TWICE ABOUT IT, BUT I'M SURE...
WASTE
SACHI!!
STAB
DON'T WASTE YOUR FOOD LIKE THAT!
And don't be sneaky about it!
BIIIII...
...THIS WAS THE KIND OF ENVIRONMENT MOM GREW UP IN.
SHE HATED ALL THINGS DECEITFUL...
IF YOU'RE GOOD, I'LL MAKE YOU MY SPECIAL HAMBURGER TOMORROW.
REALLY? THE ONE WITH THE EGG IN IT?!
IT'S YOUR BIRTHDAY TOMORROW, SACHI.
WE'VE GOTTA CELEBRATE.
AND...
...SHE WAS ALWAYS SUCH A STRAIGHT SHOOTER.

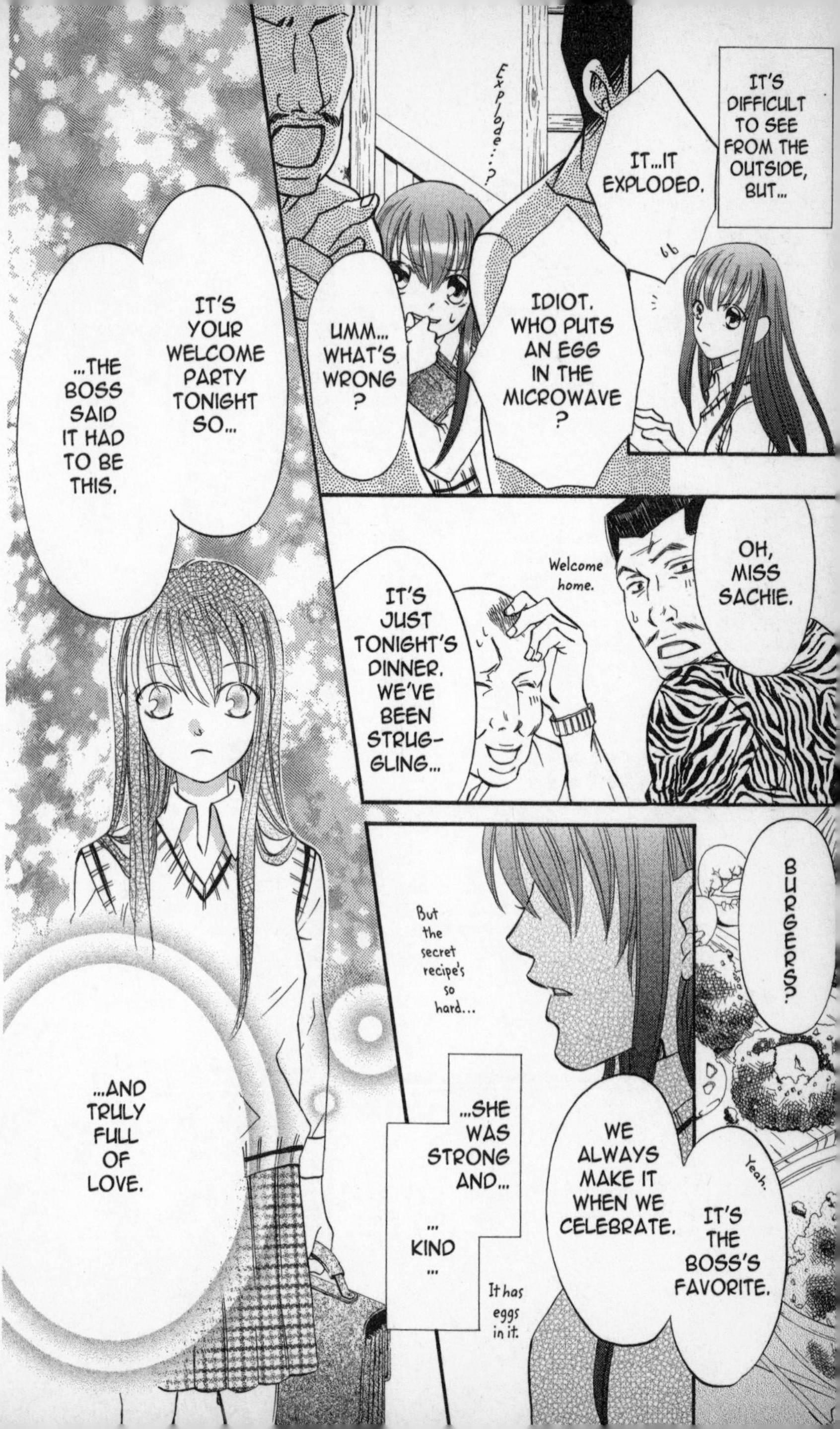

IT'S DIFFICULT TO SEE FROM THE OUTSIDE, BUT...
IT...IT EXPLODED.
Explode...?
IDIOT. WHO PUTS AN EGG IN THE MICROWAVE?
UMM... WHAT'S WRONG?
OH, MISS SACHIE.
Welcome home.
IT'S JUST TONIGHT'S DINNER. WE'VE BEEN STRUG-GLING...
BURGERS?
But the secret recipe's so hard...
Yeah.
IT'S THE BOSS'S FAVORITE.
WE ALWAYS MAKE IT WHEN WE CELEBRATE.
It has eggs in it.
...SHE WAS STRONG AND...
...KIND...
IT'S YOUR WELCOME PARTY TONIGHT SO...
...THE BOSS SAID IT HAD TO BE THIS.
...AND TRULY FULL OF LOVE.

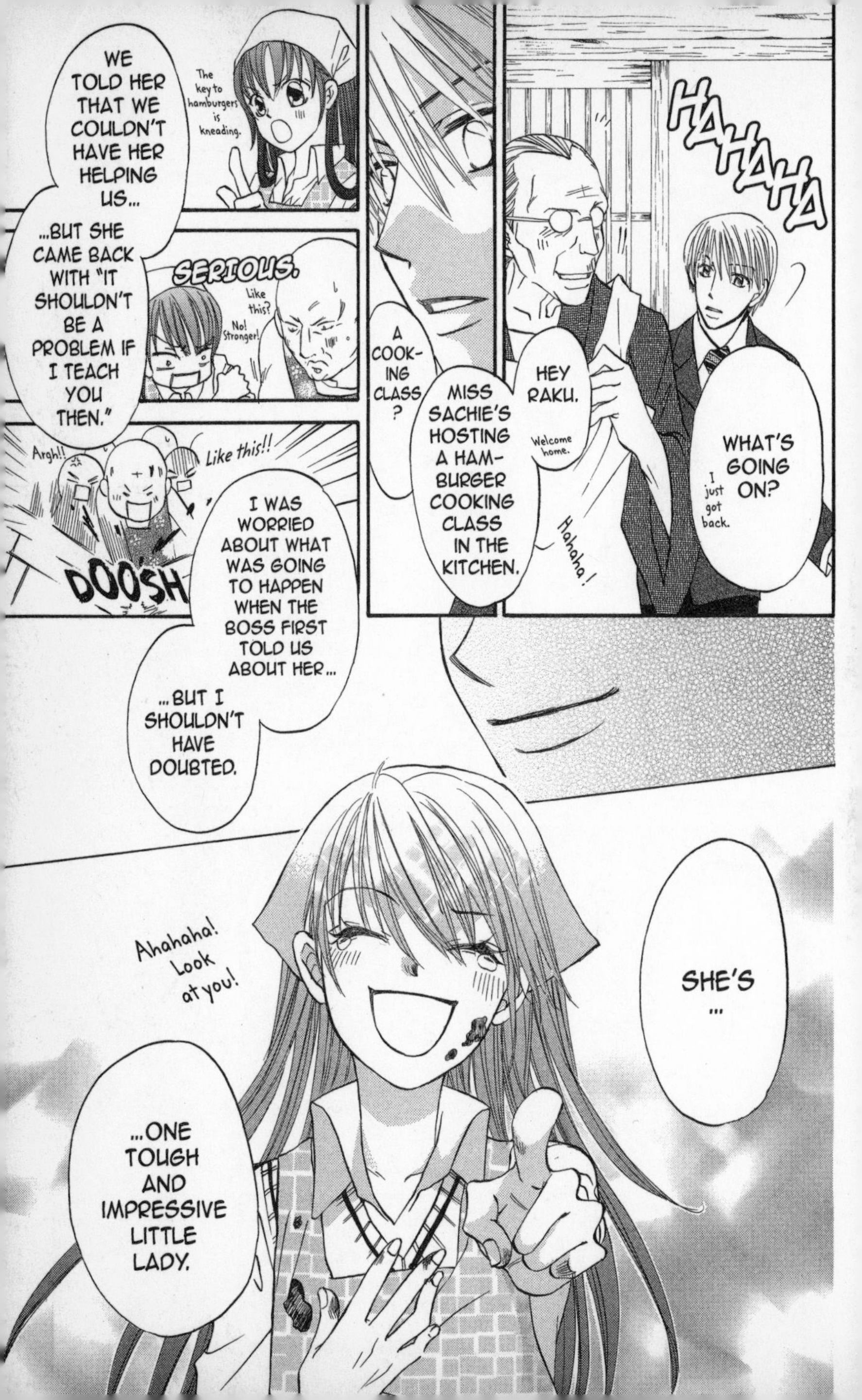
HAHAHAHA
WHAT'S GOING ON?
I just got back.
HEY RAKU.
Welcome home.
MISS SACHIE'S HOSTING A HAMBURGER COOKING CLASS IN THE KITCHEN.
Hahaha!
A COOKING CLASS?
WE TOLD HER THAT WE COULDN'T HAVE HER HELPING US...
The key to hamburgers is kneading.
...BUT SHE CAME BACK WITH "IT SHOULDN'T BE A PROBLEM IF I TEACH YOU THEN."
SERIOUS.
Like this?
No! Stronger!
Like this!!
Argh!!
DOOSH
I WAS WORRIED ABOUT WHAT WAS GOING TO HAPPEN WHEN THE BOSS FIRST TOLD US ABOUT HER...
...BUT I SHOULDN'T HAVE DOUBTED.
SHE'S...
...ONE TOUGH AND IMPRESSIVE LITTLE LADY.
Ahahaha! Look at you!

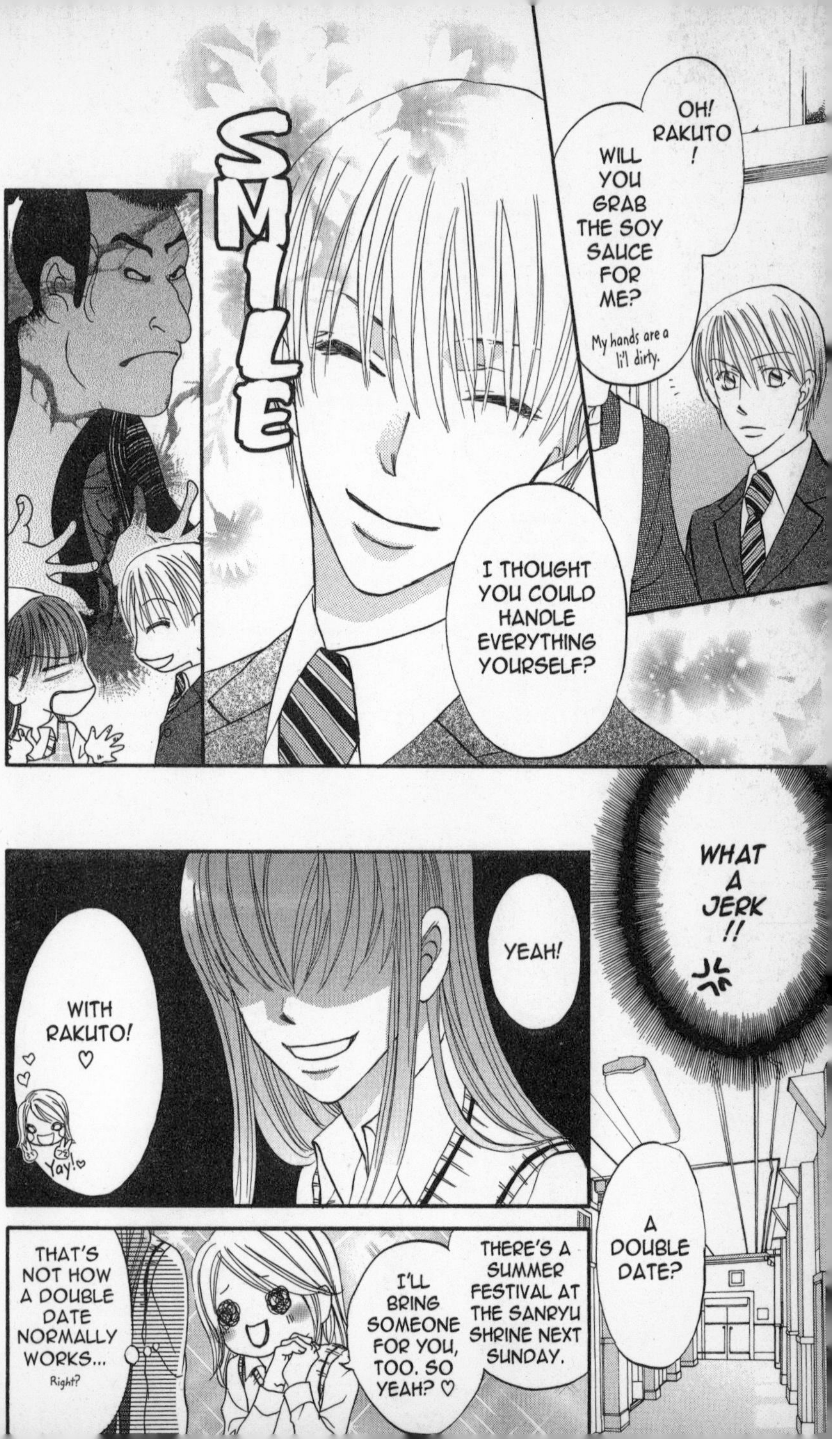
OH! RAKUTO!
WILL YOU GRAB THE SOY SAUCE FOR ME?
My hands are a li'l dirty.
SMILE
I THOUGHT YOU COULD HANDLE EVERYTHING YOURSELF?
WHAT A JERK!!
A DOUBLE DATE?
YEAH!
WITH RAKUTO! ♡
Yay!♡
THERE'S A SUMMER FESTIVAL AT THE SANRYU SHRINE NEXT SUNDAY.
I'LL BRING SOMEONE FOR YOU, TOO. SO YEAH? ♡
THAT'S NOT HOW A DOUBLE DATE NORMALLY WORKS...
Right?

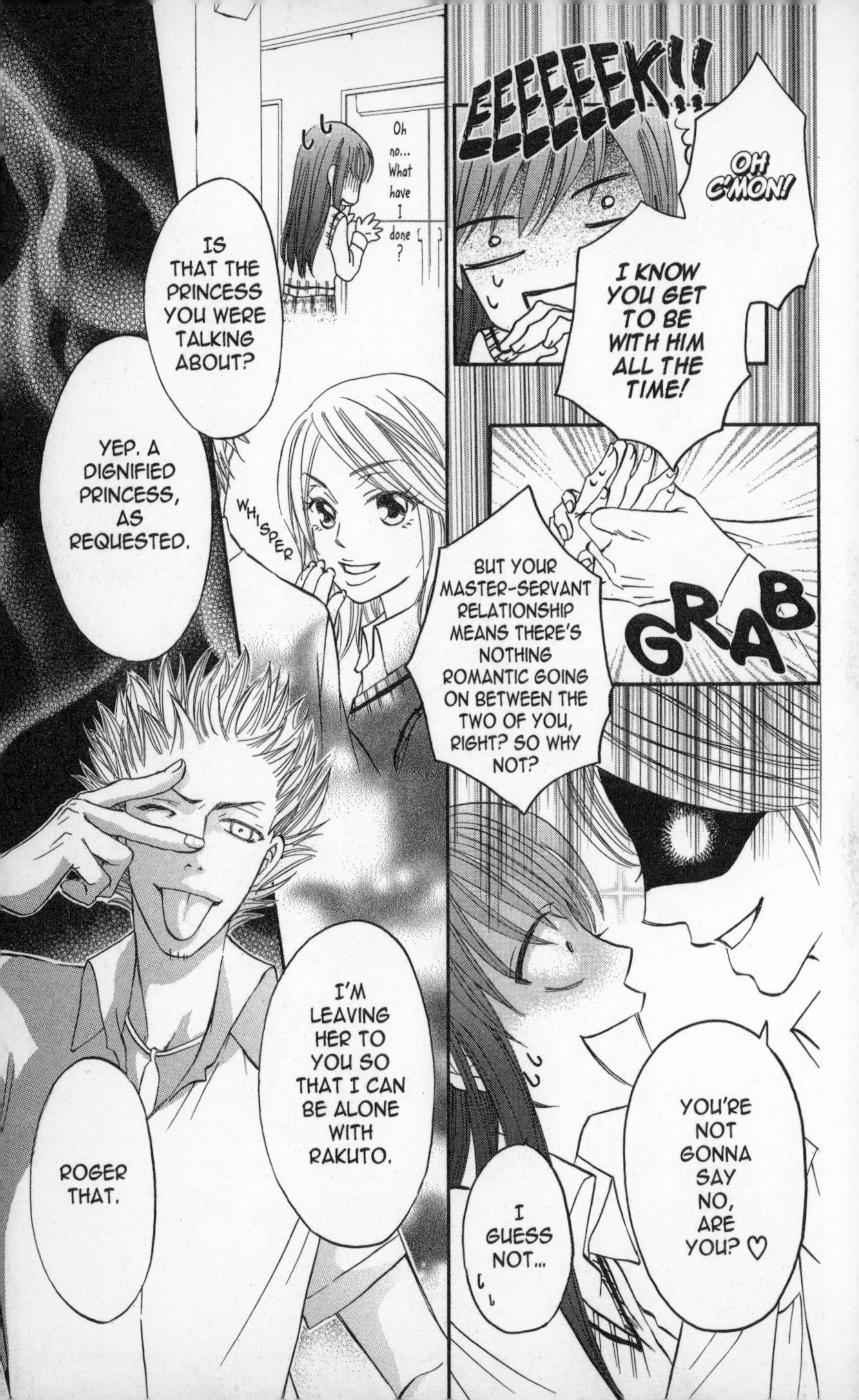
EEEEEEEK!!
OH C'MON!
I KNOW YOU GET TO BE WITH HIM ALL THE TIME!
GRAB
BUT YOUR MASTER-SERVANT RELATIONSHIP MEANS THERE'S NOTHING ROMANTIC GOING ON BETWEEN THE TWO OF YOU, RIGHT? SO WHY NOT?
YOU'RE NOT GONNA SAY NO, ARE YOU? ♡
I GUESS NOT...
Oh no... What have I done?
IS THAT THE PRINCESS YOU WERE TALKING ABOUT?
YEP. A DIGNIFIED PRINCESS, AS REQUESTED.
WHISPER
I'M LEAVING HER TO YOU SO THAT I CAN BE ALONE WITH RAKUTO.
ROGER THAT.

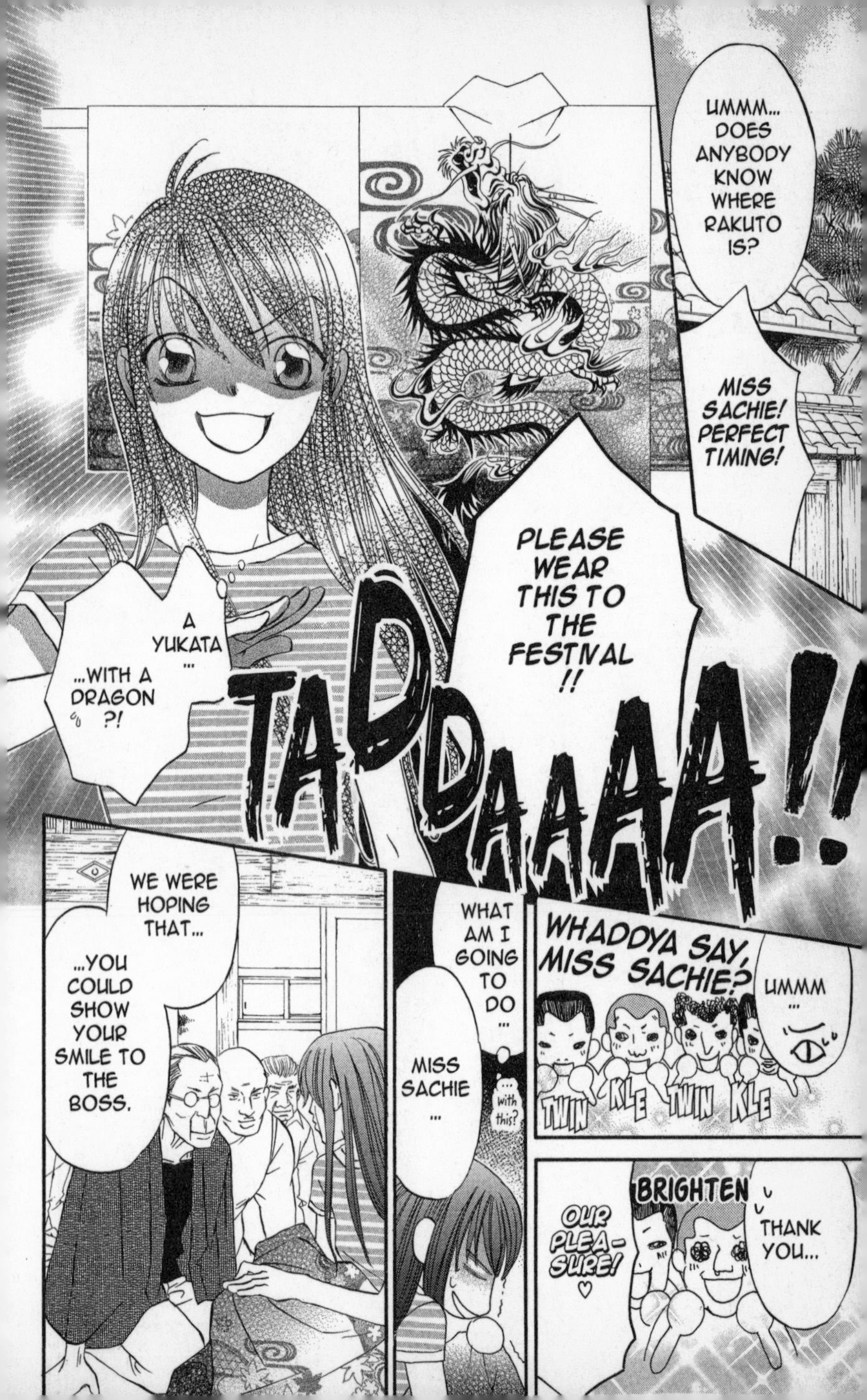
UMMM... DOES ANYBODY KNOW WHERE RAKUTO IS?
MISS SACHIE! PERFECT TIMING!
PLEASE WEAR THIS TO THE FESTIVAL !!
TADAAAA!!
A YUKATA ...
...WITH A DRAGON ?!
WHADDYA SAY, MISS SACHIE?
UMMM ...
TWINKLE TWINKLE
BRIGHTEN
THANK YOU...
OUR PLEA-SURE! ♥
WHAT AM I GOING TO DO ...
... with this?
MISS SACHIE ...
WE WERE HOPING THAT...
...YOU COULD SHOW YOUR SMILE TO THE BOSS.

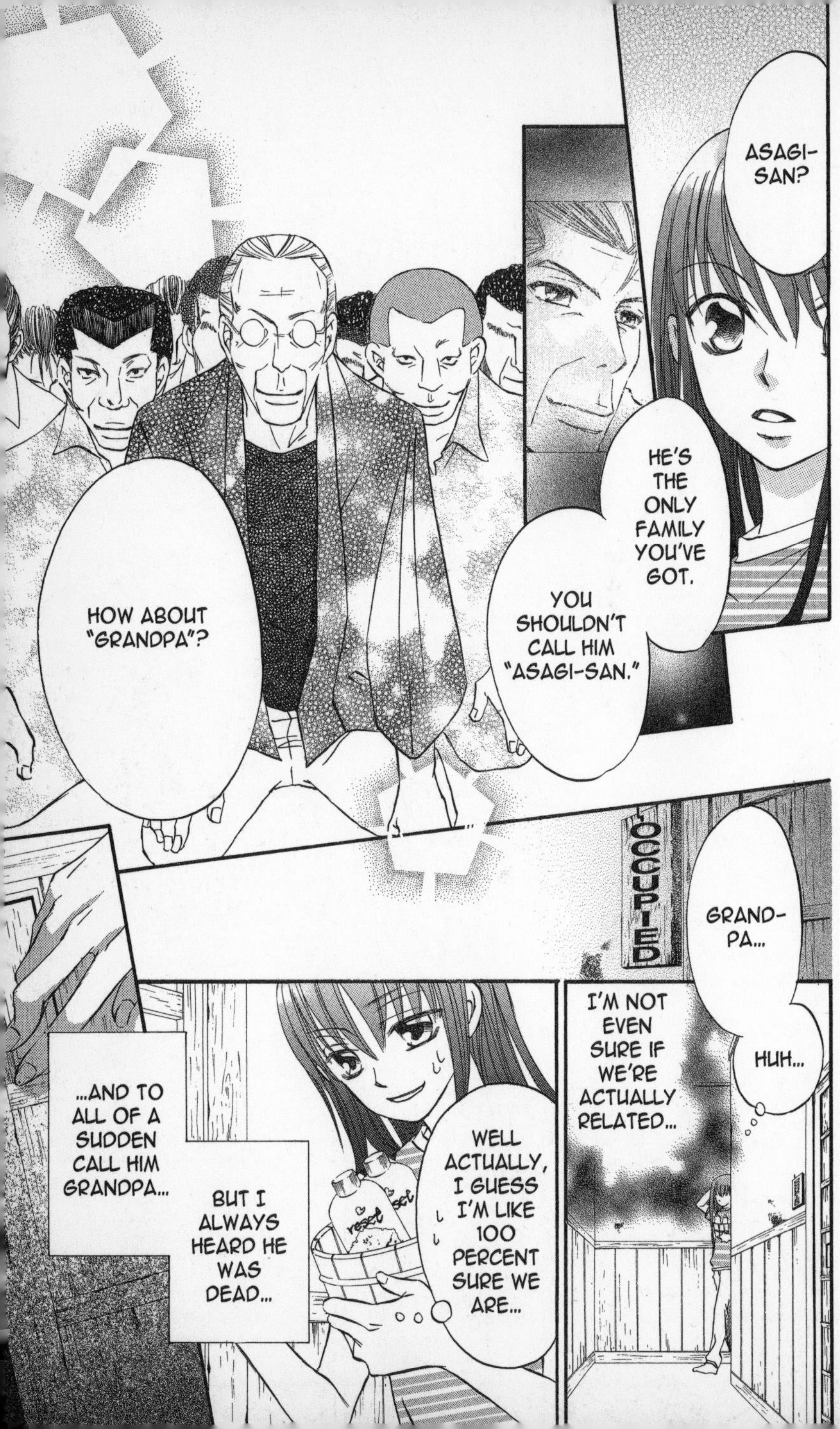
ASAGI-SAN?
HE'S THE ONLY FAMILY YOU'VE GOT.
YOU SHOULDN'T CALL HIM "ASAGI-SAN."
HOW ABOUT "GRANDPA"?
OCCUPIED
GRAND-PA...
HUH...
I'M NOT EVEN SURE IF WE'RE ACTUALLY RELATED...
WELL ACTUALLY, I GUESS I'M LIKE 100 PERCENT SURE WE ARE...
BUT I ALWAYS HEARD HE WAS DEAD...
...AND TO ALL OF A SUDDEN CALL HIM GRANDPA...
reset

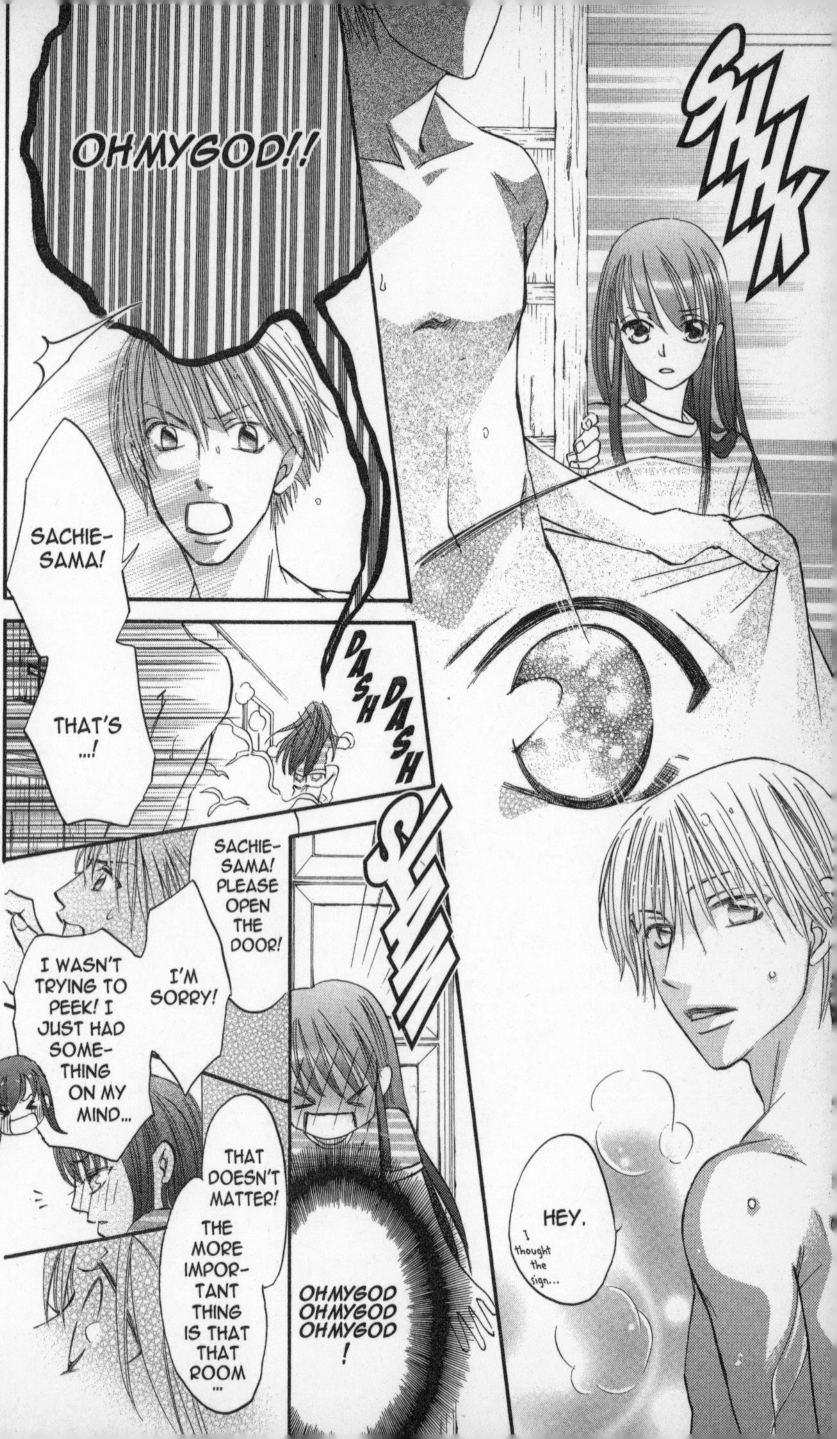

SHHK
HEY.
I thought the sign...
OHMYGOD!!
SACHIE-SAMA!
THAT'S ...!
DASH DASH
SACHIE-SAMA! PLEASE OPEN THE DOOR!
I'M SORRY!
I WASN'T TRYING TO PEEK! I JUST HAD SOMETHING ON MY MIND...
OHMYGOD OHMYGOD OHMYGOD!
THAT DOESN'T MATTER!
THE MORE IMPORTANT THING IS THAT THAT ROOM ...

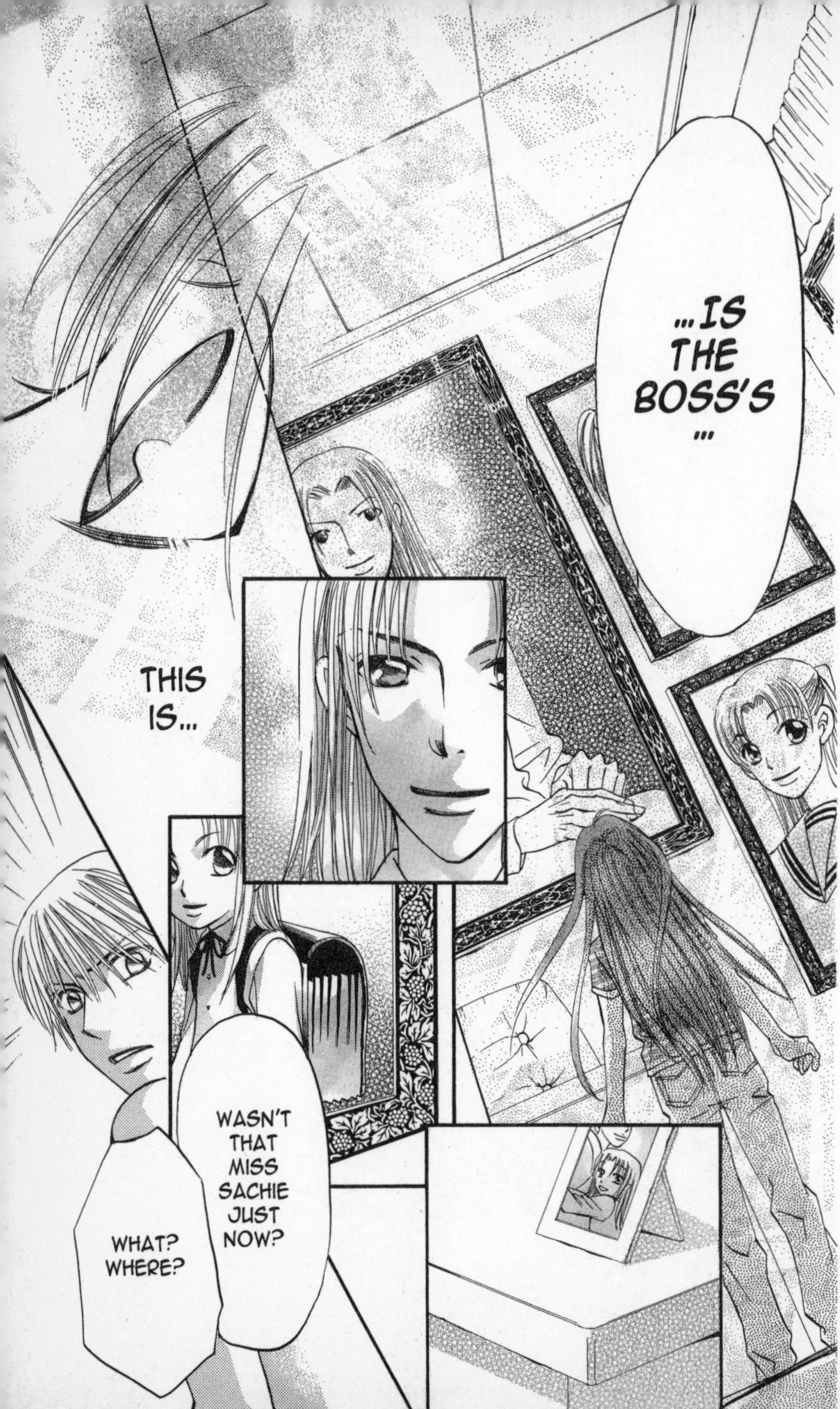
...IS THE BOSS'S ...
THIS IS...
WASN'T THAT MISS SACHIE JUST NOW?
WHAT? WHERE?

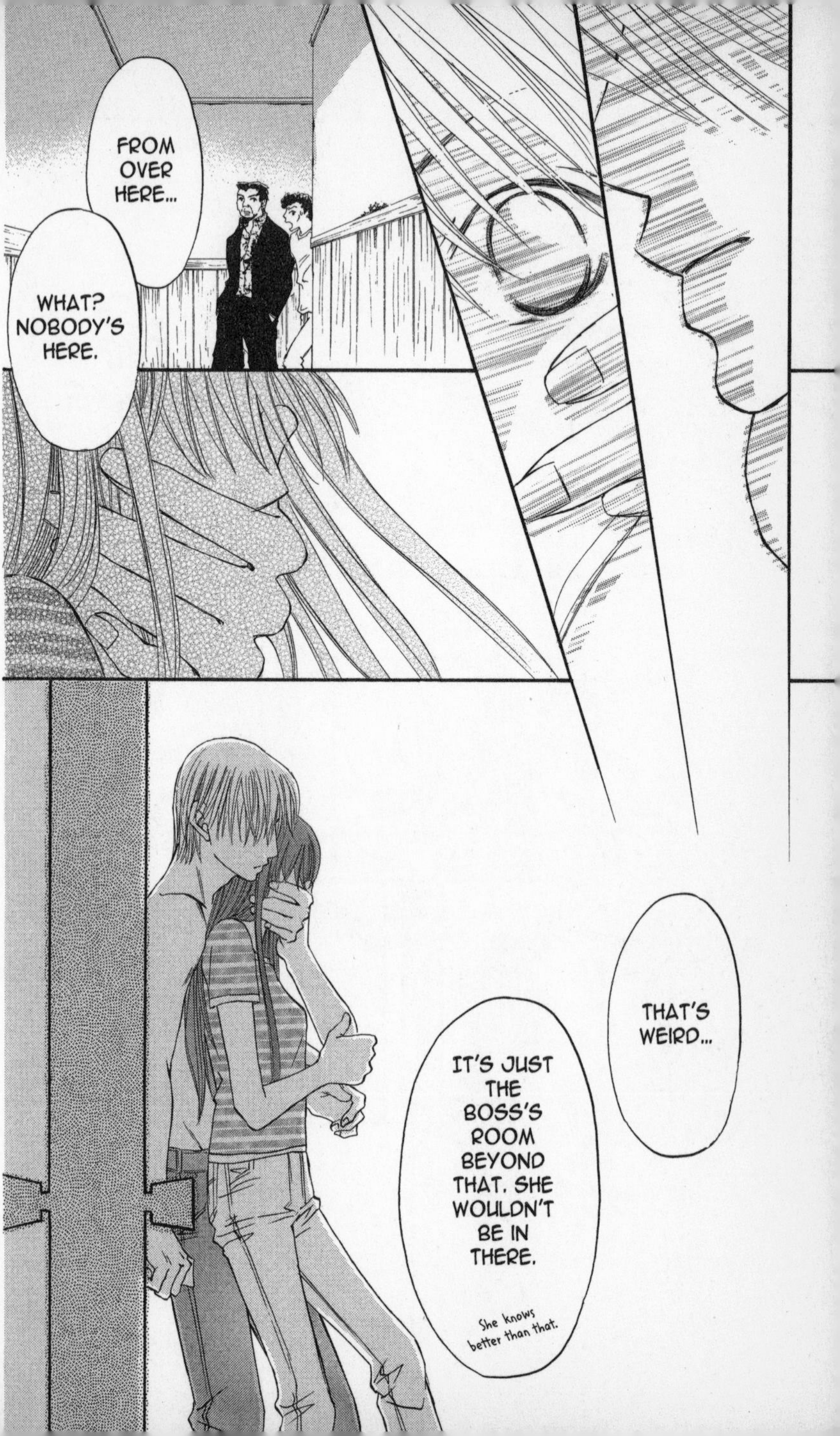
FROM OVER HERE...
WHAT? NOBODY'S HERE.
THAT'S WEIRD...
IT'S JUST THE BOSS'S ROOM BEYOND THAT. SHE WOULDN'T BE IN THERE.
She knows better than that.

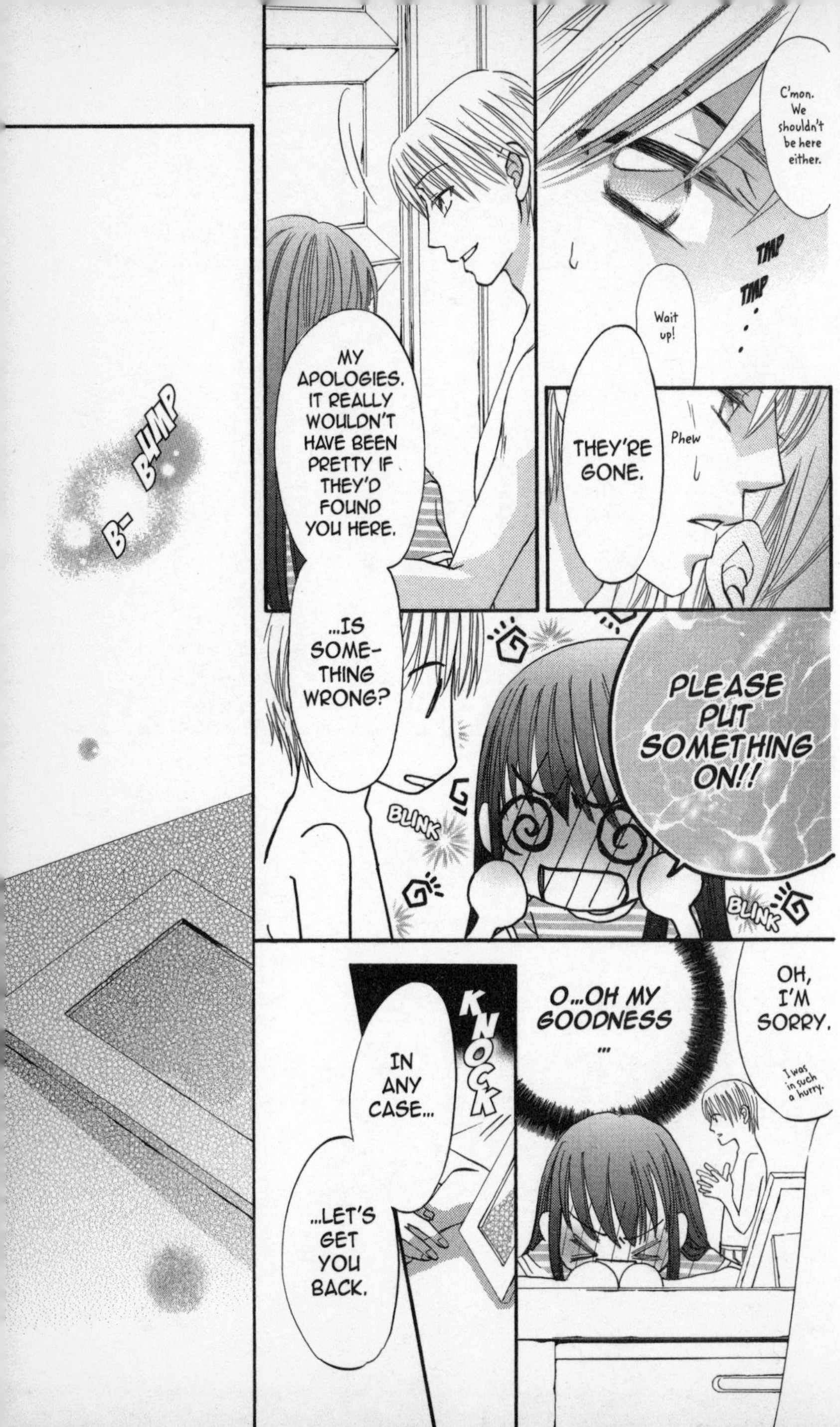
C'mon. We shouldn't be here either.
TMP TMP...
Wait up!
Phew
THEY'RE GONE.
MY APOLOGIES. IT REALLY WOULDN'T HAVE BEEN PRETTY IF THEY'D FOUND YOU HERE.
...IS SOMETHING WRONG?
PLEASE PUT SOMETHING ON!!
BLINK
BLINK
OH, I'M SORRY.
I was in such a hurry.
O...OH MY GOODNESS...
KNOCK
IN ANY CASE...
...LET'S GET YOU BACK.
B-BUMP

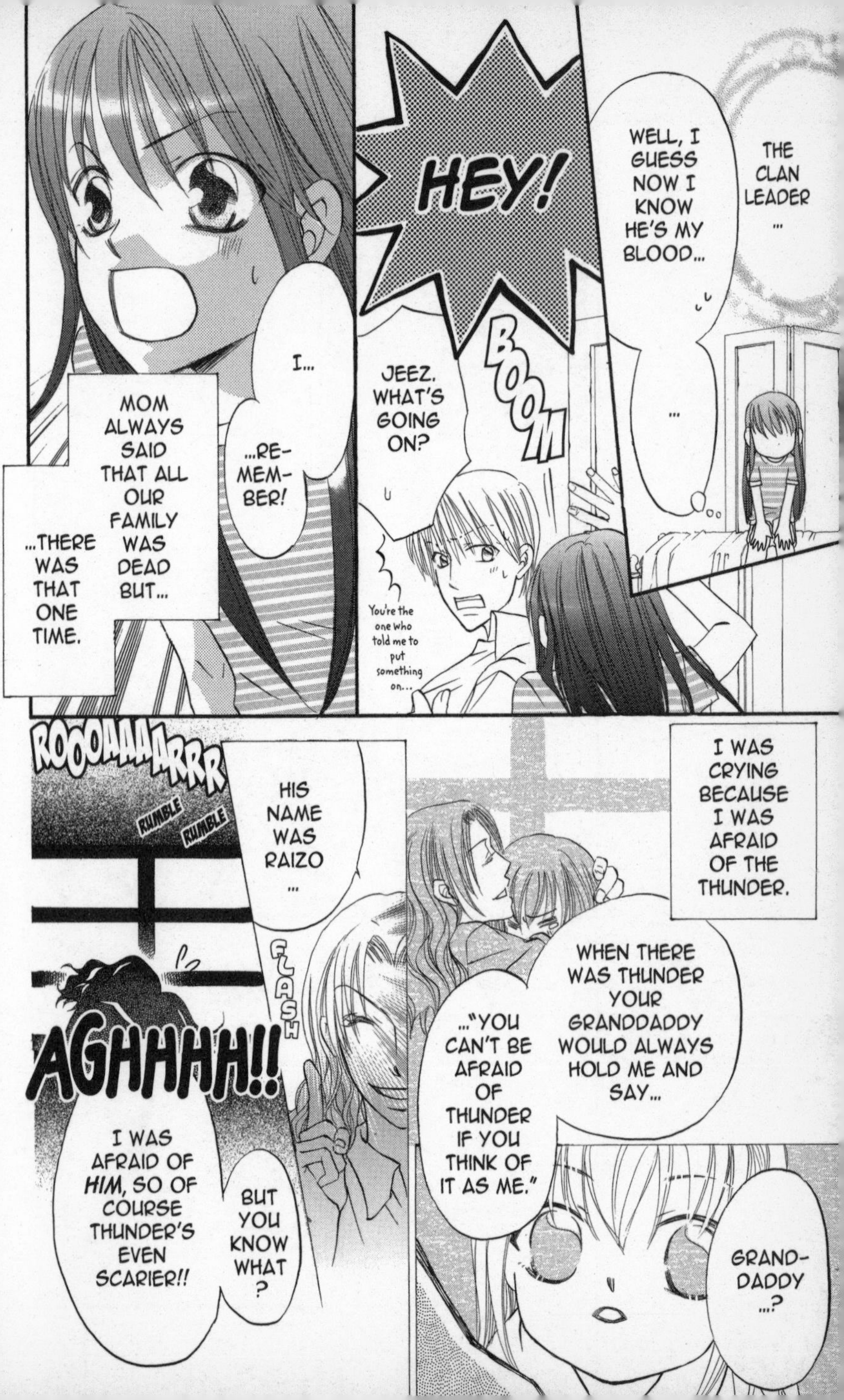
THE CLAN LEADER ...
WELL, I GUESS NOW I KNOW HE'S MY BLOOD...
...
HEY!
BOOM
JEEZ. WHAT'S GOING ON?
You're the one who told me to put something on...
I...
...RE-MEM-BER!
MOM ALWAYS SAID THAT ALL OUR FAMILY WAS DEAD BUT...
...THERE WAS THAT ONE TIME.
I WAS CRYING BECAUSE I WAS AFRAID OF THE THUNDER.
WHEN THERE WAS THUNDER YOUR GRANDDADDY WOULD ALWAYS HOLD ME AND SAY...
..."YOU CAN'T BE AFRAID OF THUNDER IF YOU THINK OF IT AS ME."
GRAND-DADDY ...?
ROOOAAAARRR
RUMBLE
RUMBLE
HIS NAME WAS RAIZO ...
FLASH
AGHHHH!!
BUT YOU KNOW WHAT?
I WAS AFRAID OF *HIM*, SO OF COURSE THUNDER'S EVEN SCARIER!!

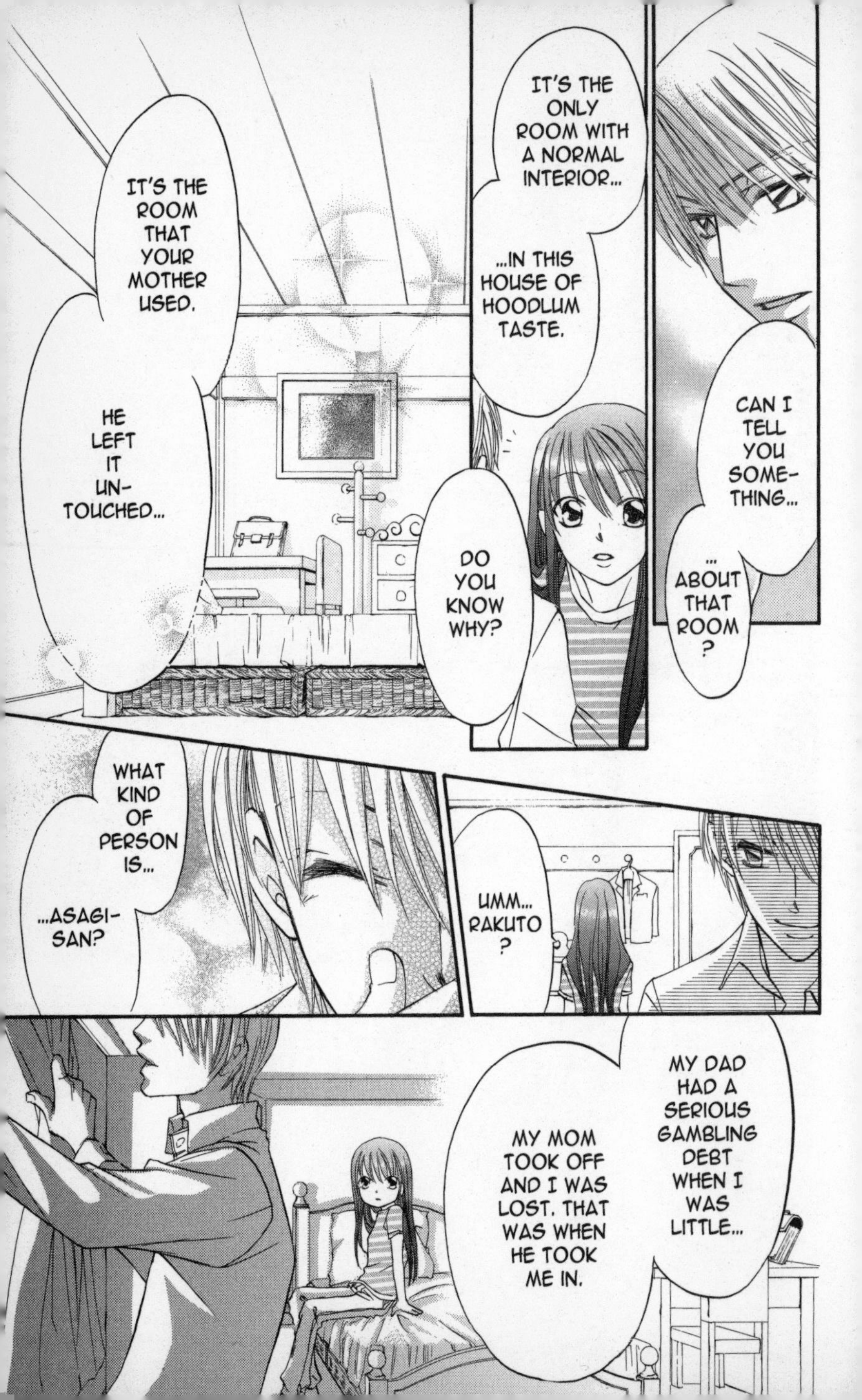
CAN I TELL YOU SOME-THING...
...ABOUT THAT ROOM?
IT'S THE ONLY ROOM WITH A NORMAL INTERIOR...
...IN THIS HOUSE OF HOODLUM TASTE.
DO YOU KNOW WHY?
IT'S THE ROOM THAT YOUR MOTHER USED.
HE LEFT IT UN-TOUCHED...
UMM... RAKUTO?
WHAT KIND OF PERSON IS...
...ASAGI-SAN?
MY DAD HAD A SERIOUS GAMBLING DEBT WHEN I WAS LITTLE...
MY MOM TOOK OFF AND I WAS LOST. THAT WAS WHEN HE TOOK ME IN.

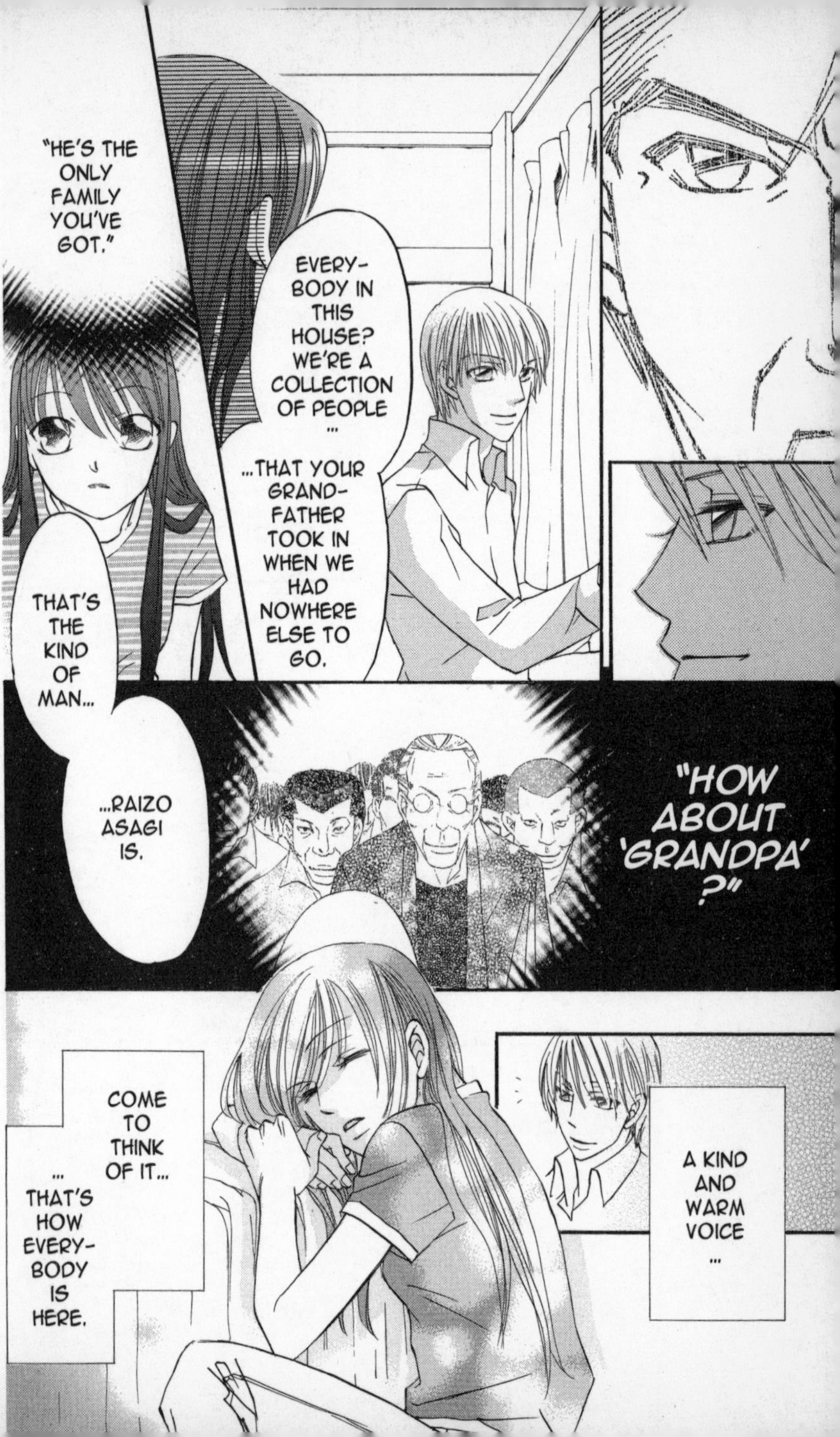
"HE'S THE ONLY FAMILY YOU'VE GOT."
EVERYBODY IN THIS HOUSE? WE'RE A COLLECTION OF PEOPLE ...
...THAT YOUR GRANDFATHER TOOK IN WHEN WE HAD NOWHERE ELSE TO GO.
THAT'S THE KIND OF MAN...
...RAIZO ASAGI IS.
"HOW ABOUT 'GRANDPA'?"
A KIND AND WARM VOICE ...
COME TO THINK OF IT...
...THAT'S HOW EVERYBODY IS HERE.

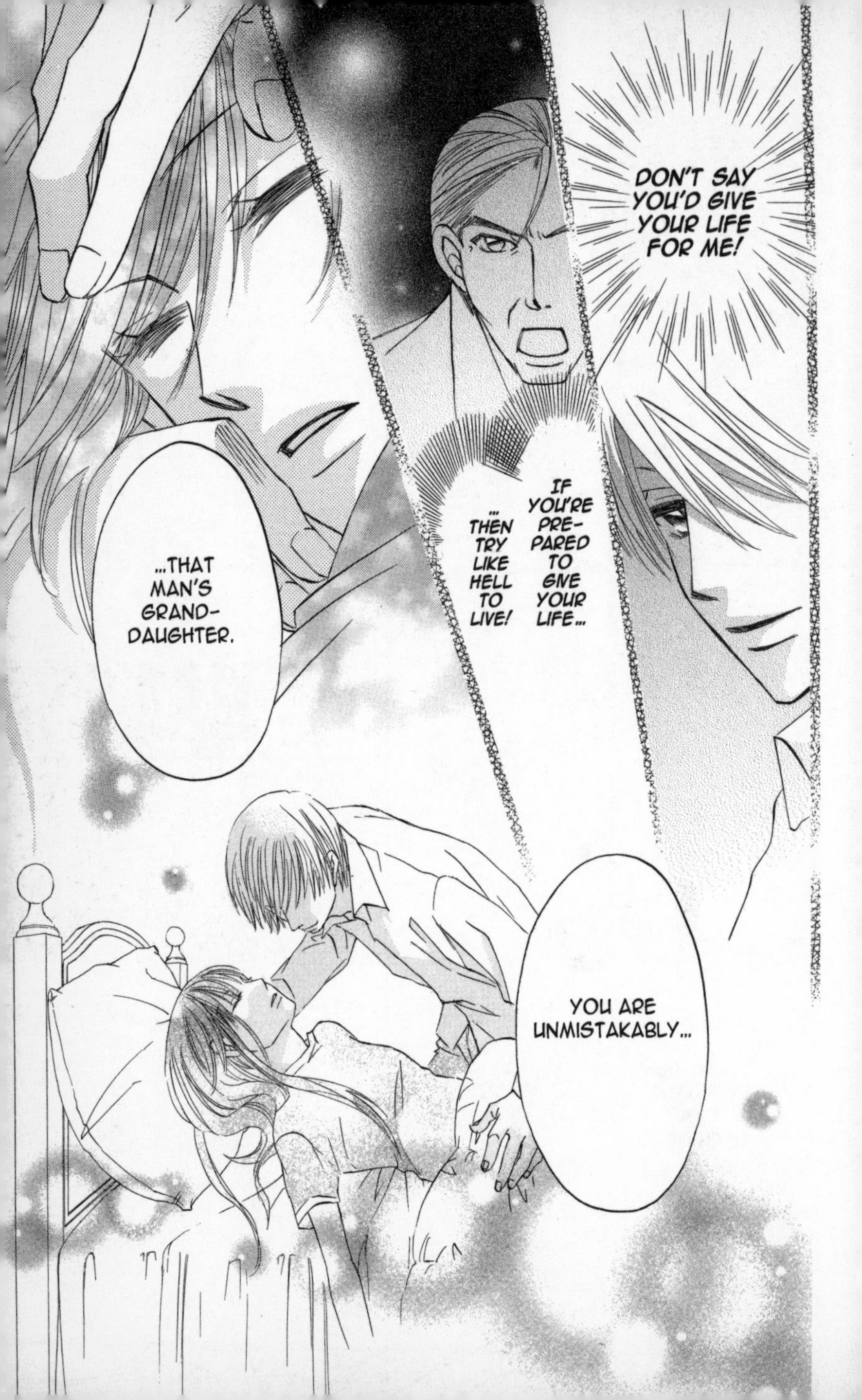
DON'T SAY YOU'D GIVE YOUR LIFE FOR ME!
IF YOU'RE PRE-PARED TO GIVE YOUR LIFE...
...THEN TRY LIKE HELL TO LIVE!
...THAT MAN'S GRAND-DAUGHTER.
YOU ARE UNMISTAKABLY...

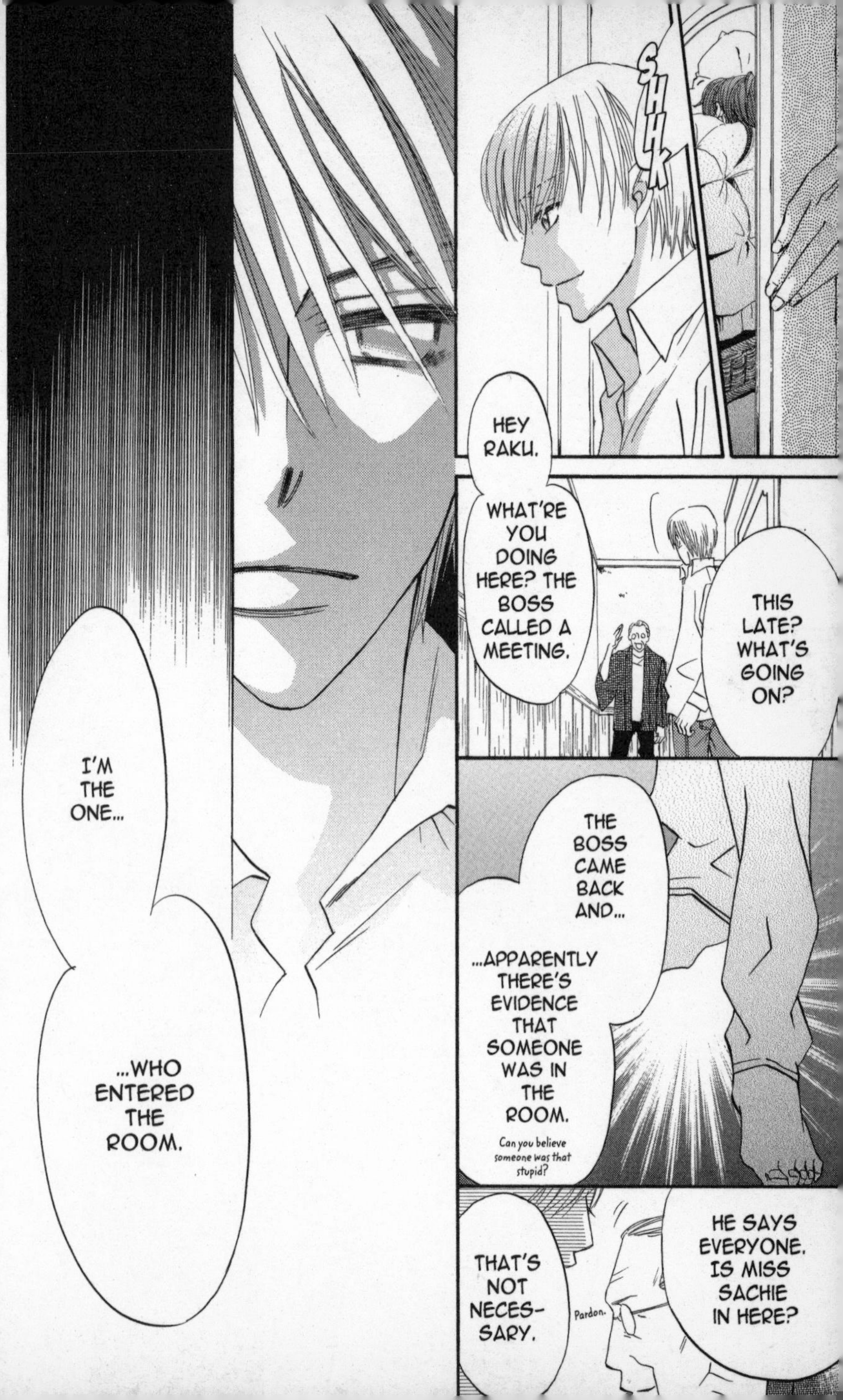
SHHK
HEY RAKU.
WHAT'RE YOU DOING HERE? THE BOSS CALLED A MEETING.
THIS LATE? WHAT'S GOING ON?
THE BOSS CAME BACK AND...
...APPARENTLY THERE'S EVIDENCE THAT SOMEONE WAS IN THE ROOM.
Can you believe someone was that stupid?
HE SAYS EVERYONE. IS MISS SACHIE IN HERE?
Pardon.
THAT'S NOT NECES-SARY.
I'M THE ONE...
...WHO ENTERED THE ROOM.

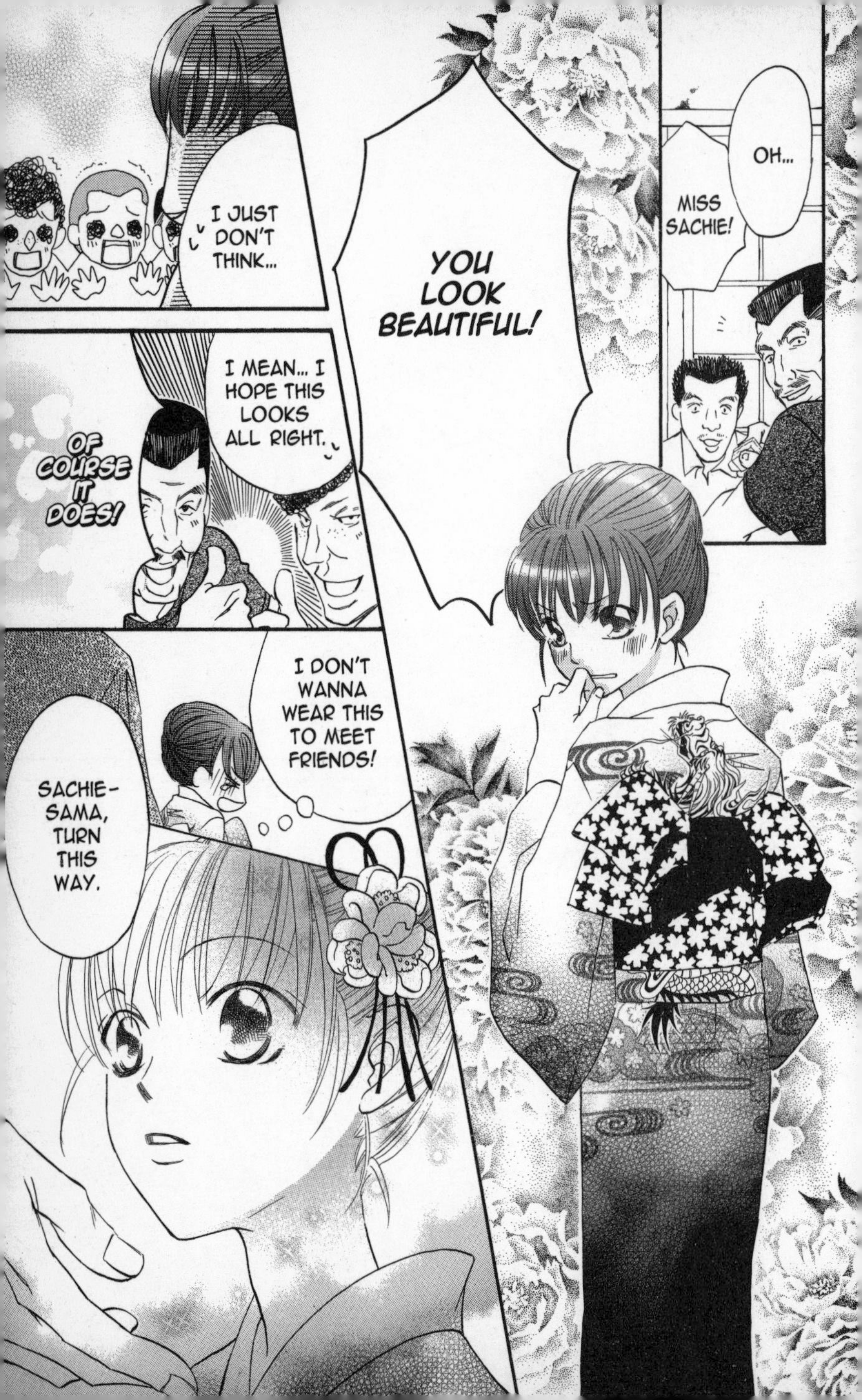
OH...
MISS SACHIE!
YOU LOOK BEAUTIFUL!
I JUST DON'T THINK...
I MEAN... I HOPE THIS LOOKS ALL RIGHT.
OF COURSE IT DOES!
I DON'T WANNA WEAR THIS TO MEET FRIENDS!
SACHIE-SAMA, TURN THIS WAY.

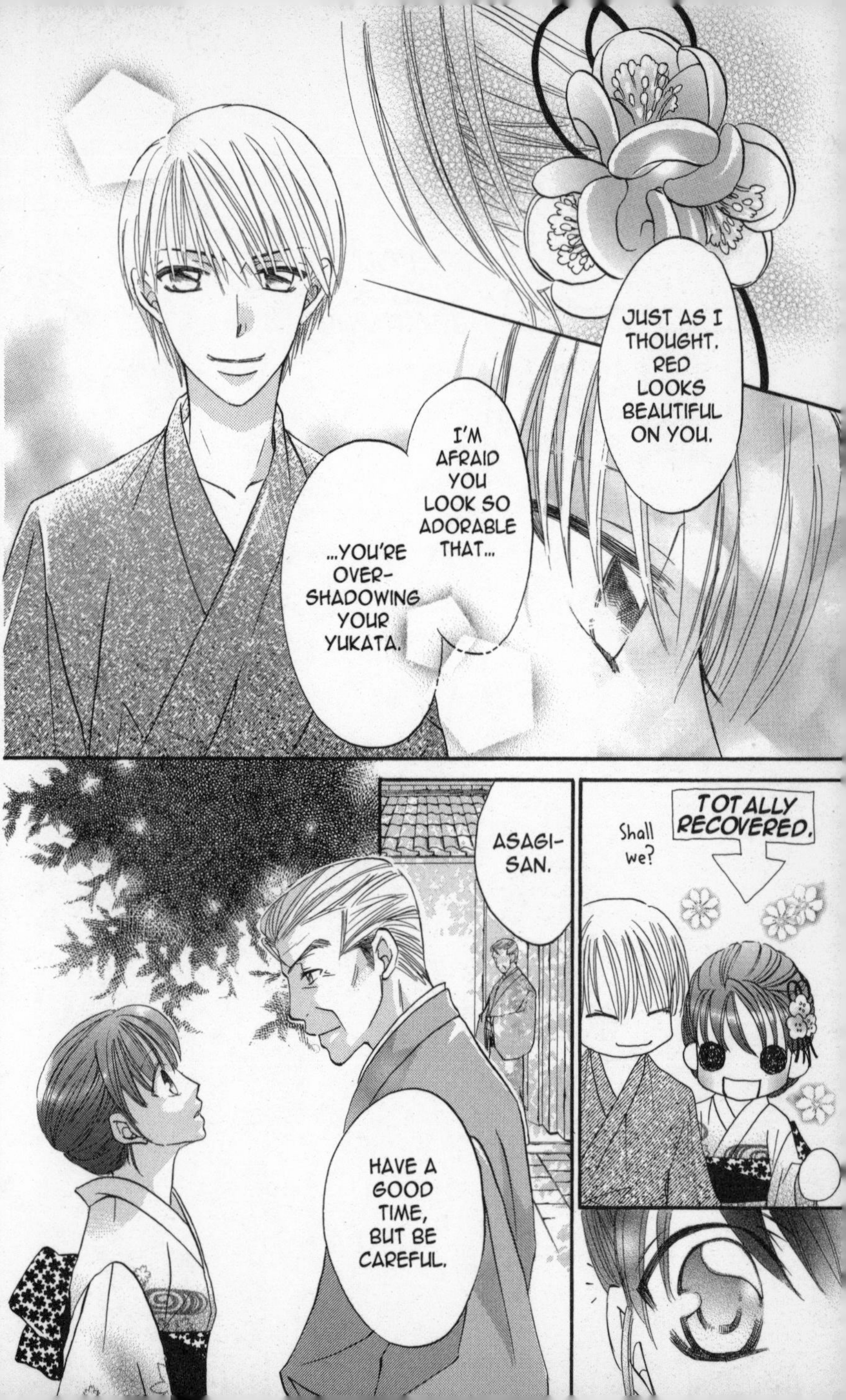
JUST AS I THOUGHT. RED LOOKS BEAUTIFUL ON YOU.
I'M AFRAID YOU LOOK SO ADORABLE THAT...
...YOU'RE OVER-SHADOWING YOUR YUKATA.
TOTALLY RECOVERED.
Shall we?
ASAGI-SAN.
HAVE A GOOD TIME, BUT BE CAREFUL.

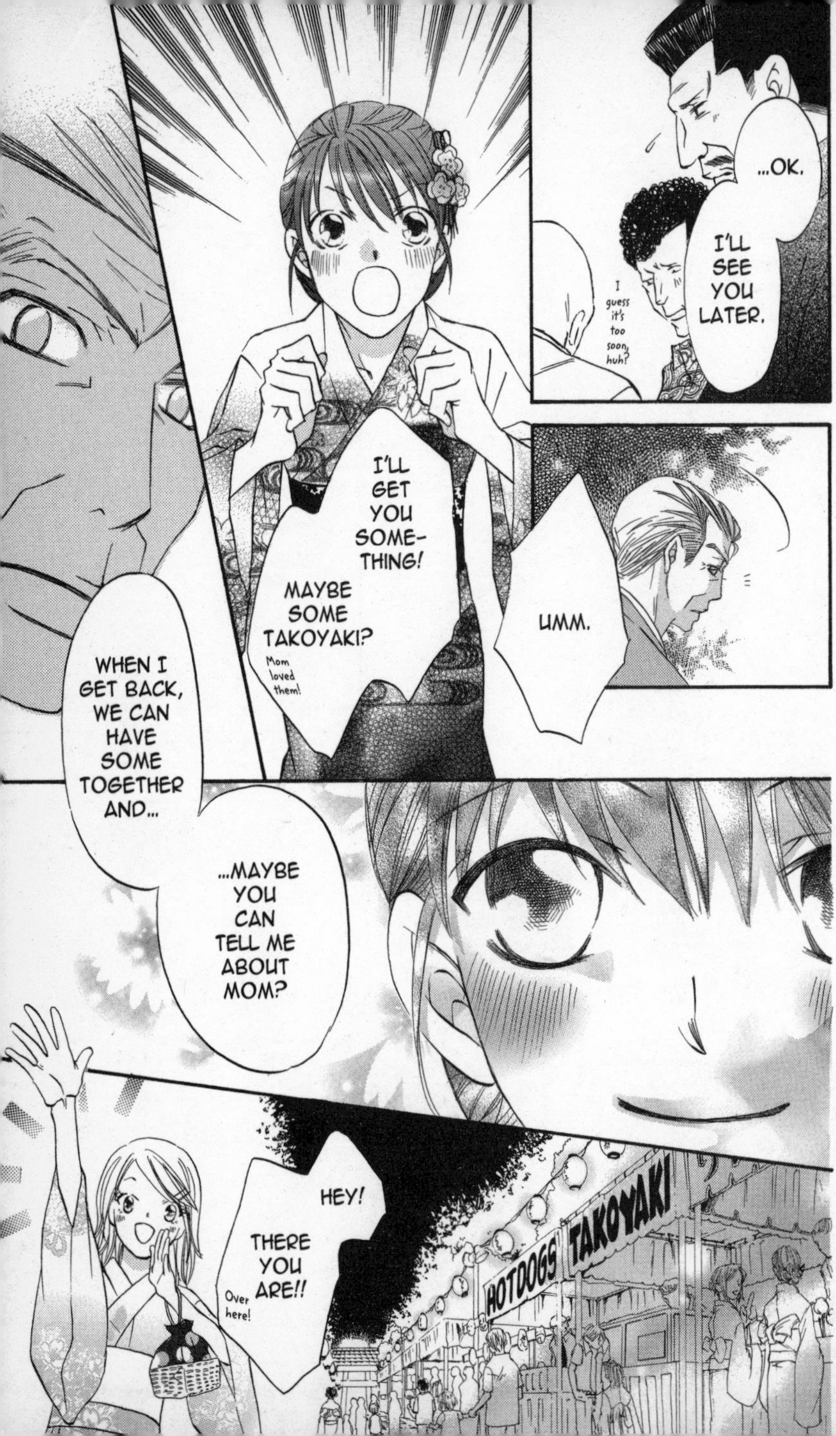
...OK.
I'LL SEE YOU LATER.
I guess it's too soon, huh?
UMM.
I'LL GET YOU SOME-THING!
MAYBE SOME TAKOYAKI?
Mom loved them!
WHEN I GET BACK, WE CAN HAVE SOME TOGETHER AND...
...MAYBE YOU CAN TELL ME ABOUT MOM?
TAKOYAKI
HOTDOGS
HEY!
THERE YOU ARE!!
Over here!

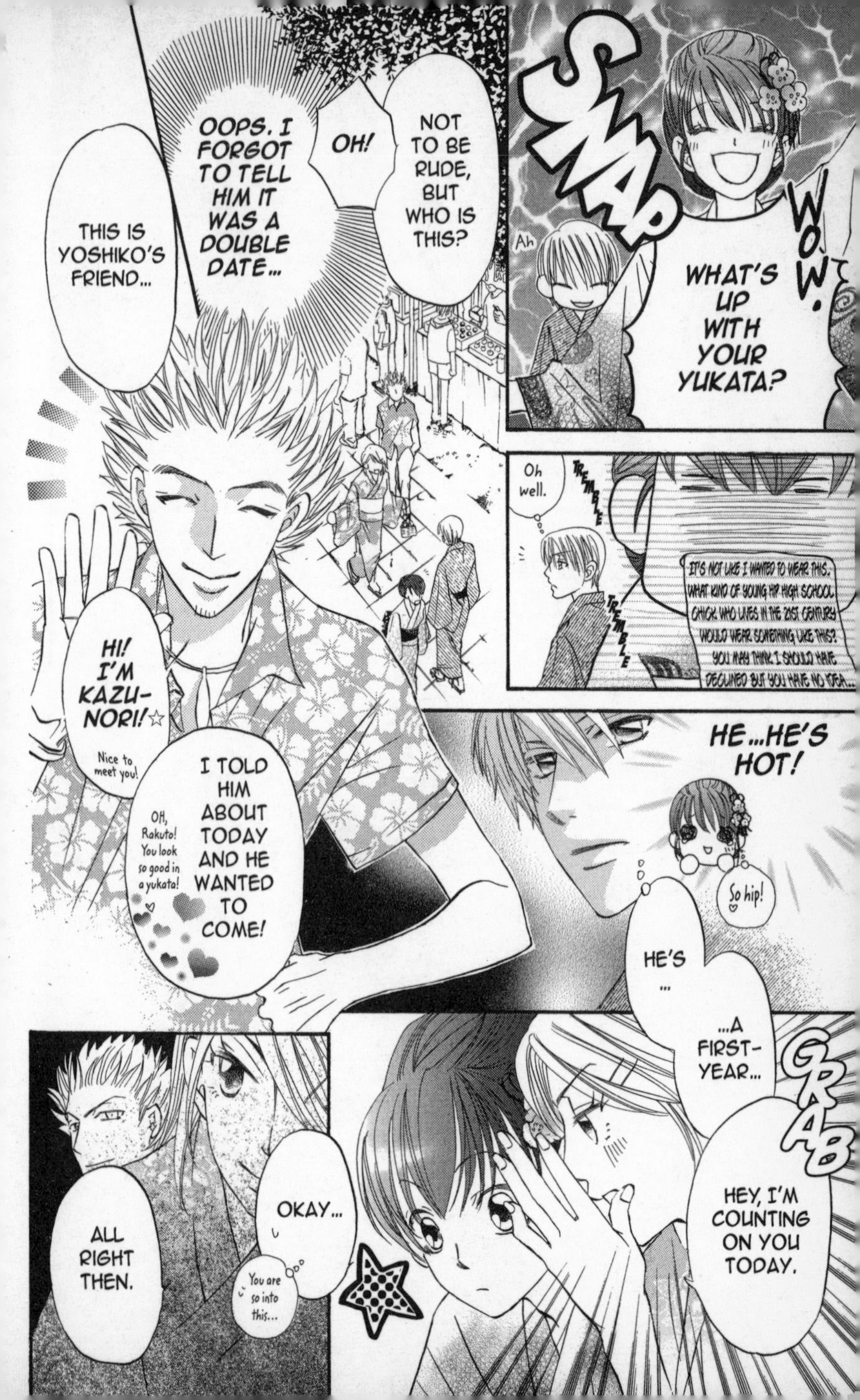
SMAP
WOW.
WHAT'S UP WITH YOUR YUKATA?
Ah
IT'S NOT LIKE I WANTED TO WEAR THIS. WHAT KIND OF YOUNG HIP HIGH SCHOOL CHICK WHO LIVES IN THE 21ST CENTURY WOULD WEAR SOMETHING LIKE THIS? YOU MAY THINK I SHOULD HAVE DECLINED BUT YOU HAVE NO IDEA...
TREMBLE
TREMBLE
Oh well.
HE...HE'S HOT!
So hip!
HE'S ...
NOT TO BE RUDE, BUT WHO IS THIS?
OH!
OOPS. I FORGOT TO TELL HIM IT WAS A DOUBLE DATE...
THIS IS YOSHIKO'S FRIEND...
HI! I'M KAZUNORI!☆
Nice to meet you!
I TOLD HIM ABOUT TODAY AND HE WANTED TO COME!
OH, Rakuto! You look so good in a yukata!
...A FIRST-YEAR...
GRAB
HEY, I'M COUNTING ON YOU TODAY.
OKAY...
You are so into this...
ALL RIGHT THEN.

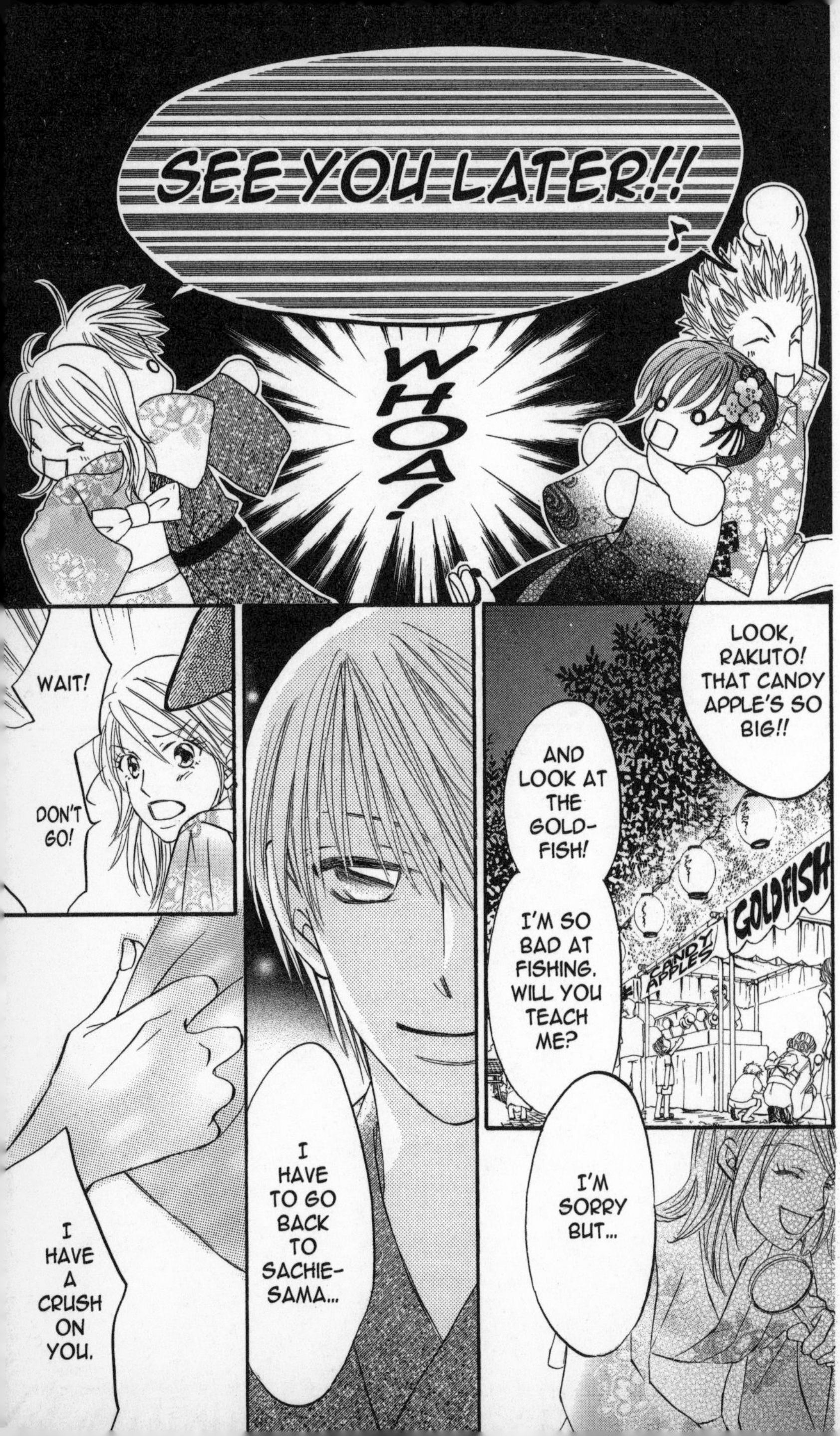
SEE YOU LATER!! ♪
WHOA!
LOOK, RAKUTO! THAT CANDY APPLE'S SO BIG!!
AND LOOK AT THE GOLD-FISH!
I'M SO BAD AT FISHING. WILL YOU TEACH ME?
GOLDFISH
CANDY APPLES
I'M SORRY BUT...
I HAVE TO GO BACK TO SACHIE-SAMA...
WAIT!
DON'T GO!
I HAVE A CRUSH ON YOU.

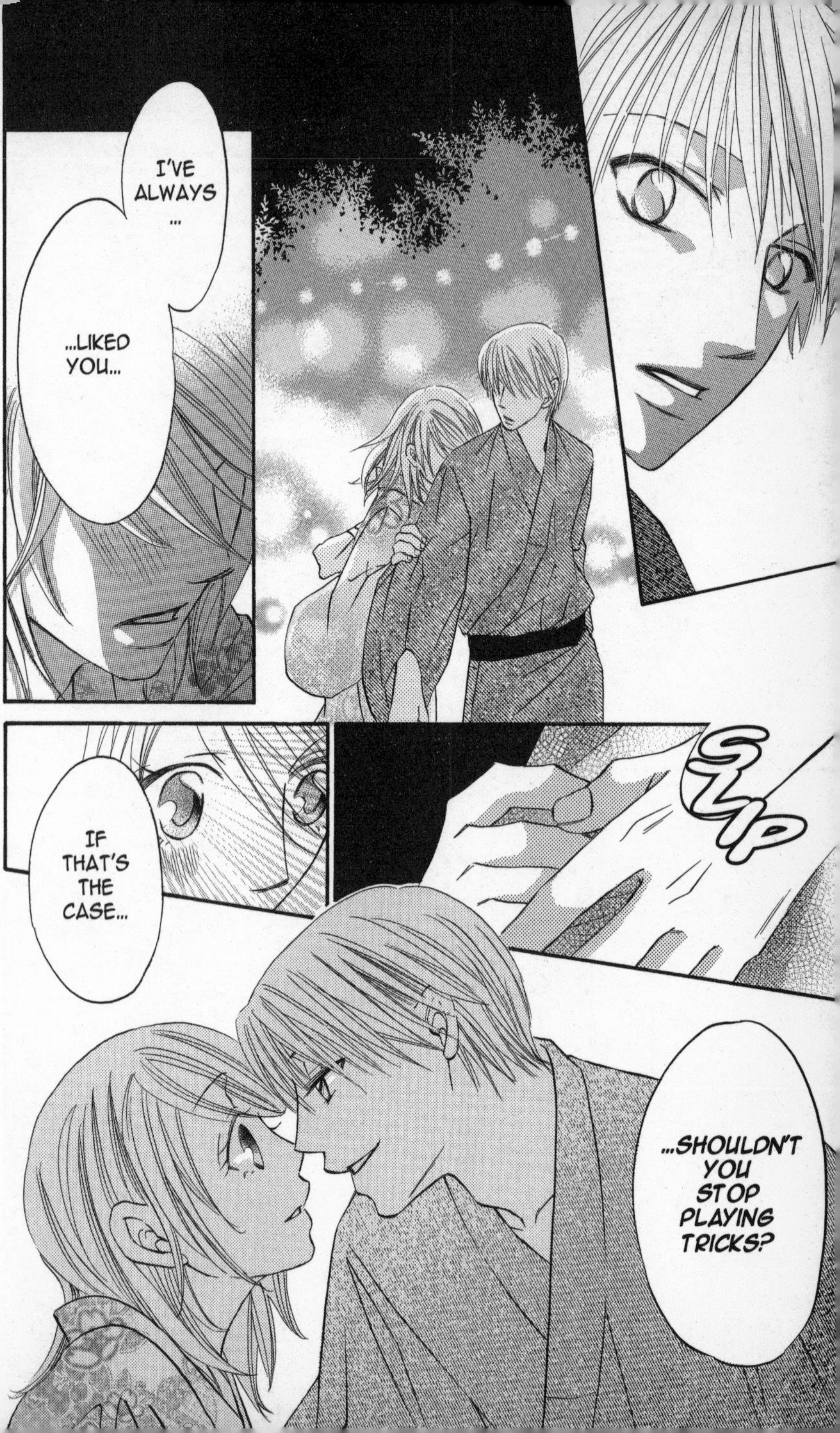
I'VE ALWAYS ...
...LIKED YOU...
SLIP
IF THAT'S THE CASE...
...SHOULDN'T YOU STOP PLAYING TRICKS?

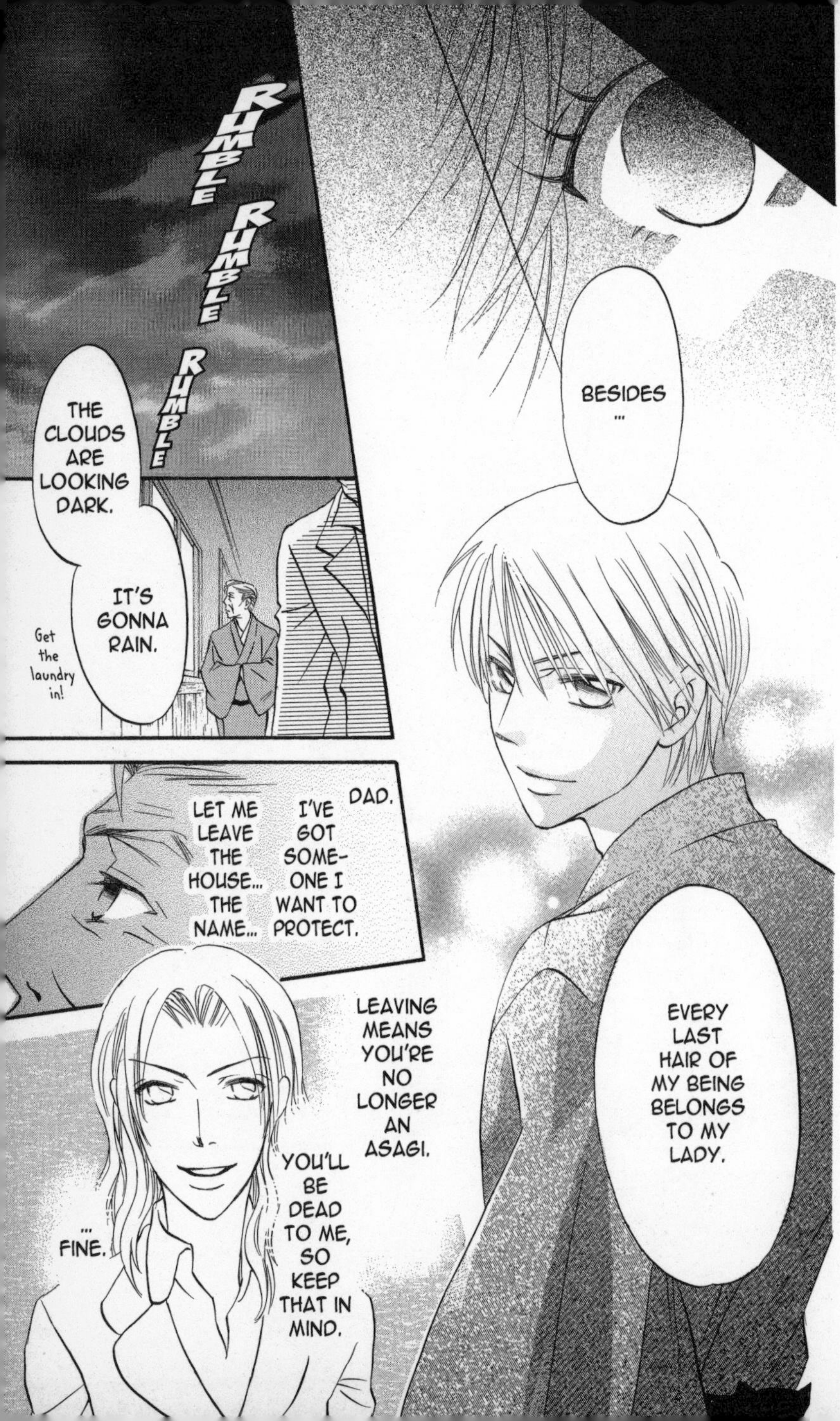
RUMBLE RUMBLE RUMBLE
THE CLOUDS ARE LOOKING DARK.
IT'S GONNA RAIN.
Get the laundry in!
DAD.
I'VE GOT SOME-ONE I WANT TO PROTECT.
LET ME LEAVE THE HOUSE... THE NAME...
LEAVING MEANS YOU'RE NO LONGER AN ASAGI.
YOU'LL BE DEAD TO ME, SO KEEP THAT IN MIND.
... FINE.
BESIDES ...
EVERY LAST HAIR OF MY BEING BELONGS TO MY LADY.

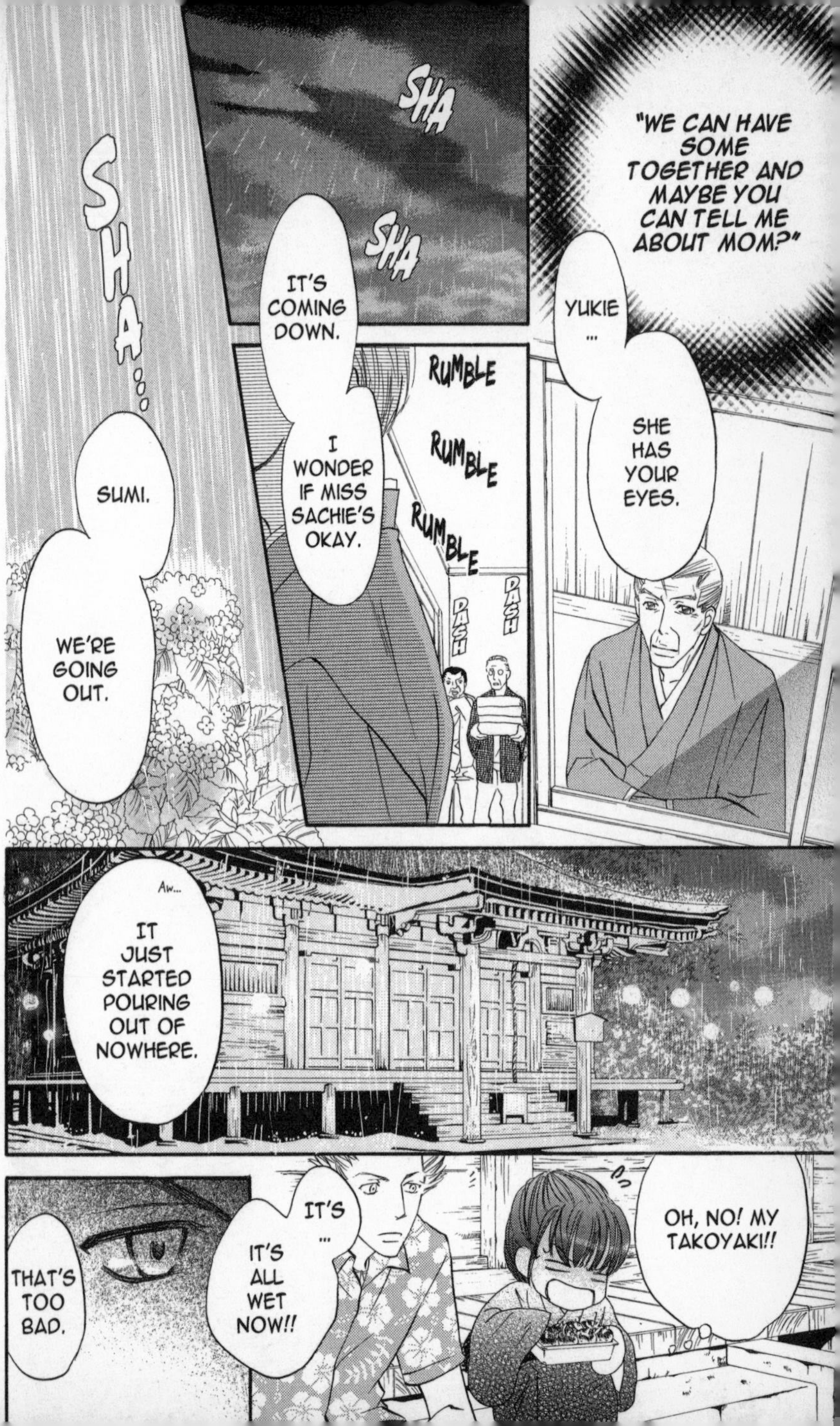
"WE CAN HAVE SOME TOGETHER AND MAYBE YOU CAN TELL ME ABOUT MOM?"
YUKIE ...
SHE HAS YOUR EYES.
SHA
SHA
IT'S COMING DOWN.
RUMBLE
RUMBLE
RUMBLE
I WONDER IF MISS SACHIE'S OKAY.
DASH
DASH
SHA...
SUMI.
WE'RE GOING OUT.
Aw...
IT JUST STARTED POURING OUT OF NOWHERE.
OH, NO! MY TAKOYAKI!!
IT'S ...
IT'S ALL WET NOW!!
THAT'S TOO BAD.

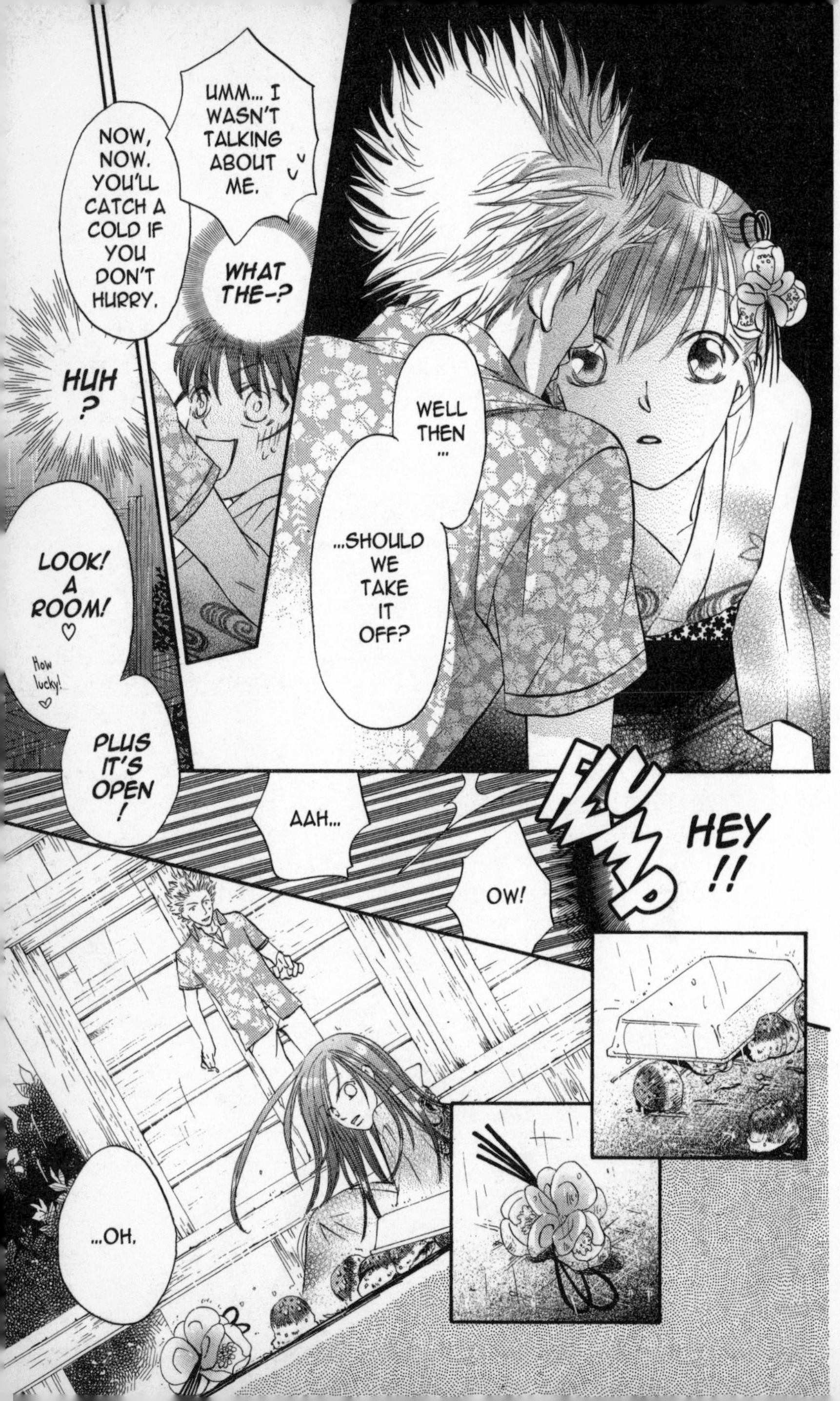
WELL THEN ...
...SHOULD WE TAKE IT OFF?
UMM... I WASN'T TALKING ABOUT ME.
WHAT THE-?
NOW, NOW. YOU'LL CATCH A COLD IF YOU DON'T HURRY.
HUH?
LOOK! A ROOM! ♡
How lucky! ♡
PLUS IT'S OPEN!
FLUMP
HEY!!
AAH...
OW!
...OH.

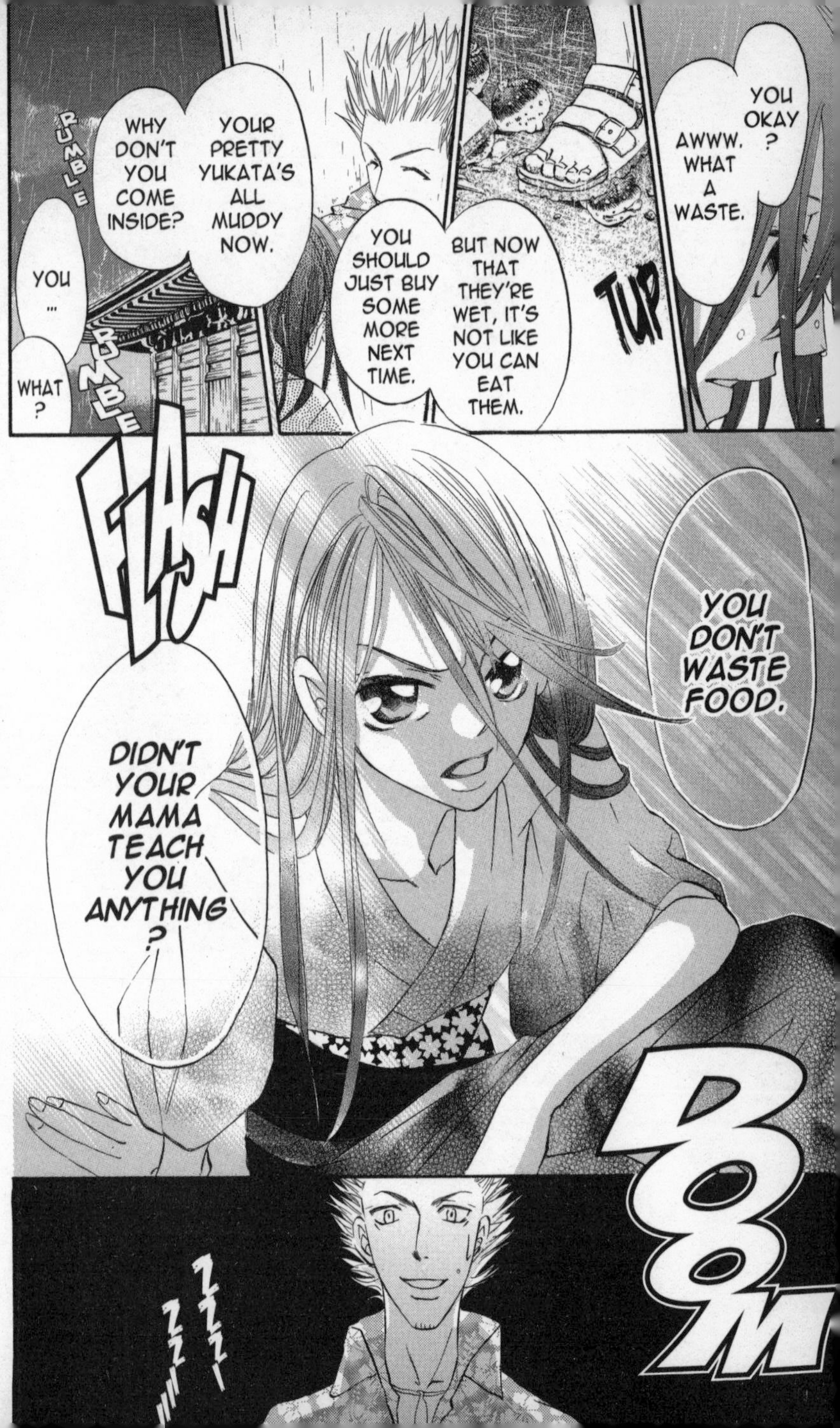
YOU OKAY?
AWWW. WHAT A WASTE.
TUP
BUT NOW THAT THEY'RE WET, IT'S NOT LIKE YOU CAN EAT THEM.
YOU SHOULD JUST BUY SOME MORE NEXT TIME.
YOUR PRETTY YUKATA'S ALL MUDDY NOW.
WHY DON'T YOU COME INSIDE?
RUMBLE
YOU ...
WHAT?
RUMBLE
FLASH
YOU DON'T WASTE FOOD.
DIDN'T YOUR MAMA TEACH YOU ANYTHING?
BOOM
ZZZ

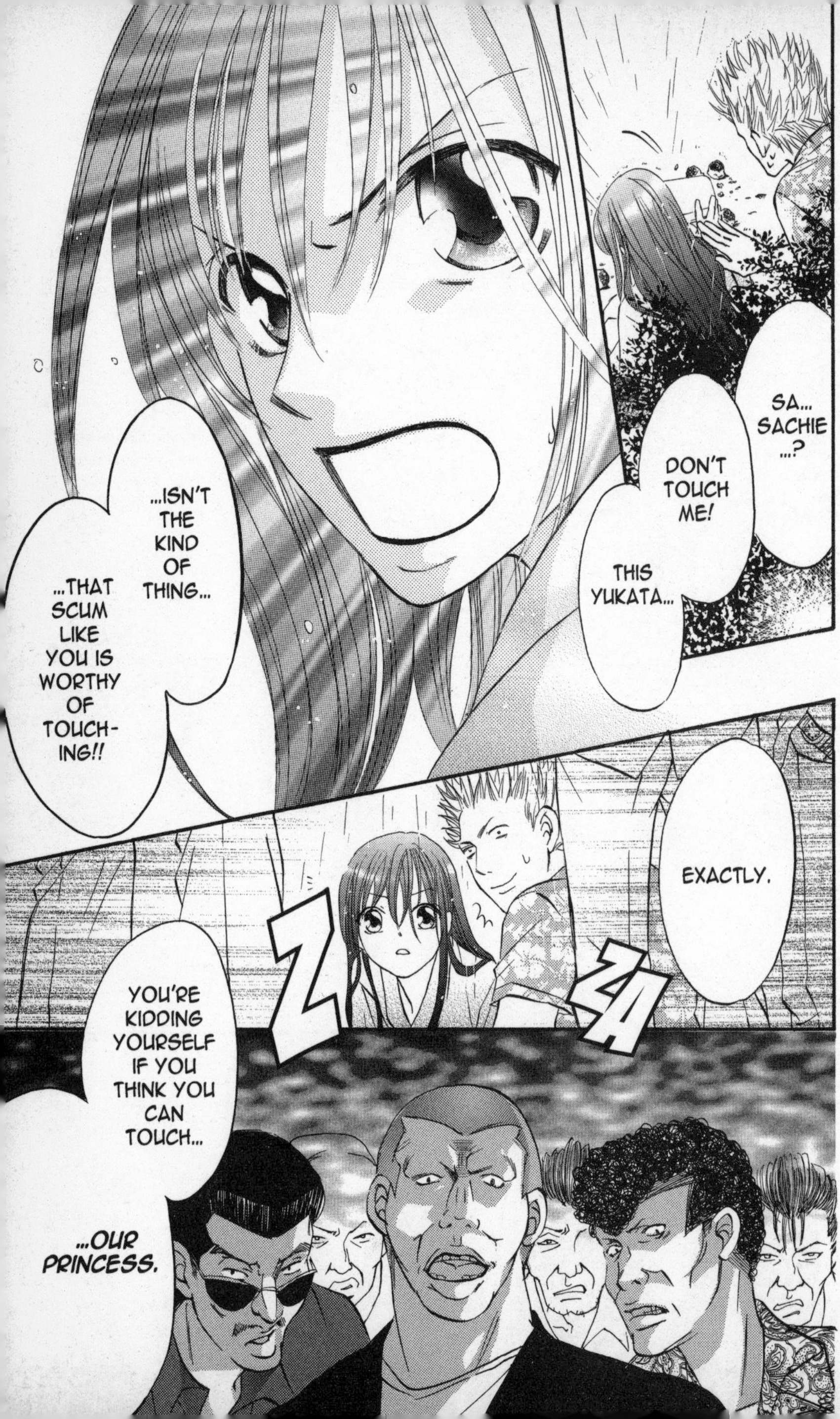
SA... SACHIE ...?
DON'T TOUCH ME!
THIS YUKATA...
...ISN'T THE KIND OF THING...
...THAT SCUM LIKE YOU IS WORTHY OF TOUCHING!!
EXACTLY.
ZA
Z
YOU'RE KIDDING YOURSELF IF YOU THINK YOU CAN TOUCH...
...OUR PRINCESS.

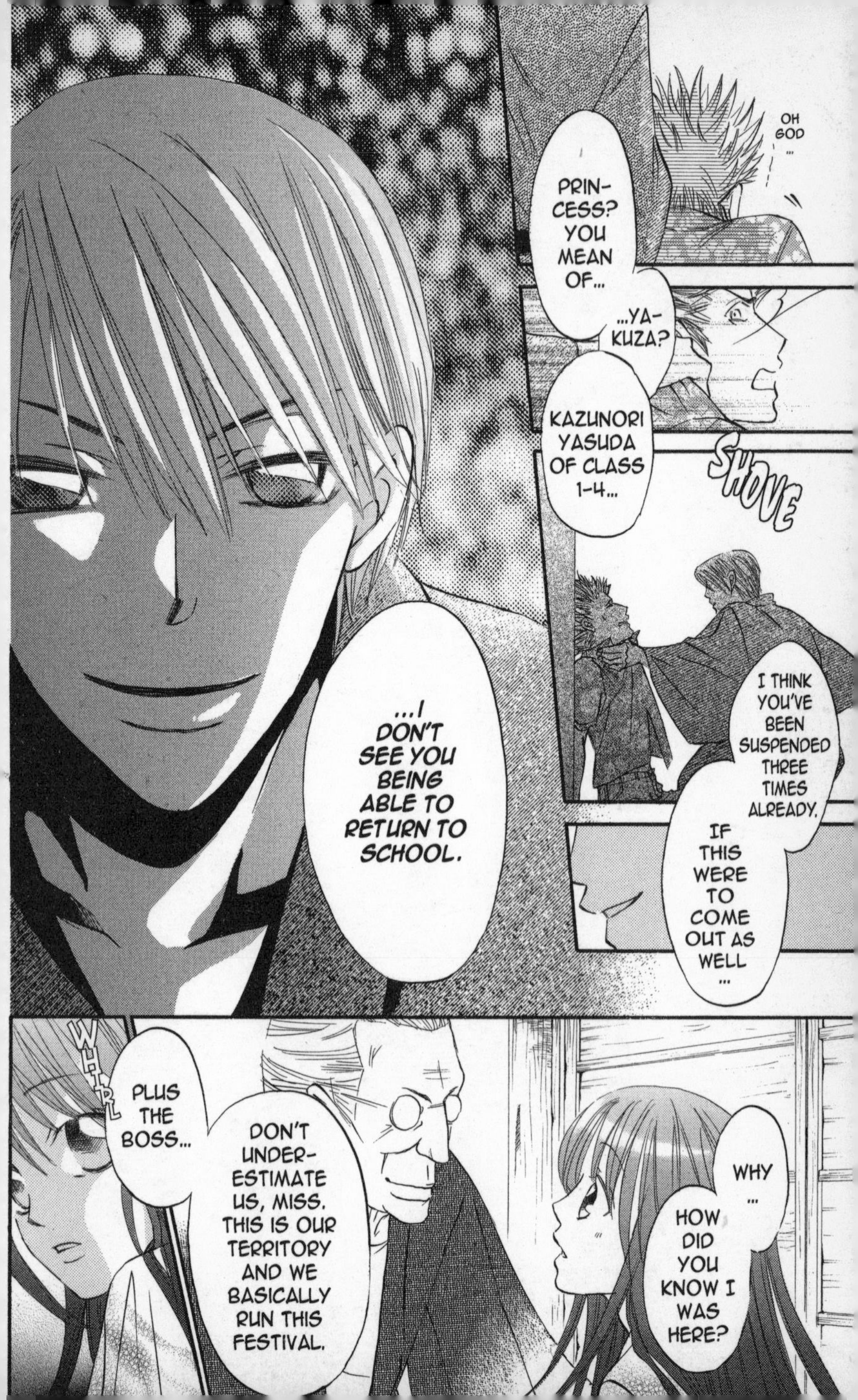
OH GOD ...
PRIN-CESS? YOU MEAN OF...
...YA-KUZA?
KAZUNORI YASUDA OF CLASS 1-4...
SHOVE
I THINK YOU'VE BEEN SUSPENDED THREE TIMES ALREADY.
IF THIS WERE TO COME OUT AS WELL ...
...I DON'T SEE YOU BEING ABLE TO RETURN TO SCHOOL.
WHY ...
HOW DID YOU KNOW I WAS HERE?
DON'T UNDER-ESTIMATE US, MISS. THIS IS OUR TERRITORY AND WE BASICALLY RUN THIS FESTIVAL.
PLUS THE BOSS...
WHIRL

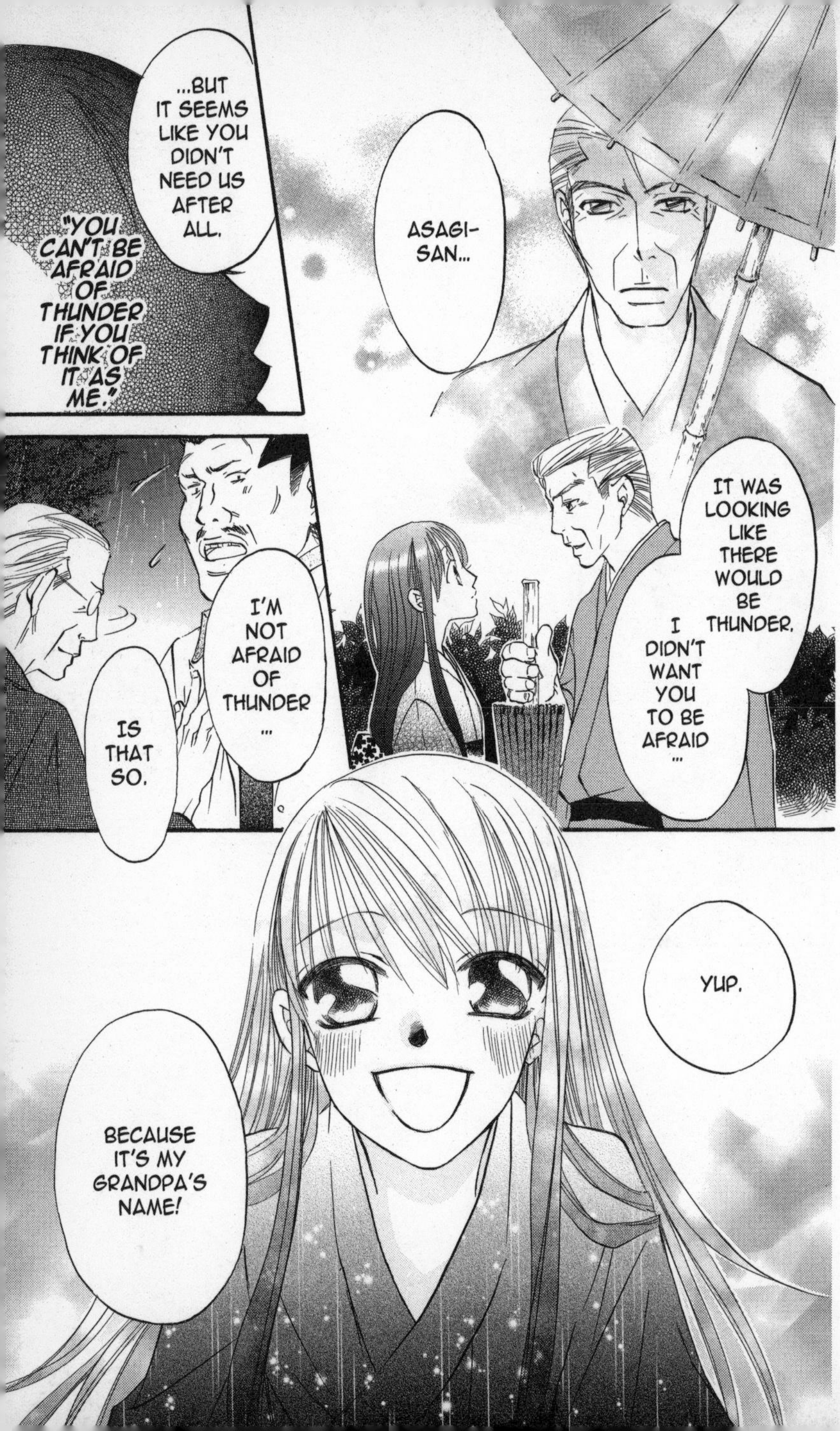
ASAGI-SAN...
...BUT IT SEEMS LIKE YOU DIDN'T NEED US AFTER ALL.
"YOU CAN'T BE AFRAID OF THUNDER IF YOU THINK OF IT AS ME."
IT WAS LOOKING LIKE THERE WOULD BE THUNDER.
I DIDN'T WANT YOU TO BE AFRAID...
I'M NOT AFRAID OF THUNDER...
IS THAT SO.
YUP.
BECAUSE IT'S MY GRANDPA'S NAME!

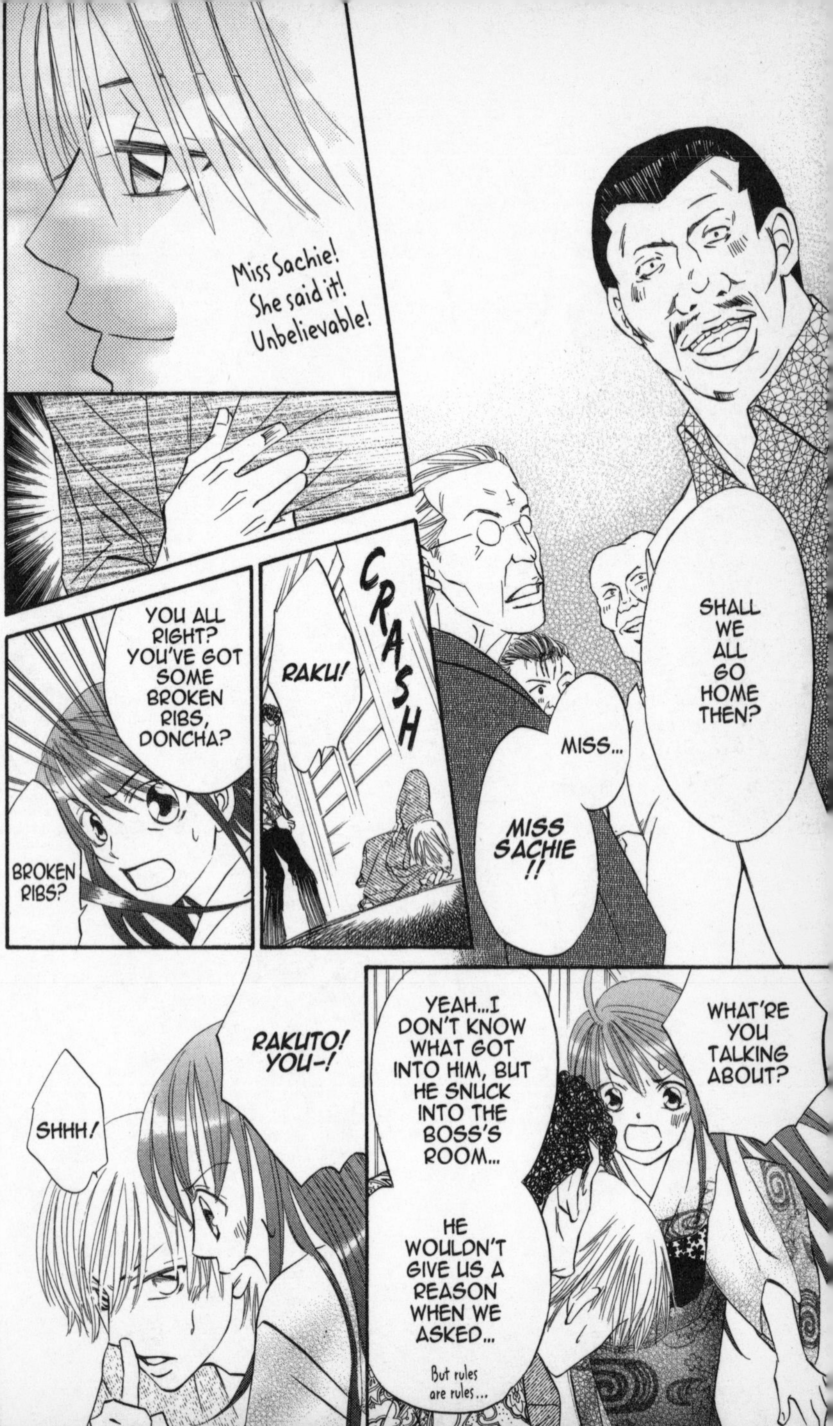
SHALL WE ALL GO HOME THEN?
MISS...
MISS SACHIE !!
Miss Sachie! She said it! Unbelievable!
CRASH
RAKU!
YOU ALL RIGHT? YOU'VE GOT SOME BROKEN RIBS, DONCHA?
BROKEN RIBS?
WHAT'RE YOU TALKING ABOUT?
YEAH...I DON'T KNOW WHAT GOT INTO HIM, BUT HE SNUCK INTO THE BOSS'S ROOM...
HE WOULDN'T GIVE US A REASON WHEN WE ASKED...
But rules are rules...
RAKUTO! YOU-!
SHHH!

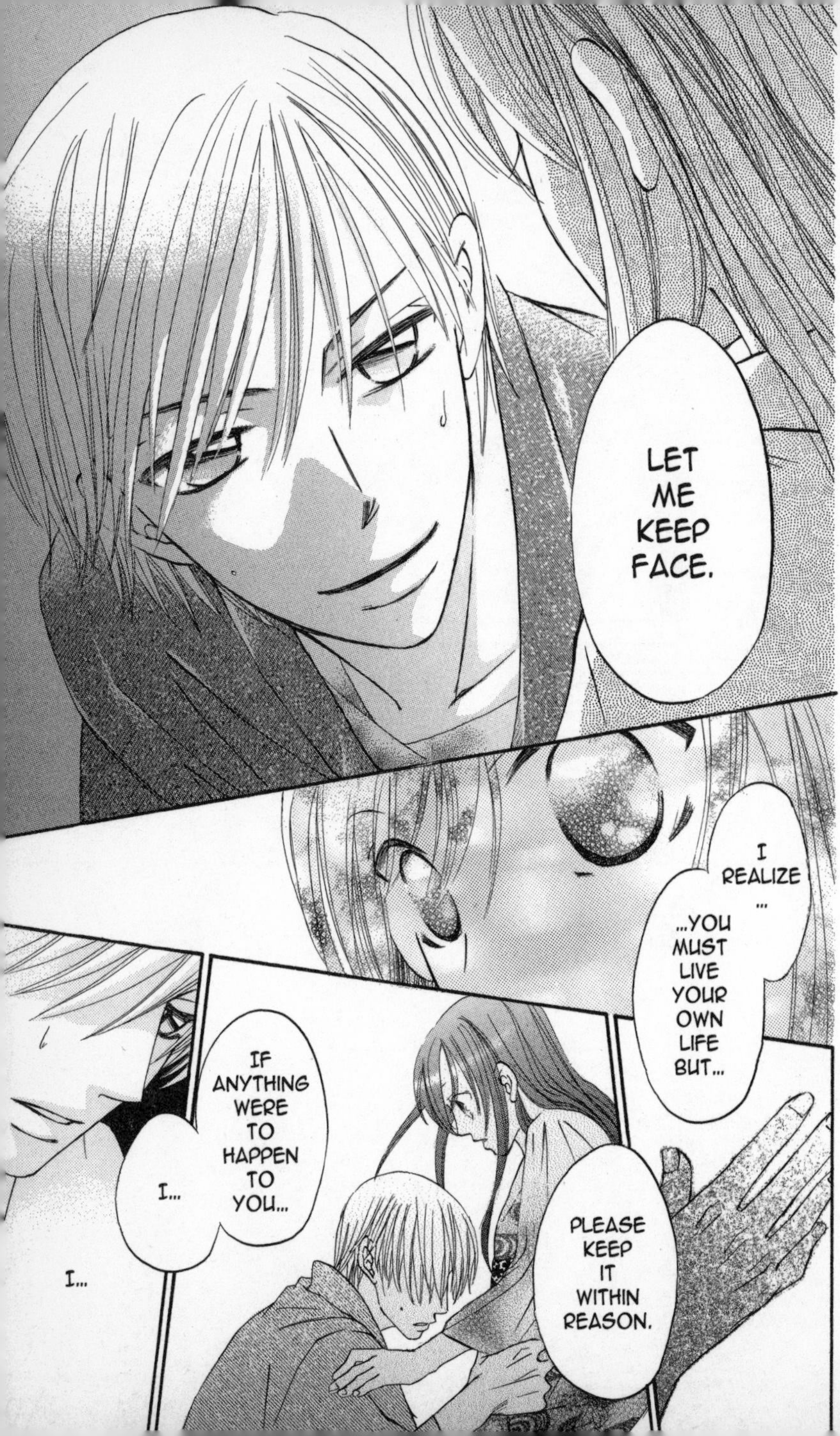
LET ME KEEP FACE.
I REALIZE ...
...YOU MUST LIVE YOUR OWN LIFE BUT...
PLEASE KEEP IT WITHIN REASON.
IF ANYTHING WERE TO HAPPEN TO YOU...
I...
I...

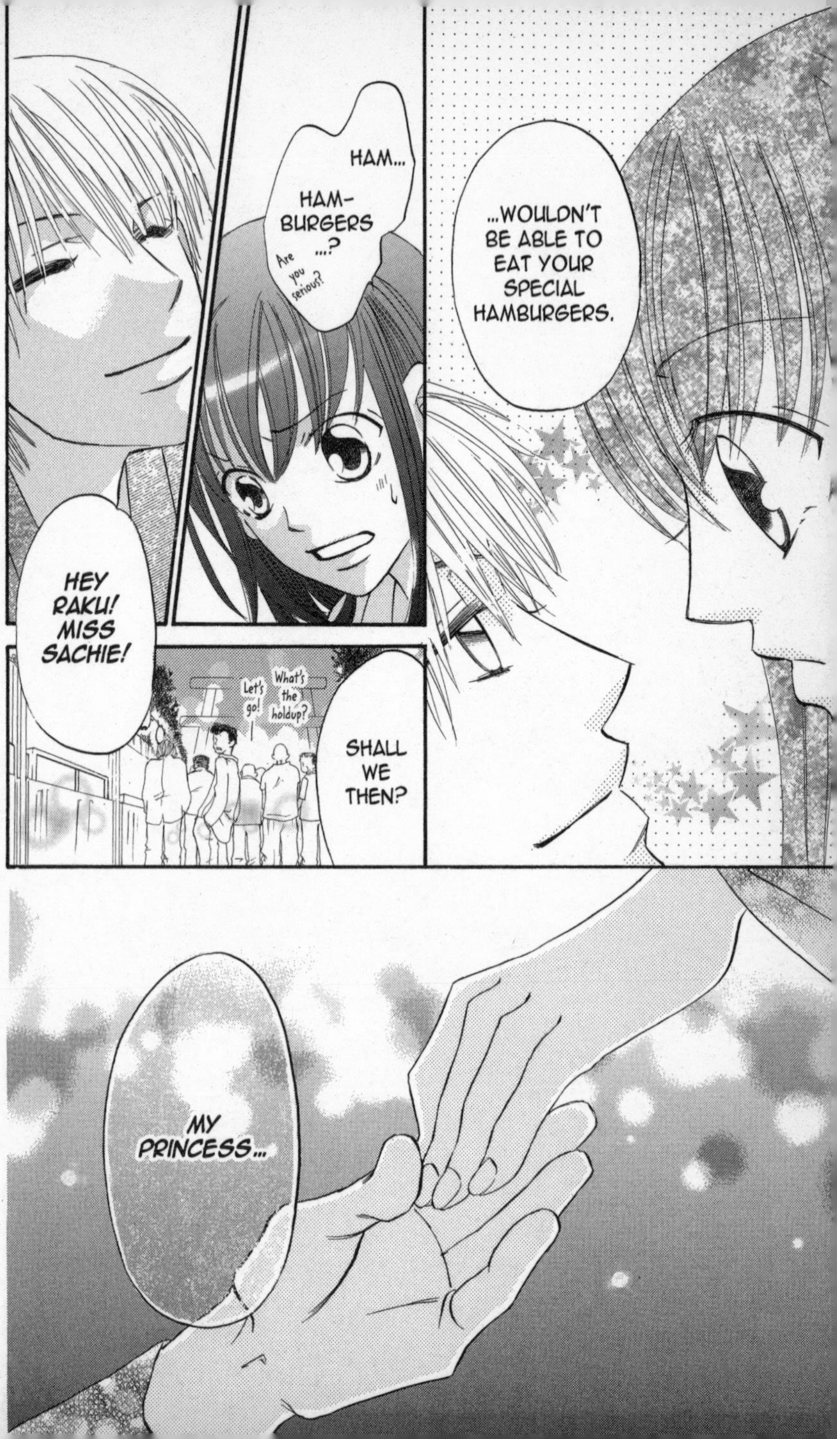
...WOULDN'T BE ABLE TO EAT YOUR SPECIAL HAMBURGERS.
HAM...
HAM- BURGERS ...?
Are you serious?
HEY RAKU! MISS SACHIE!
What's the holdup?
Let's go!
SHALL WE THEN?
MY PRINCESS...

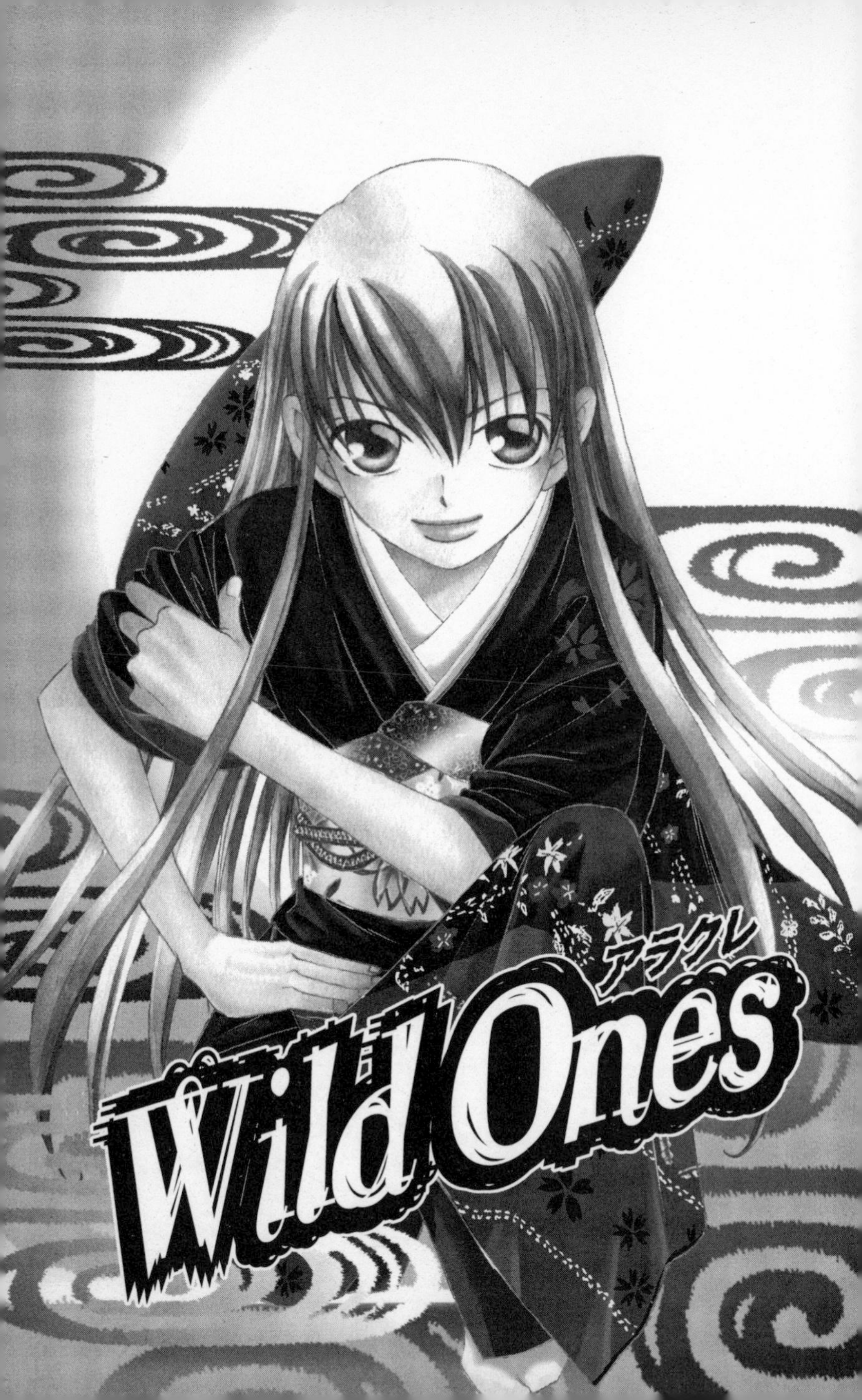
アラクレ
Wild Ones

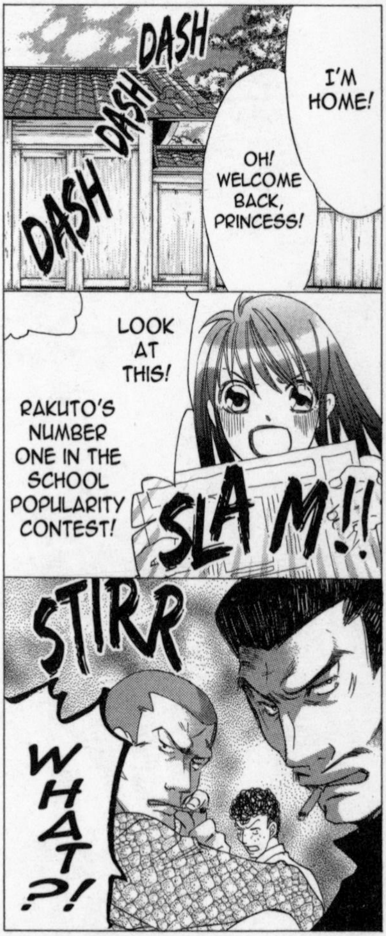
I'M HOME!
DASH DASH DASH
OH! WELCOME BACK, PRINCESS!
LOOK AT THIS!
RAKUTO'S NUMBER ONE IN THE SCHOOL POPULARITY CONTEST!
SLAM!!
STIRR
WHAT?!

TO BE CONTINUED...

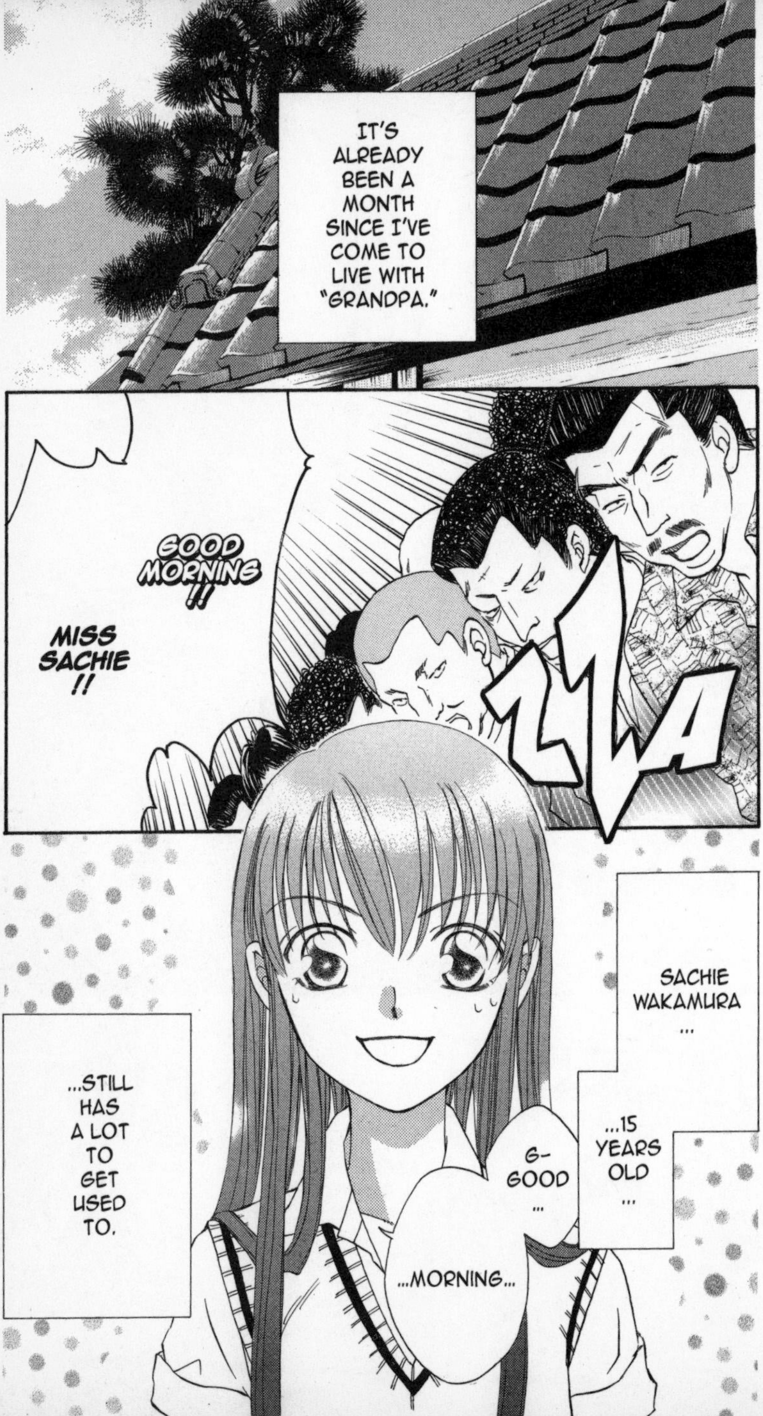
IT'S ALREADY BEEN A MONTH SINCE I'VE COME TO LIVE WITH "GRANDPA."
ZA
GOOD MORNING!!
MISS SACHIE!!
SACHIE WAKAMURA...
...15 YEARS OLD...
G-GOOD...
...MORNING...
...STILL HAS A LOT TO GET USED TO.

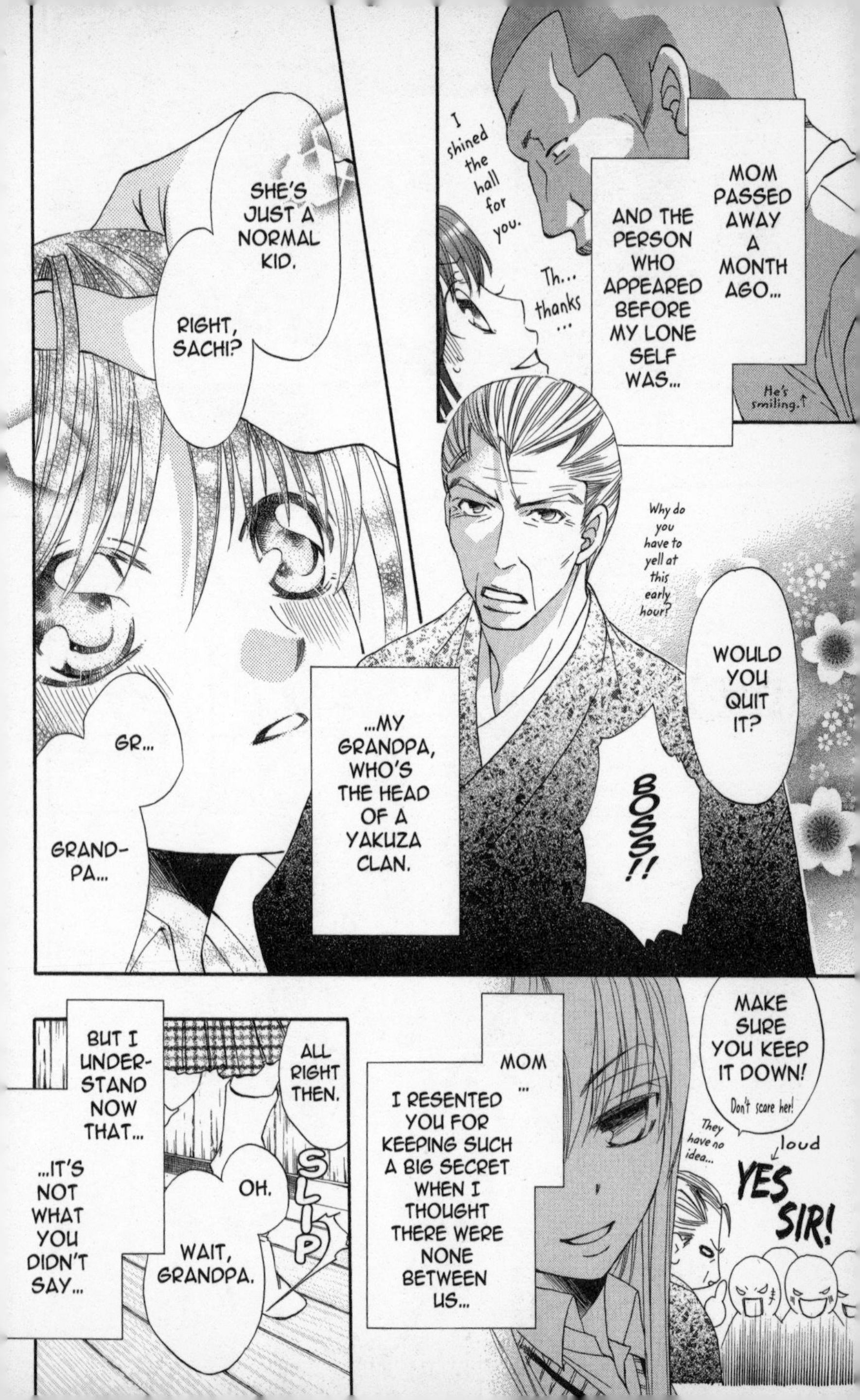
MOM PASSED AWAY A MONTH AGO...
AND THE PERSON WHO APPEARED BEFORE MY LONE SELF WAS...
I shined the hall for you.
Th... thanks...
He's smiling.↑
WOULD YOU QUIT IT?
Why do you have to yell at this early hour?
BOSS!!
...MY GRANDPA, WHO'S THE HEAD OF A YAKUZA CLAN.
SHE'S JUST A NORMAL KID.
RIGHT, SACHI?
GR...
GRAND-PA...
MAKE SURE YOU KEEP IT DOWN!
Don't scare her!
loud
YES SIR!
They have no idea...
MOM...
I RESENTED YOU FOR KEEPING SUCH A BIG SECRET WHEN I THOUGHT THERE WERE NONE BETWEEN US...
ALL RIGHT THEN.
BUT I UNDER-STAND NOW THAT...
OH.
SLIP
WAIT, GRANDPA.
...IT'S NOT WHAT YOU DIDN'T SAY...

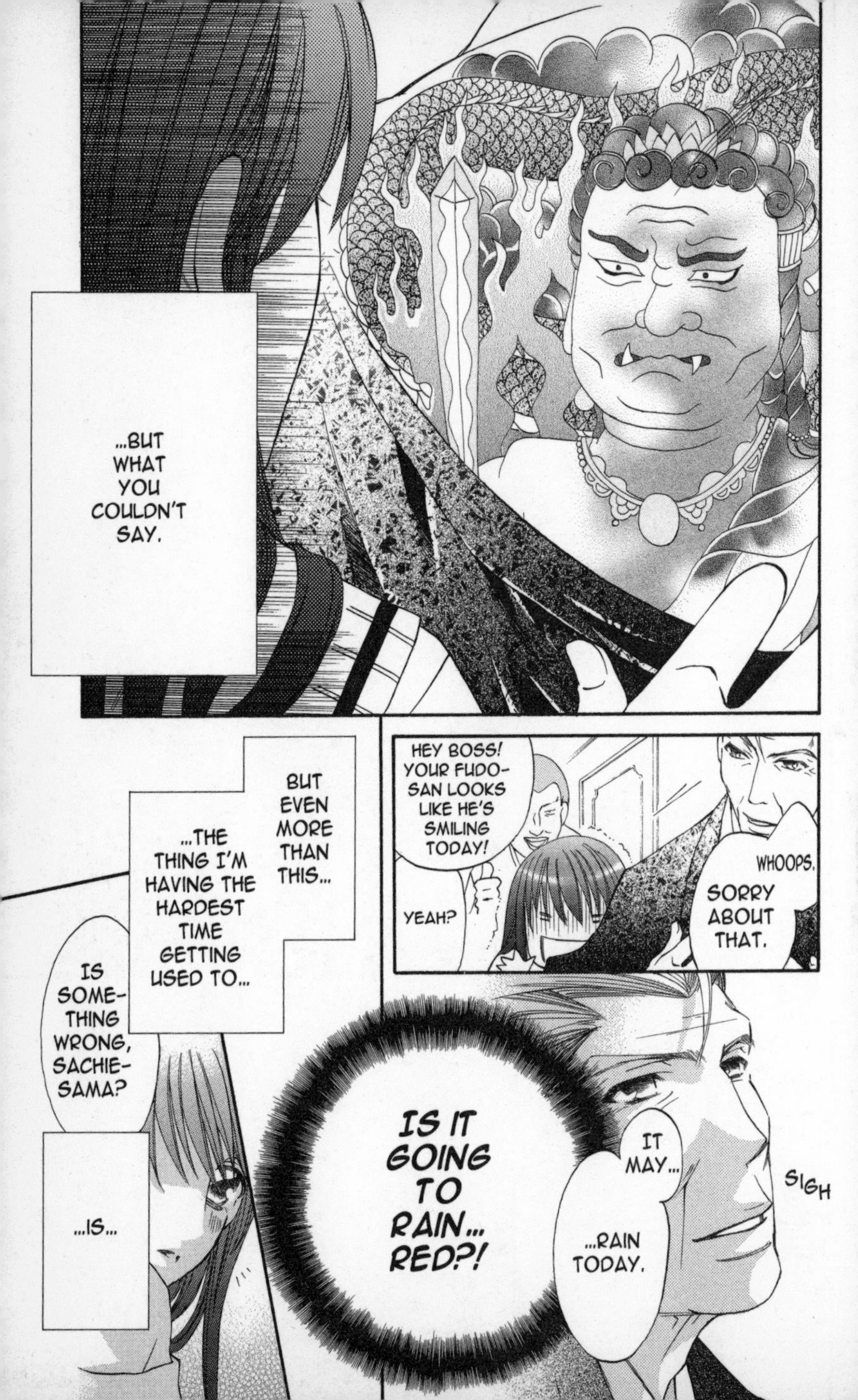
...BUT WHAT YOU COULDN'T SAY.
HEY BOSS! YOUR FUDO-SAN LOOKS LIKE HE'S SMILING TODAY!
WHOOPS.
SORRY ABOUT THAT.
YEAH?
SIGH
IT MAY...
...RAIN TODAY.
IS IT GOING TO RAIN... RED?!
BUT EVEN MORE THAN THIS...
...THE THING I'M HAVING THE HARDEST TIME GETTING USED TO...
IS SOMETHING WRONG, SACHIE-SAMA?
...IS...

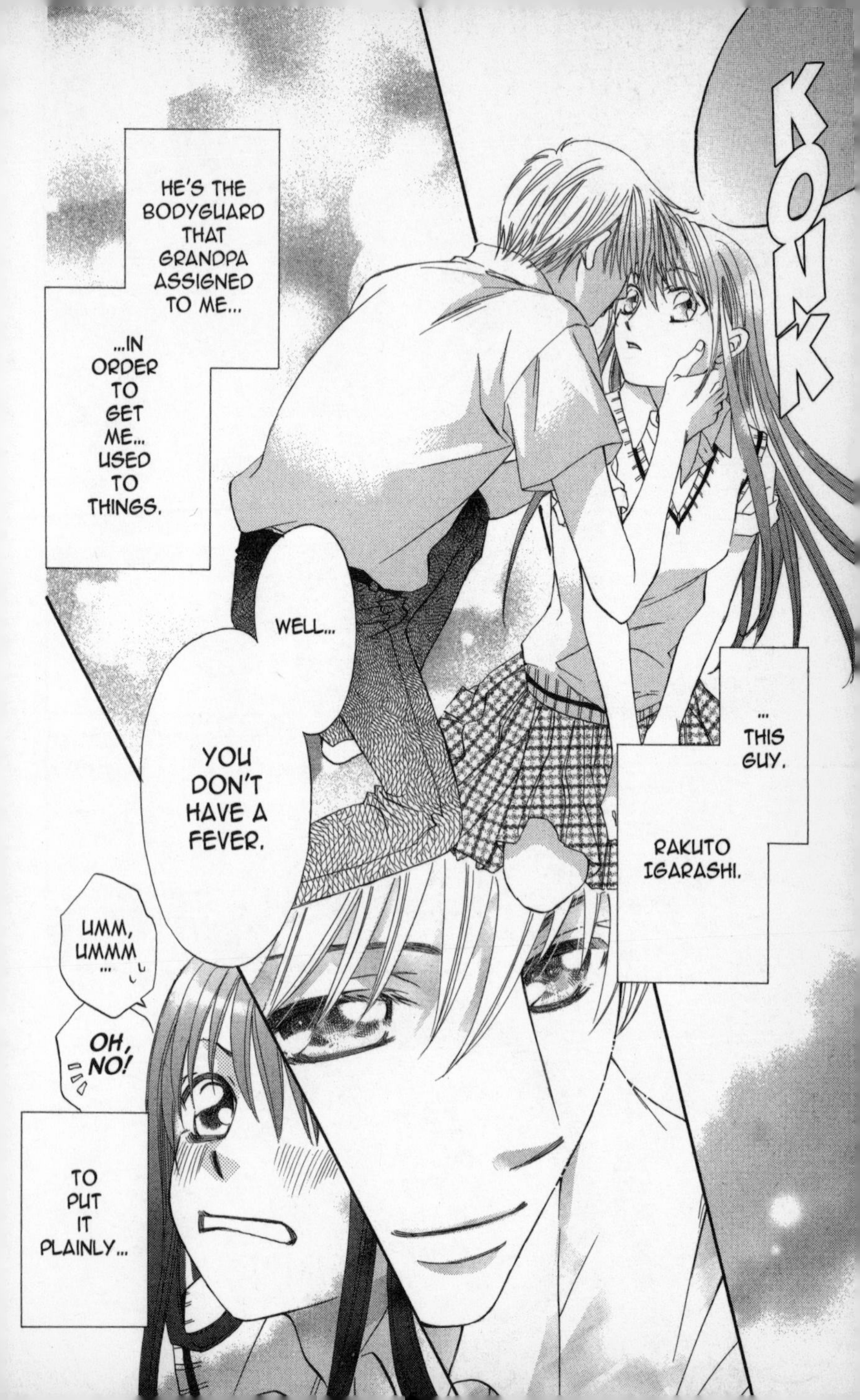
KONK
HE'S THE BODYGUARD THAT GRANDPA ASSIGNED TO ME...
...IN ORDER TO GET ME... USED TO THINGS.
... THIS GUY.
RAKUTO IGARASHI.
WELL...
YOU DON'T HAVE A FEVER.
UMM, UMMM ...
OH, NO!
TO PUT IT PLAINLY...

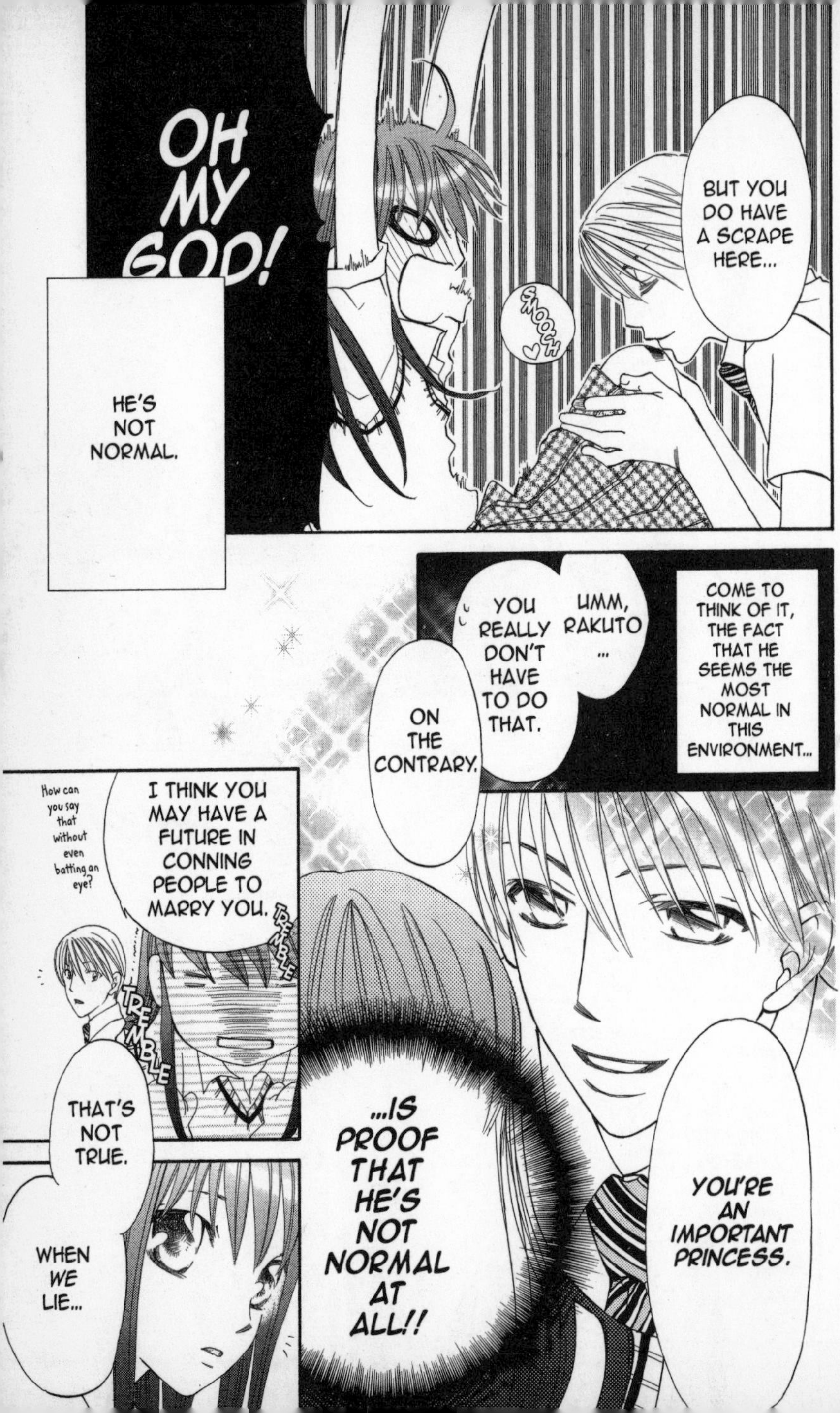
BUT YOU DO HAVE A SCRAPE HERE...
SMOOCH
OH MY GOD!
HE'S NOT NORMAL.
COME TO THINK OF IT, THE FACT THAT HE SEEMS THE MOST NORMAL IN THIS ENVIRONMENT...
UMM, RAKUTO...
YOU REALLY DON'T HAVE TO DO THAT.
ON THE CONTRARY.
YOU'RE AN IMPORTANT PRINCESS.
...IS PROOF THAT HE'S NOT NORMAL AT ALL!!
I THINK YOU MAY HAVE A FUTURE IN CONNING PEOPLE TO MARRY YOU.
How can you say that without even batting an eye?
TREMBLE
TREMBLE
THAT'S NOT TRUE.
WHEN WE LIE...

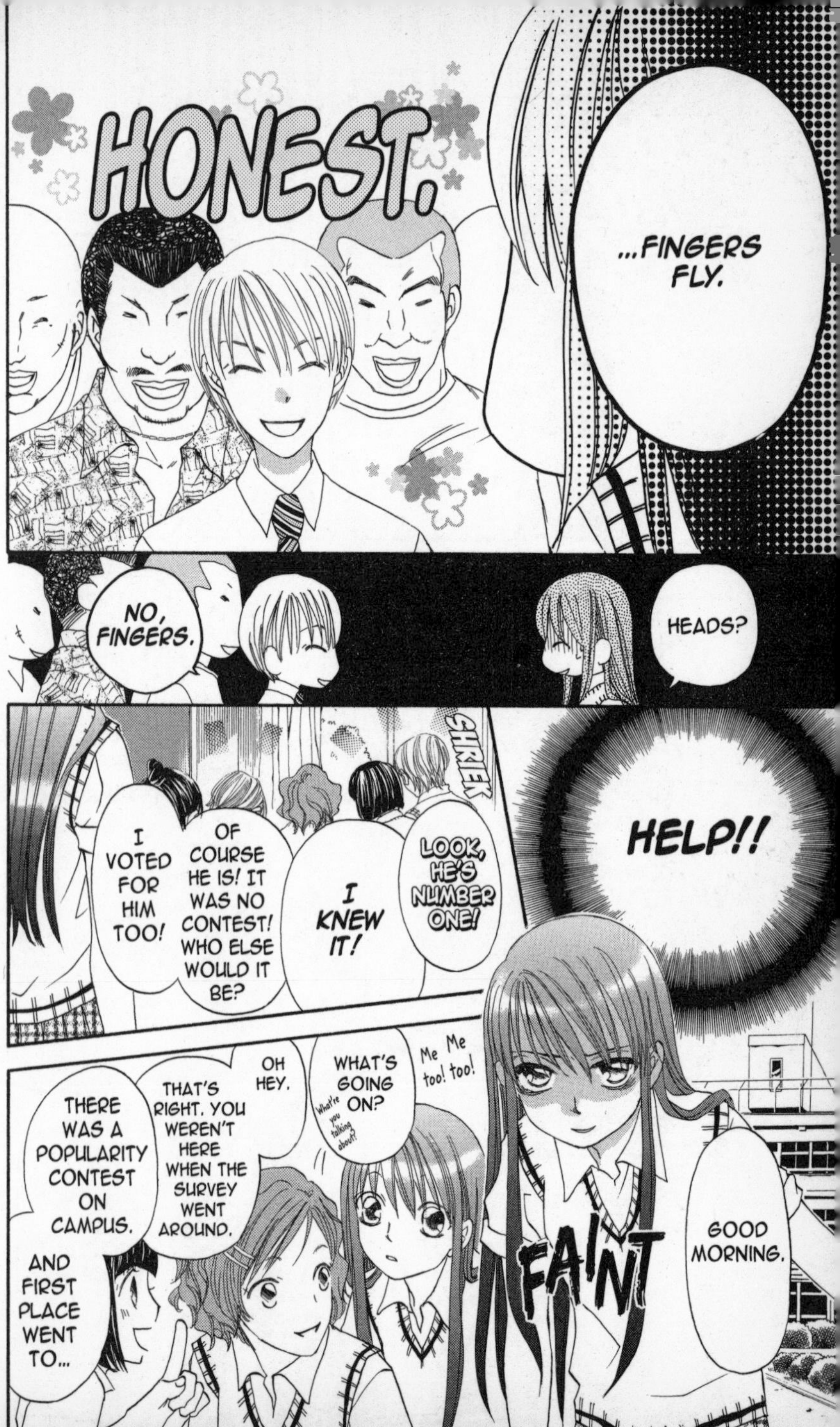
...FINGERS FLY.
HONEST.
HEADS?
NO, FINGERS.
HELP!!
SHRIEK
LOOK, HE'S NUMBER ONE!
I KNEW IT!
OF COURSE HE IS! IT WAS NO CONTEST! WHO ELSE WOULD IT BE?
I VOTED FOR HIM TOO!
GOOD MORNING.
FAINT
Me too! Me too!
WHAT'S GOING ON?
What're you talking about?
OH HEY.
THAT'S RIGHT. YOU WEREN'T HERE WHEN THE SURVEY WENT AROUND.
THERE WAS A POPULARITY CONTEST ON CAMPUS.
AND FIRST PLACE WENT TO...

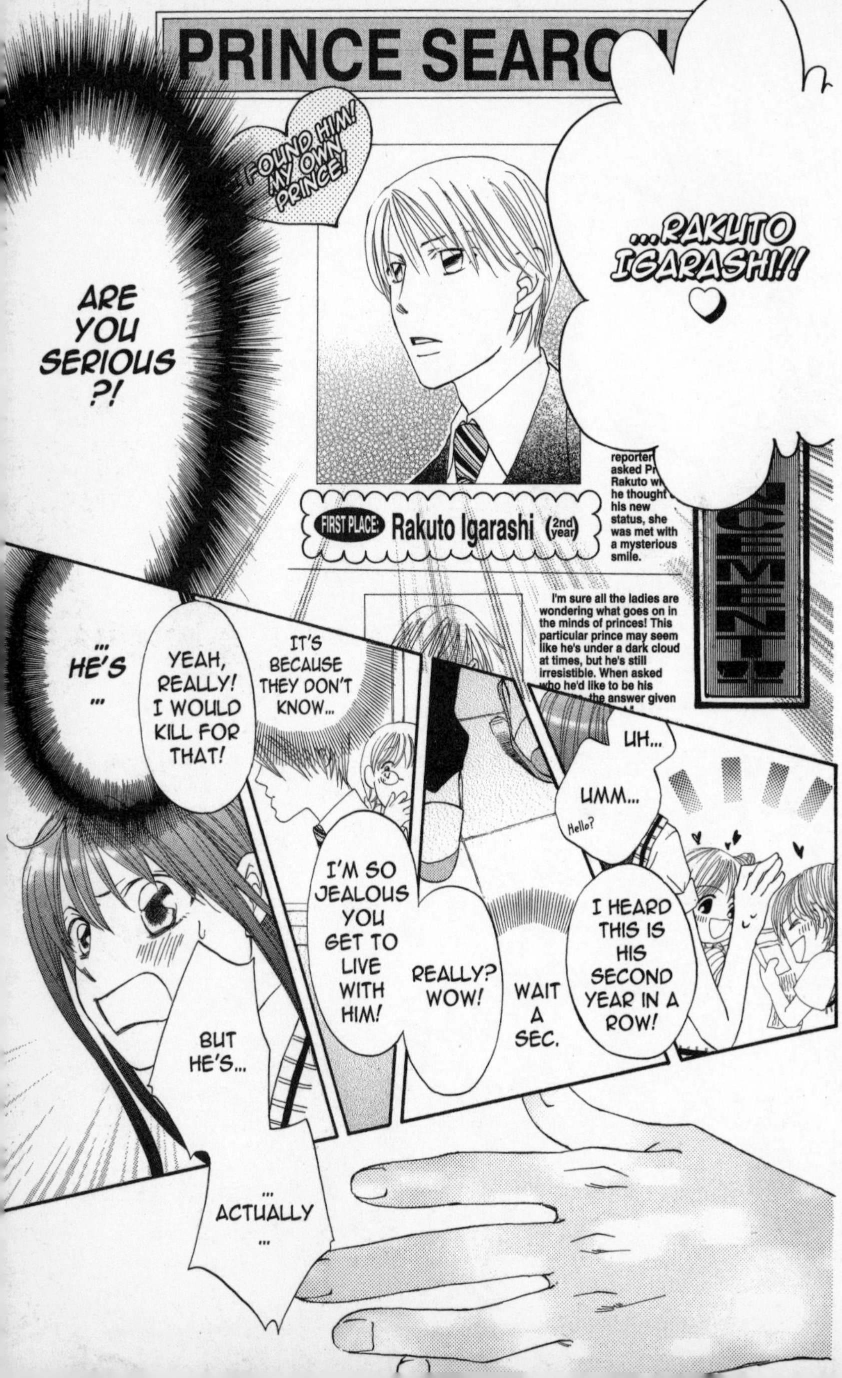
PRINCE SEARC
I FOUND HIM! MY OWN PRINCE!
...RAKUTO IGARASHI!! ♥
FIRST PLACE: Rakuto Igarashi (2nd year)
reporter asked Pr Rakuto wh he thought his new status, she was met with a mysterious smile.
I'm sure all the ladies are wondering what goes on in the minds of princes! This particular prince may seem like he's under a dark cloud at times, but he's still irresistible. When asked who he'd like to be his
the answer given
ARE YOU SERIOUS ?!
UH...
UMM...
Hello?
I HEARD THIS IS HIS SECOND YEAR IN A ROW!
WAIT A SEC.
REALLY? WOW!
I'M SO JEALOUS YOU GET TO LIVE WITH HIM!
IT'S BECAUSE THEY DON'T KNOW...
YEAH, REALLY! I WOULD KILL FOR THAT!
...HE'S...
BUT HE'S...
...ACTUALLY...

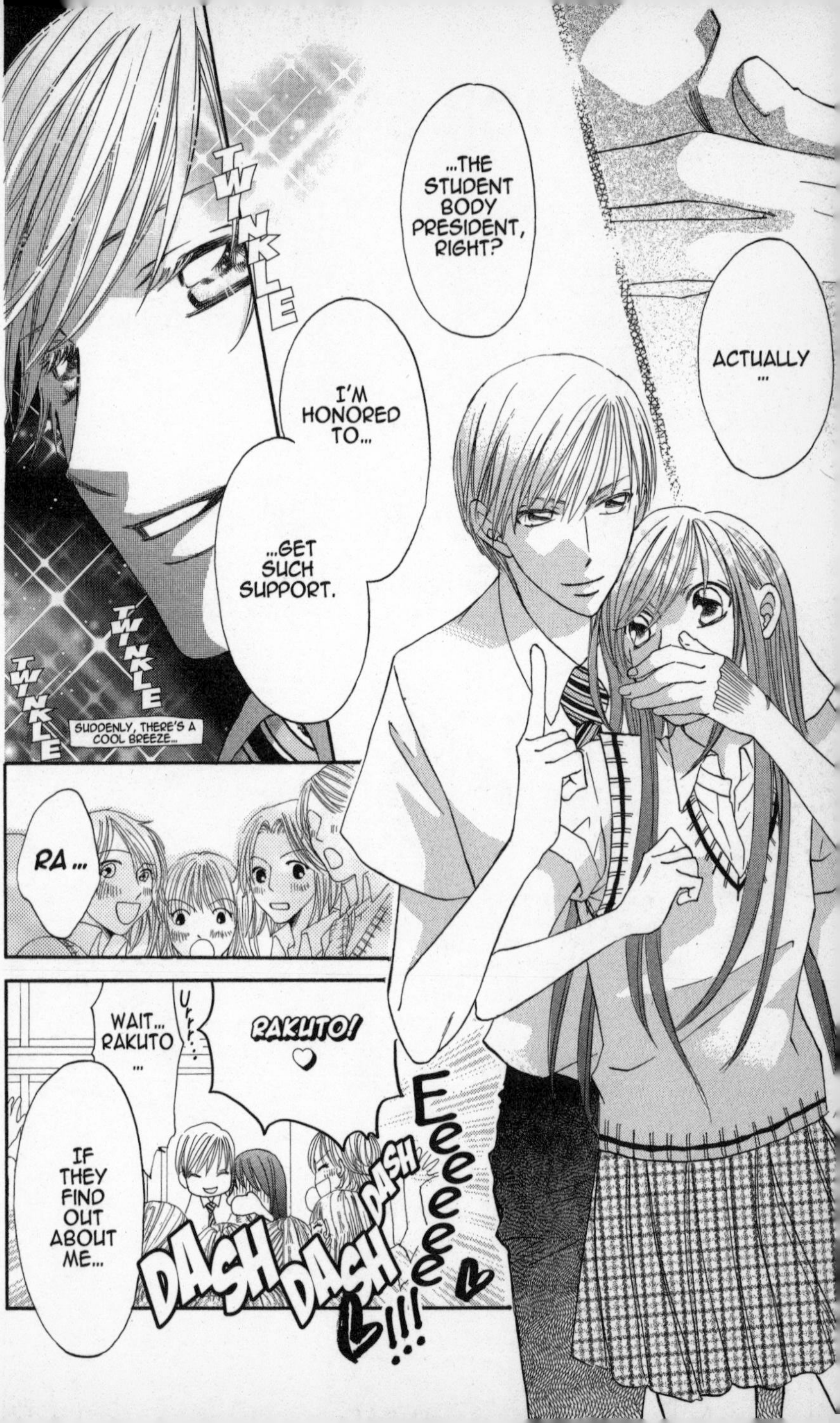
ACTUALLY...
...THE STUDENT BODY PRESIDENT, RIGHT?
TWINKLE
I'M HONORED TO...
...GET SUCH SUPPORT.
TWINKLE
TWINKLE
SUDDENLY, THERE'S A COOL BREEZE...
RA...
Eeeeeee!!!
DASH
DASH
DASH
RAKUTO!
Urrr...
WAIT... RAKUTO...
IF THEY FIND OUT ABOUT ME...

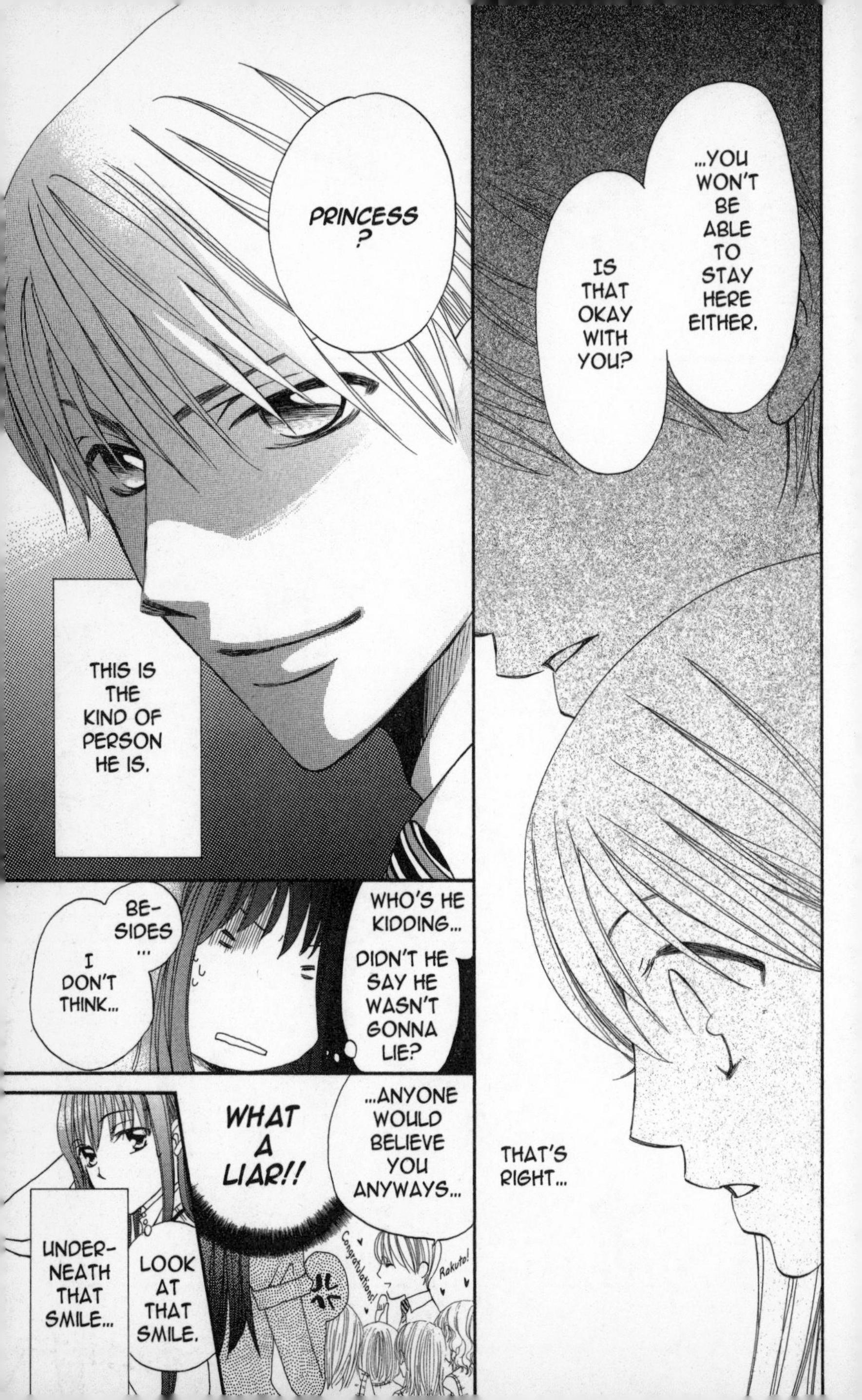
...YOU WON'T BE ABLE TO STAY HERE EITHER.
IS THAT OKAY WITH YOU?
THAT'S RIGHT...
PRINCESS?
THIS IS THE KIND OF PERSON HE IS.
WHO'S HE KIDDING...
DIDN'T HE SAY HE WASN'T GONNA LIE?
BESIDES...
I DON'T THINK...
...ANYONE WOULD BELIEVE YOU ANYWAYS...
WHAT A LIAR!!
Rakuto!
Congratulations!
LOOK AT THAT SMILE.
UNDERNEATH THAT SMILE...

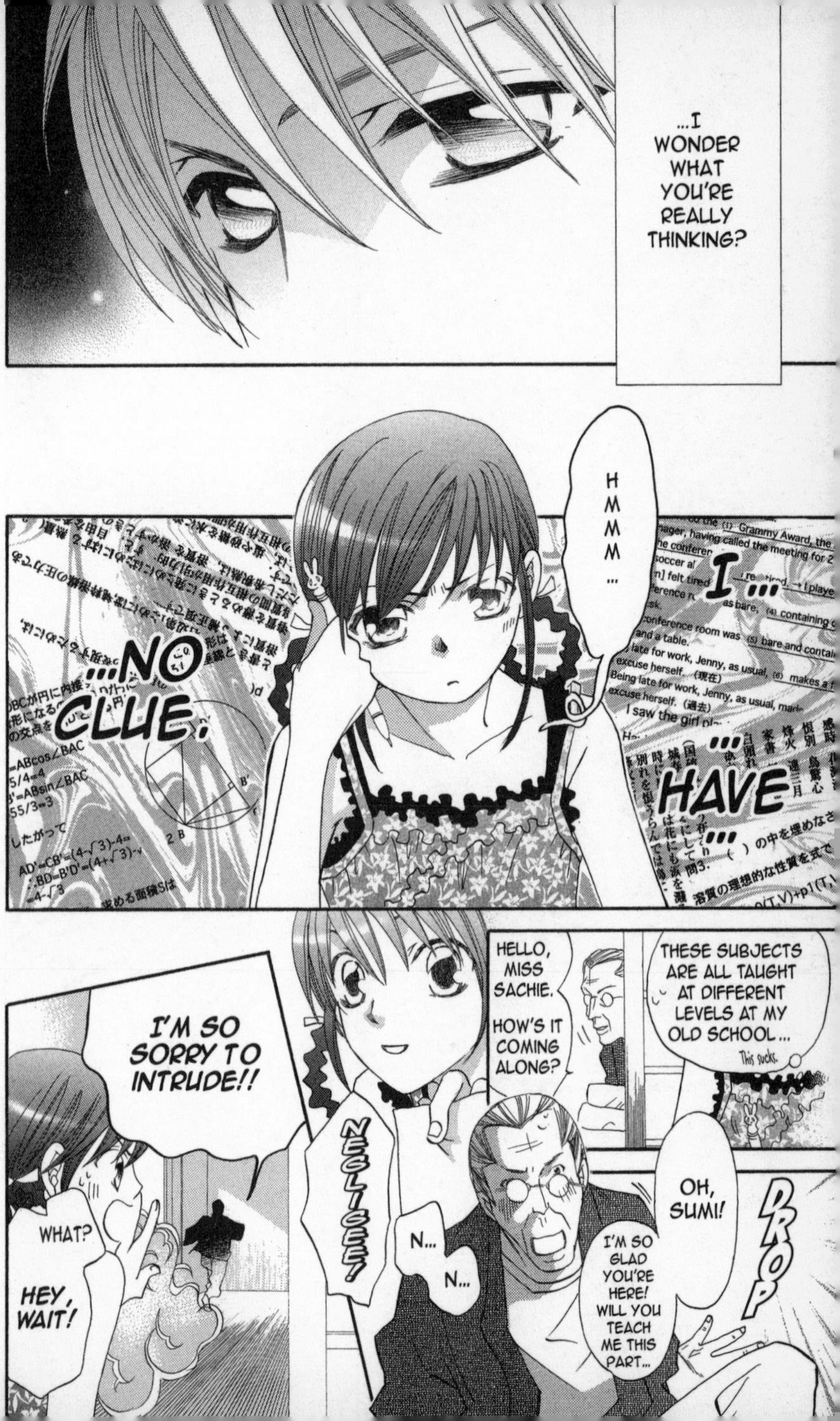
...I WONDER WHAT YOU'RE REALLY THINKING?
HMMM...
I...
HAVE...
...NO CLUE.
THESE SUBJECTS ARE ALL TAUGHT AT DIFFERENT LEVELS AT MY OLD SCHOOL...
This sucks.
HELLO, MISS SACHIE.
HOW'S IT COMING ALONG?
DROP
OH, SUMI!
I'M SO GLAD YOU'RE HERE! WILL YOU TEACH ME THIS PART...
N...
N...
NEGLIGEE!
I'M SO SORRY TO INTRUDE!!
WHAT?
HEY, WAIT!

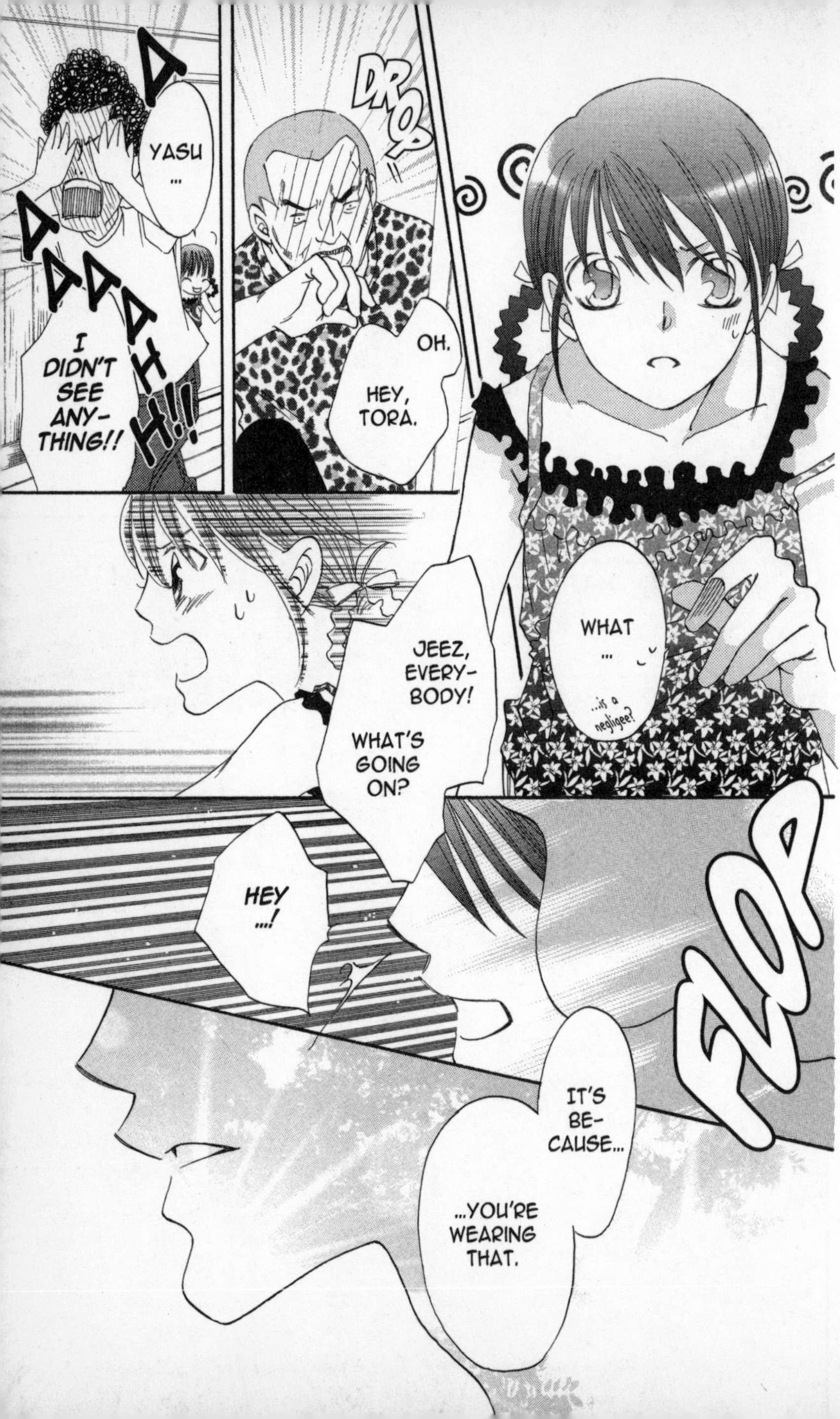
WHAT ...
...is a negligee?
DROP
OH.
HEY, TORA.
YASU ...
AAAAAH!!
I DIDN'T SEE ANYTHING!!
JEEZ, EVERYBODY!
WHAT'S GOING ON?
ZOOP
HEY ...!
IT'S BECAUSE...
...YOU'RE WEARING THAT.

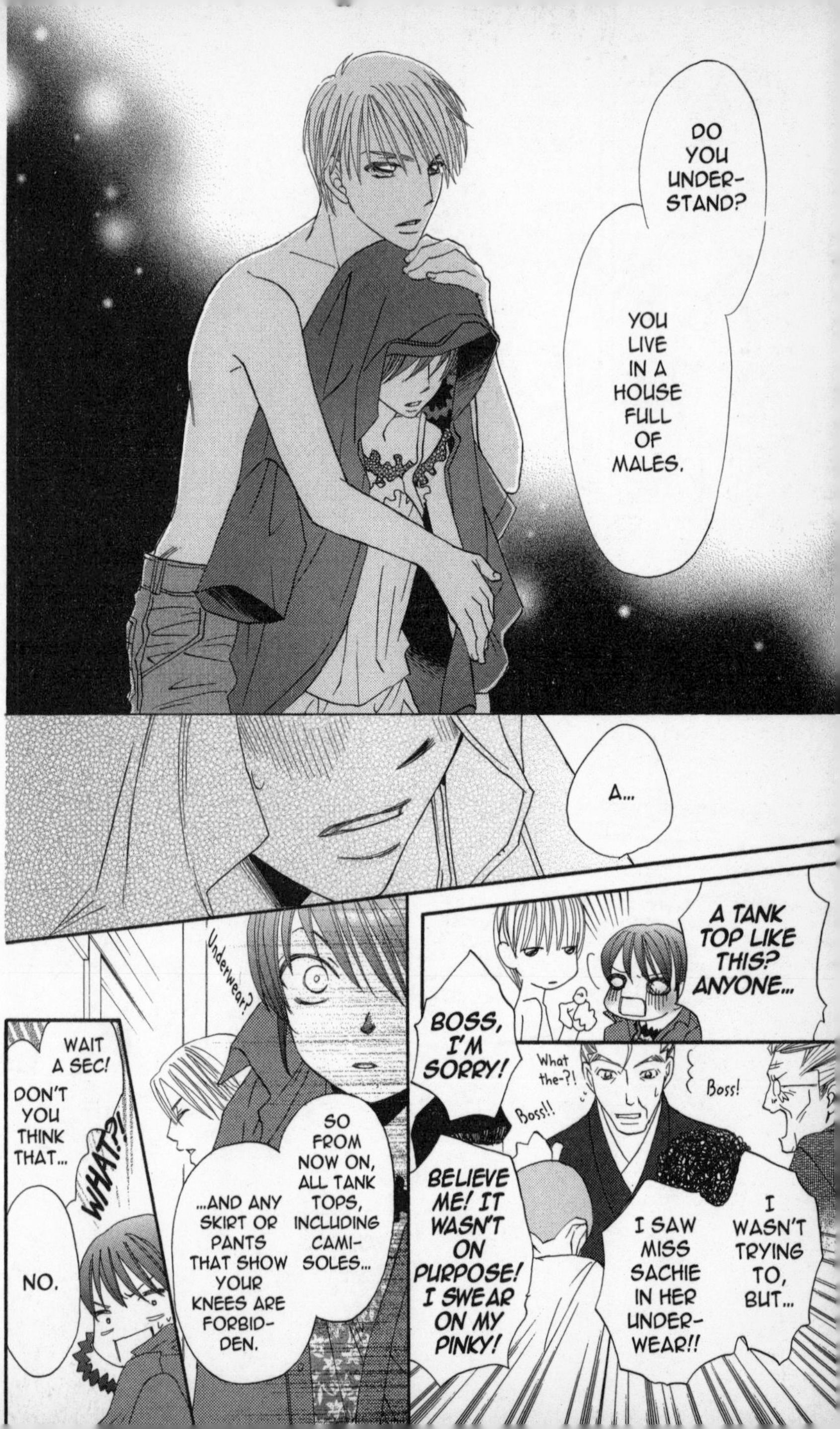
DO YOU UNDER-STAND?
YOU LIVE IN A HOUSE FULL OF MALES.
A...
A TANK TOP LIKE THIS? ANYONE...
Boss!
I WASN'T TRYING TO, BUT...
I SAW MISS SACHIE IN HER UNDER-WEAR!!
What the-?!
Boss!!
BOSS, I'M SORRY!
BELIEVE ME! IT WASN'T ON PURPOSE! I SWEAR ON MY PINKY!
Underwear?
SO FROM NOW ON, ALL TANK TOPS, INCLUDING CAMI-SOLES...
...AND ANY SKIRT OR PANTS THAT SHOW YOUR KNEES ARE FORBID-DEN.
WAIT A SEC! DON'T YOU THINK THAT...
WHAT?!
NO.

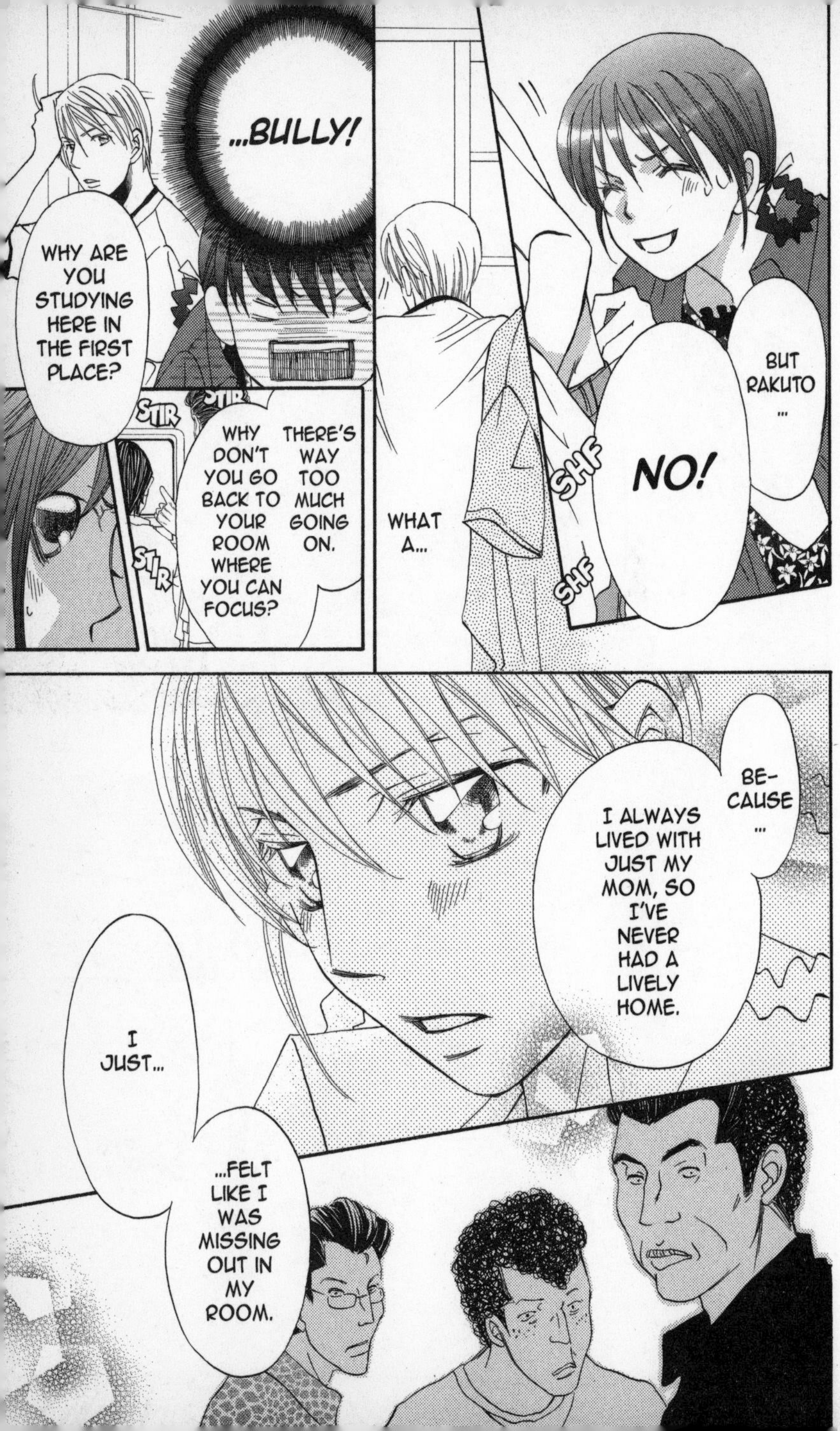
BUT RAKUTO...
NO!
SHF
SHF
WHAT A...
...BULLY!
WHY ARE YOU STUDYING HERE IN THE FIRST PLACE?
STIR
STIR
STIR
THERE'S WAY TOO MUCH GOING ON.
WHY DON'T YOU GO BACK TO YOUR ROOM WHERE YOU CAN FOCUS?
BE-CAUSE...
I ALWAYS LIVED WITH JUST MY MOM, SO I'VE NEVER HAD A LIVELY HOME.
I JUST...
...FELT LIKE I WAS MISSING OUT IN MY ROOM.

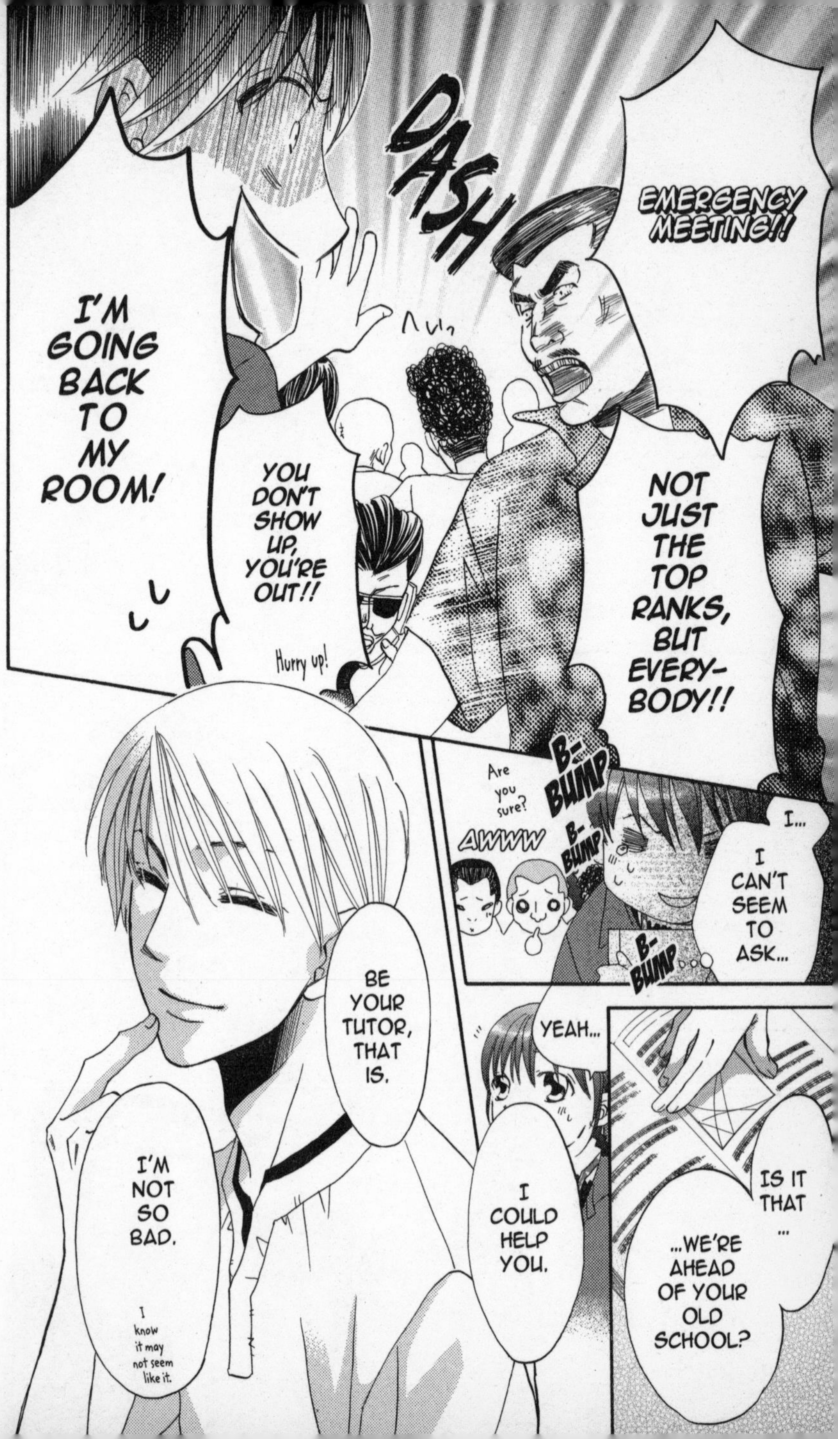
EMERGENCY MEETING!!
DASH
NOT JUST THE TOP RANKS, BUT EVERY-BODY!!
YOU DON'T SHOW UP, YOU'RE OUT!!
Hurry up!
I'M GOING BACK TO MY ROOM!
I... I CAN'T SEEM TO ASK...
B-BUMP
B-BUMP
B-BUMP
Are you sure?
AWWW
IS IT THAT ...
...WE'RE AHEAD OF YOUR OLD SCHOOL?
YEAH...
I'M NOT SO BAD.
I know it may not seem like it.
I COULD HELP YOU.
BE YOUR TUTOR, THAT IS.

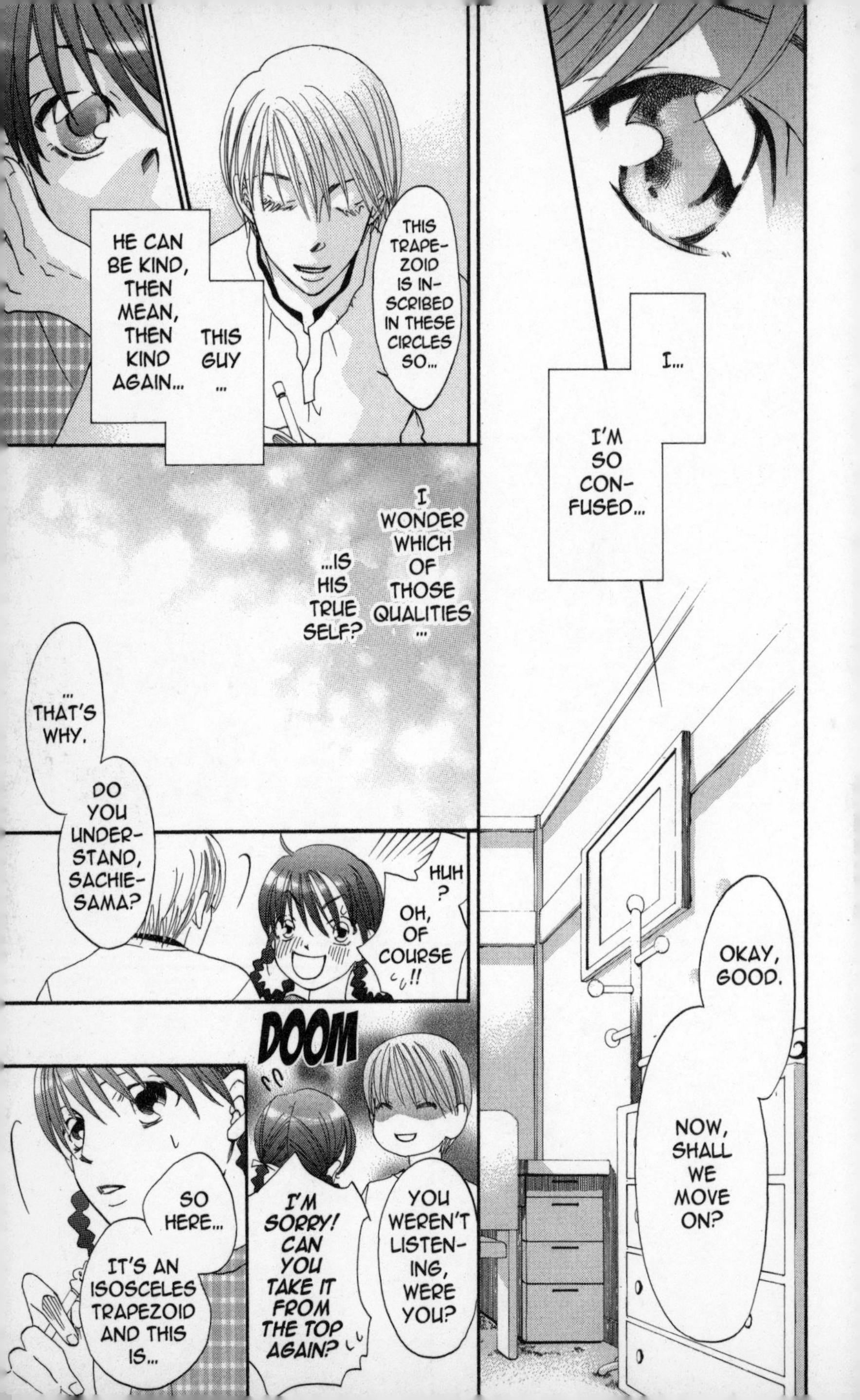
I...
I'M SO CON-FUSED...
OKAY, GOOD.
NOW, SHALL WE MOVE ON?
THIS TRAPE-ZOID IS IN-SCRIBED IN THESE CIRCLES SO...
THIS GUY ...
HE CAN BE KIND, THEN MEAN, THEN KIND AGAIN...
I WONDER WHICH OF THOSE QUALITIES ...
...IS HIS TRUE SELF?
... THAT'S WHY.
DO YOU UNDER-STAND, SACHIE-SAMA?
HUH? OH, OF COURSE!!
DOOM
YOU WEREN'T LISTEN-ING, WERE YOU?
I'M SORRY! CAN YOU TAKE IT FROM THE TOP AGAIN?
SO HERE...
IT'S AN ISOSCELES TRAPEZOID AND THIS IS...

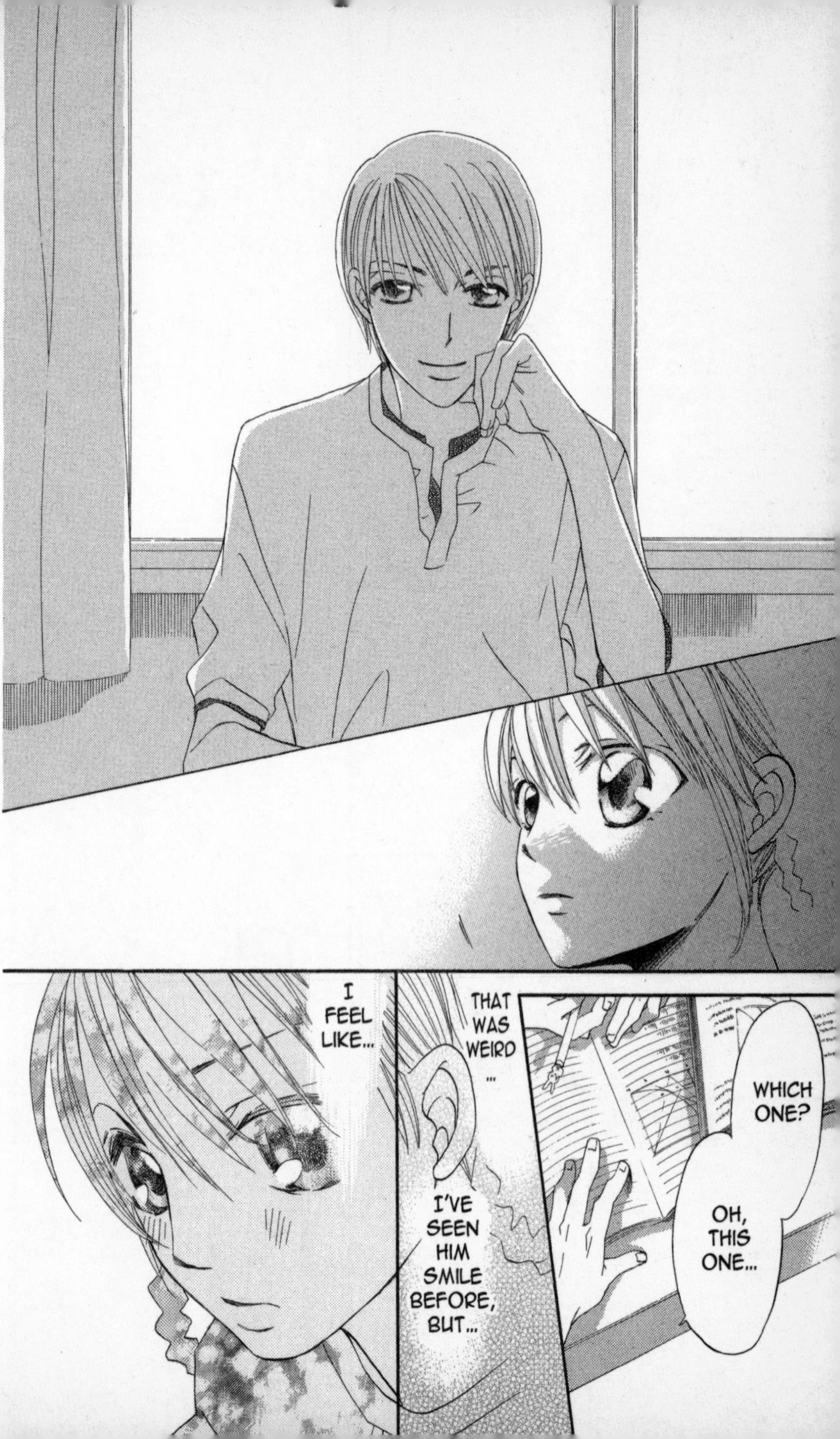
WHICH ONE?
OH, THIS ONE...
THAT WAS WEIRD...
I'VE SEEN HIM SMILE BEFORE, BUT...
I FEEL LIKE...

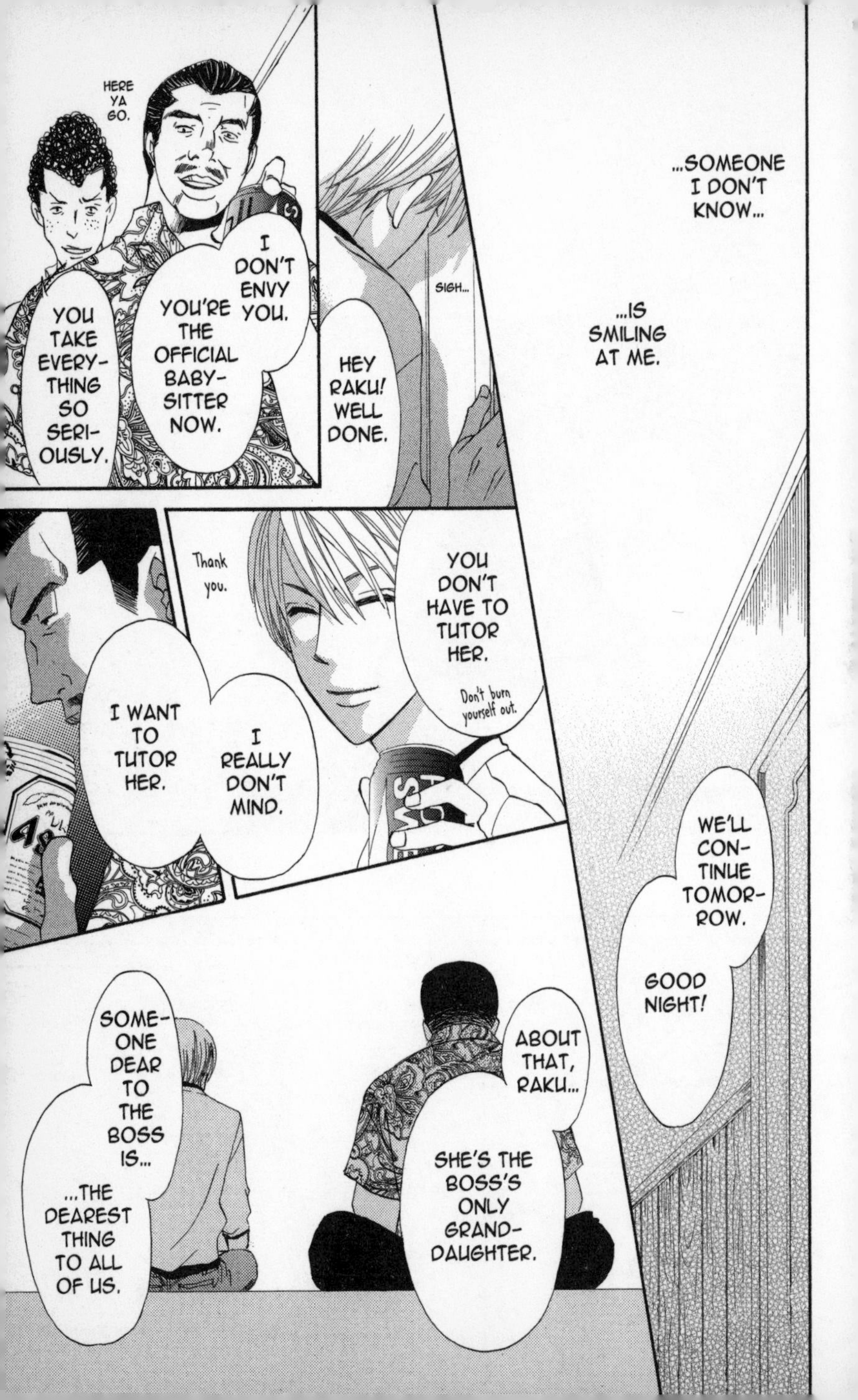
...SOMEONE I DON'T KNOW...
...IS SMILING AT ME.
WE'LL CONTINUE TOMORROW.
GOOD NIGHT!
SIGH...
HEY RAKU! WELL DONE.
HERE YA GO.
I DON'T ENVY YOU.
YOU'RE THE OFFICIAL BABY-SITTER NOW.
YOU TAKE EVERY-THING SO SERI-OUSLY.
Thank you.
YOU DON'T HAVE TO TUTOR HER.
Don't burn yourself out.
I REALLY DON'T MIND.
I WANT TO TUTOR HER.
ABOUT THAT, RAKU...
SHE'S THE BOSS'S ONLY GRAND-DAUGHTER.
SOME-ONE DEAR TO THE BOSS IS...
...THE DEAREST THING TO ALL OF US.

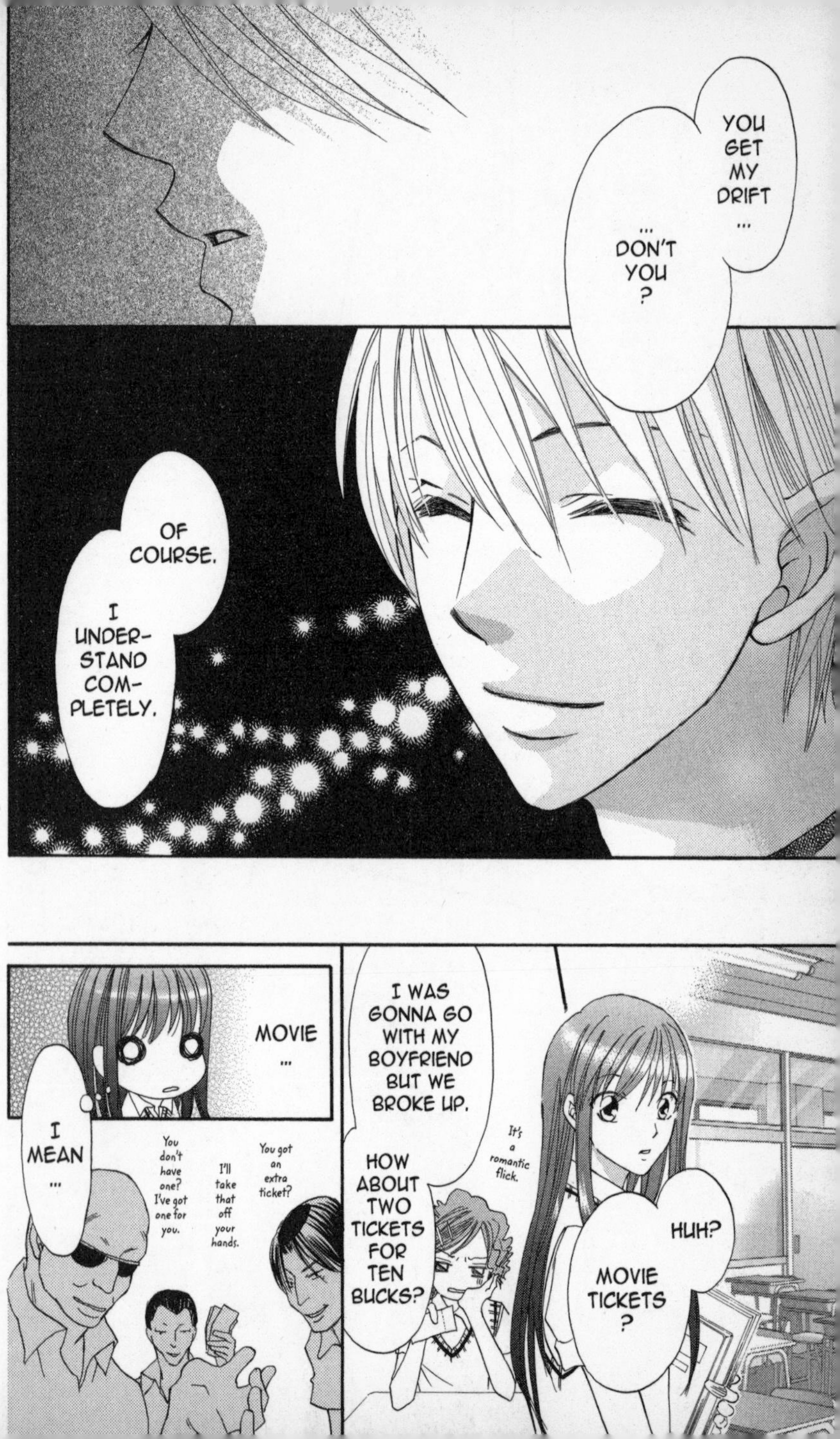
YOU GET MY DRIFT ... ... DON'T YOU ?
OF COURSE.
I UNDER-STAND COM-PLETELY.
I WAS GONNA GO WITH MY BOYFRIEND BUT WE BROKE UP.
HOW ABOUT TWO TICKETS FOR TEN BUCKS?
It's a romantic flick.
HUH?
MOVIE TICKETS ?
MOVIE ...
You got an extra ticket?
I'll take that off your hands.
You don't have one? I've got one for you.
I MEAN ...

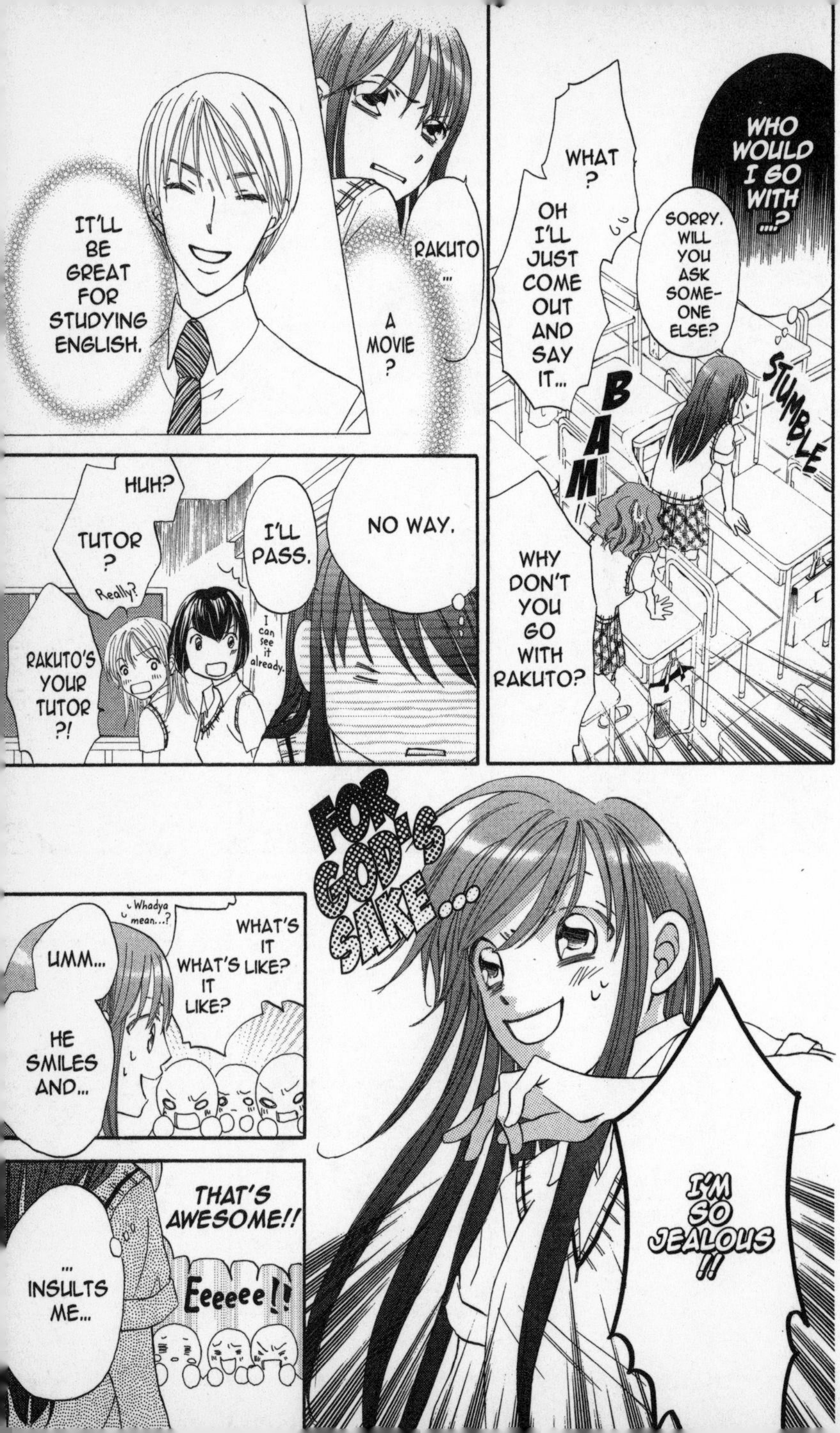

WHO WOULD I GO WITH ...?
SORRY. WILL YOU ASK SOME-ONE ELSE?
WHAT ?
OH I'LL JUST COME OUT AND SAY IT...
STUMBLE
BAM
WHY DON'T YOU GO WITH RAKUTO?
RAKUTO ...
A MOVIE ?
IT'LL BE GREAT FOR STUDYING ENGLISH.
NO WAY.
I'LL PASS.
I can see it already.
HUH?
TUTOR ?
Really?
RAKUTO'S YOUR TUTOR ?!
FOR GOD'S SAKE...
I'M SO JEALOUS !!
WHAT'S IT LIKE?
WHAT'S IT LIKE?
Whadya mean...?
UMM...
HE SMILES AND...
THAT'S AWESOME!!
Eeeeee!!
... INSULTS ME...

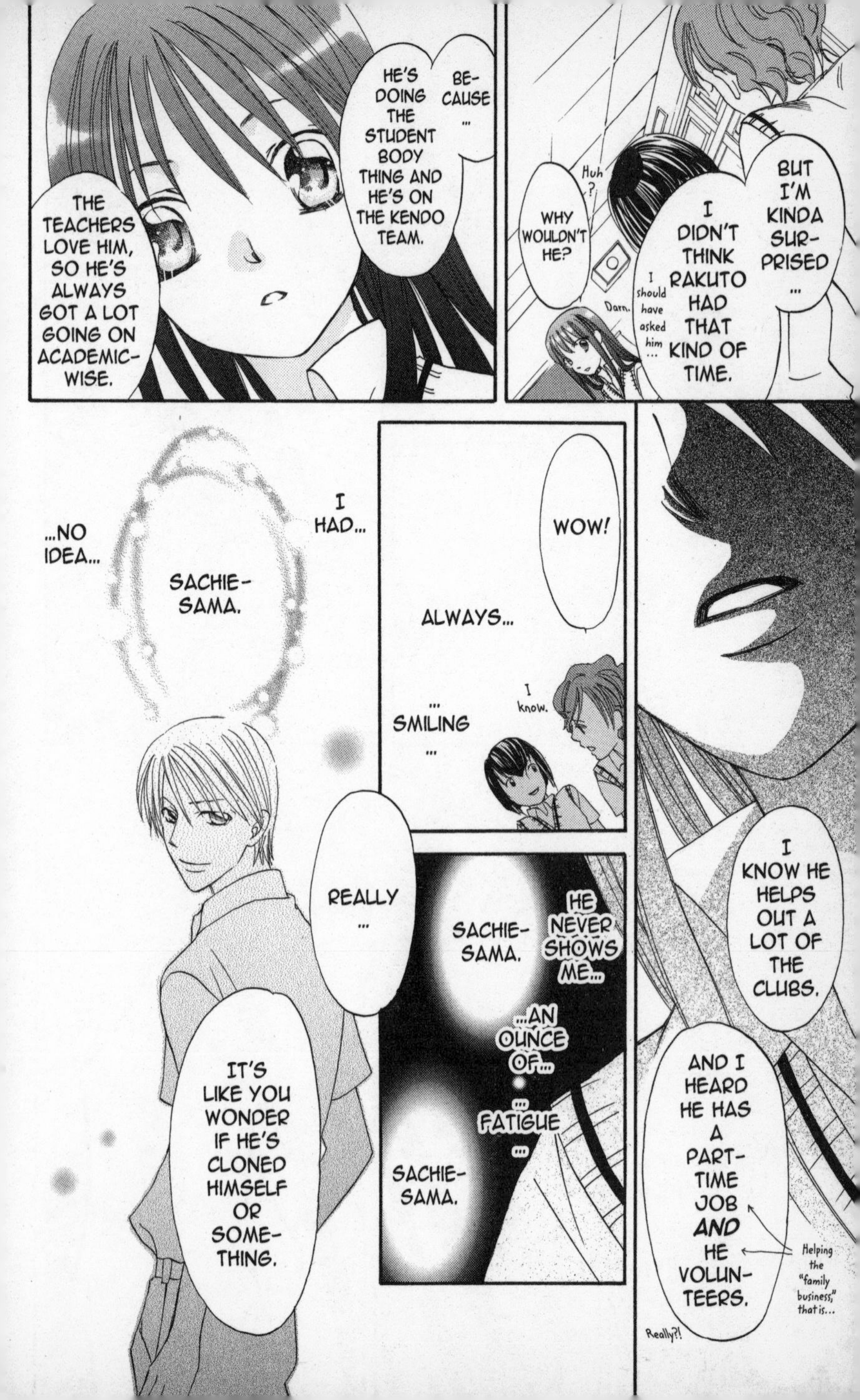
BUT I'M KINDA SURPRISED...
I DIDN'T THINK RAKUTO HAD THAT KIND OF TIME.
I should have asked him...
Darn.
Huh?
WHY WOULDN'T HE?
BE-CAUSE...
HE'S DOING THE STUDENT BODY THING AND HE'S ON THE KENDO TEAM.
THE TEACHERS LOVE HIM, SO HE'S ALWAYS GOT A LOT GOING ON ACADEMIC-WISE.
I KNOW HE HELPS OUT A LOT OF THE CLUBS.
AND I HEARD HE HAS A PART-TIME JOB AND HE VOLUNTEERS.
Helping the "family business," that is...
Really?!
WOW!
I know.
ALWAYS...
...SMILING...
HE NEVER SHOWS ME...
SACHIE-SAMA.
...AN OUNCE OF...
...FATIGUE...
SACHIE-SAMA.
I HAD...
...NO IDEA...
SACHIE-SAMA.
REALLY...
IT'S LIKE YOU WONDER IF HE'S CLONED HIMSELF OR SOMETHING.

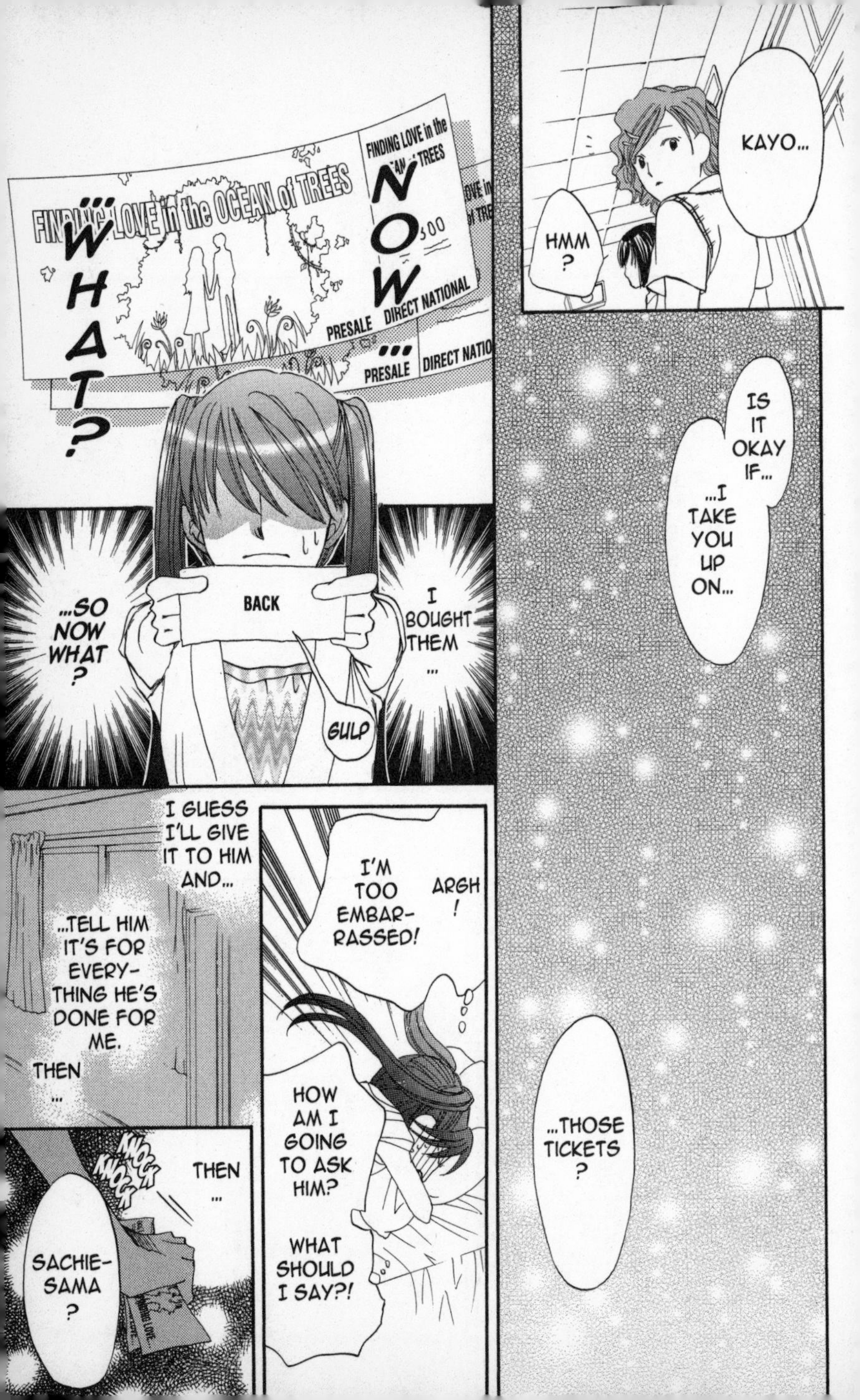
KAYO...
HMM?
IS IT OKAY IF...
...I TAKE YOU UP ON...
...THOSE TICKETS?
...WHAT?
NOW...
LOVE in the OCEAN of TREES
FINDING LOVE in the
TREES
PRESALE
DIRECT NATIONAL
PRESALE
DIRECT NATIO
BACK
I BOUGHT THEM...
...SO NOW WHAT?
GULP
I'M TOO EMBARRASSED!
ARGH!
HOW AM I GOING TO ASK HIM?
WHAT SHOULD I SAY?!
I GUESS I'LL GIVE IT TO HIM AND...
...TELL HIM IT'S FOR EVERYTHING HE'S DONE FOR ME.
THEN...
KNOCK KNOCK
THEN...
SACHIE-SAMA?

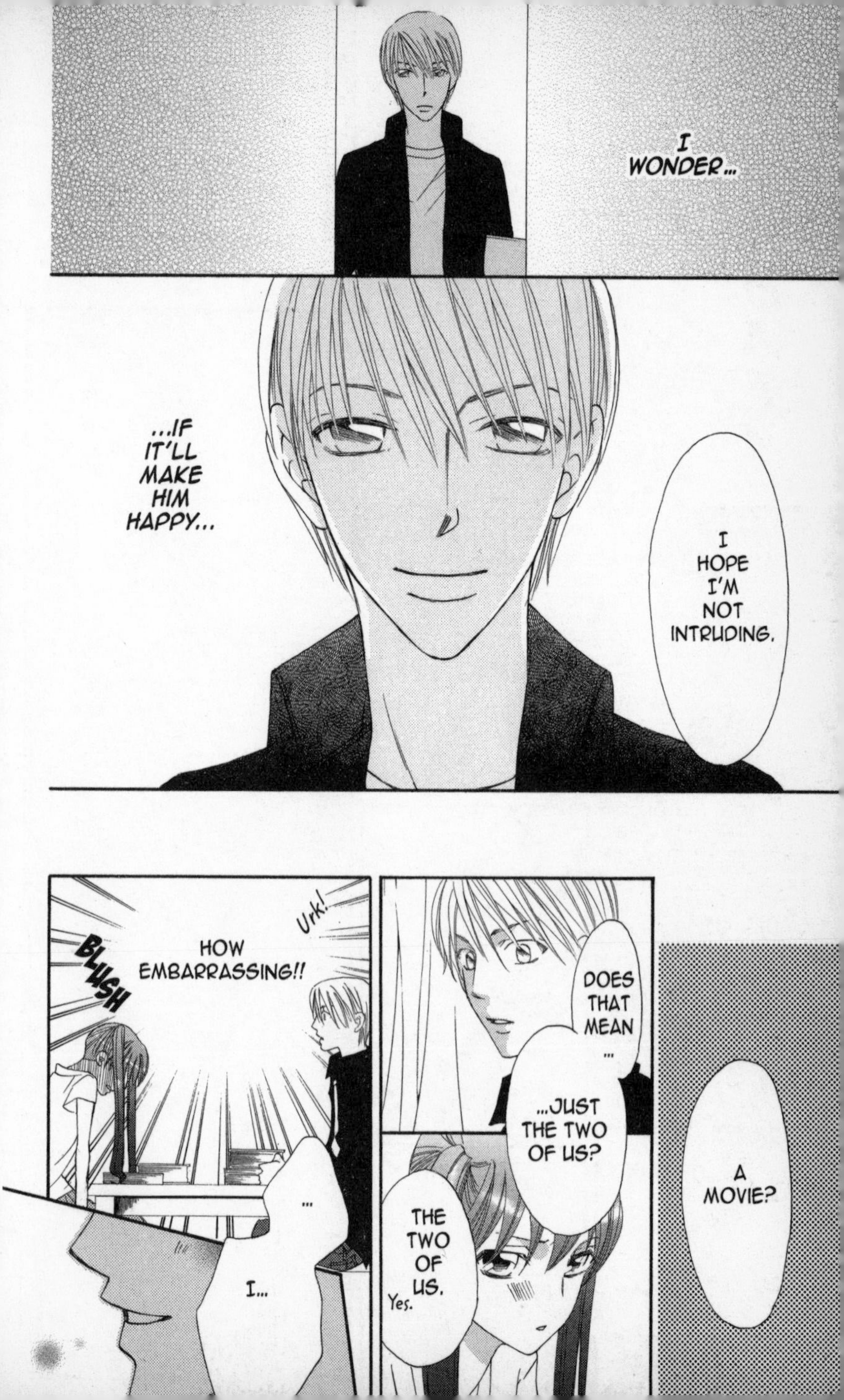
I WONDER...
I HOPE I'M NOT INTRUDING.
...IF IT'LL MAKE HIM HAPPY...
A MOVIE?
DOES THAT MEAN...
...JUST THE TWO OF US?
THE TWO OF US.
Yes.
Urk!
HOW EMBARRASSING!!
BLUSH
...
I...

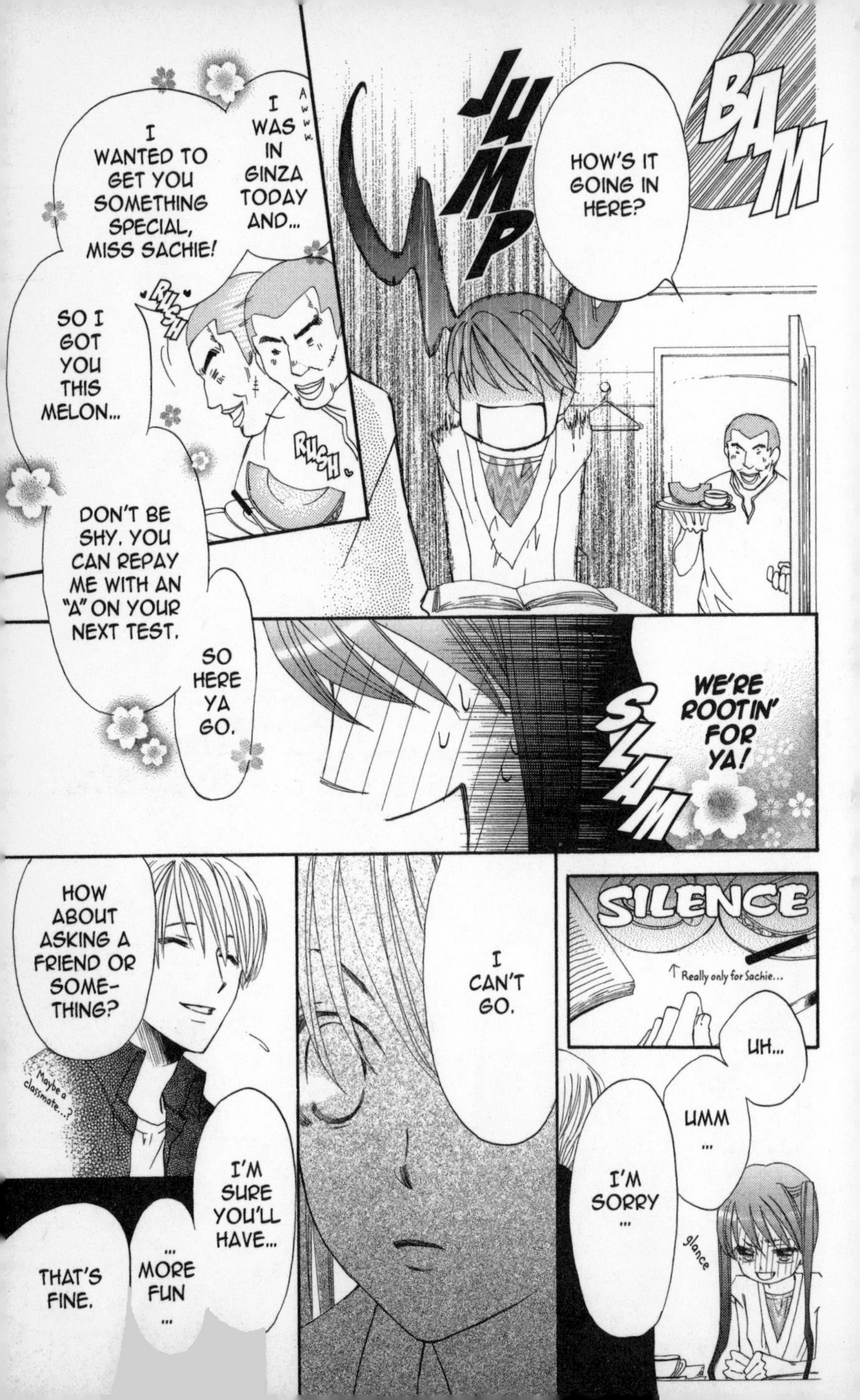
BAM
HOW'S IT GOING IN HERE?
JUMP
I WAS IN GINZA TODAY AND...
AWWW.
I WANTED TO GET YOU SOMETHING SPECIAL, MISS SACHIE!
RUSH
SO I GOT YOU THIS MELON...
RUSH
DON'T BE SHY. YOU CAN REPAY ME WITH AN "A" ON YOUR NEXT TEST.
SO HERE YA GO.
WE'RE ROOTIN' FOR YA!
SLAM
SILENCE
↑ Really only for Sachie...
UH...
UMM ...
I'M SORRY ...
glance
I CAN'T GO.
HOW ABOUT ASKING A FRIEND OR SOME-THING?
Maybe a classmate...?
I'M SURE YOU'LL HAVE...
... MORE FUN ...
THAT'S FINE.

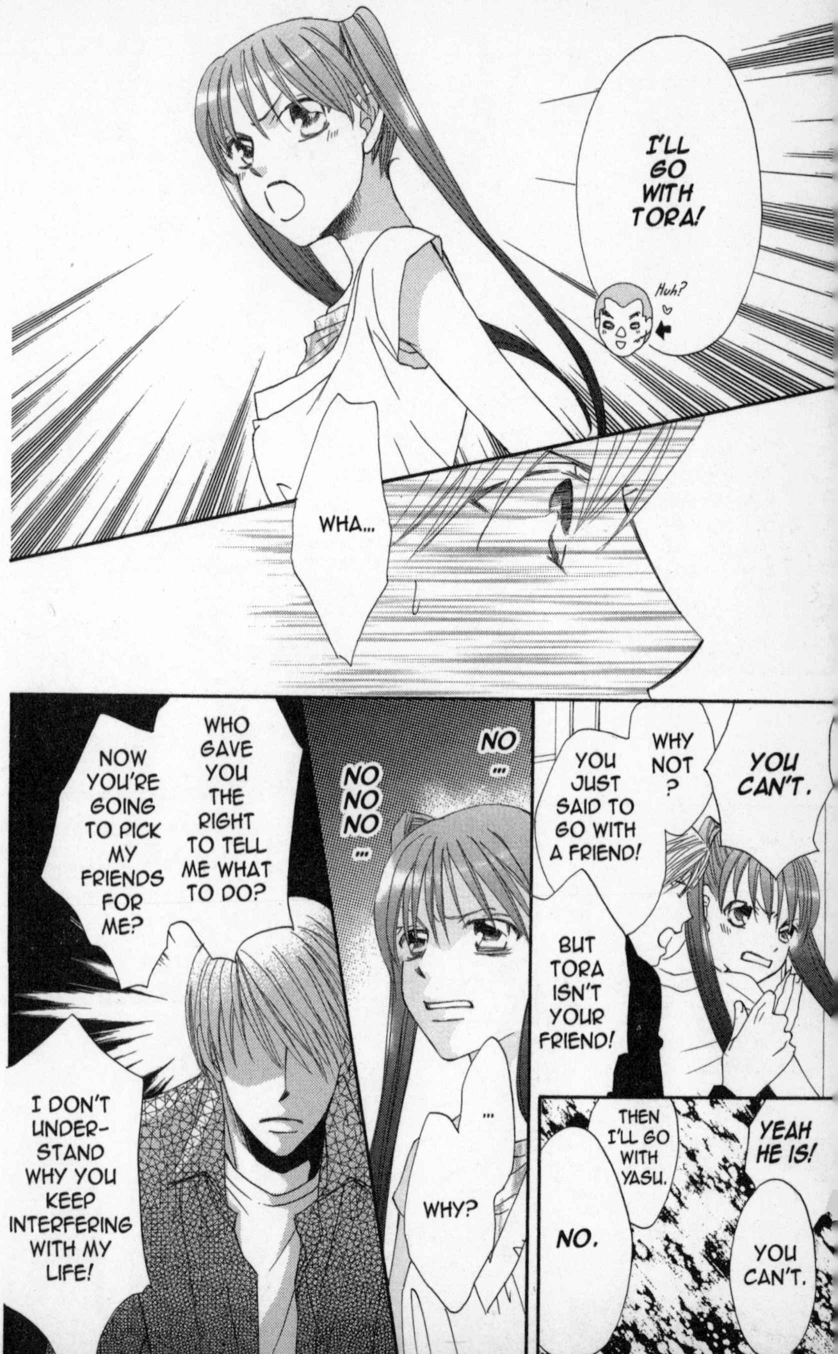
I'LL GO WITH TORA!
Huh?
WHA...
YOU CAN'T.
WHY NOT?
YOU JUST SAID TO GO WITH A FRIEND!
BUT TORA ISN'T YOUR FRIEND!
YEAH HE IS!
YOU CAN'T.
THEN I'LL GO WITH YASU.
NO.
NO...
NO NO NO...
WHO GAVE YOU THE RIGHT TO TELL ME WHAT TO DO?
NOW YOU'RE GOING TO PICK MY FRIENDS FOR ME?
...
WHY?
I DON'T UNDER-STAND WHY YOU KEEP INTERFERING WITH MY LIFE!

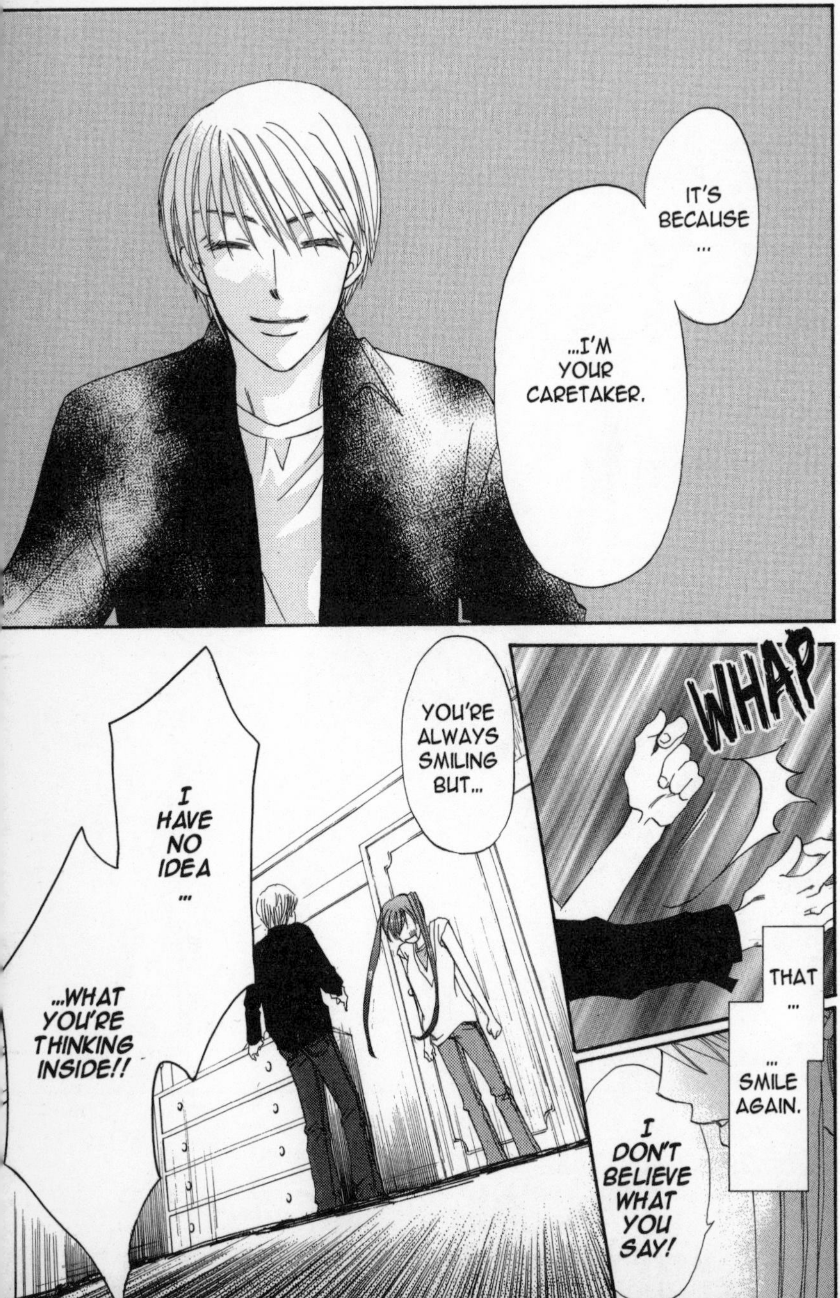
IT'S BECAUSE ...
...I'M YOUR CARETAKER.
WHAP
THAT ... ... SMILE AGAIN.
I DON'T BELIEVE WHAT YOU SAY!
YOU'RE ALWAYS SMILING BUT...
I HAVE NO IDEA ...
...WHAT YOU'RE THINKING INSIDE!!

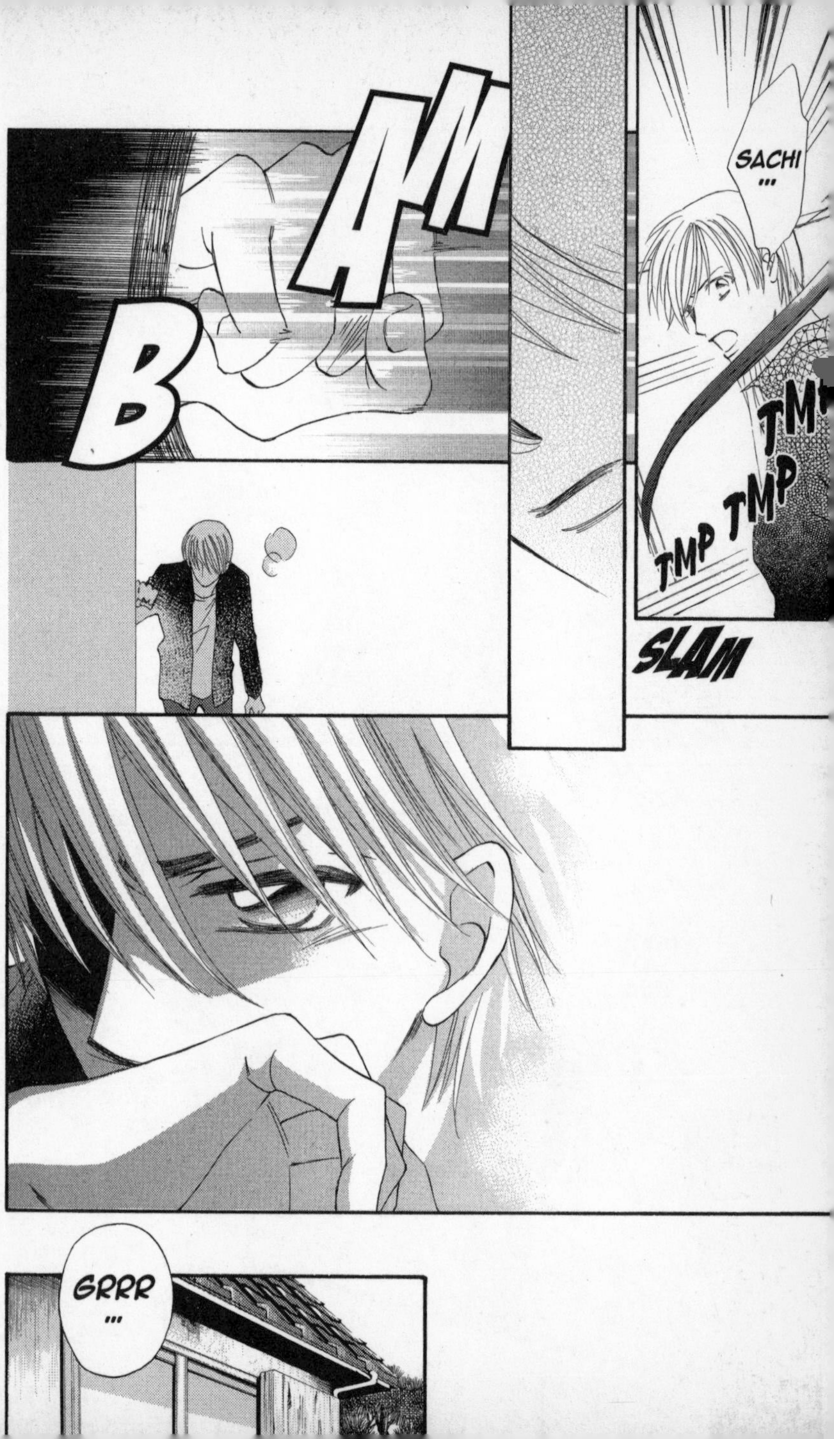
SACHI ...
TMP TMP TMP TMP
SLAM
BAM
GRRR ...

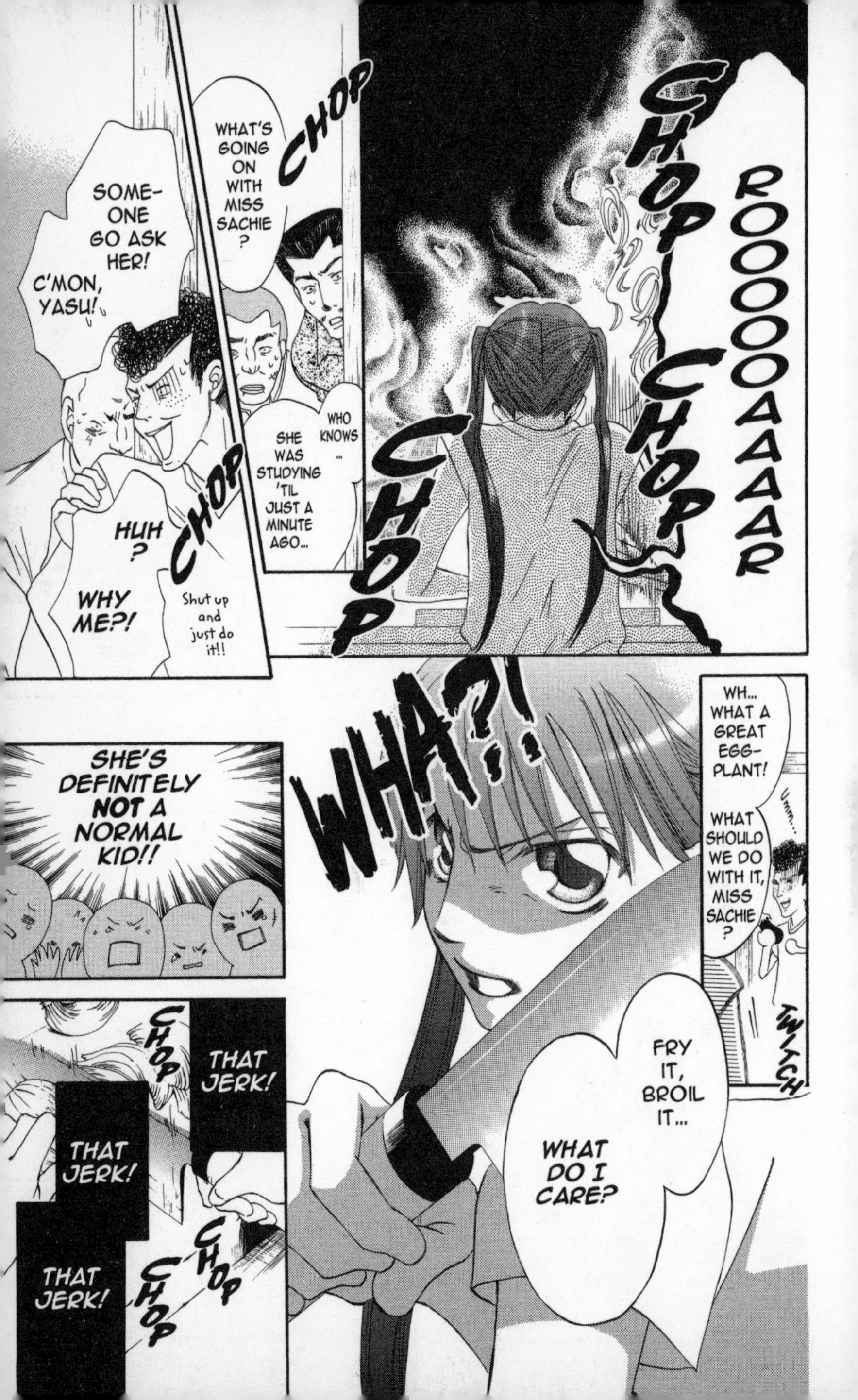
ROOOOOOAAAAAR
CHOP CHOP
CHOP
CHOP
WHAT'S GOING ON WITH MISS SACHIE?
CHOP
SOME-ONE GO ASK HER!
C'MON, YASU!
WHO KNOWS...
SHE WAS STUDYING 'TIL JUST A MINUTE AGO...
CHOP
HUH?
WHY ME?!
Shut up and just do it!!
WH... WHAT A GREAT EGG-PLANT!
Umm...
WHAT SHOULD WE DO WITH IT, MISS SACHIE?
WHA?!
SHE'S DEFINITELY NOT A NORMAL KID!!
TWITCH
FRY IT, BROIL IT...
WHAT DO I CARE?
CHOP
THAT JERK!
THAT JERK!
THAT JERK!
CHOP
CHOP

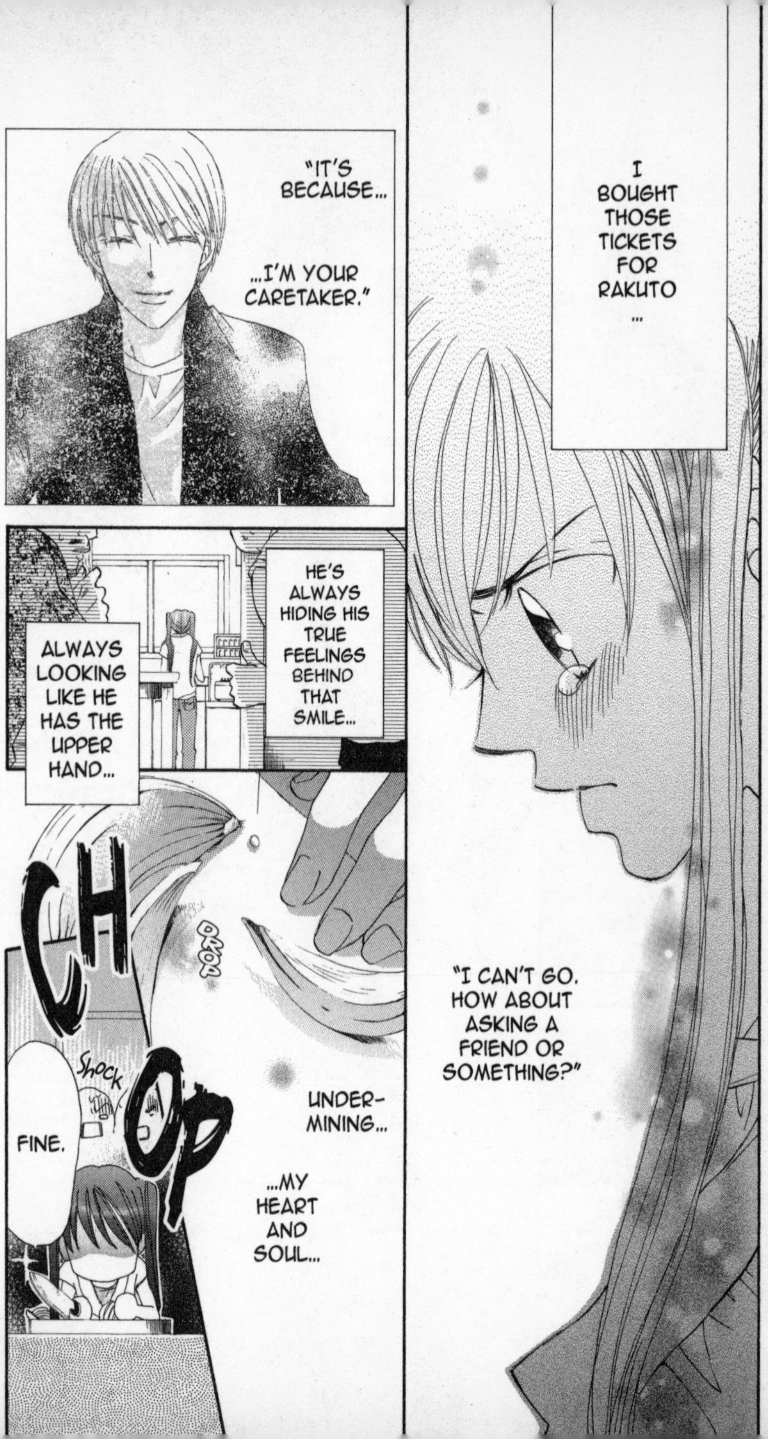
I BOUGHT THOSE TICKETS FOR RAKUTO ...
"I CAN'T GO. HOW ABOUT ASKING A FRIEND OR SOMETHING?"
"IT'S BECAUSE...
...I'M YOUR CARETAKER."
HE'S ALWAYS HIDING HIS TRUE FEELINGS BEHIND THAT SMILE...
ALWAYS LOOKING LIKE HE HAS THE UPPER HAND...
DROP
UNDER-MINING...
...MY HEART AND SOUL...
CHOP
Shock
FINE.

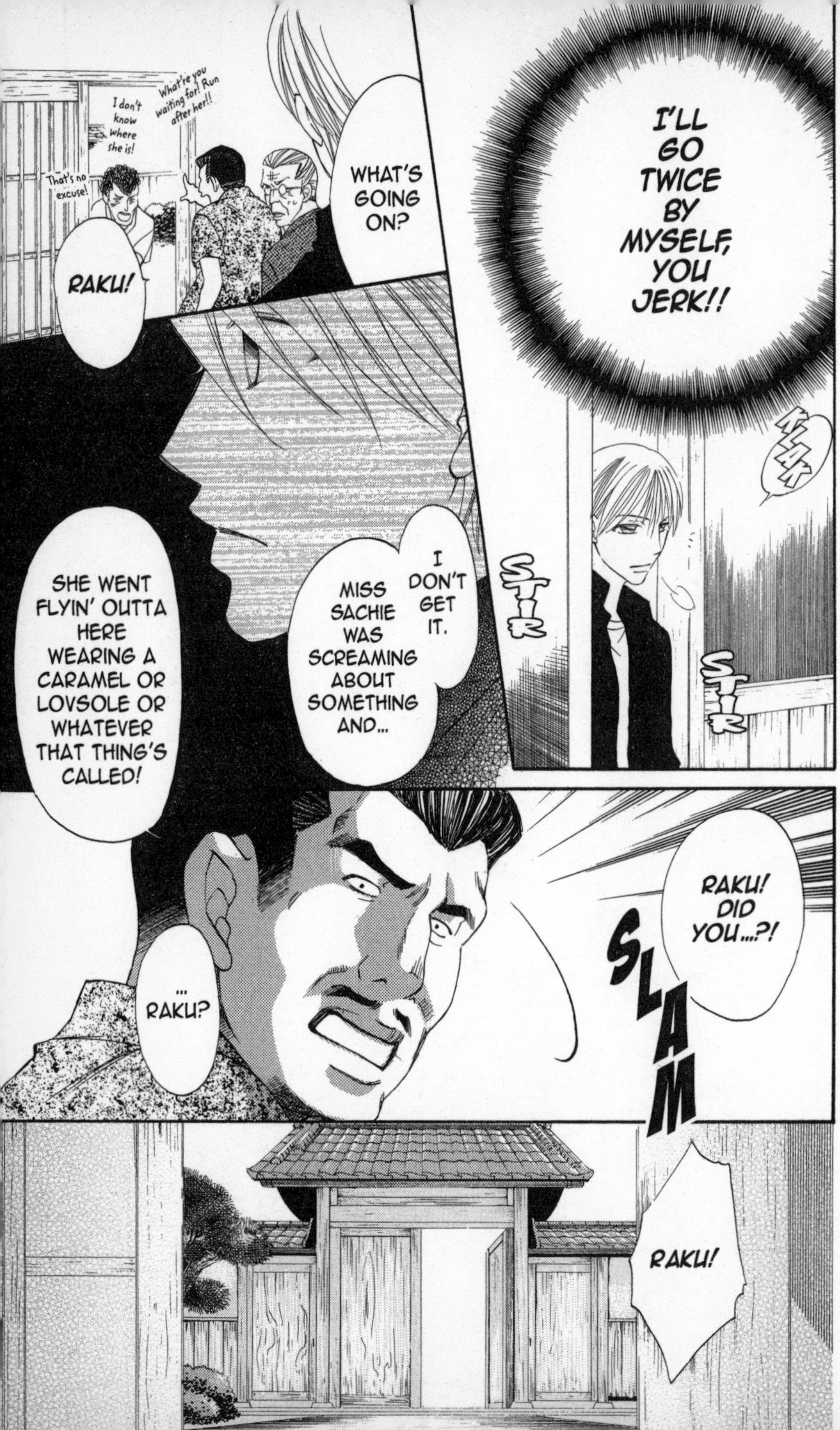
I'LL GO TWICE BY MYSELF, YOU JERK!!
KLAK
STIR
STIR
WHAT'S GOING ON?
What're you waiting for! Run after her!!
I don't know where she is!
That's no excuse!
RAKU!
I DON'T GET IT.
MISS SACHIE WAS SCREAMING ABOUT SOMETHING AND...
SHE WENT FLYIN' OUTTA HERE WEARING A CARAMEL OR LOVSOLE OR WHATEVER THAT THING'S CALLED!
RAKU! DID YOU...?!
SLAM
... RAKU?
RAKU!

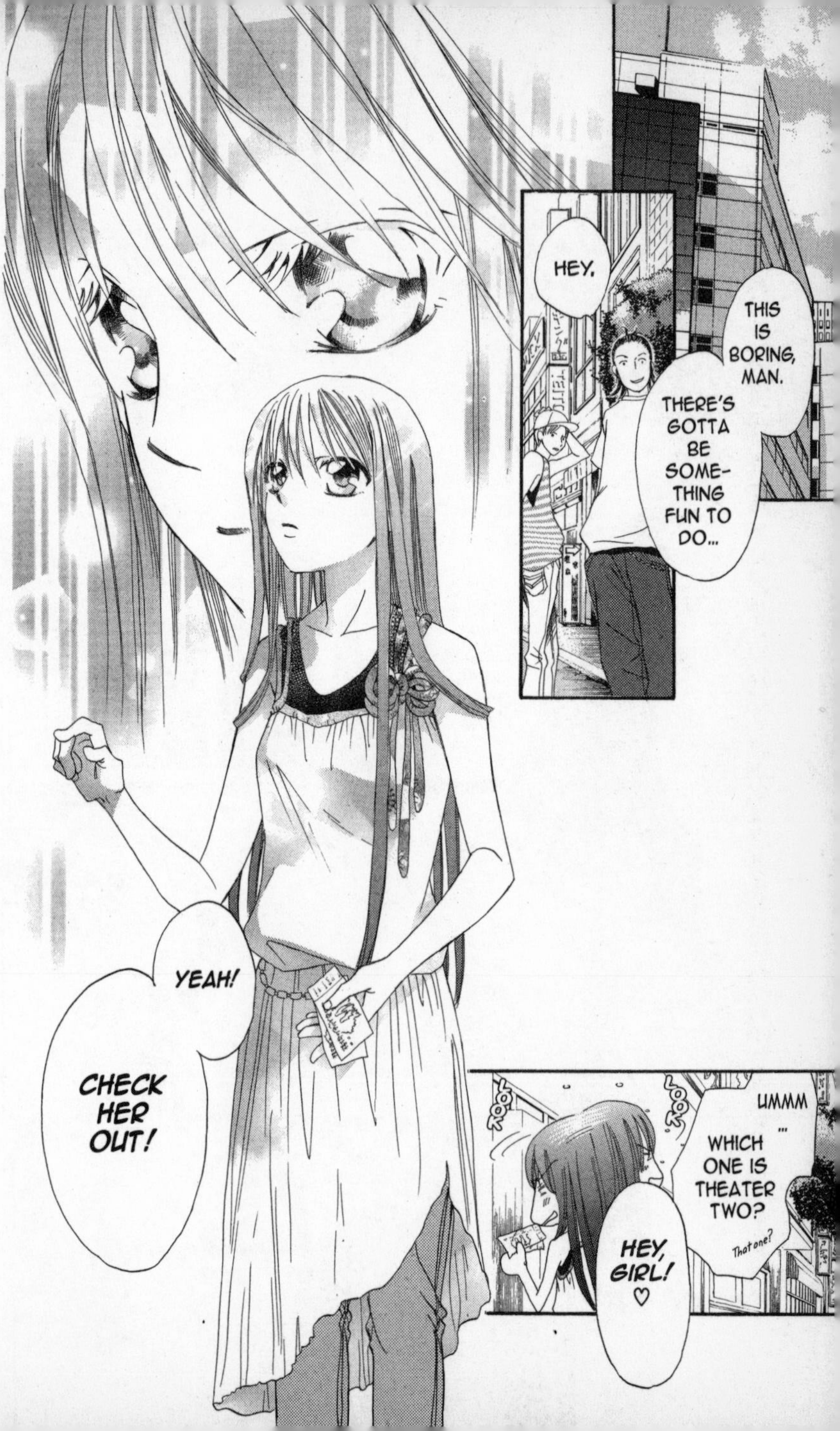
HEY.
THIS IS BORING, MAN.
THERE'S GOTTA BE SOME-THING FUN TO DO...
LOOK
LOOK
UMMM... WHICH ONE IS THEATER TWO?
That one?
HEY, GIRL! ♡
YEAH!
CHECK HER OUT!

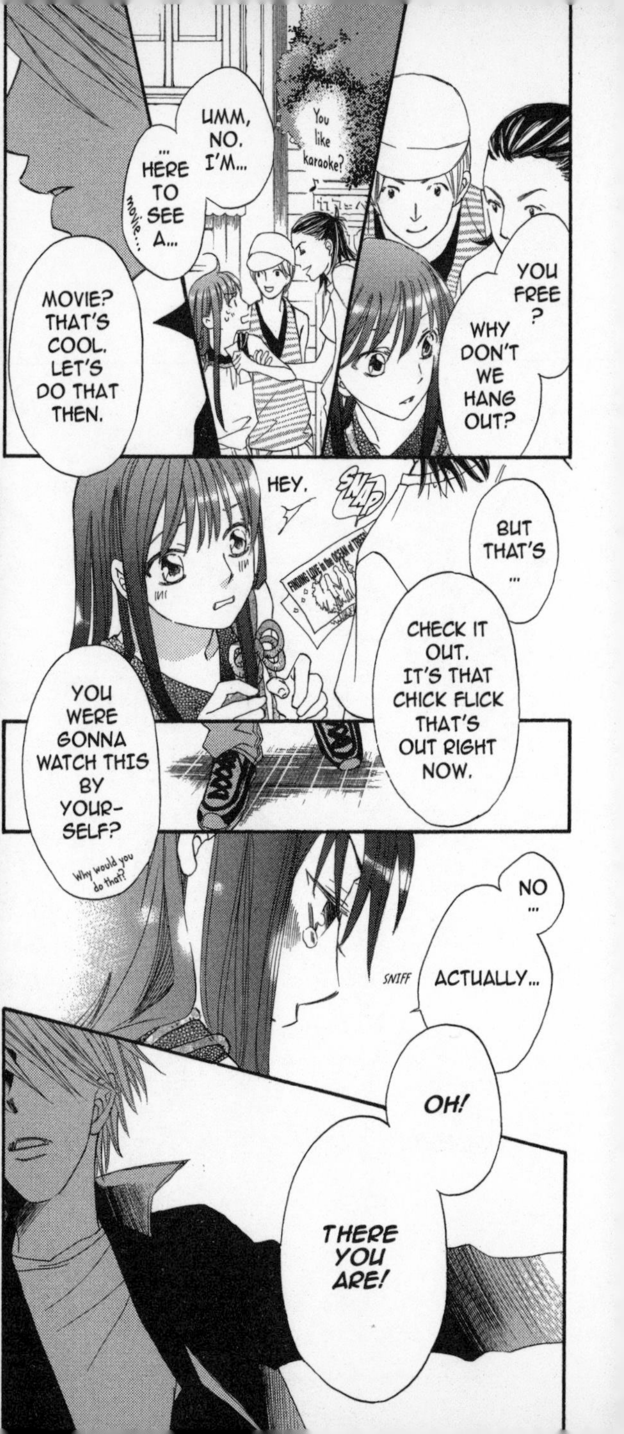
YOU FREE?
WHY DON'T WE HANG OUT?
You like karaoke?
UMM, NO. I'M...
... HERE TO SEE A...
movie...
MOVIE? THAT'S COOL. LET'S DO THAT THEN.
HEY.
SNAP
BUT THAT'S ...
CHECK IT OUT. IT'S THAT CHICK FLICK THAT'S OUT RIGHT NOW.
YOU WERE GONNA WATCH THIS BY YOURSELF?
Why would you do that?
NO ... ACTUALLY...
SNIFF
OH!
THERE YOU ARE!

I DREW THE YUKATA WITH THE DRAGON ON IT IN THE FIRST STORY, LAUGHING TO MYSELF ABOUT HOW CRUDE IT WAS. BUT THEN I WAS IN SHINJUKU AND I SAW IT... THE DRAGON PATTERN, THAT IS... AND IT LOOKED PRETTY NORMAL. ARGUABLY EVEN FASHIONABLE...

THERE WERE A LOT OF SCREW-UPS IN THE STORY. LIKE DRAWING TOO MANY FINGERS ON SACHIE'S MOM. (I FIXED IT, OF COURSE!) SACHIE WAS ALSO 17 YEARS OLD IN THE MAGAZINE BUT NOW SHE'S 15. I WASN'T EVEN REALLY THINKING ABOUT IT AND DEEMED HER 17 WHEN I REALIZED THAT RAKUTO WOULD HAVE ALREADY GRADUATED IF HE WERE OLDER THAN HER... SO SHE BECAME YOUNGER. MAGAZINE READERS MAY HAVE CAUGHT ON, BUT THAT'S THE REASON FOR HER BEING 15 NOW...

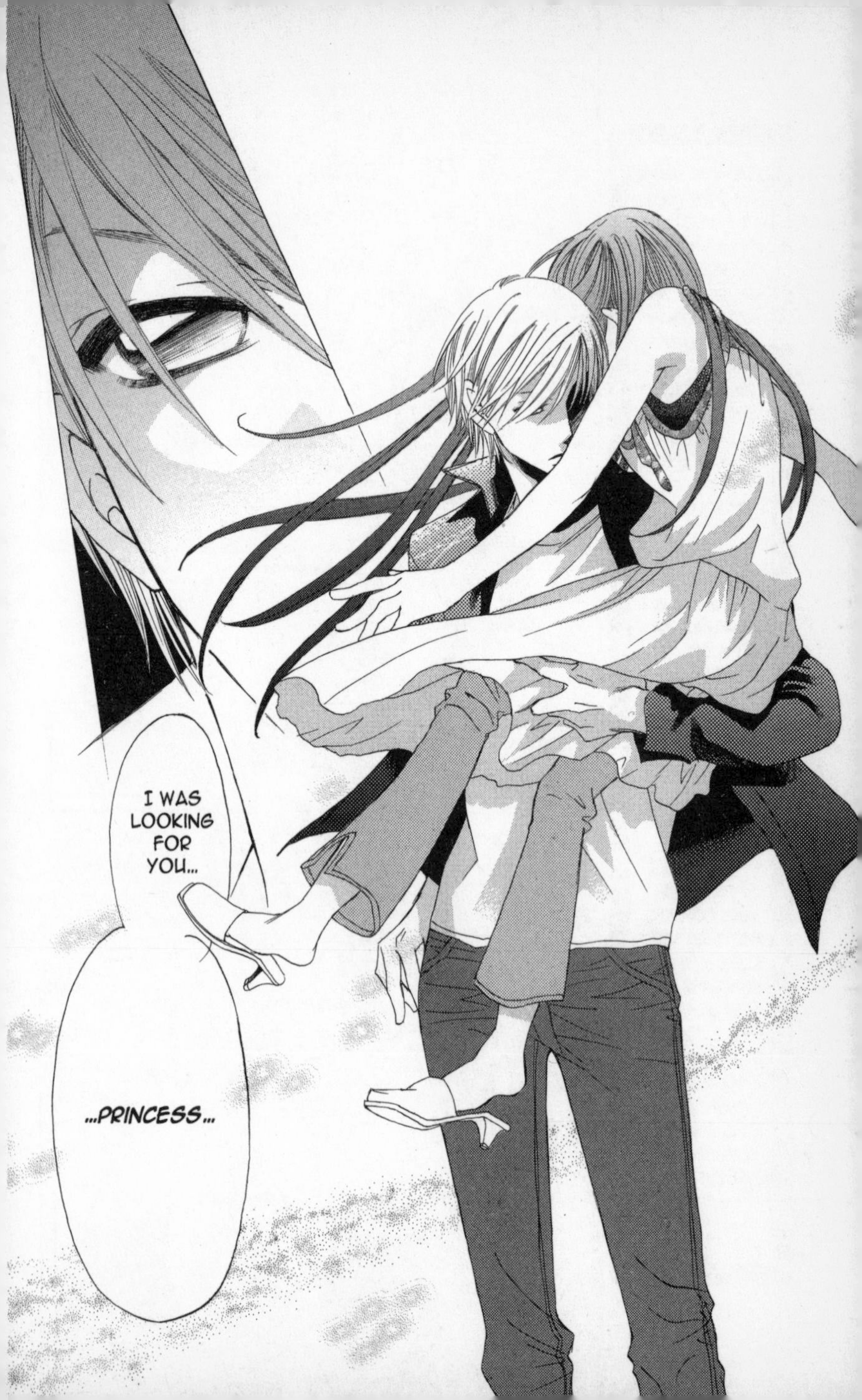
I WAS LOOKING FOR YOU...
...PRINCESS...

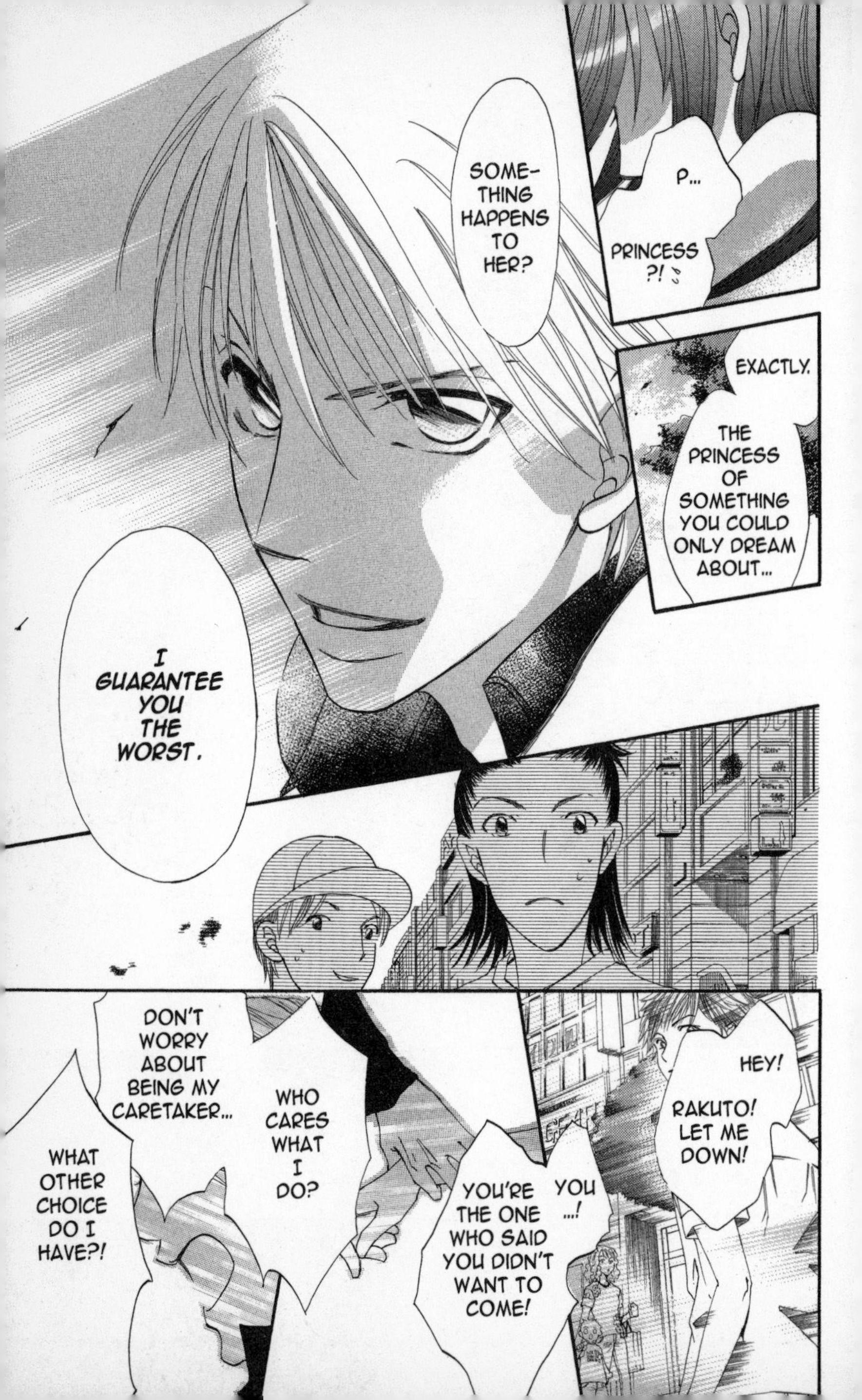
P...
PRINCESS ?!
EXACTLY.
THE PRINCESS OF SOMETHING YOU COULD ONLY DREAM ABOUT...
SOME-THING HAPPENS TO HER?
I GUARANTEE YOU THE WORST.
HEY!
RAKUTO! LET ME DOWN!
YOU ...!
YOU'RE THE ONE WHO SAID YOU DIDN'T WANT TO COME!
WHO CARES WHAT I DO?
DON'T WORRY ABOUT BEING MY CARETAKER...
WHAT OTHER CHOICE DO I HAVE?!

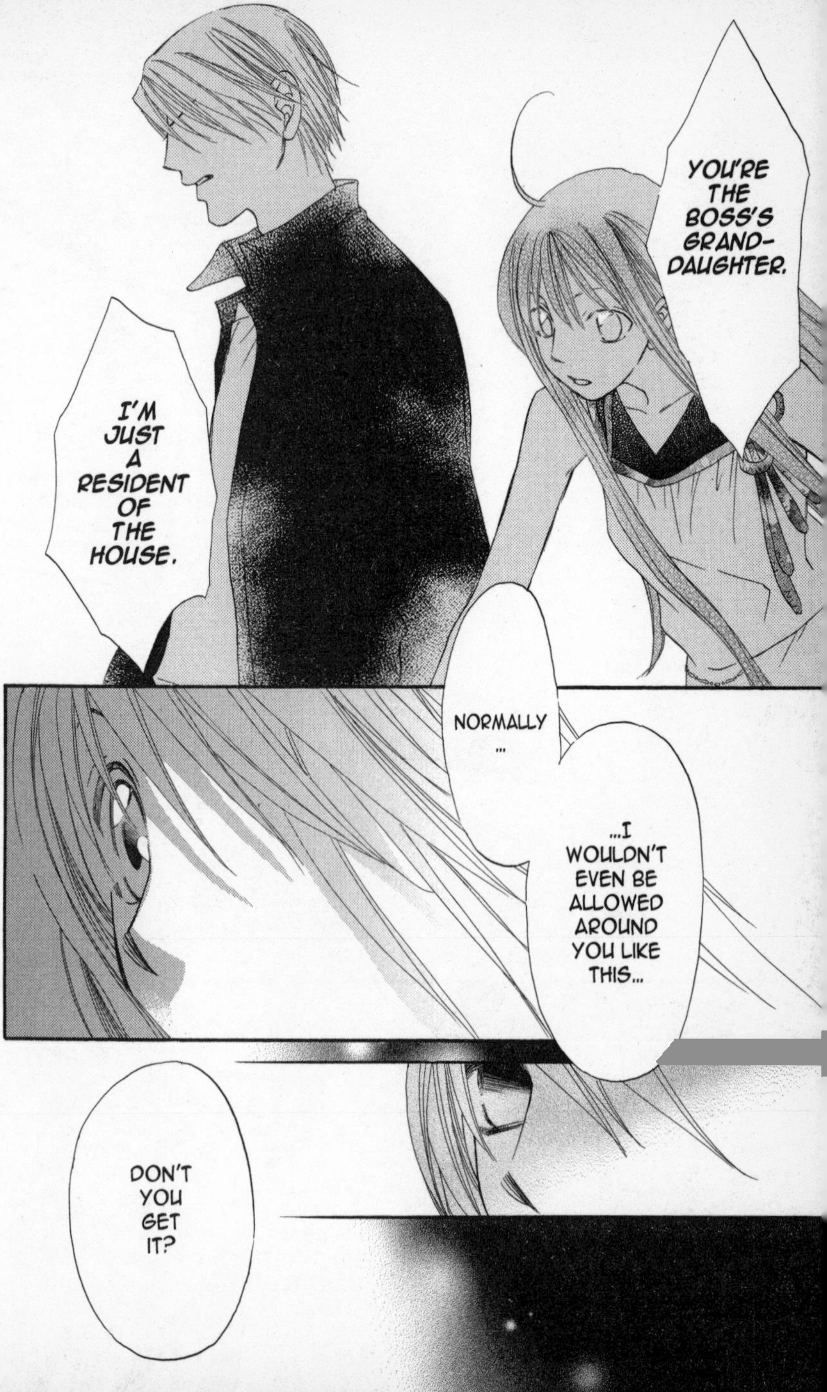
YOU'RE THE BOSS'S GRAND-DAUGHTER.
I'M JUST A RESIDENT OF THE HOUSE.
NORMALLY...
...I WOULDN'T EVEN BE ALLOWED AROUND YOU LIKE THIS...
DON'T YOU GET IT?

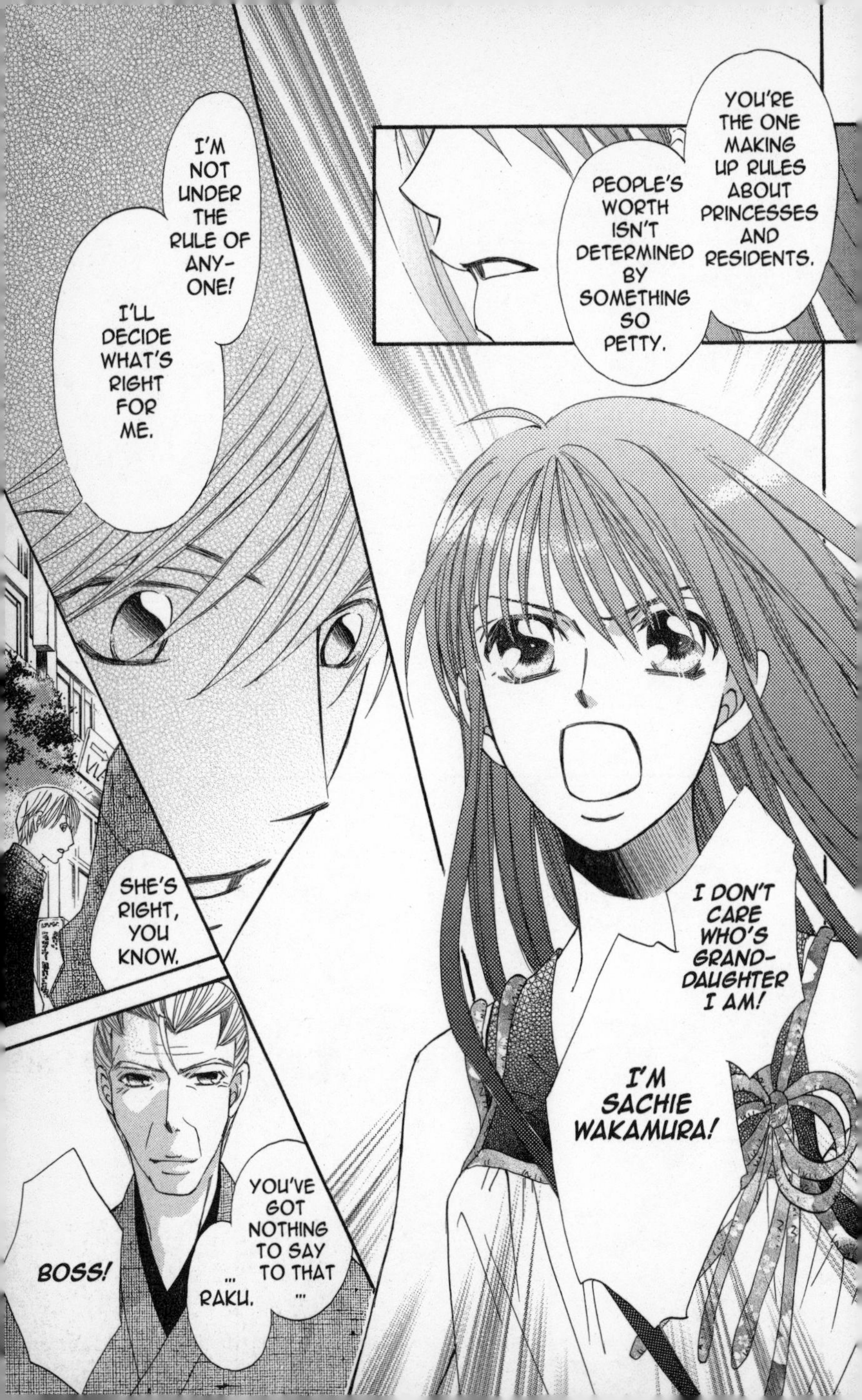

YOU'RE THE ONE MAKING UP RULES ABOUT PRINCESSES AND RESIDENTS.
PEOPLE'S WORTH ISN'T DETERMINED BY SOMETHING SO PETTY.
I DON'T CARE WHO'S GRAND-DAUGHTER I AM!
I'M SACHIE WAKAMURA!
I'M NOT UNDER THE RULE OF ANY-ONE!
I'LL DECIDE WHAT'S RIGHT FOR ME.
SHE'S RIGHT, YOU KNOW.
YOU'VE GOT NOTHING TO SAY TO THAT ...
... RAKU.
BOSS!

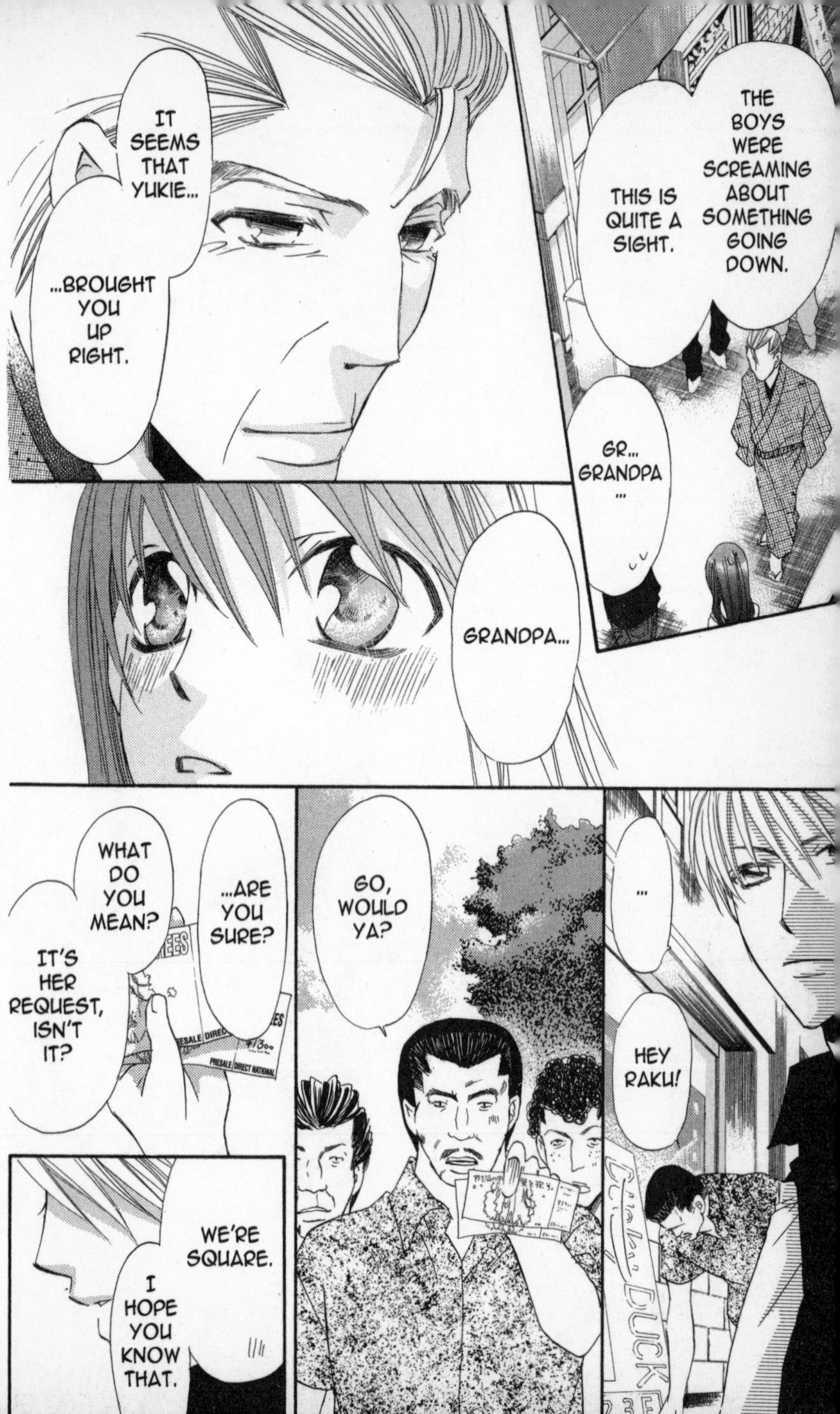
THE BOYS WERE SCREAMING ABOUT SOMETHING GOING DOWN.
THIS IS QUITE A SIGHT.
GR... GRANDPA ...
IT SEEMS THAT YUKIE...
...BROUGHT YOU UP RIGHT.
GRANDPA...
...
HEY RAKU!
GO, WOULD YA?
...ARE YOU SURE?
WHAT DO YOU MEAN?
IT'S HER REQUEST, ISN'T IT?
PRESALE DIRECT NATIONAL
WE'RE SQUARE.
I HOPE YOU KNOW THAT.

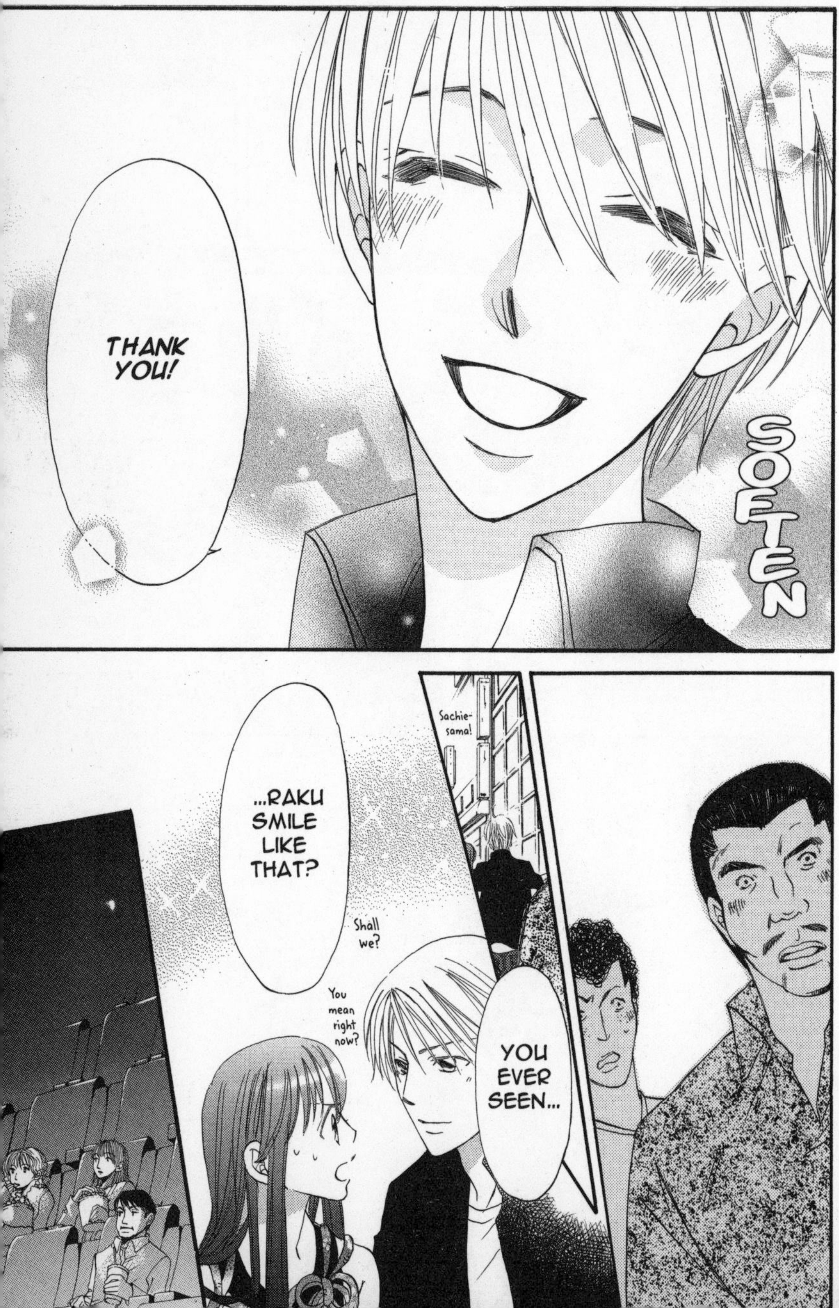
THANK YOU!
SOFTEN
YOU EVER SEEN...
Sachie-sama!
...RAKU SMILE LIKE THAT?
Shall we?
You mean right now?

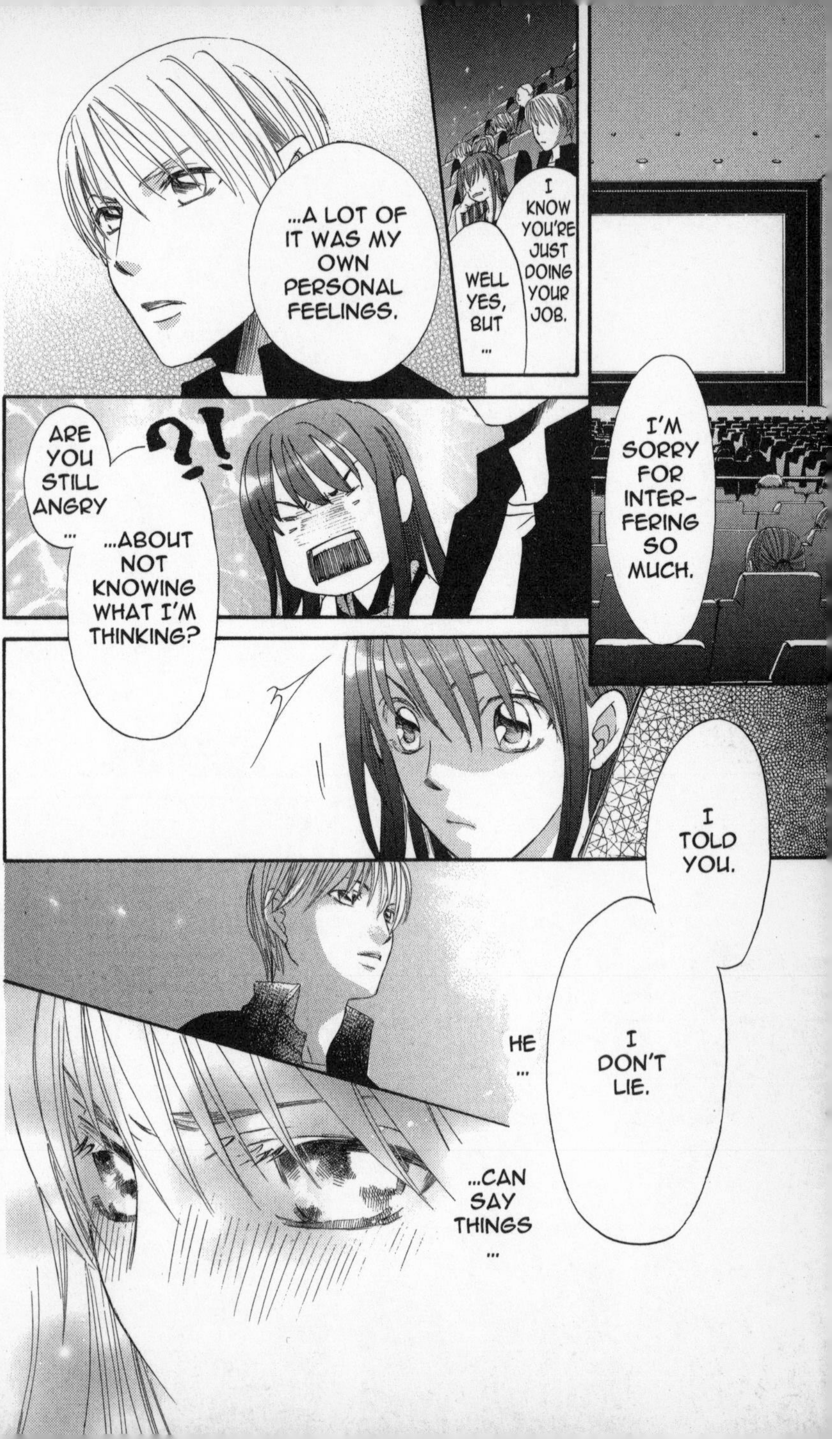
I'M SORRY FOR INTERFERING SO MUCH.
I KNOW YOU'RE JUST DOING YOUR JOB.
WELL YES, BUT ...
...A LOT OF IT WAS MY OWN PERSONAL FEELINGS.
?!
ARE YOU STILL ANGRY ...
...ABOUT NOT KNOWING WHAT I'M THINKING?
I TOLD YOU.
I DON'T LIE.
HE ...
...CAN SAY THINGS ...

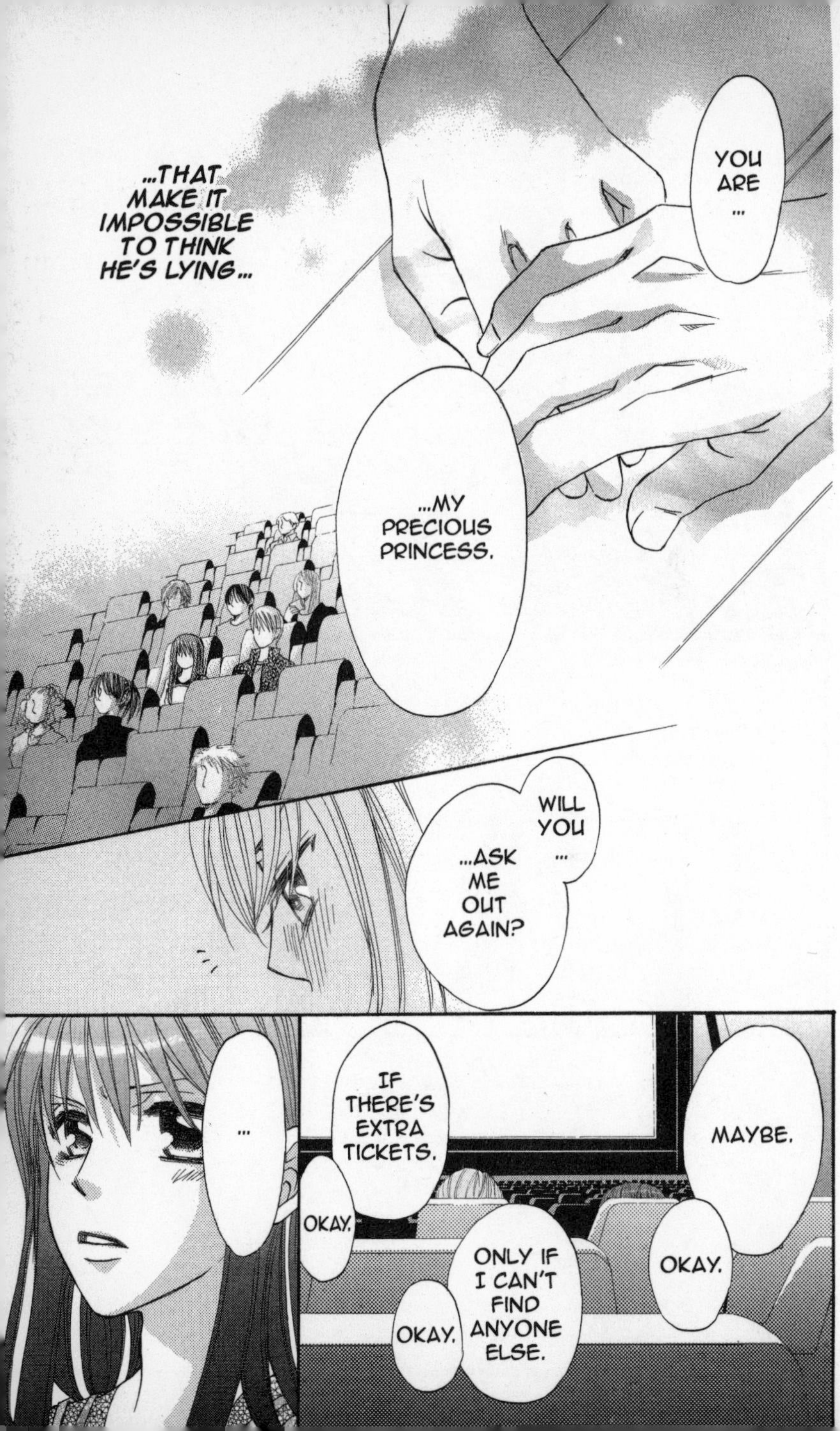
YOU ARE ...
...MY PRECIOUS PRINCESS.
...THAT MAKE IT IMPOSSIBLE TO THINK HE'S LYING...
WILL YOU ...
...ASK ME OUT AGAIN?
MAYBE.
OKAY.
IF THERE'S EXTRA TICKETS.
OKAY.
ONLY IF I CAN'T FIND ANYONE ELSE.
OKAY.
...

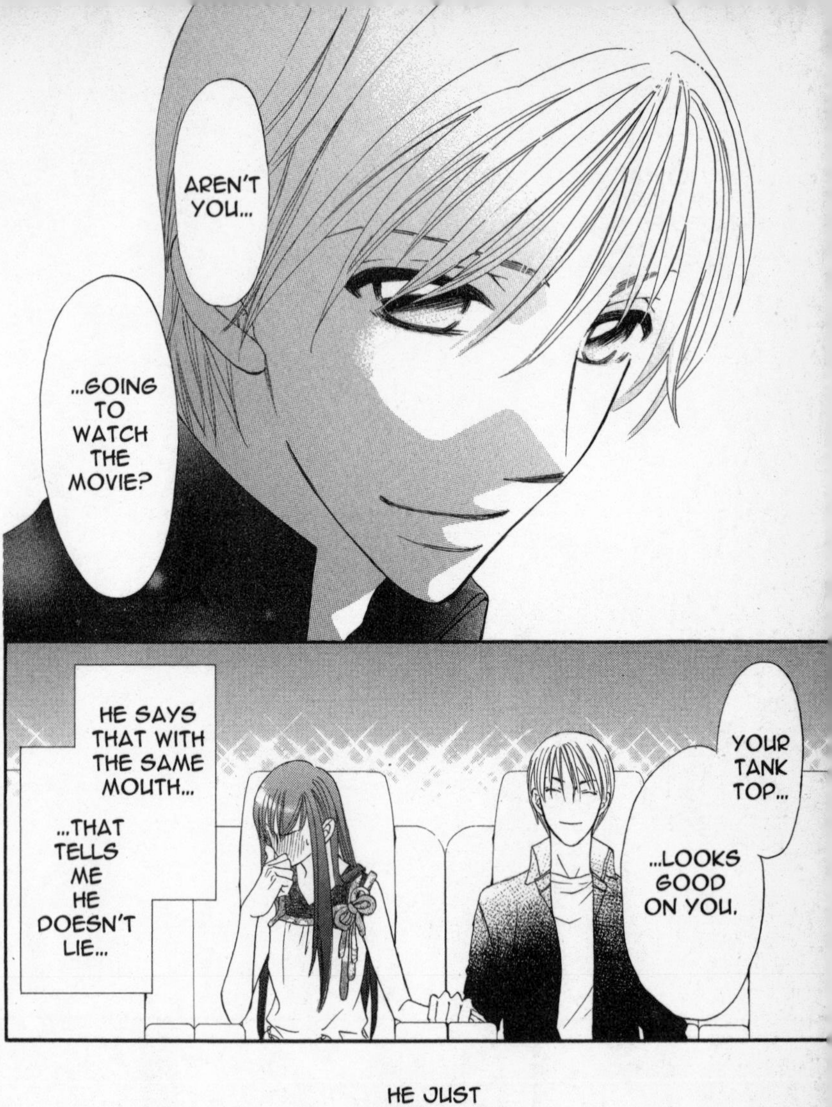
AREN'T YOU...
...GOING TO WATCH THE MOVIE?
YOUR TANK TOP...
...LOOKS GOOD ON YOU.
HE SAYS THAT WITH THE SAME MOUTH...
...THAT TELLS ME HE DOESN'T LIE...

HE JUST MIGHT BE THE DEADLIEST ONE OF THEM ALL...

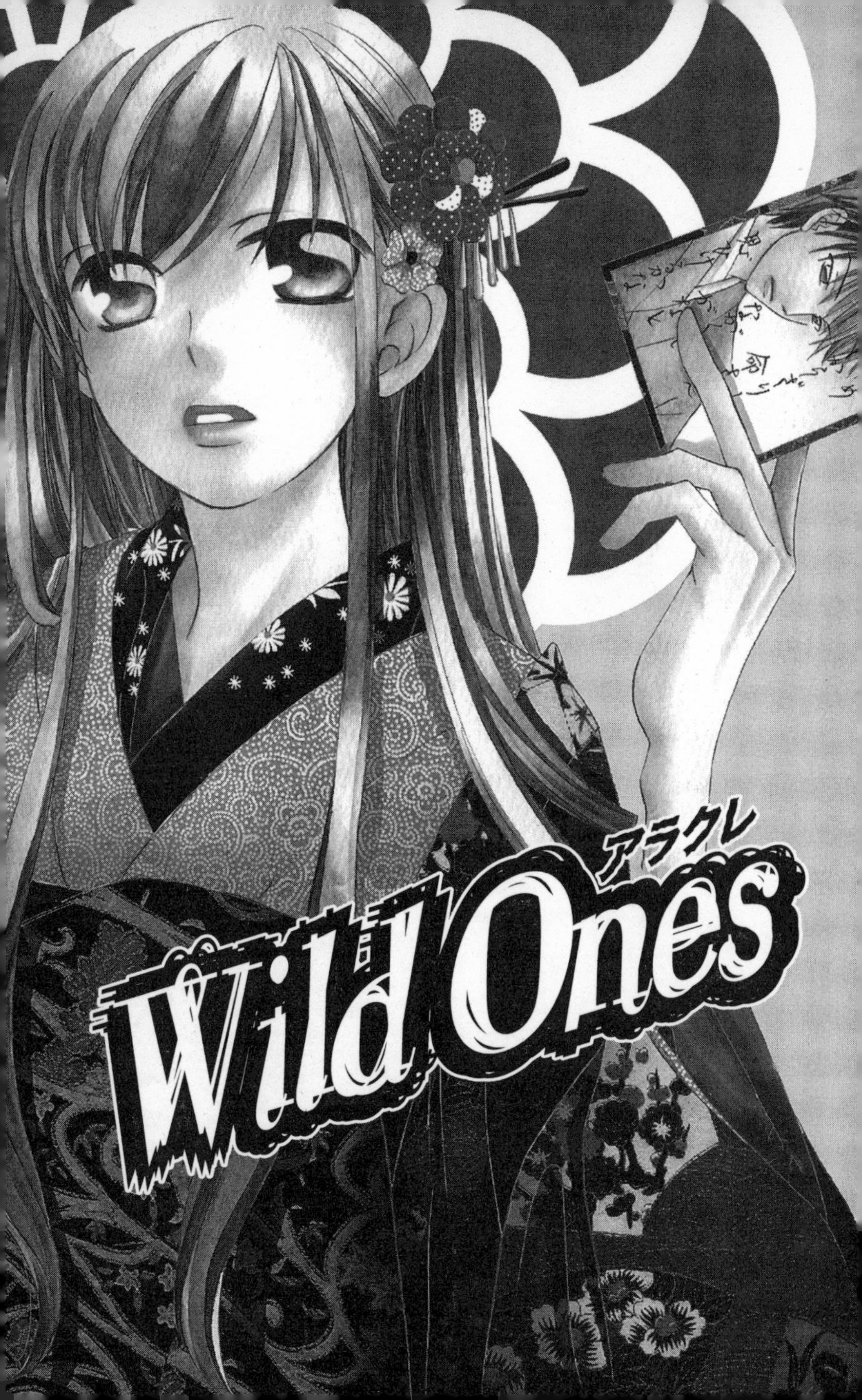
アラクレ
Wild Ones

AR

GHHHHH

NICE! I KNEW YOU'D COME THROUGH!

THANKS BUD! ♡

I LOST AGAIN!

HEY RAKU. IF THERE'S A CHANCE TO WIN, YOU SHOULD SPEAK UP.

JEEZ...

WELL, IT STILL IS A GAME OF CHANCE.

A BOOKIE ?!

JUST TAKE IT.

THANK YOU. THE NEXT ONE'LL BE IN THE SUMMER.

I▷ THE END.

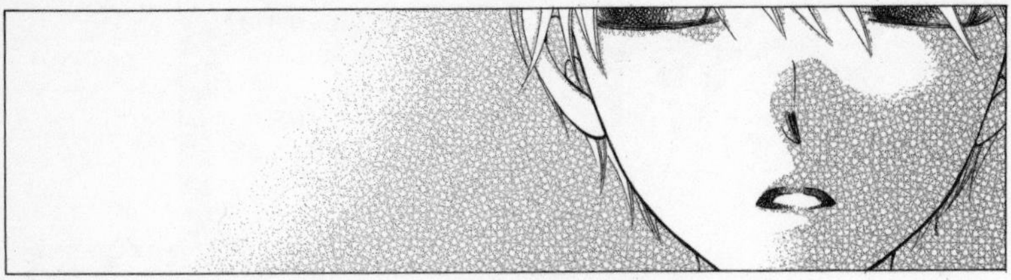

IT WAS SOMETHING...

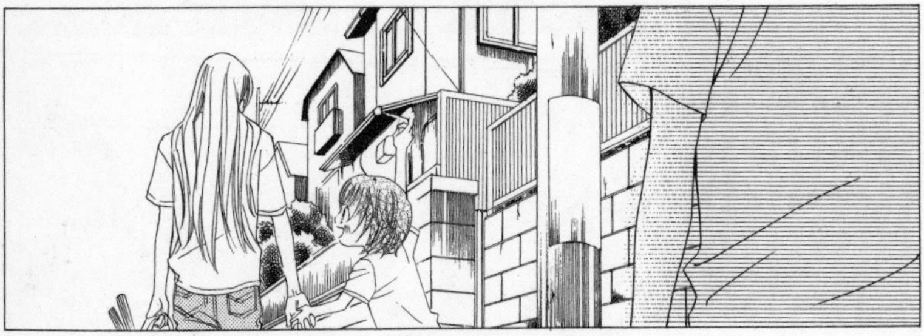

...I SWORE TO DO...

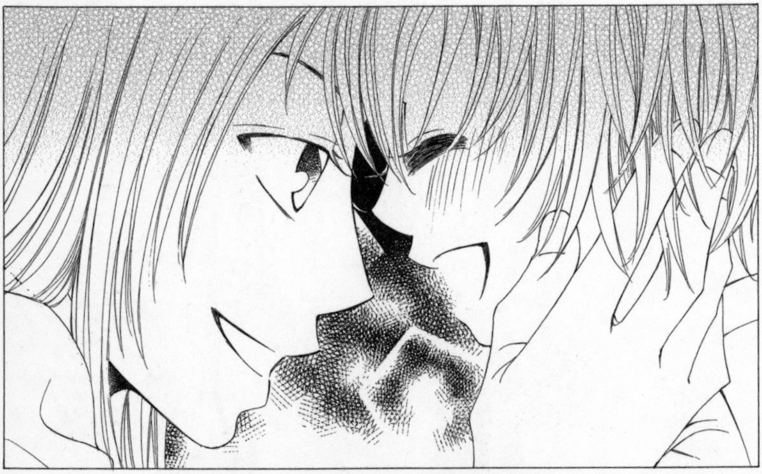

...10 YEARS AGO...

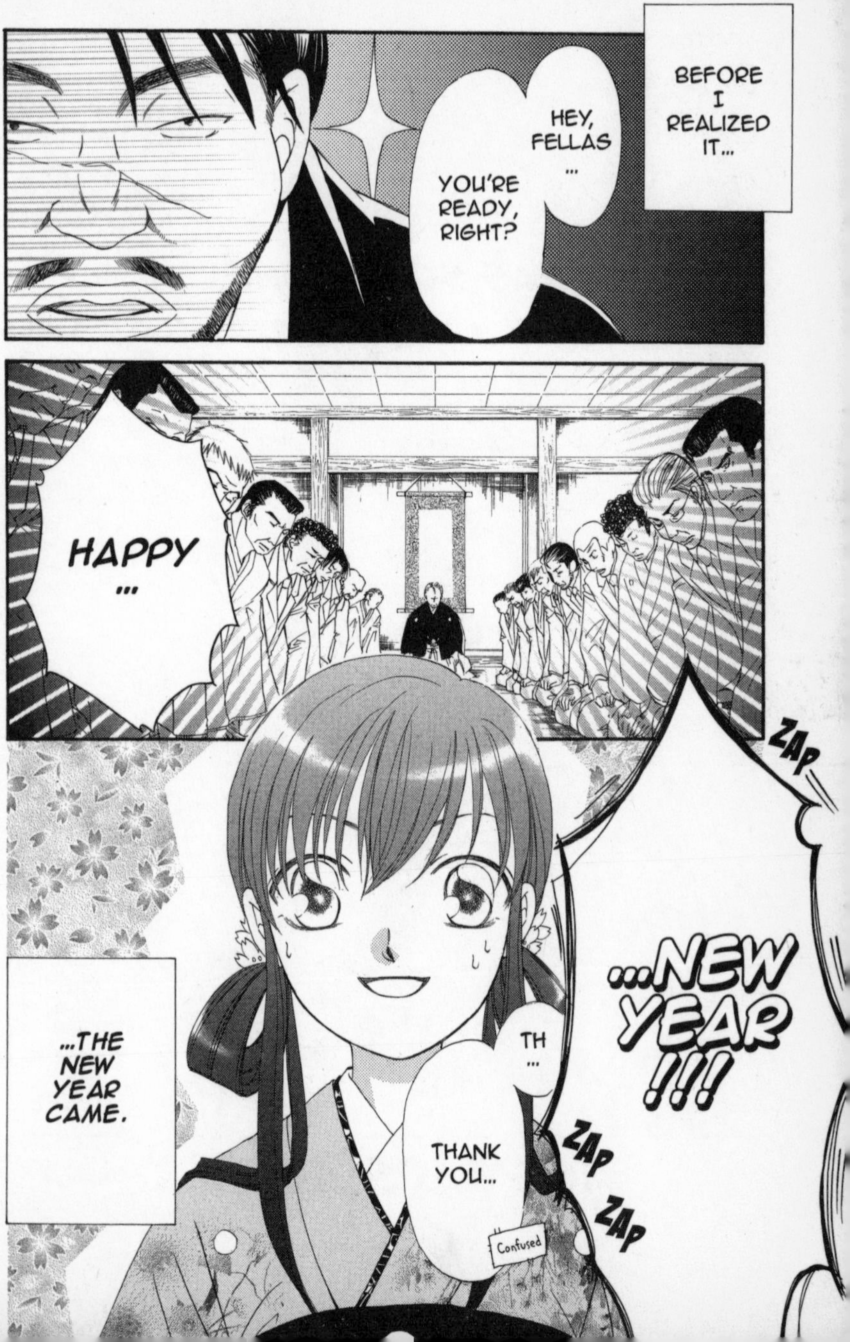
BEFORE I REALIZED IT...
HEY, FELLAS...
YOU'RE READY, RIGHT?
HAPPY...
...NEW YEAR!!!
ZAP
ZAP
ZAP
TH...
THANK YOU...
Confused
...THE NEW YEAR CAME.

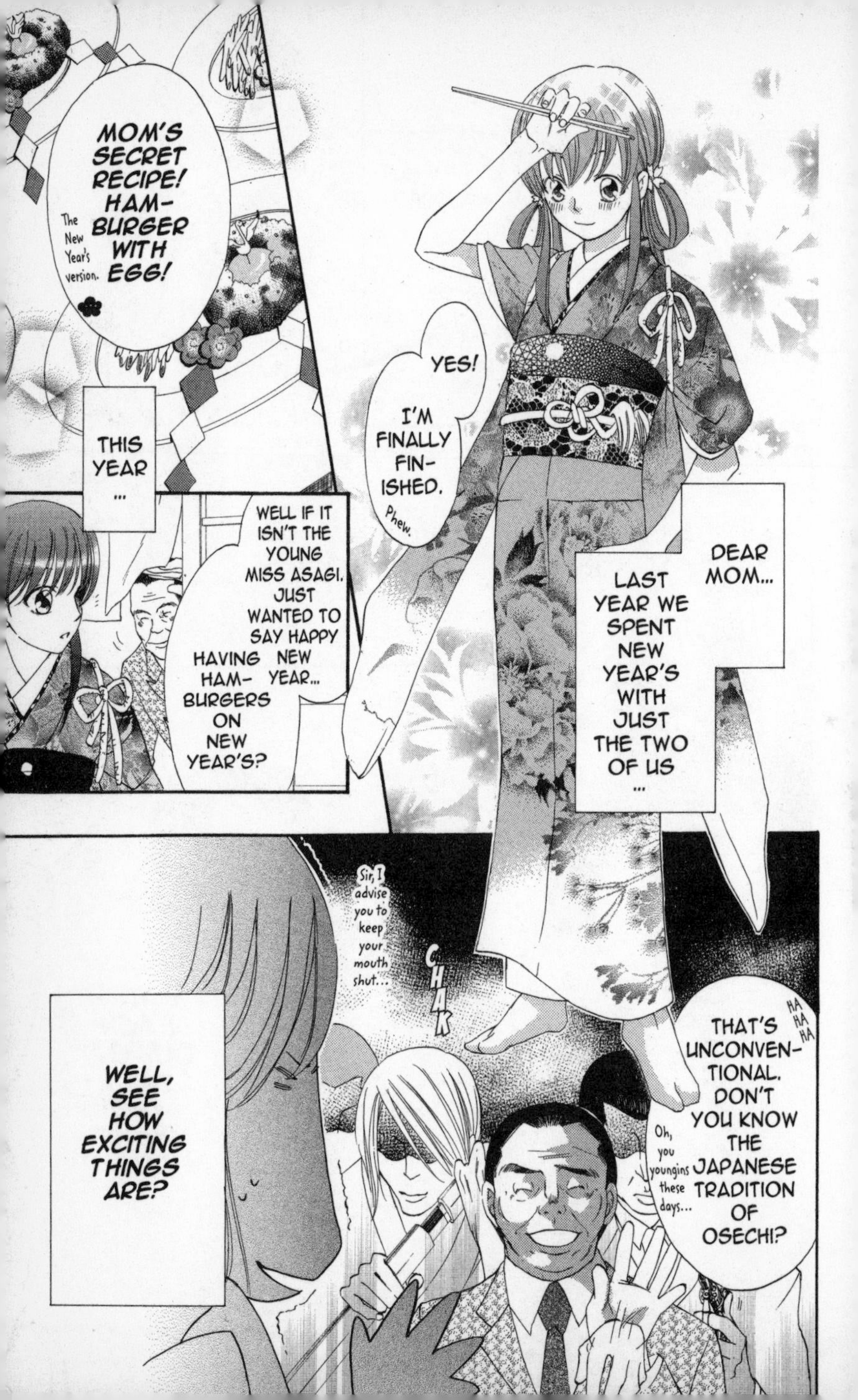
YES!
I'M FINALLY FIN-ISHED.
Phew.
DEAR MOM... LAST YEAR WE SPENT NEW YEAR'S WITH JUST THE TWO OF US ...
MOM'S SECRET RECIPE! HAM-BURGER WITH EGG!
The New Year's version.
THIS YEAR ...
WELL IF IT ISN'T THE YOUNG MISS ASAGI. JUST WANTED TO SAY HAPPY NEW YEAR...
HAVING HAM-BURGERS ON NEW YEAR'S?
HA HA HA
THAT'S UNCONVEN-TIONAL. DON'T YOU KNOW THE JAPANESE TRADITION OF OSECHI?
Oh, you youngins these days...
CHAK
Sir, I advise you to keep your mouth shut...
WELL, SEE HOW EXCITING THINGS ARE?

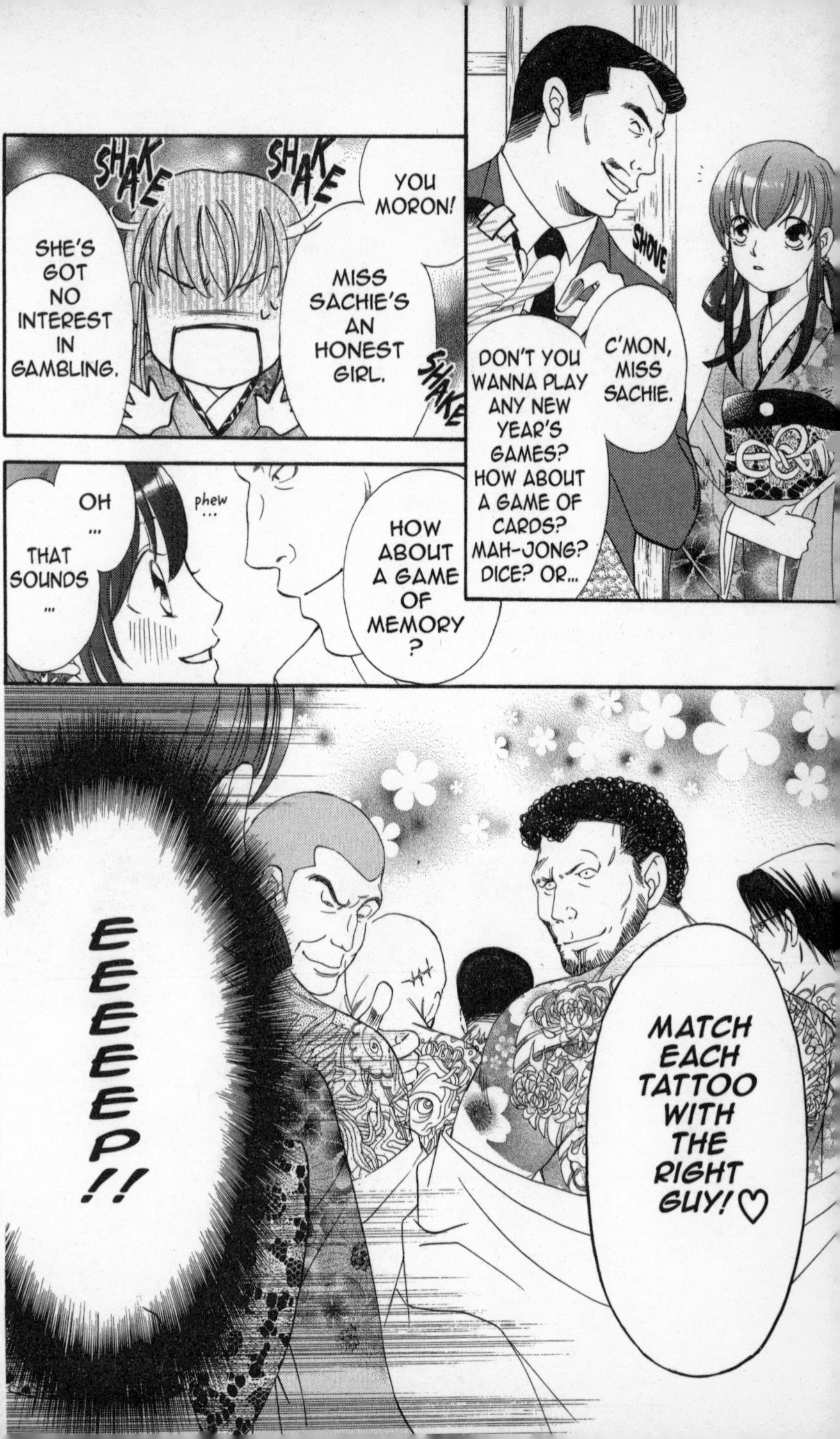
SHOVE
C'MON, MISS SACHIE.
DON'T YOU WANNA PLAY ANY NEW YEAR'S GAMES? HOW ABOUT A GAME OF CARDS? MAH-JONG? DICE? OR...
SHAKE
SHAKE
YOU MORON!
MISS SACHIE'S AN HONEST GIRL.
SHAKE
SHE'S GOT NO INTEREST IN GAMBLING.
HOW ABOUT A GAME OF MEMORY?
phew...
OH ... THAT SOUNDS ...
MATCH EACH TATTOO WITH THE RIGHT GUY! ♡
EEEEEEP!!

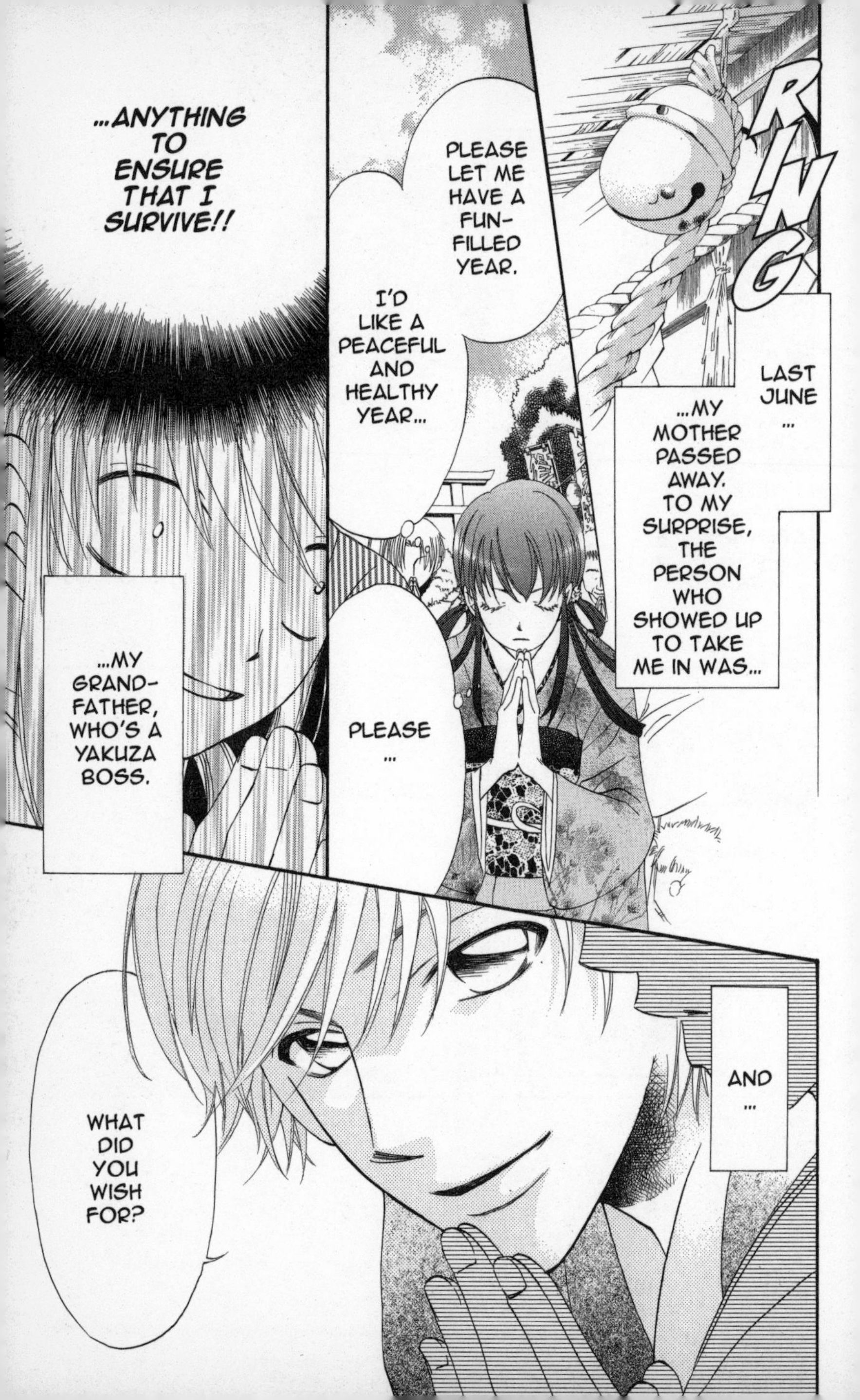

RING
LAST JUNE ...
...MY MOTHER PASSED AWAY. TO MY SURPRISE, THE PERSON WHO SHOWED UP TO TAKE ME IN WAS...
PLEASE LET ME HAVE A FUN-FILLED YEAR.
I'D LIKE A PEACEFUL AND HEALTHY YEAR...
PLEASE ...
...ANYTHING TO ENSURE THAT I SURVIVE!!
...MY GRAND-FATHER, WHO'S A YAKUZA BOSS.
AND ...
WHAT DID YOU WISH FOR?

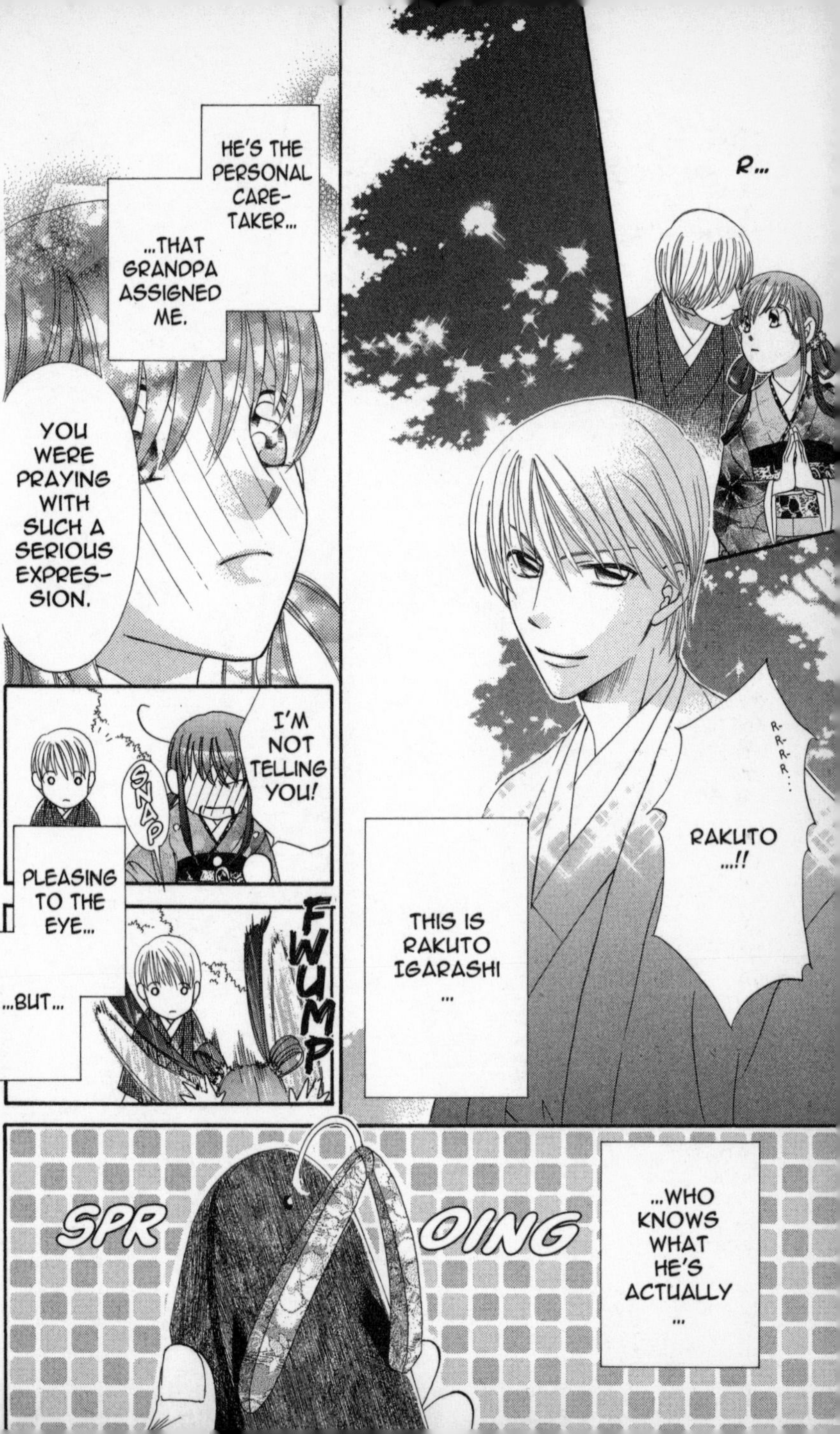
R...
R-R-R-R...
RAKUTO ...!!
THIS IS RAKUTO IGARASHI ...
HE'S THE PERSONAL CARE-TAKER...
...THAT GRANDPA ASSIGNED ME.
YOU WERE PRAYING WITH SUCH A SERIOUS EXPRES-SION.
I'M NOT TELLING YOU!
SNAP
PLEASING TO THE EYE...
...BUT...
FWUMP
...WHO KNOWS WHAT HE'S ACTUALLY ...
SPR
OING

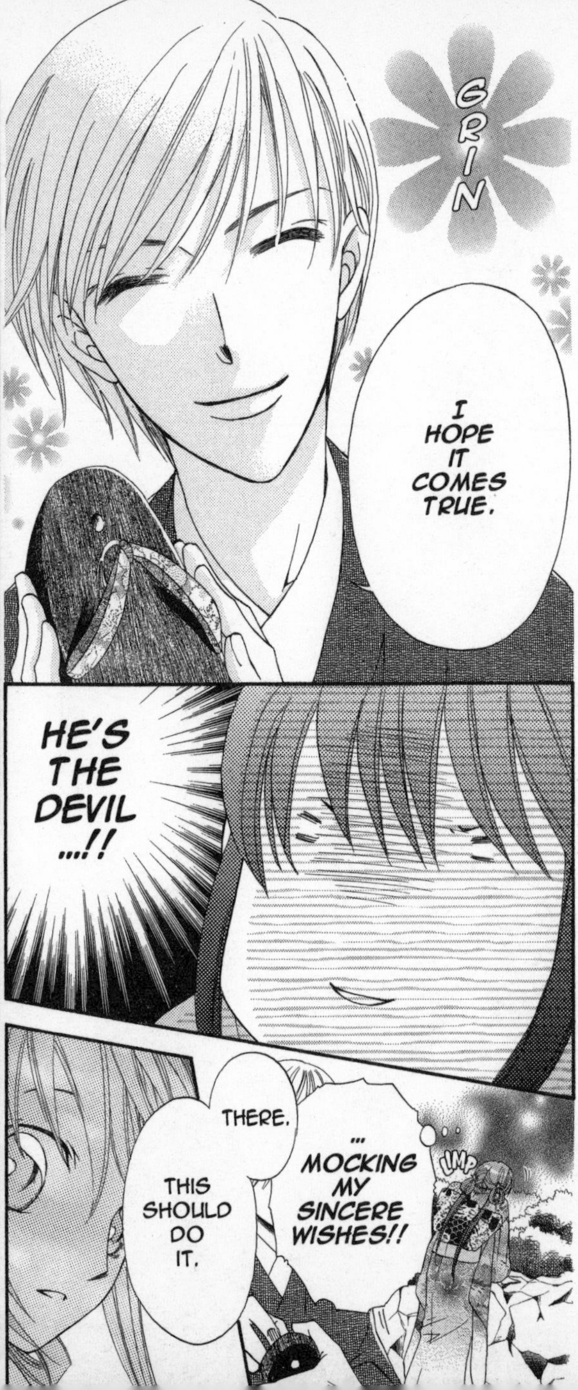
GRIN
I HOPE IT COMES TRUE.
HE'S THE DEVIL ...!!
... MOCKING MY SINCERE WISHES!!
LIMP
THERE.
THIS SHOULD DO IT.

I DREW THE SPREAD FOR THIS CHAPTER AFTER MY EDITOR SUGGESTED THAT I DO A DUO SHOT. I'M SURE HE SAW IT AND WAS RIGHTLY DISAP-POINTED... SORRY. THIS WAS THE BEST I COULD DO... I WAS TRYING TO DECIDE ON A POEM FOR RAKUTO ON THE COVER BUT WAS SHOCKED WHEN I ACTUALLY LOOKED INTO THE KARUTA GAME FOR HYAKUNIN ISSHU THAT I WAS GOING TO BASE IT ON. I HAD A VERY DIFFERENT IMAGE OF THAT FAMOUS OPENING PHRASE, "KIMI GA TAME"... I THOUGHT IT WAS LIKE THIS:

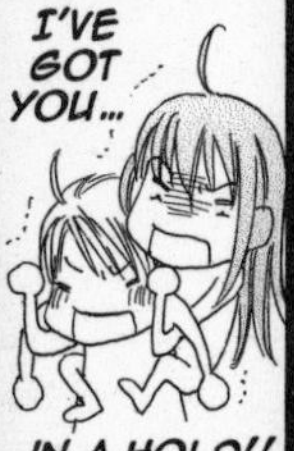
I'VE GOT YOU...

...IN A HOLD!!

PATHETIC THAT I THOUGHT THAT FOR ALL THESE YEARS. I HONESTLY SHOCKED MYSELF.
I'VE BEEN PLAYING HYAKUNIN ISSHU SINCE I WAS YOUNG, BUT I GUESS YOU TEND TO REMEMBER THINGS BY IMAGE WHEN YOU'RE THAT YOUNG... I REALIZE WE WERE PROBABLY TAUGHT THIS IN MIDDLE SCHOOL...

MUMBLE MUMBLE

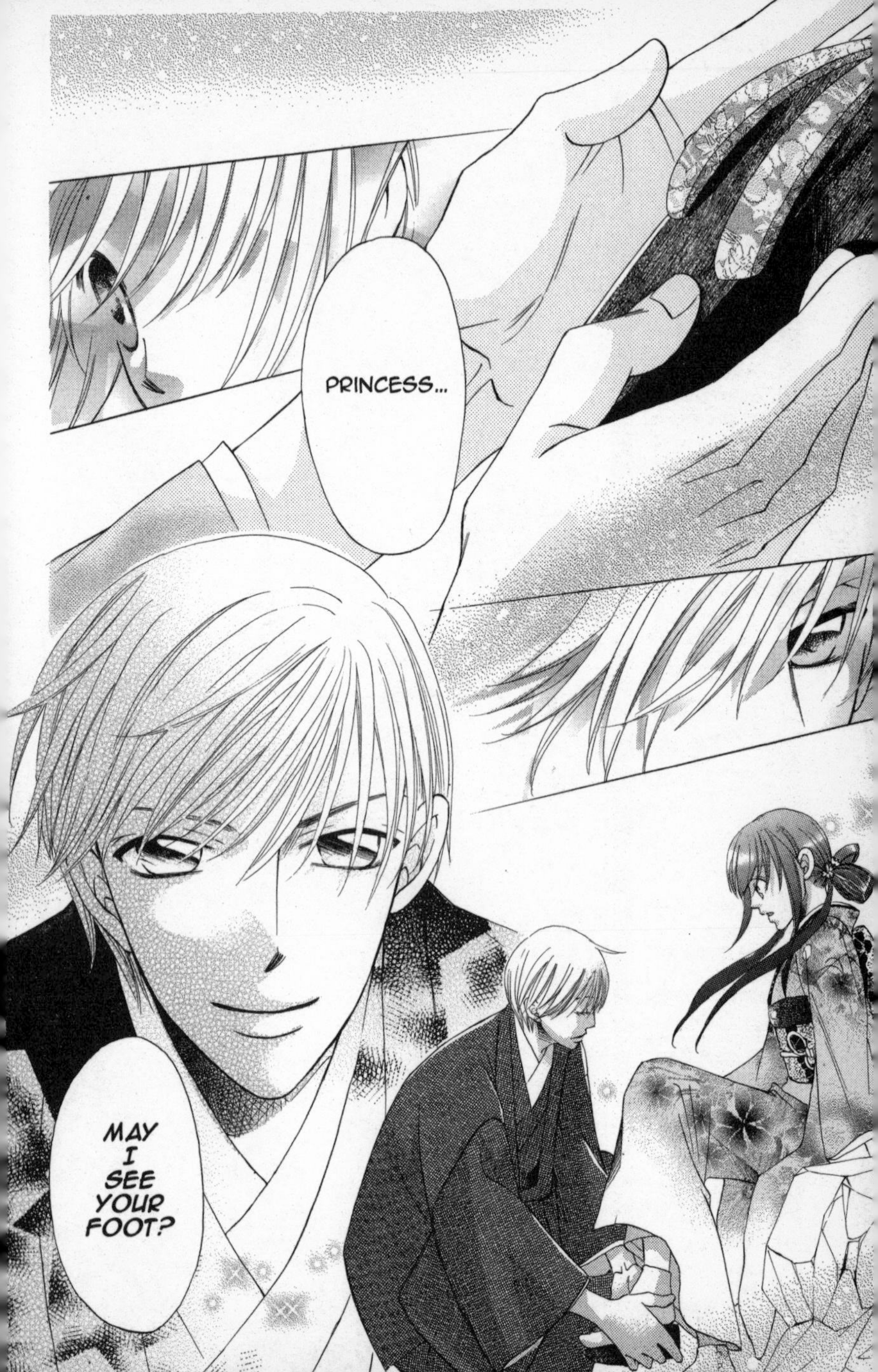
PRINCESS...
MAY I SEE YOUR FOOT?

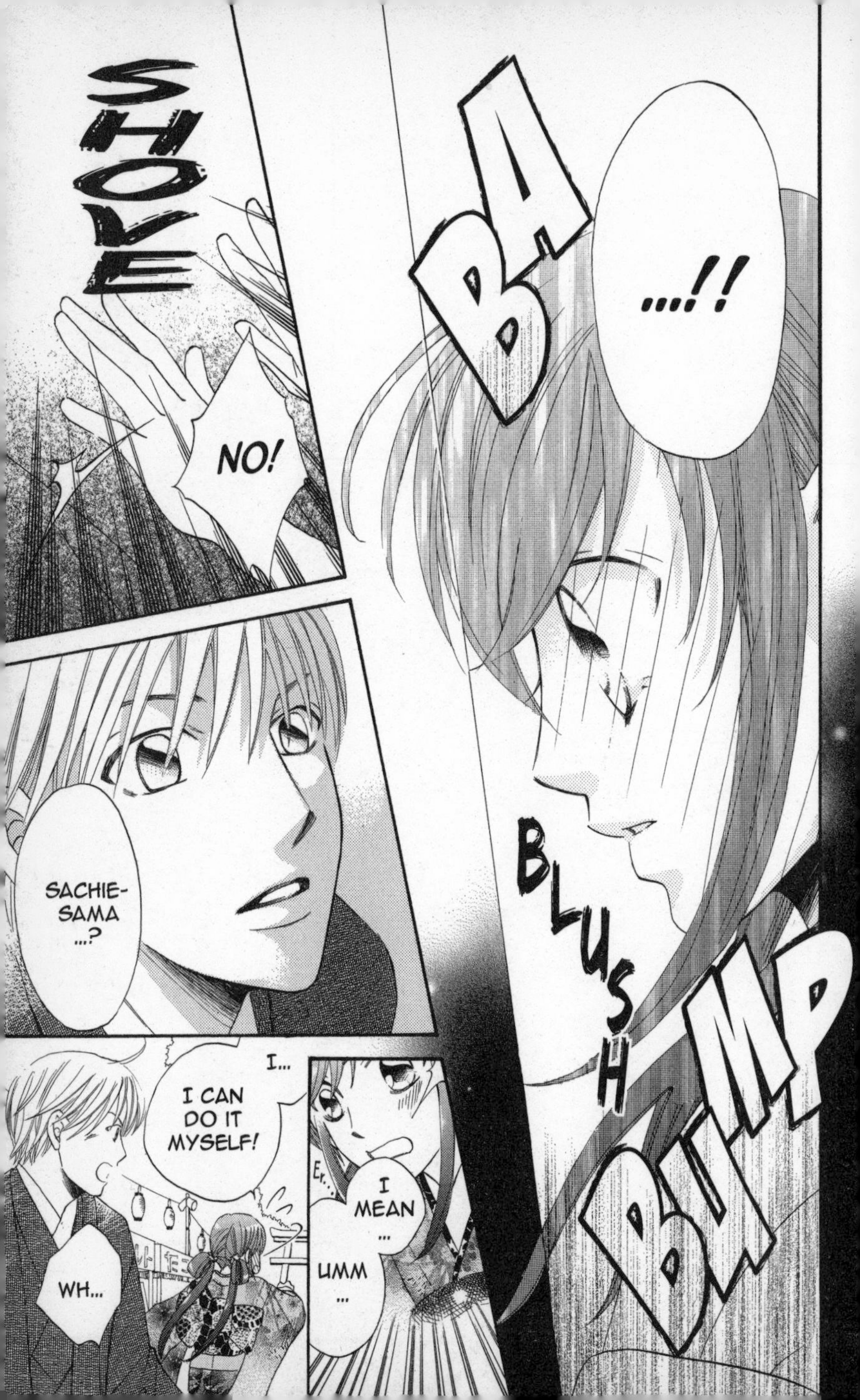
BA
...!!
BLUSH
BUMP
SHOVE
NO!
SACHIE-SAMA ...?
Er...
I MEAN ...
UMM ...
I...
I CAN DO IT MYSELF!
WH...

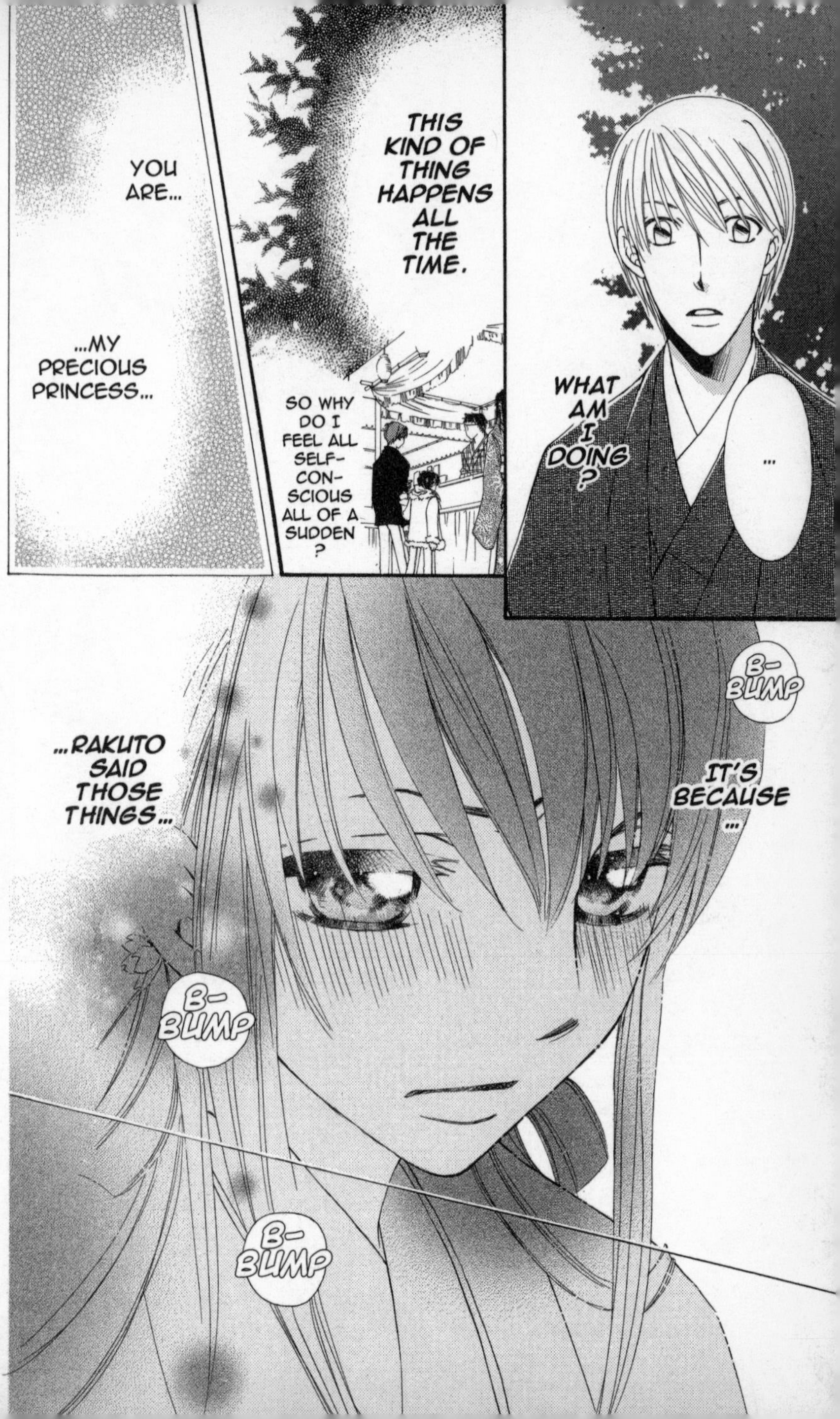
...
WHAT AM I DOING?
THIS KIND OF THING HAPPENS ALL THE TIME.
SO WHY DO I FEEL ALL SELF-CONSCIOUS ALL OF A SUDDEN?
YOU ARE...
...MY PRECIOUS PRINCESS...
B-BUMP
IT'S BECAUSE...
...RAKUTO SAID THOSE THINGS...
B-BUMP
B-BUMP

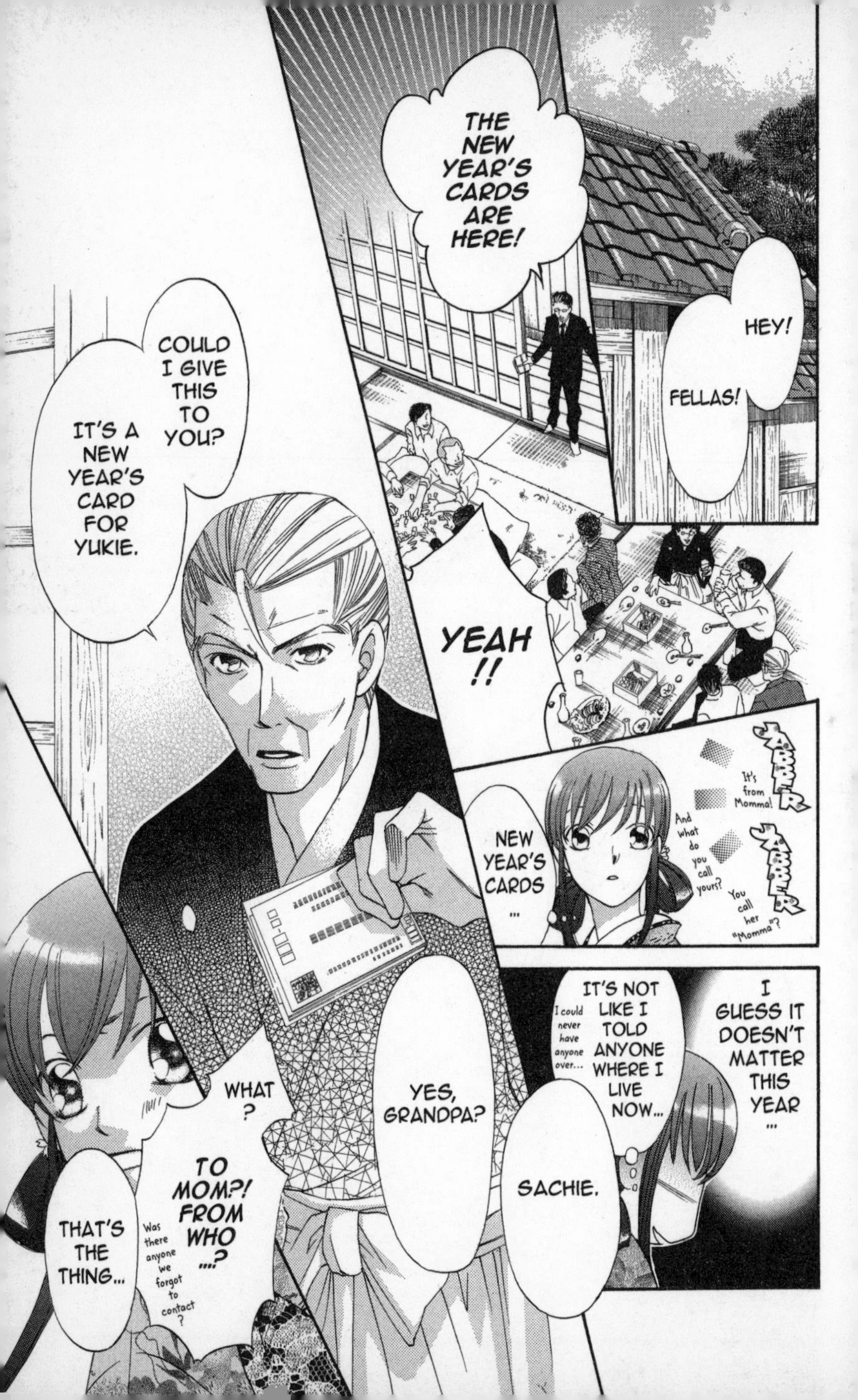
HEY!
FELLAS!
THE NEW YEAR'S CARDS ARE HERE!
YEAH!!
JABBER
It's from Momma!
JABBER
You call her "Momma"?
And what do you call yours?
NEW YEAR'S CARDS ...
I GUESS IT DOESN'T MATTER THIS YEAR ...
IT'S NOT LIKE I TOLD ANYONE WHERE I LIVE NOW...
I could never have anyone over...
SACHIE.
YES, GRANDPA?
COULD I GIVE THIS TO YOU?
IT'S A NEW YEAR'S CARD FOR YUKIE.
WHAT?
TO MOM?! FROM WHO ...?
Was there anyone we forgot to contact?
THAT'S THE THING...

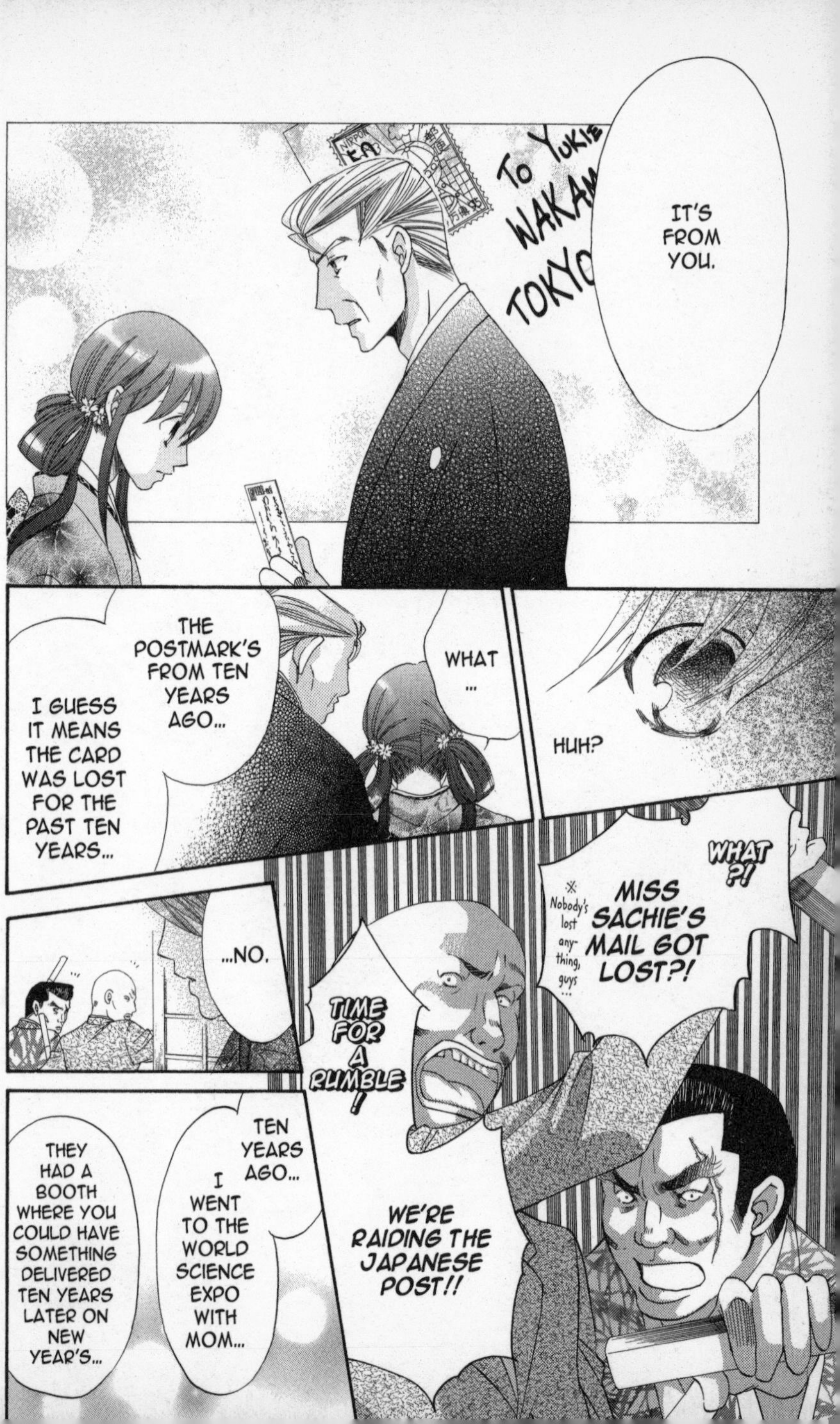
IT'S FROM YOU.
To Yukie
HUH?
WHAT ...
THE POSTMARK'S FROM TEN YEARS AGO...
I GUESS IT MEANS THE CARD WAS LOST FOR THE PAST TEN YEARS...
WHAT ?!
MISS SACHIE'S MAIL GOT LOST?!
※ Nobody's lost anything, guys ...
TIME FOR A RUMBLE!
WE'RE RAIDING THE JAPANESE POST!!
...NO.
TEN YEARS AGO...
I WENT TO THE WORLD SCIENCE EXPO WITH MOM...
THEY HAD A BOOTH WHERE YOU COULD HAVE SOMETHING DELIVERED TEN YEARS LATER ON NEW YEAR'S...

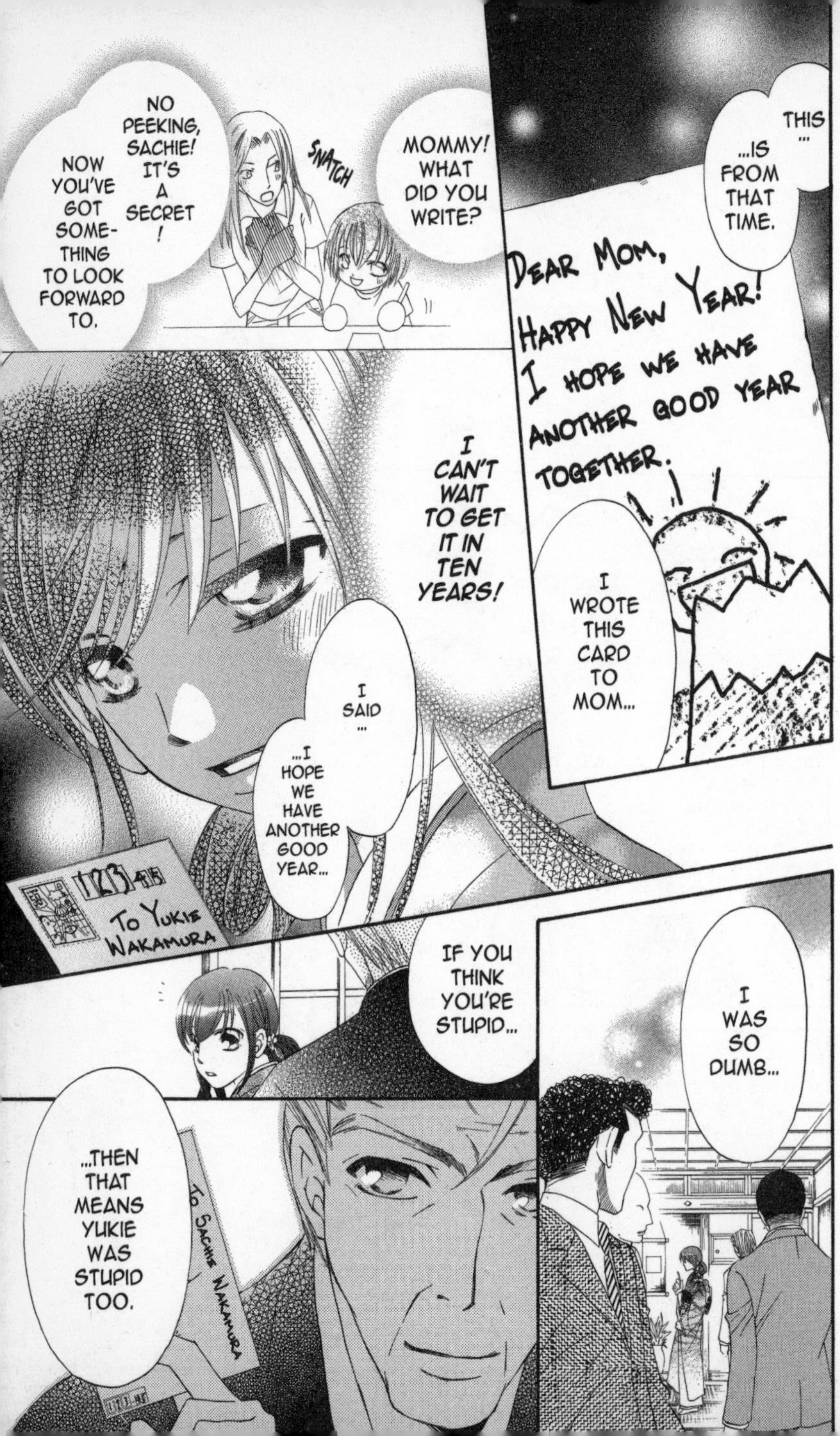
THIS...
...IS FROM THAT TIME.
DEAR MOM, HAPPY NEW YEAR! I HOPE WE HAVE ANOTHER GOOD YEAR TOGETHER.
I WROTE THIS CARD TO MOM...
MOMMY! WHAT DID YOU WRITE?
SNATCH
NO PEEKING, SACHIE! IT'S A SECRET!
NOW YOU'VE GOT SOME-THING TO LOOK FORWARD TO.
I CAN'T WAIT TO GET IT IN TEN YEARS!
I SAID...
...I HOPE WE HAVE ANOTHER GOOD YEAR...
123 45
TO YUKIE WAKAMURA
I WAS SO DUMB...
IF YOU THINK YOU'RE STUPID...
...THEN THAT MEANS YUKIE WAS STUPID TOO.
TO SACHIE WAKAMURA

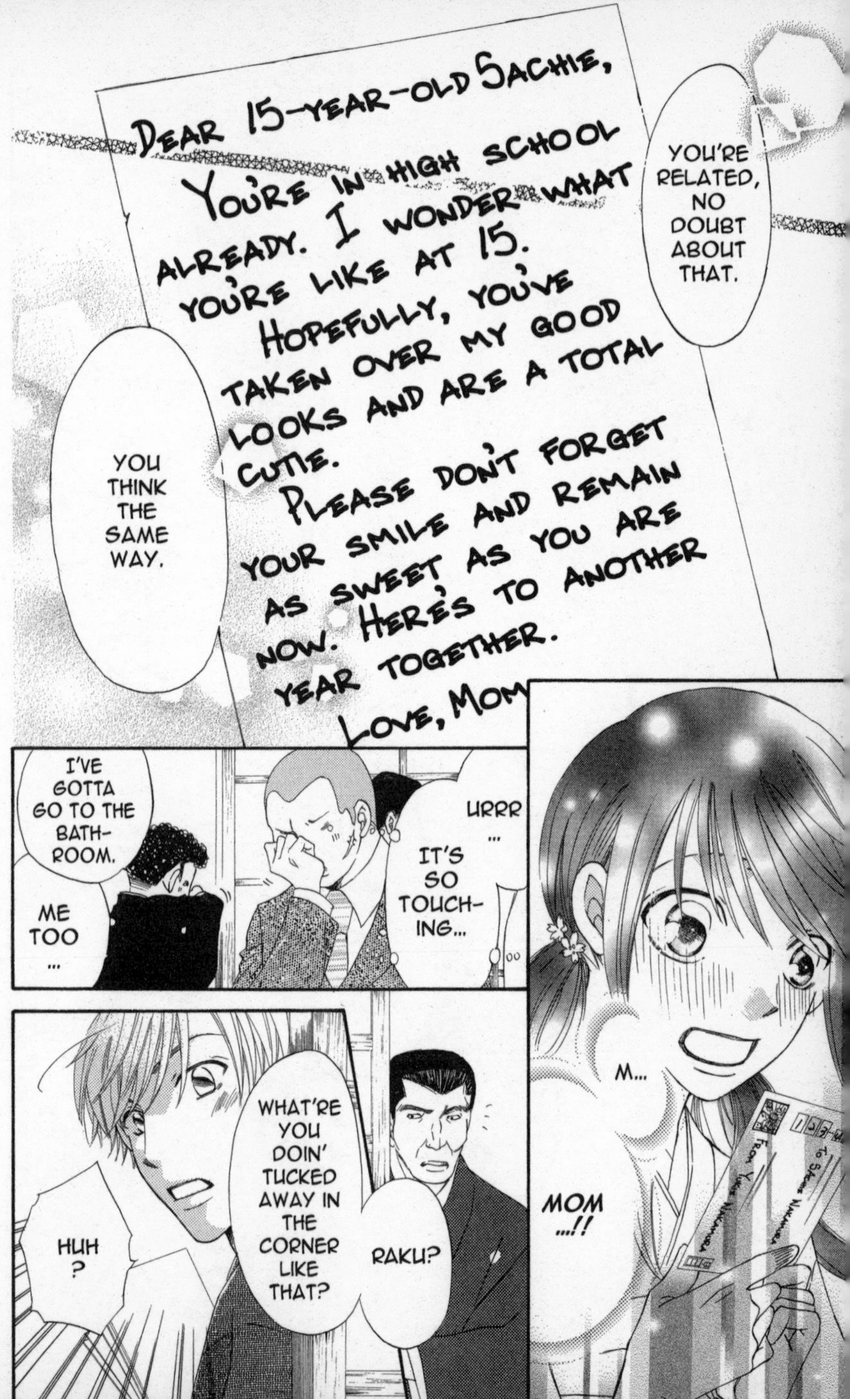
YOU'RE RELATED, NO DOUBT ABOUT THAT.
Dear 15-year-old Sachie,
You're in high school already. I wonder what you're like at 15.
Hopefully, you've taken over my good looks and are a total cutie.
Please don't forget your smile and remain as sweet as you are now. Here's to another year together.
Love, Mom
YOU THINK THE SAME WAY.
M...
MOM ...!!
URRR ...
IT'S SO TOUCHING...
I'VE GOTTA GO TO THE BATHROOM.
ME TOO ...
RAKU?
WHAT'RE YOU DOIN' TUCKED AWAY IN THE CORNER LIKE THAT?
HUH ?

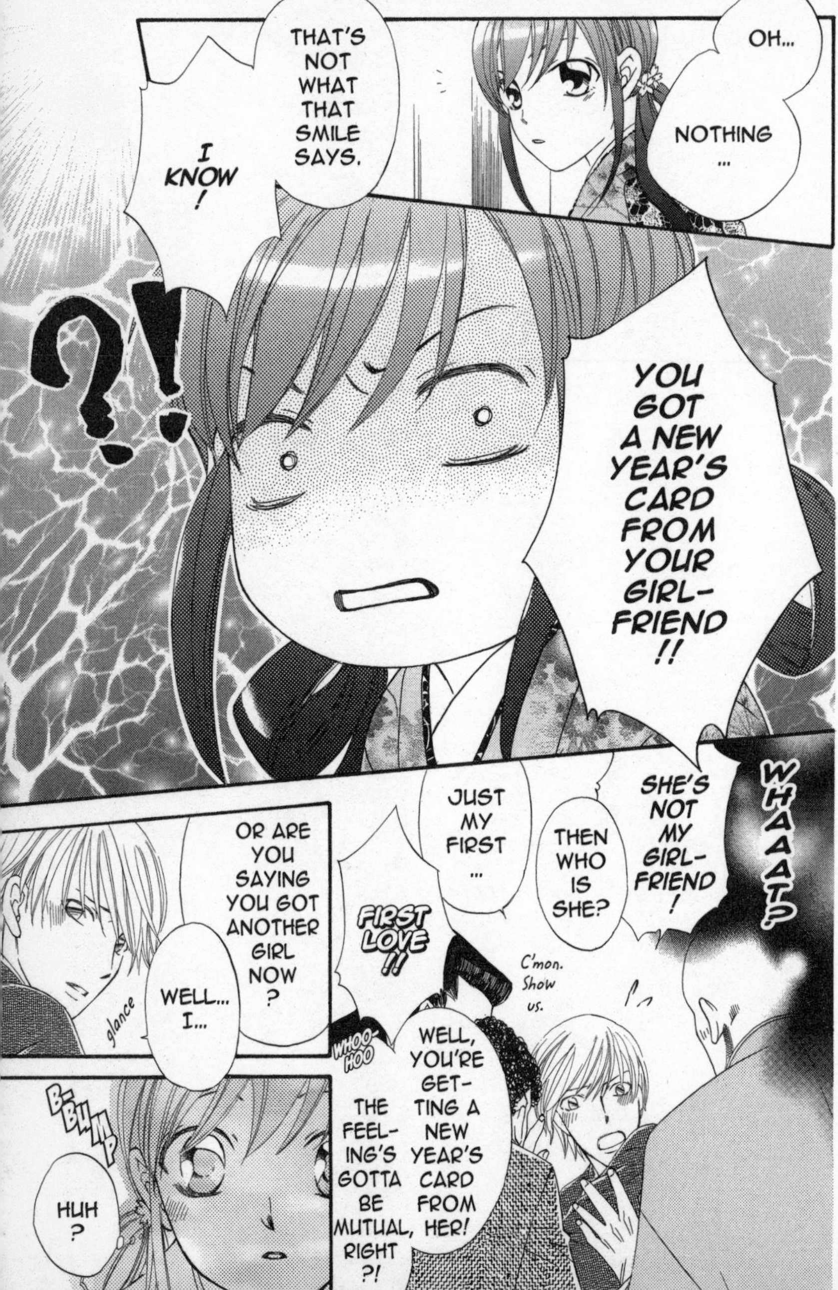
OH... NOTHING ...
THAT'S NOT WHAT THAT SMILE SAYS.
I KNOW!
?!
YOU GOT A NEW YEAR'S CARD FROM YOUR GIRLFRIEND!!
WHAAAAT?
SHE'S NOT MY GIRLFRIEND!
THEN WHO IS SHE?
JUST MY FIRST ...
FIRST LOVE!!
C'mon. Show us.
WELL, YOU'RE GETTING A NEW YEAR'S CARD FROM HER!
WHOO-HOO
THE FEELING'S GOTTA BE MUTUAL, RIGHT?!
OR ARE YOU SAYING YOU GOT ANOTHER GIRL NOW?
WELL... I...
glance
B-BUMP
HUH?

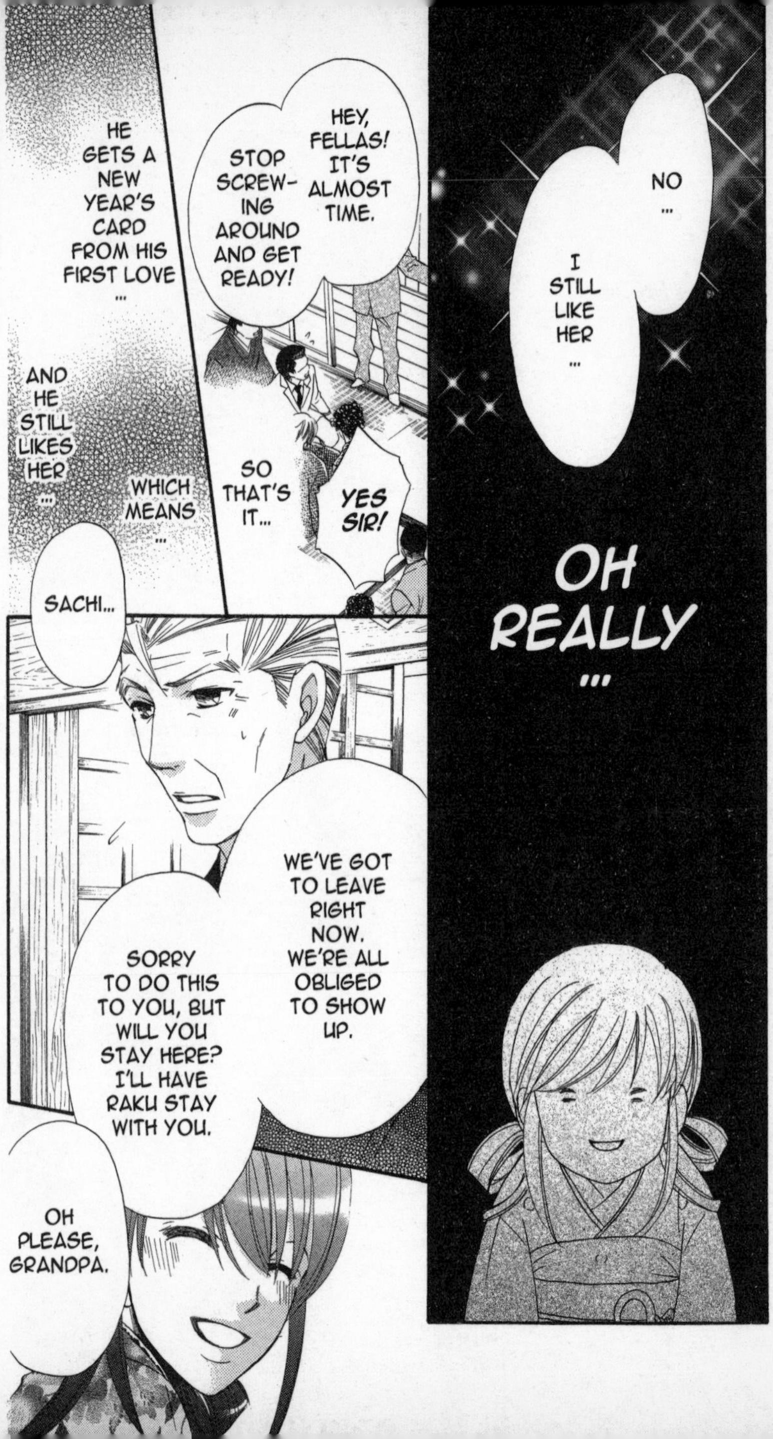
NO ...
I STILL LIKE HER ...
OH REALLY ...
HEY, FELLAS! IT'S ALMOST TIME.
STOP SCREWING AROUND AND GET READY!
YES SIR!
SO THAT'S IT...
HE GETS A NEW YEAR'S CARD FROM HIS FIRST LOVE ...
AND HE STILL LIKES HER ...
WHICH MEANS ...
SACHI...
WE'VE GOT TO LEAVE RIGHT NOW. WE'RE ALL OBLIGED TO SHOW UP.
SORRY TO DO THIS TO YOU, BUT WILL YOU STAY HERE? I'LL HAVE RAKU STAY WITH YOU.
OH PLEASE, GRANDPA.

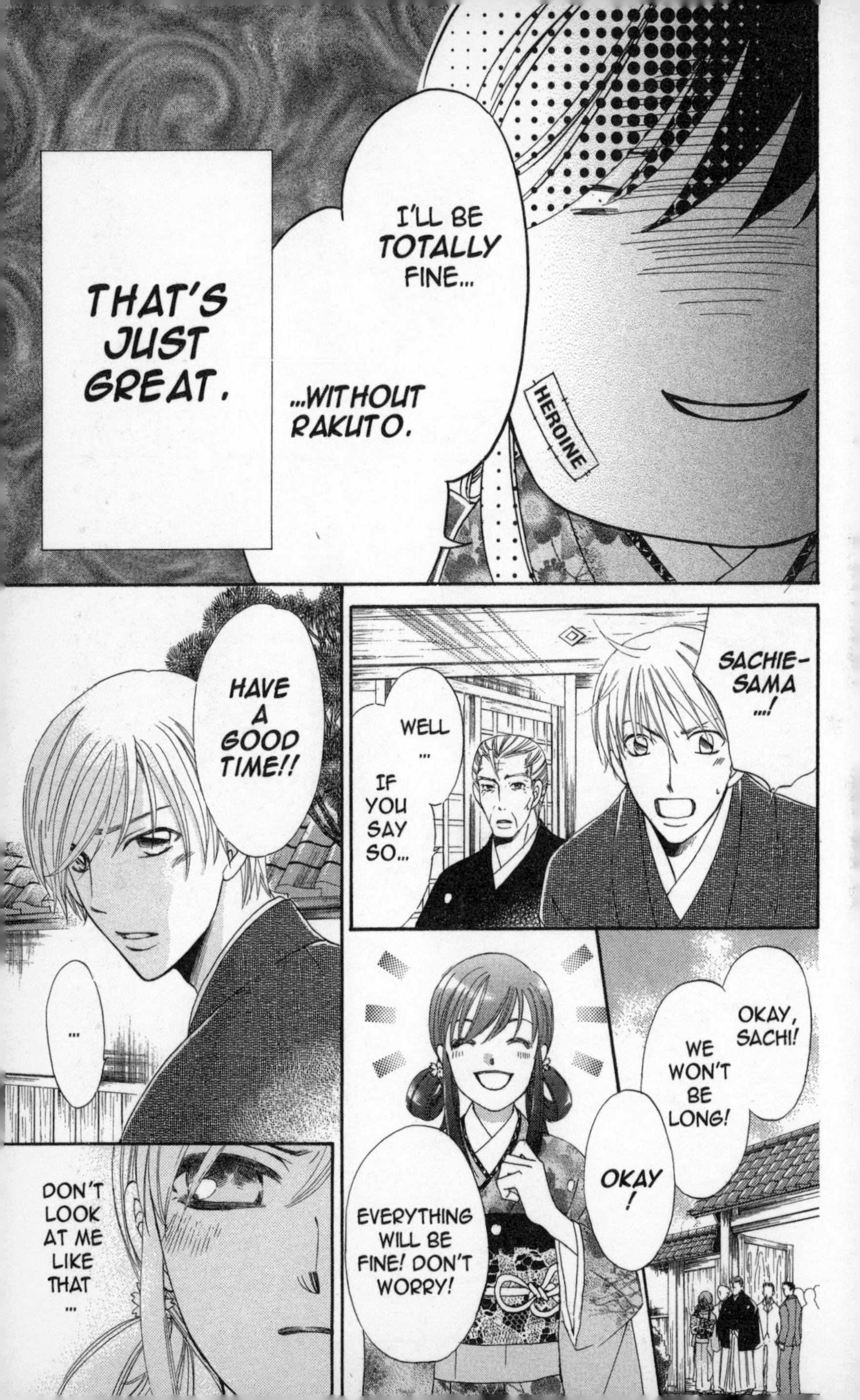
I'LL BE TOTALLY FINE...
...WITHOUT RAKUTO.
HEROINE
THAT'S JUST GREAT.
SACHIE-SAMA ...!
WELL ... IF YOU SAY SO...
OKAY, SACHI!
WE WON'T BE LONG!
OKAY!
EVERYTHING WILL BE FINE! DON'T WORRY!
HAVE A GOOD TIME!!
...
DON'T LOOK AT ME LIKE THAT ...

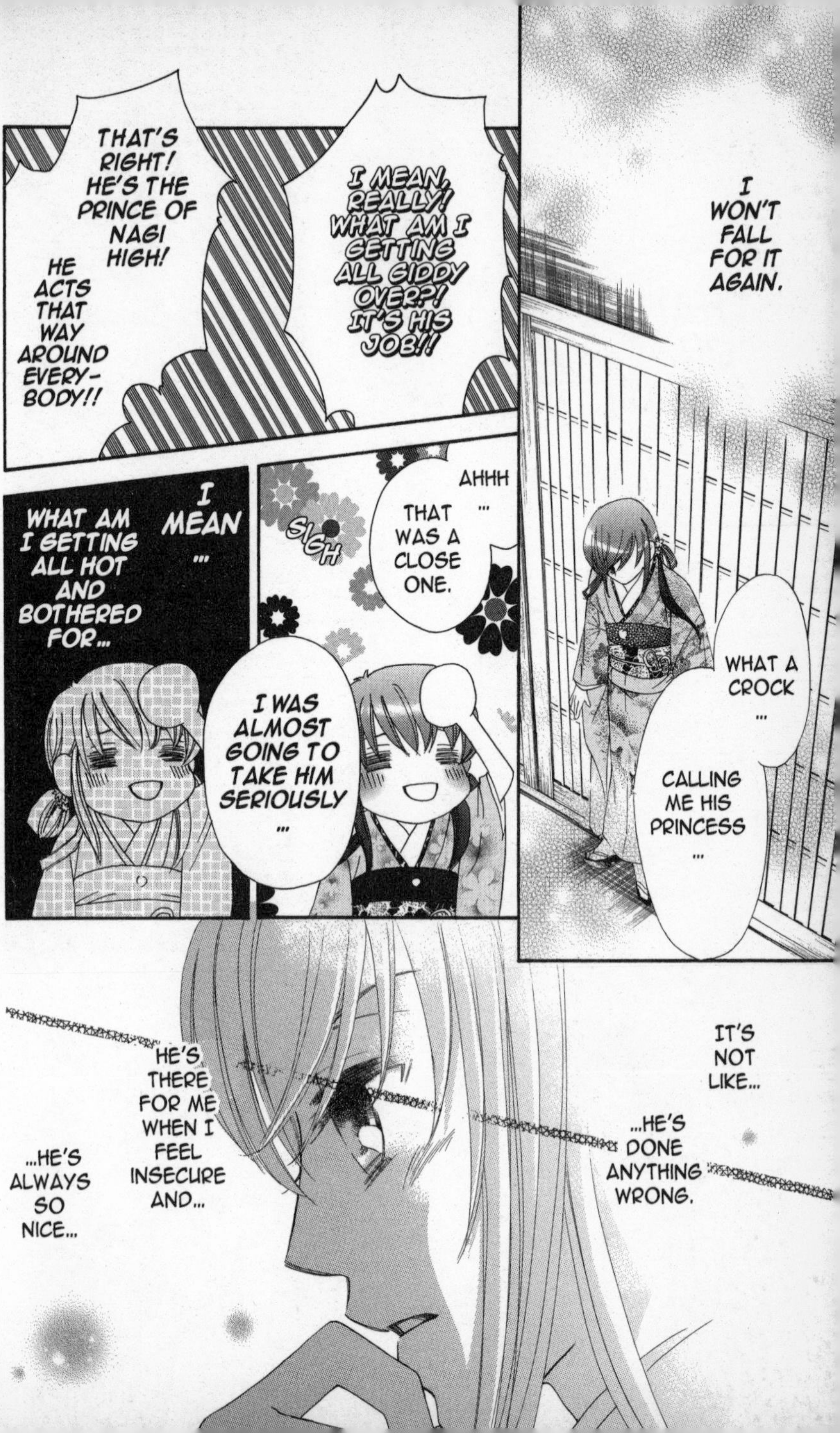
I WON'T FALL FOR IT AGAIN.
WHAT A CROCK ...
CALLING ME HIS PRINCESS ...
I MEAN, REALLY! WHAT AM I GETTING ALL GIDDY OVER?! IT'S HIS JOB!!
THAT'S RIGHT! HE'S THE PRINCE OF NAGI HIGH!
HE ACTS THAT WAY AROUND EVERY-BODY!!
AHHH ...
THAT WAS A CLOSE ONE.
SIGH
I WAS ALMOST GOING TO TAKE HIM SERIOUSLY ...
I MEAN ...
WHAT AM I GETTING ALL HOT AND BOTHERED FOR...
IT'S NOT LIKE...
...HE'S DONE ANYTHING WRONG.
HE'S THERE FOR ME WHEN I FEEL INSECURE AND...
...HE'S ALWAYS SO NICE...

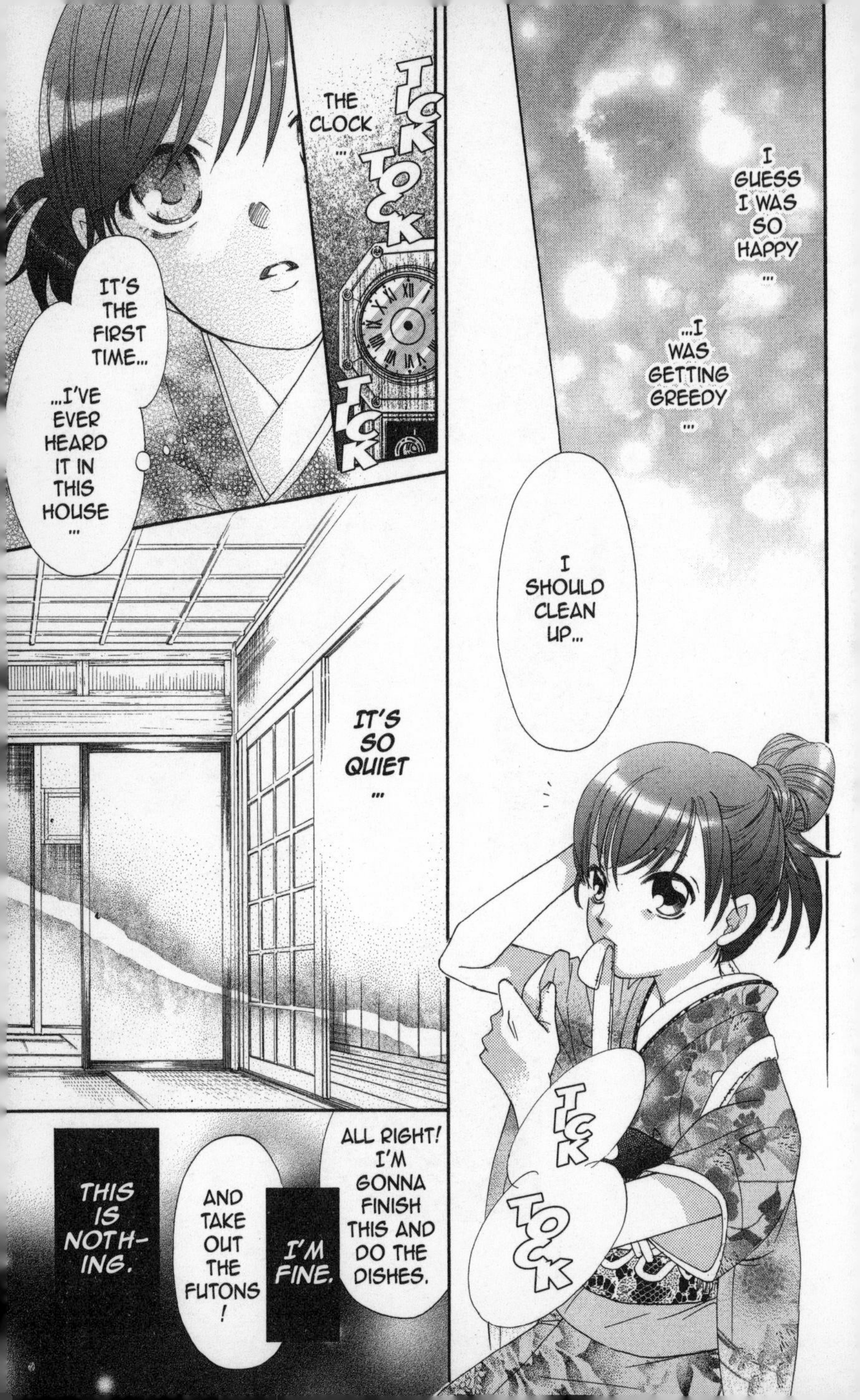
I GUESS I WAS SO HAPPY...
...I WAS GETTING GREEDY...
I SHOULD CLEAN UP...
TICK TOCK
THE CLOCK...
TICK TOCK
TICK
IT'S THE FIRST TIME...
...I'VE EVER HEARD IT IN THIS HOUSE...
IT'S SO QUIET...
ALL RIGHT! I'M GONNA FINISH THIS AND DO THE DISHES.
I'M FINE.
AND TAKE OUT THE FUTONS!
THIS IS NOTHING.

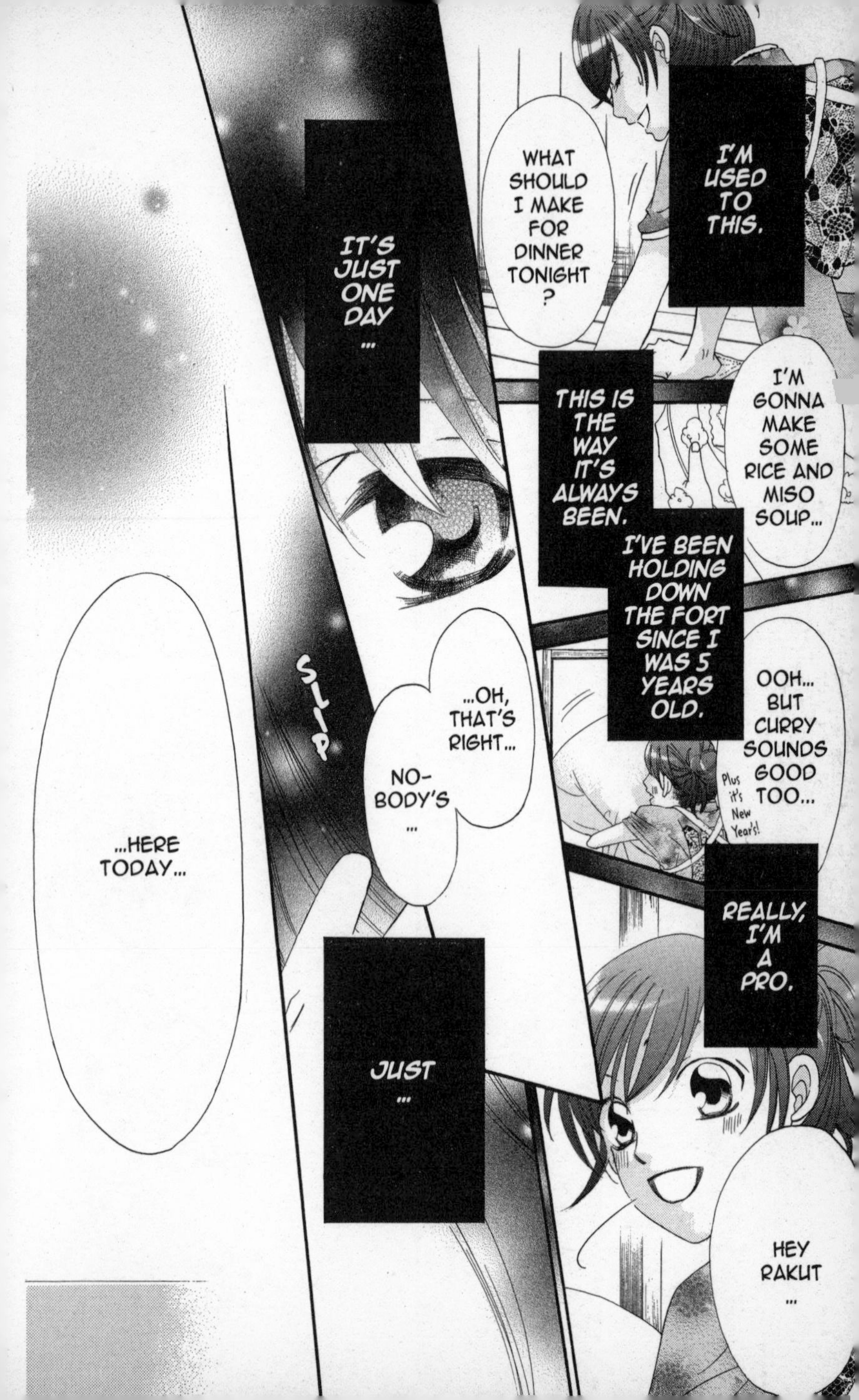
I'M USED TO THIS.
WHAT SHOULD I MAKE FOR DINNER TONIGHT?
I'M GONNA MAKE SOME RICE AND MISO SOUP...
THIS IS THE WAY IT'S ALWAYS BEEN.
I'VE BEEN HOLDING DOWN THE FORT SINCE I WAS 5 YEARS OLD.
OOH... BUT CURRY SOUNDS GOOD TOO...
Plus it's New Year's!
REALLY, I'M A PRO.
HEY RAKUT...
IT'S JUST ONE DAY...
...OH, THAT'S RIGHT...
NO-BODY'S...
SLIP
JUST...
...HERE TODAY...

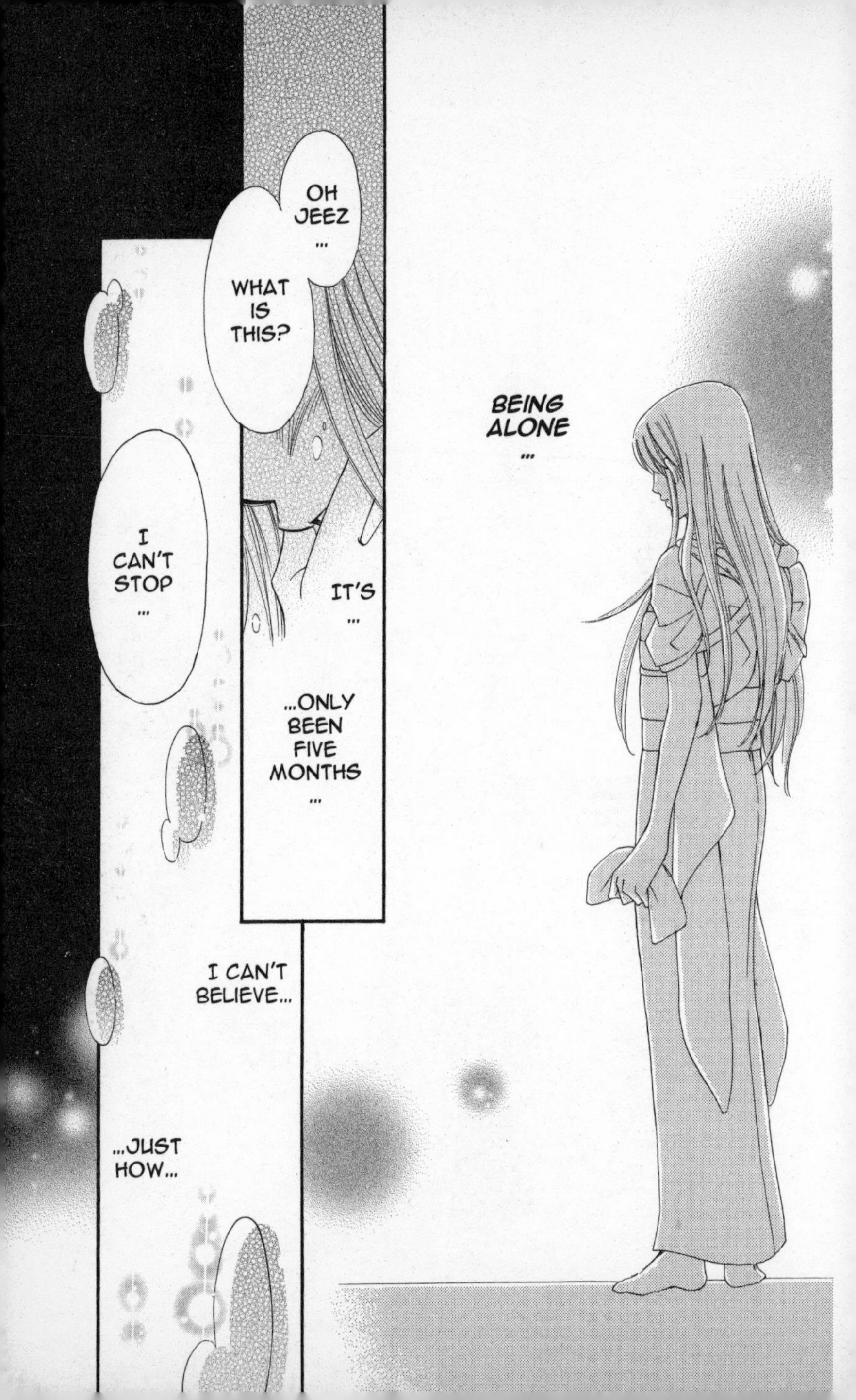
BEING ALONE ...
OH JEEZ ...
WHAT IS THIS?
IT'S ...
...ONLY BEEN FIVE MONTHS ...
I CAN'T STOP ...
I CAN'T BELIEVE...
...JUST HOW...

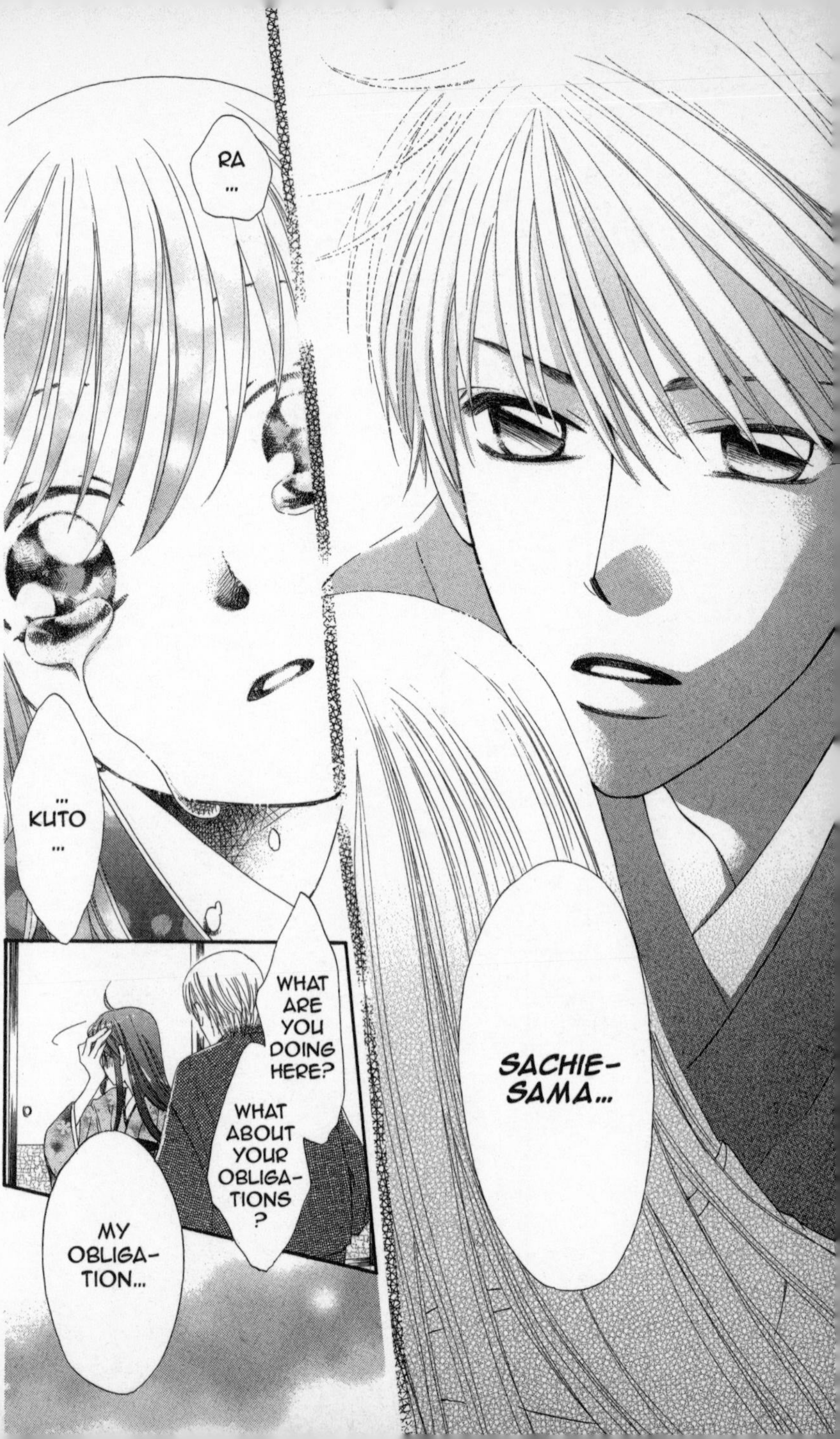
SACHIE-SAMA...
RA ...
... KUTO ...
WHAT ARE YOU DOING HERE?
WHAT ABOUT YOUR OBLIGATIONS?
MY OBLIGATION...

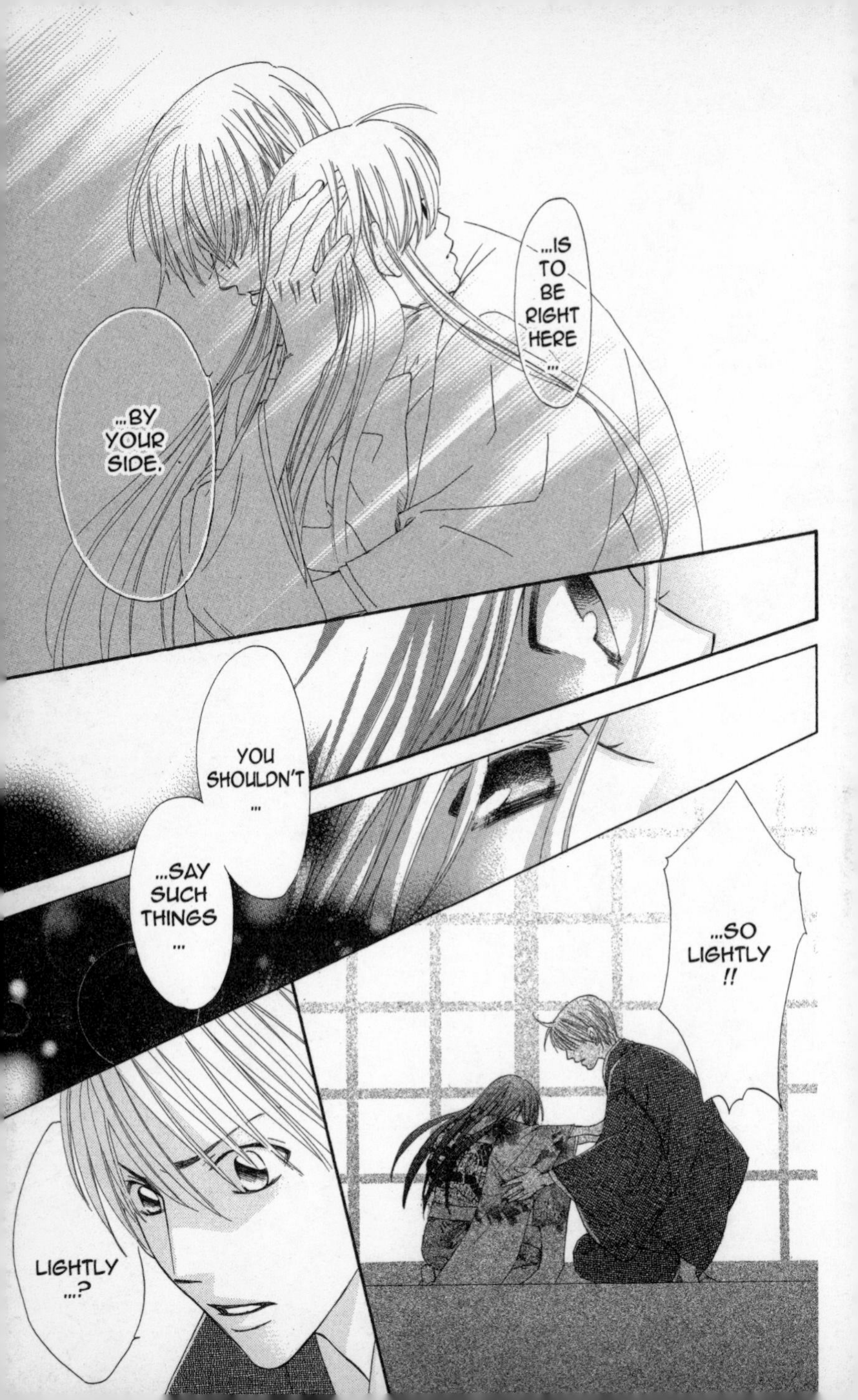
...IS TO BE RIGHT HERE...
...BY YOUR SIDE.
YOU SHOULDN'T...
...SAY SUCH THINGS...
...SO LIGHTLY!!
LIGHTLY...?

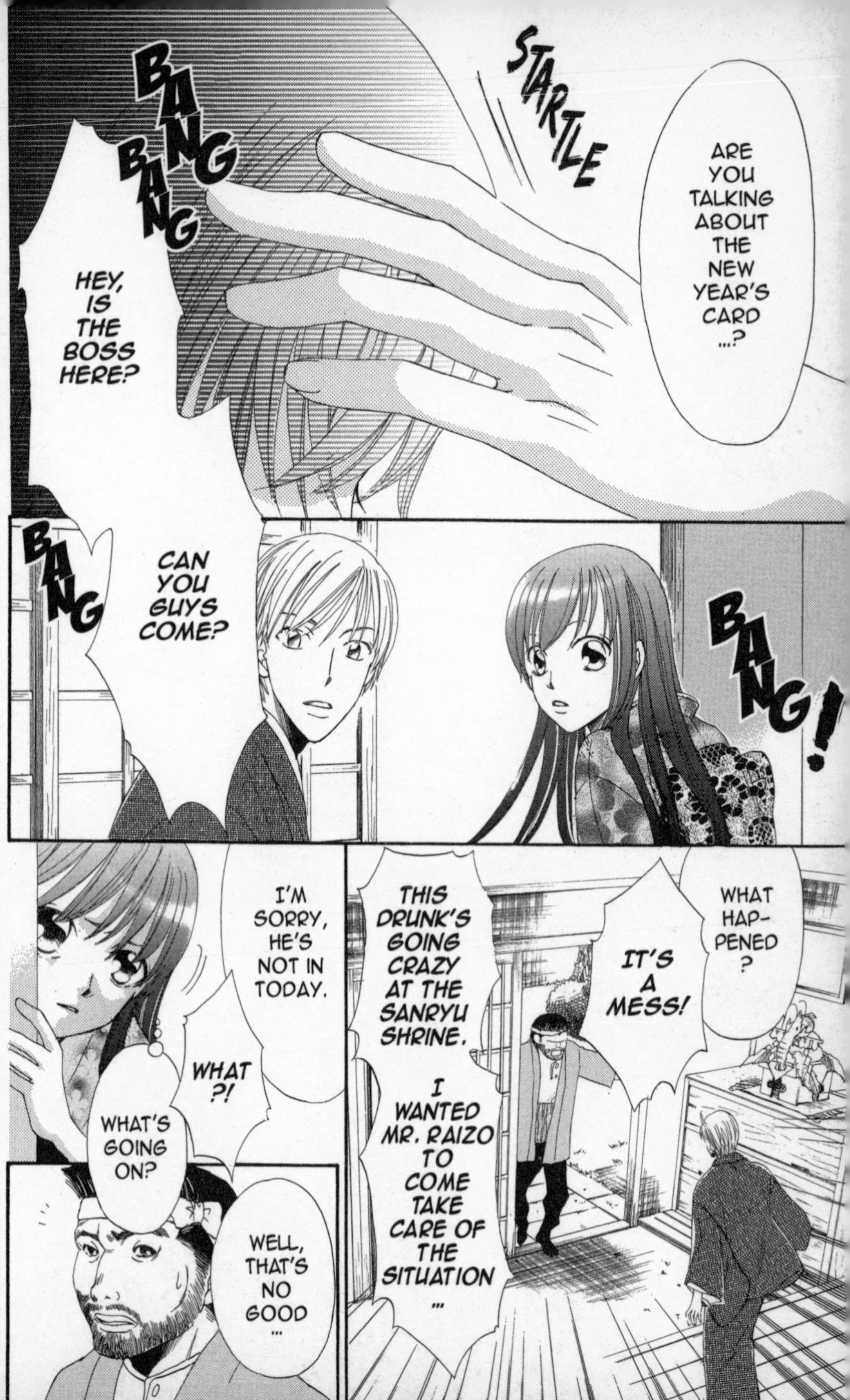
ARE YOU TALKING ABOUT THE NEW YEAR'S CARD ...?
STARTLE
BANG BANG
HEY, IS THE BOSS HERE?
BANG!
CAN YOU GUYS COME?
BANG
WHAT HAP-PENED?
IT'S A MESS!
THIS DRUNK'S GOING CRAZY AT THE SANRYU SHRINE.
I WANTED MR. RAIZO TO COME TAKE CARE OF THE SITUATION ...
I'M SORRY, HE'S NOT IN TODAY.
WHAT?!
WHAT'S GOING ON?
WELL, THAT'S NO GOOD ...

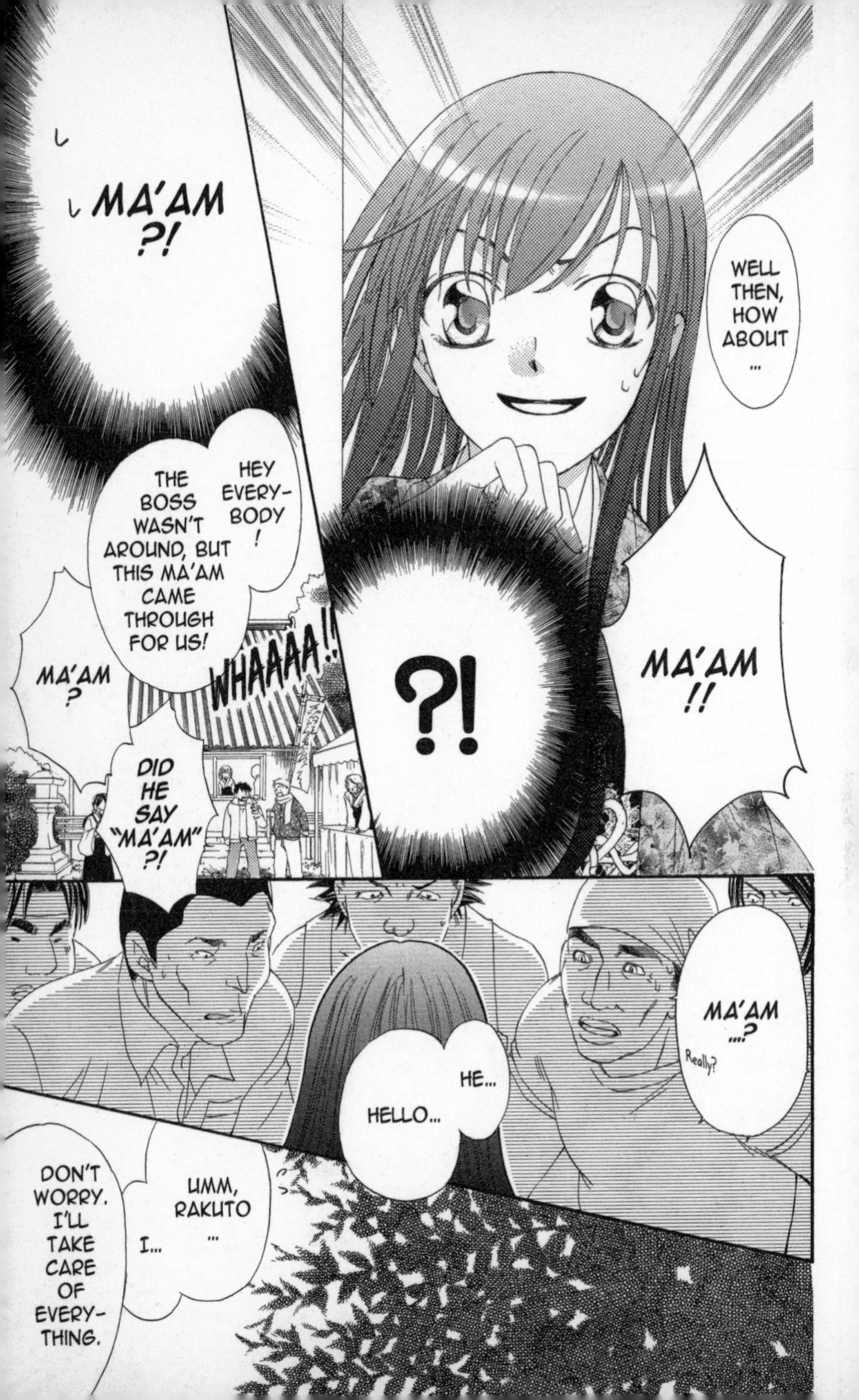
WELL THEN, HOW ABOUT ...
MA'AM !!
?!
MA'AM ?!
HEY EVERY-BODY!
THE BOSS WASN'T AROUND, BUT THIS MA'AM CAME THROUGH FOR US!
WHAAAA!!
MA'AM?
DID HE SAY "MA'AM"?!
MA'AM ...?
Really?
HE... HELLO...
UMM, RAKUTO ...
I...
DON'T WORRY. I'LL TAKE CARE OF EVERY-THING.

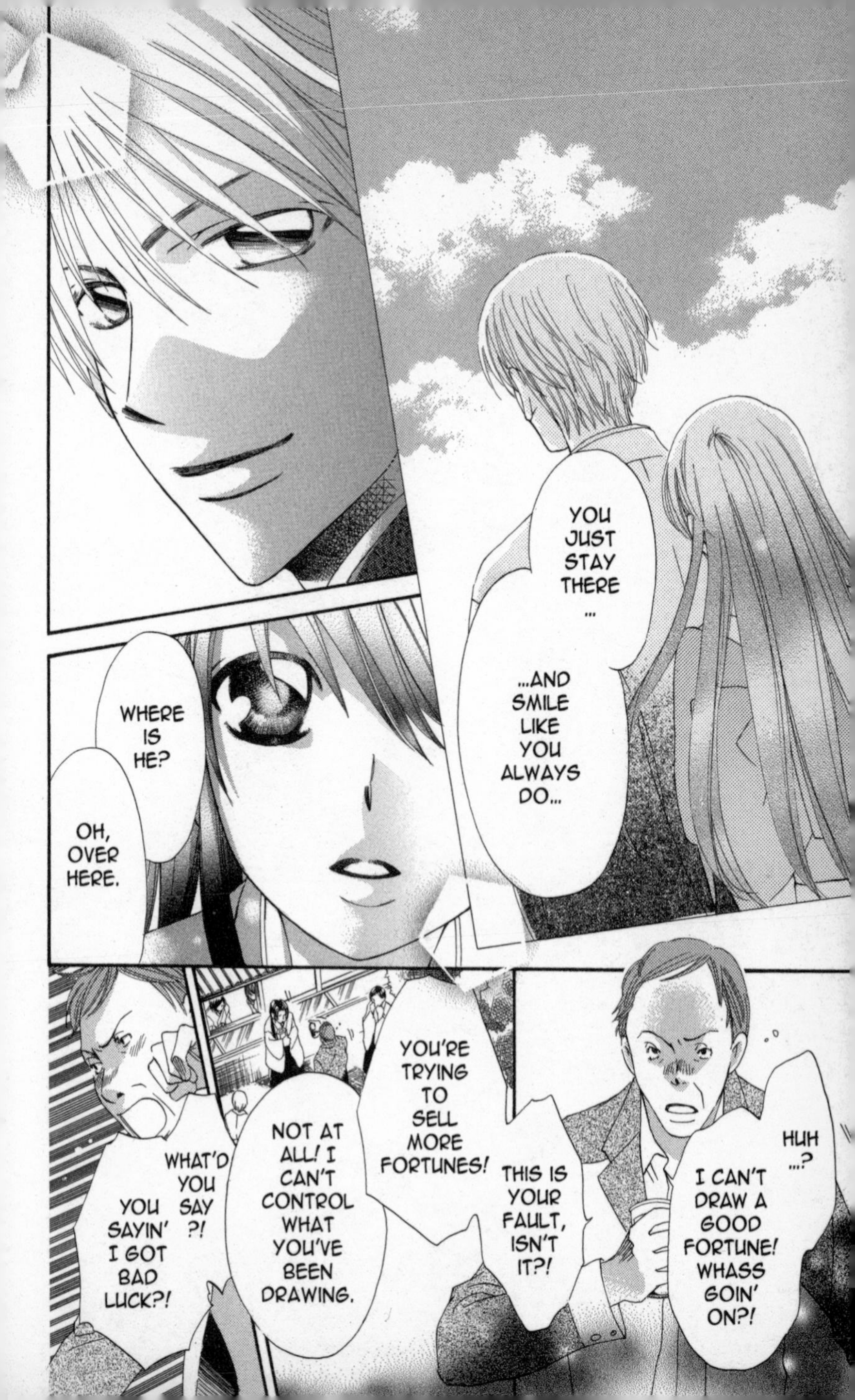
YOU JUST STAY THERE...
...AND SMILE LIKE YOU ALWAYS DO...
WHERE IS HE?
OH, OVER HERE.
HUH...?
I CAN'T DRAW A GOOD FORTUNE! WHASS GOIN' ON?!
THIS IS YOUR FAULT, ISN'T IT?!
YOU'RE TRYING TO SELL MORE FORTUNES!
NOT AT ALL! I CAN'T CONTROL WHAT YOU'VE BEEN DRAWING.
WHAT'D YOU SAY?!
YOU SAYIN' I GOT BAD LUCK?!

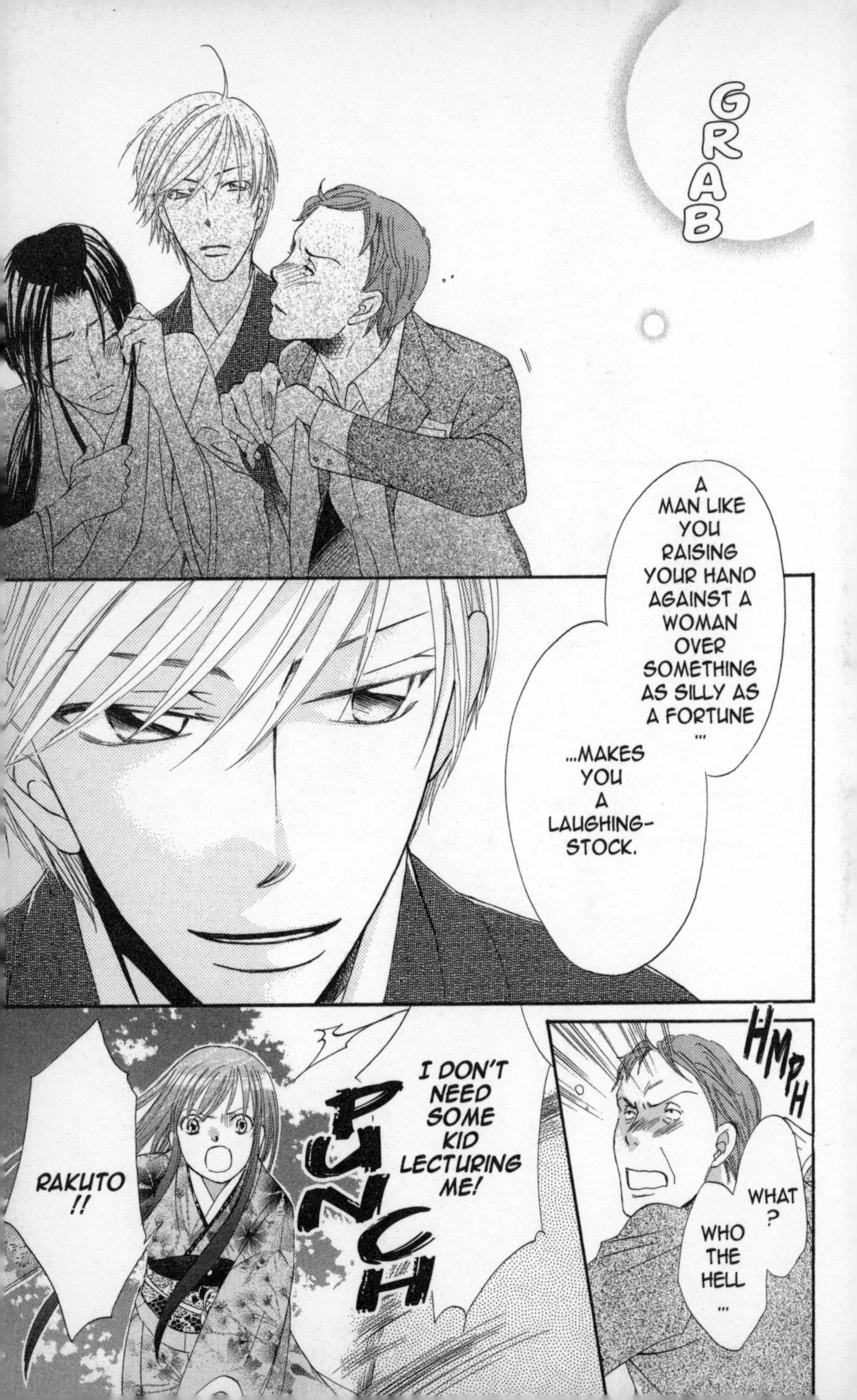
GRAB
A MAN LIKE YOU RAISING YOUR HAND AGAINST A WOMAN OVER SOMETHING AS SILLY AS A FORTUNE...
...MAKES YOU A LAUGHING-STOCK.
HMPH
WHAT? WHO THE HELL...
I DON'T NEED SOME KID LECTURING ME!
PUNCH
RAKUTO!!

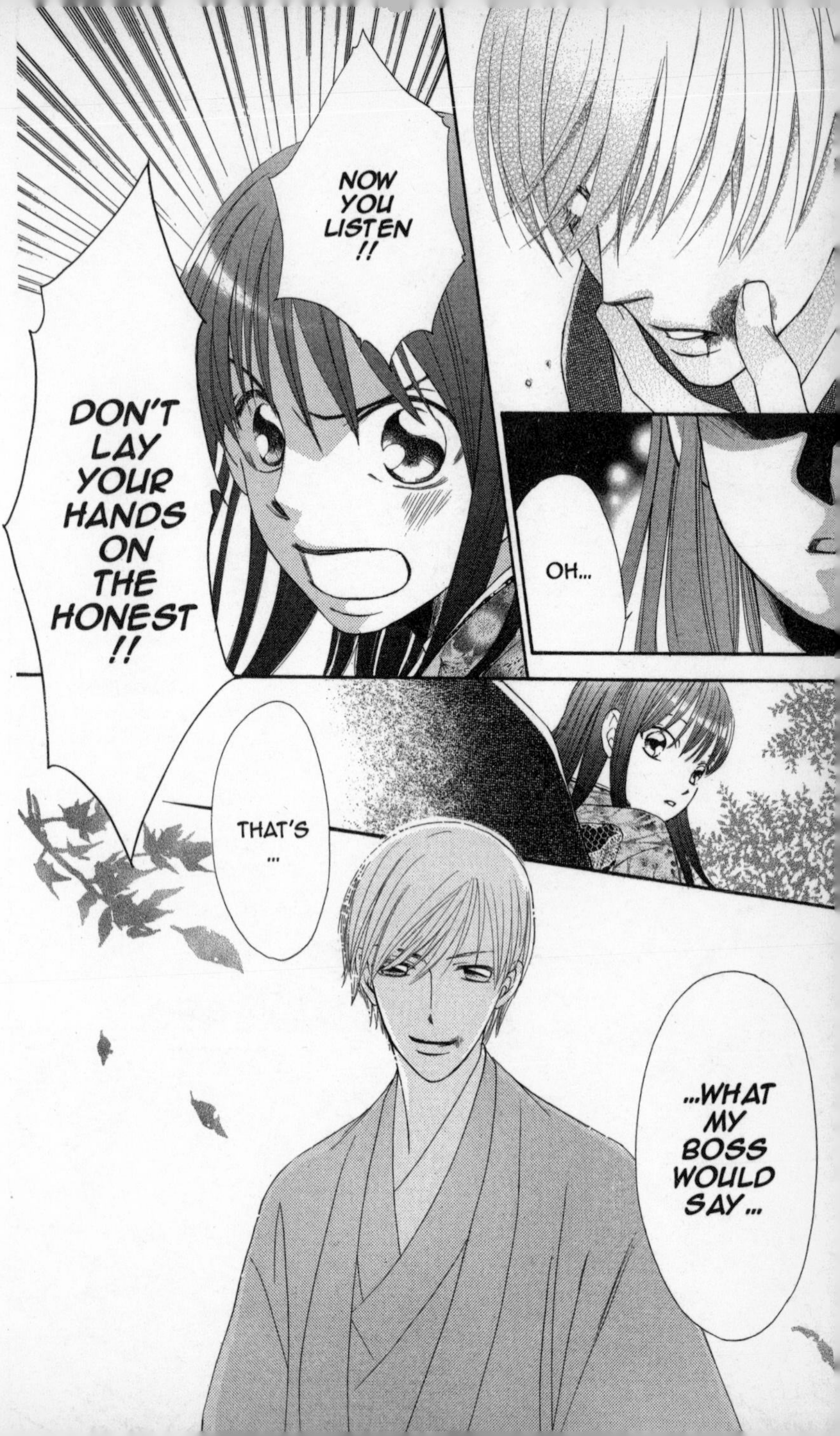
OH...
NOW YOU LISTEN!!
DON'T LAY YOUR HANDS ON THE HONEST!!
THAT'S...
...WHAT MY BOSS WOULD SAY...

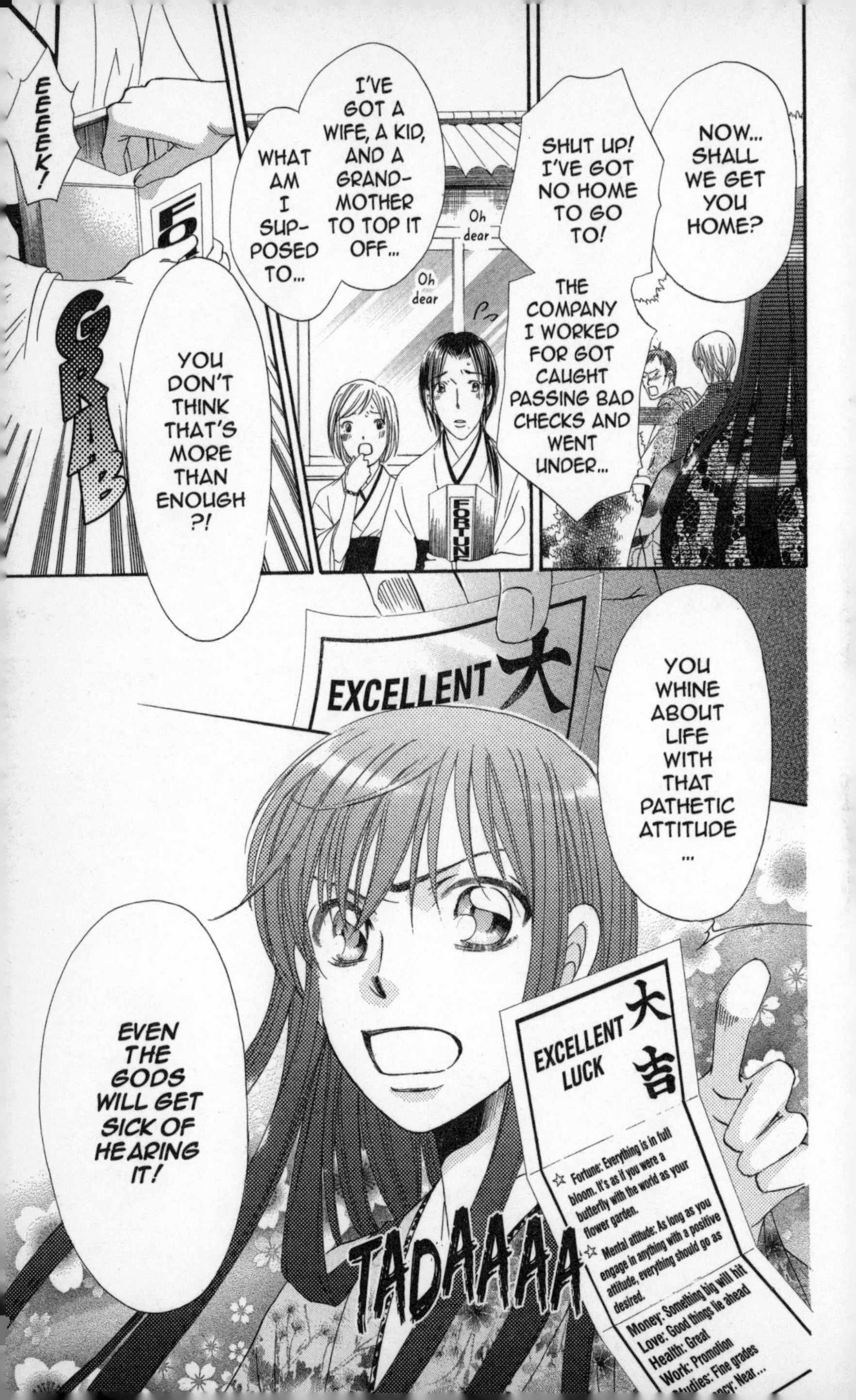
NOW... SHALL WE GET YOU HOME?
SHUT UP! I'VE GOT NO HOME TO GO TO!
THE COMPANY I WORKED FOR GOT CAUGHT PASSING BAD CHECKS AND WENT UNDER...
Oh dear
Oh dear
I'VE GOT A WIFE, A KID, AND A GRAND-MOTHER TO TOP IT OFF...
WHAT AM I SUP-POSED TO...
EEEEK!
GRAB
YOU DON'T THINK THAT'S MORE THAN ENOUGH?!
FORTUNE
EXCELLENT 大
YOU WHINE ABOUT LIFE WITH THAT PATHETIC ATTITUDE...
EVEN THE GODS WILL GET SICK OF HEARING IT!
TADAAAA
EXCELLENT LUCK 大吉
☆ Fortune: Everything is in full bloom. It's as if you were a butterfly with the world as your flower garden.
☆ Mental attitude: As long as you engage in anything with a positive attitude, everything should go as desired.
Money: Something big will hit
Love: Good things lie ahead
Health: Great
Work: Promotion

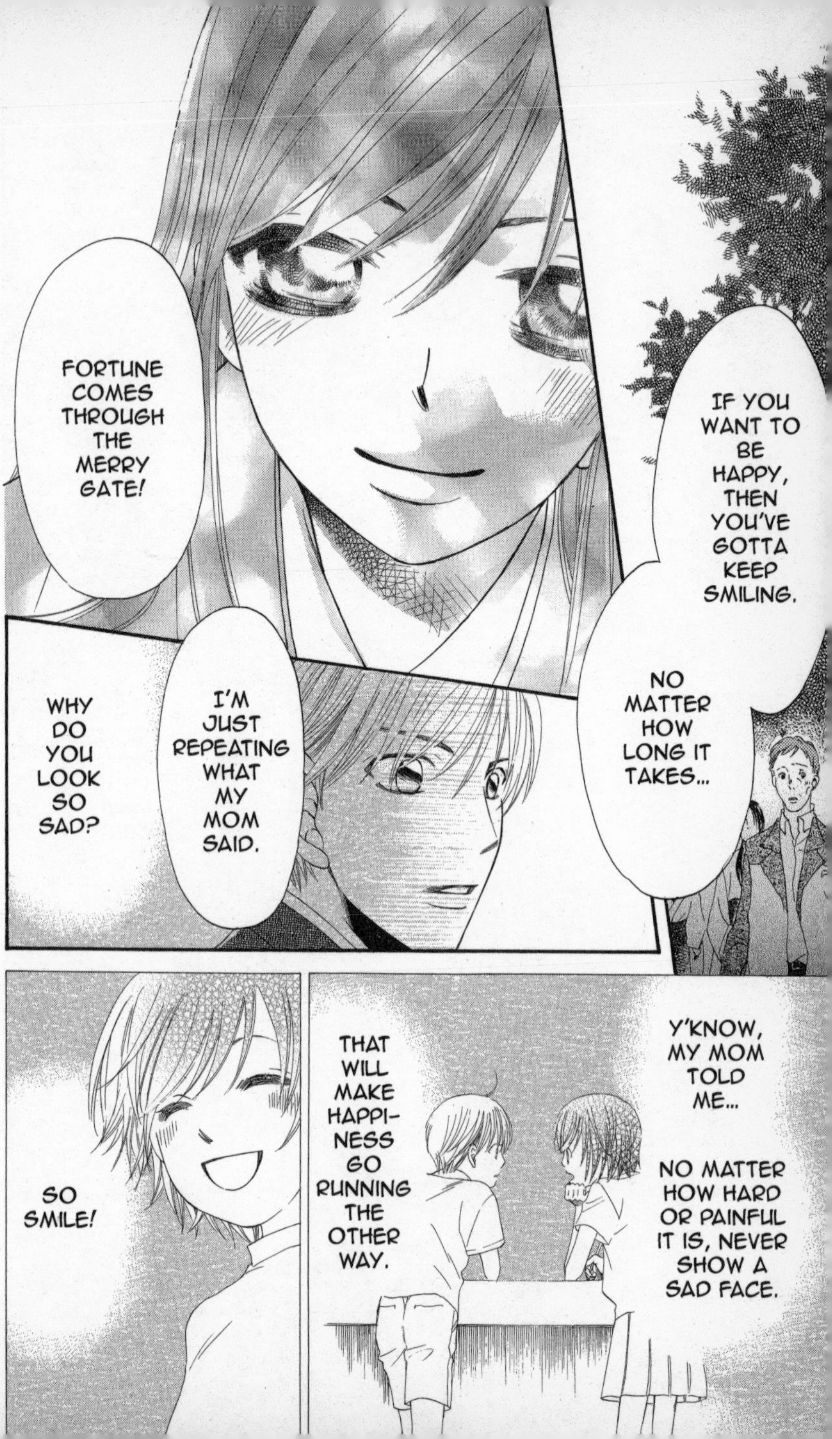
IF YOU WANT TO BE HAPPY, THEN YOU'VE GOTTA KEEP SMILING.
NO MATTER HOW LONG IT TAKES...
FORTUNE COMES THROUGH THE MERRY GATE!
I'M JUST REPEATING WHAT MY MOM SAID.
WHY DO YOU LOOK SO SAD?
Y'KNOW, MY MOM TOLD ME...
NO MATTER HOW HARD OR PAINFUL IT IS, NEVER SHOW A SAD FACE.
THAT WILL MAKE HAPPINESS GO RUNNING THE OTHER WAY.
SO SMILE!

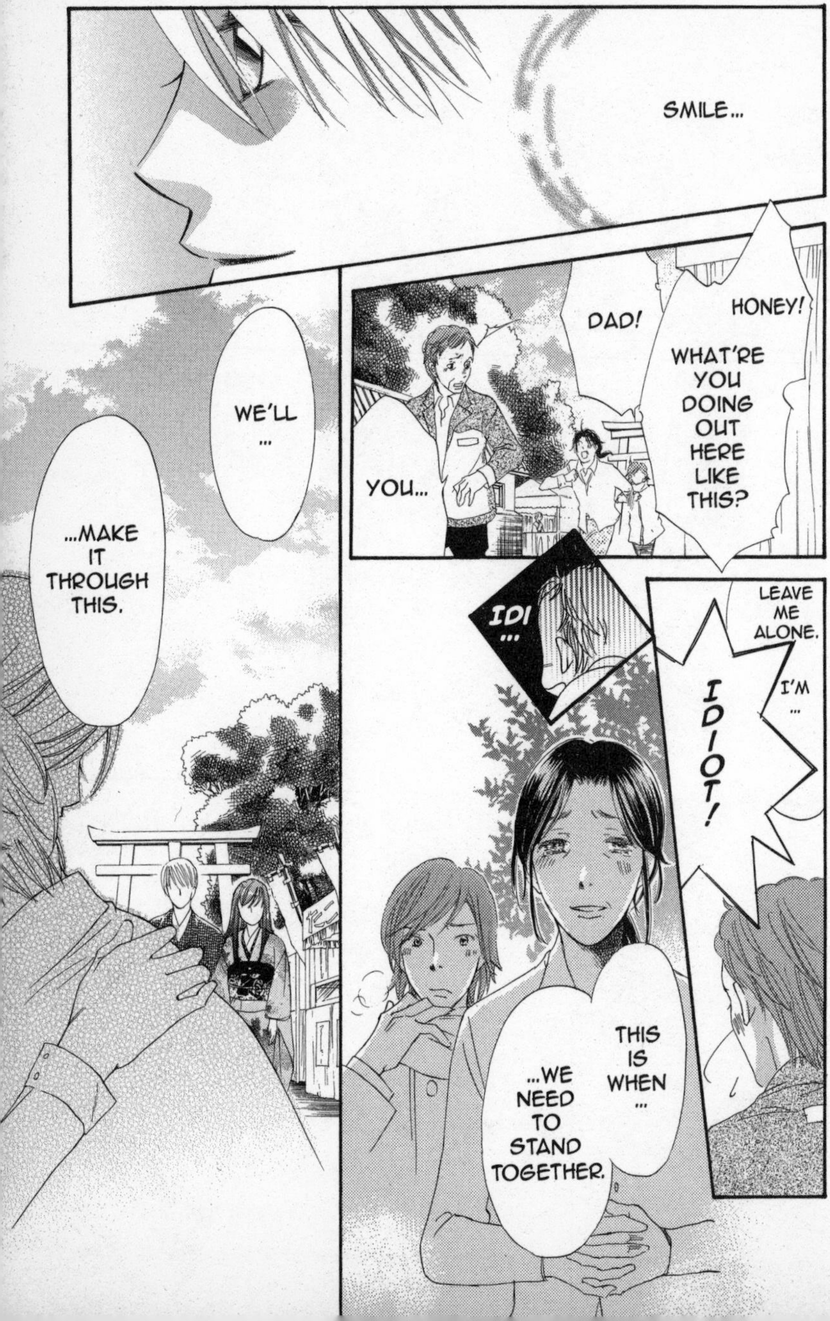
SMILE...
HONEY! WHAT'RE YOU DOING OUT HERE LIKE THIS?
DAD!
YOU...
LEAVE ME ALONE. I'M... IDIOT!
IDI...
THIS IS WHEN...
...WE NEED TO STAND TOGETHER.
WE'LL...
...MAKE IT THROUGH THIS.

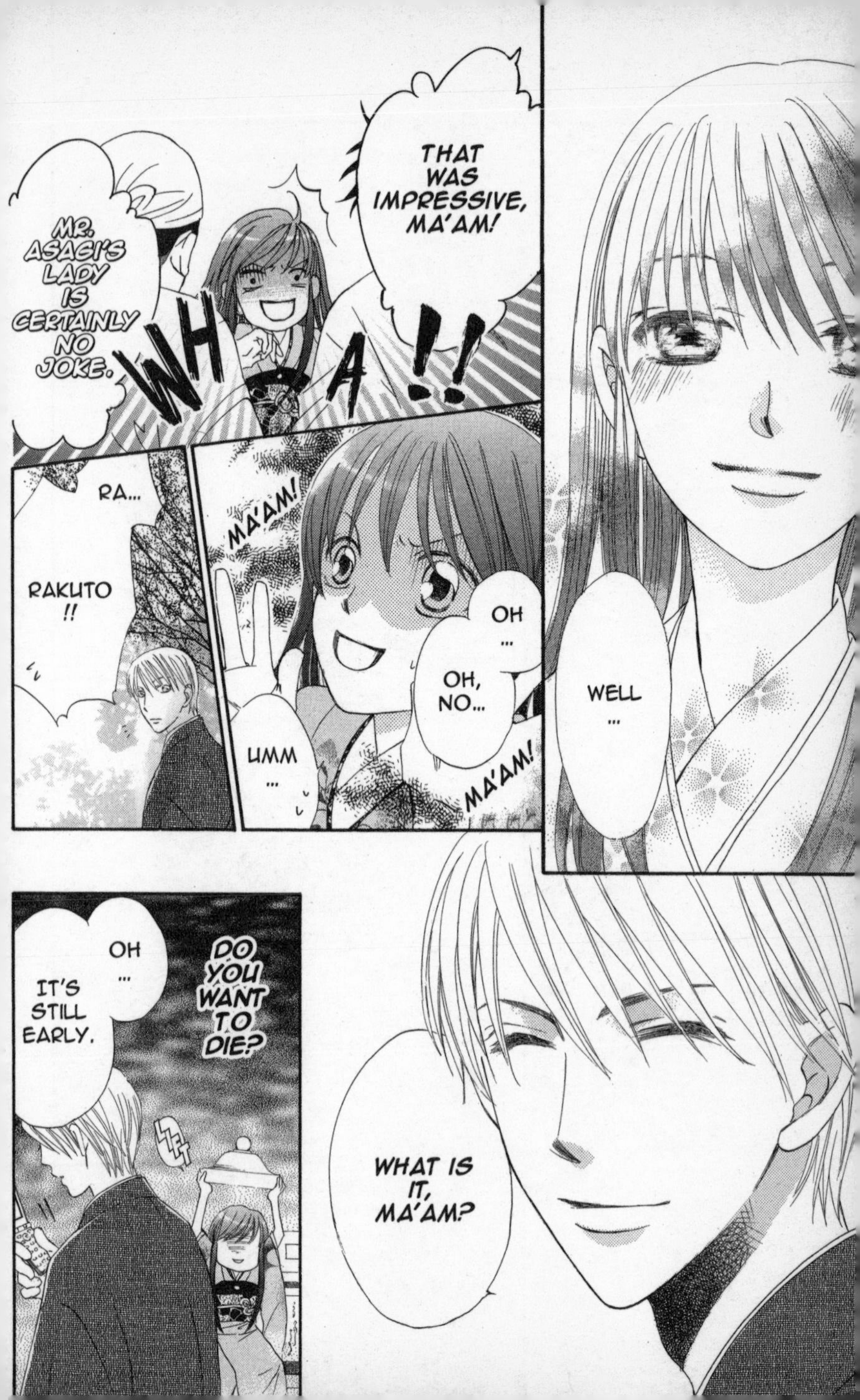
WELL ...
THAT WAS IMPRESSIVE, MA'AM!
WH A!!
MR. ASAGI'S LADY IS CERTAINLY NO JOKE.
MA'AM!
OH ...
OH, NO...
UMM ...
MA'AM!
RA...
RAKUTO !!
WHAT IS IT, MA'AM?
DO YOU WANT TO DIE?
OH ...
IT'S STILL EARLY.

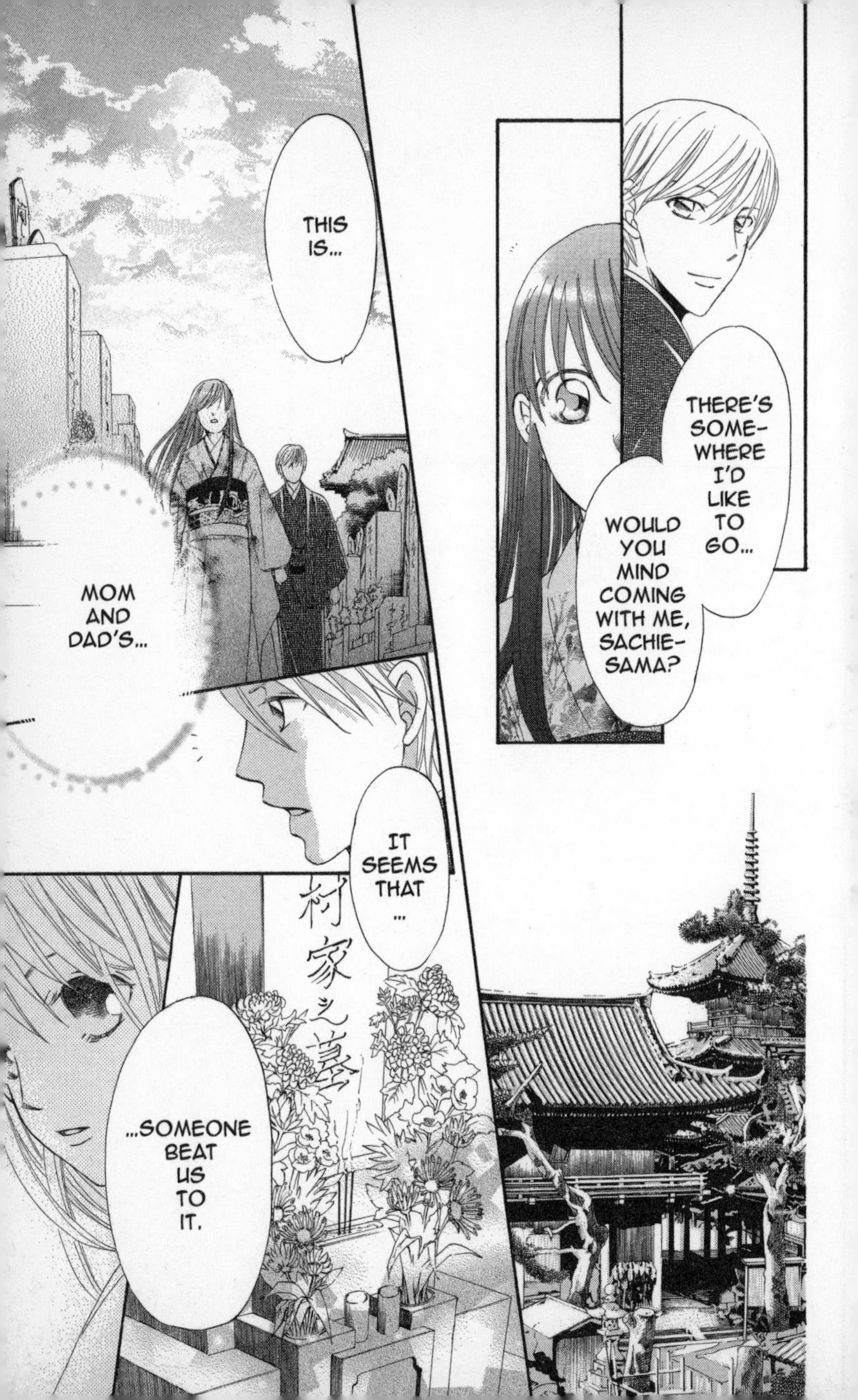
THERE'S SOMEWHERE I'D LIKE TO GO...
WOULD YOU MIND COMING WITH ME, SACHIE-SAMA?
THIS IS...
MOM AND DAD'S...
IT SEEMS THAT...
村家之墓
...SOMEONE BEAT US TO IT.

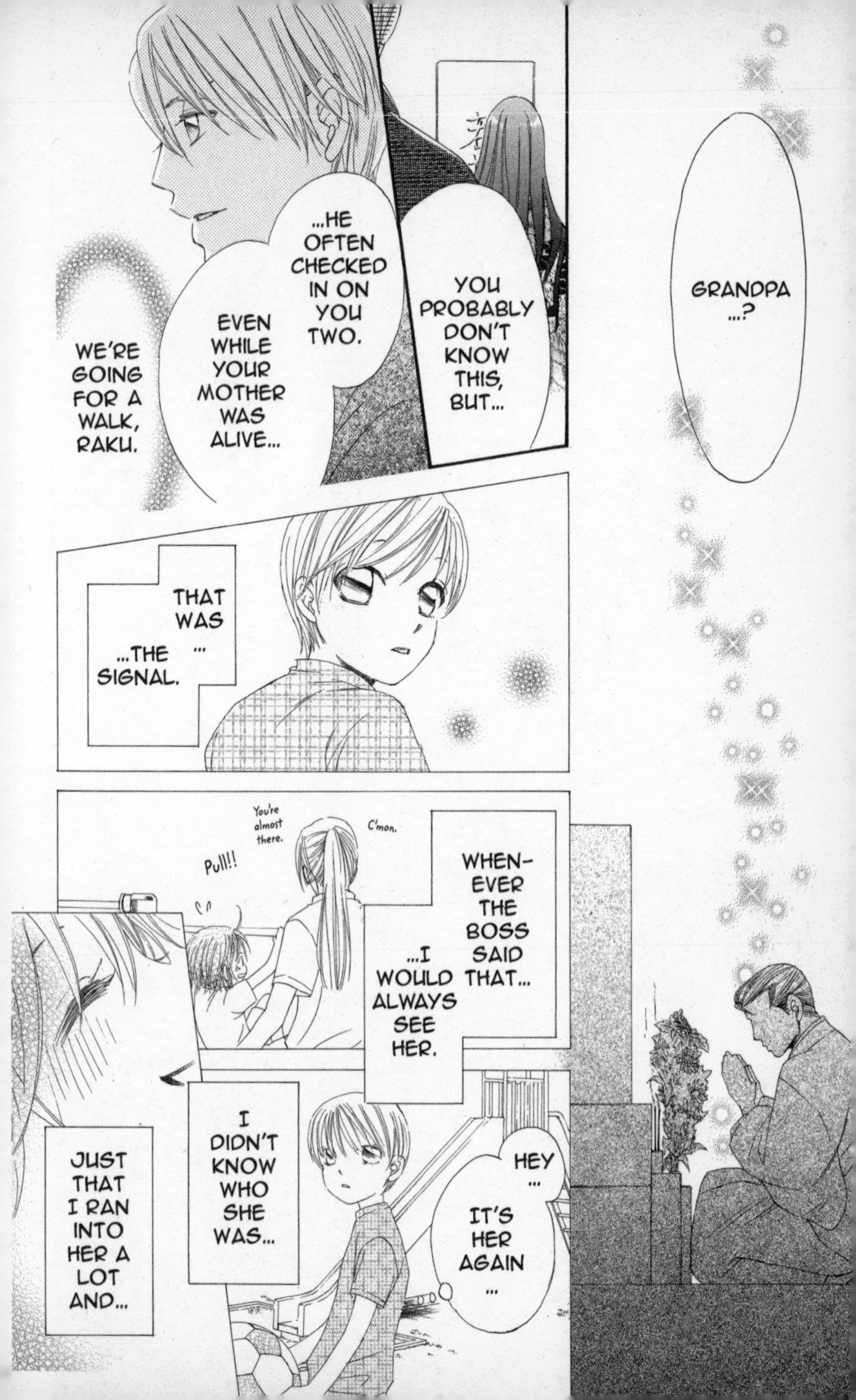
GRANDPA ...?
YOU PROBABLY DON'T KNOW THIS, BUT...
...HE OFTEN CHECKED IN ON YOU TWO.
EVEN WHILE YOUR MOTHER WAS ALIVE...
WE'RE GOING FOR A WALK, RAKU.
THAT WAS ...
...THE SIGNAL.
WHEN-EVER THE BOSS SAID THAT...
...I WOULD ALWAYS SEE HER.
C'mon.
You're almost there.
Pull!!
HEY ... IT'S HER AGAIN ...
I DIDN'T KNOW WHO SHE WAS...
JUST THAT I RAN INTO HER A LOT AND...

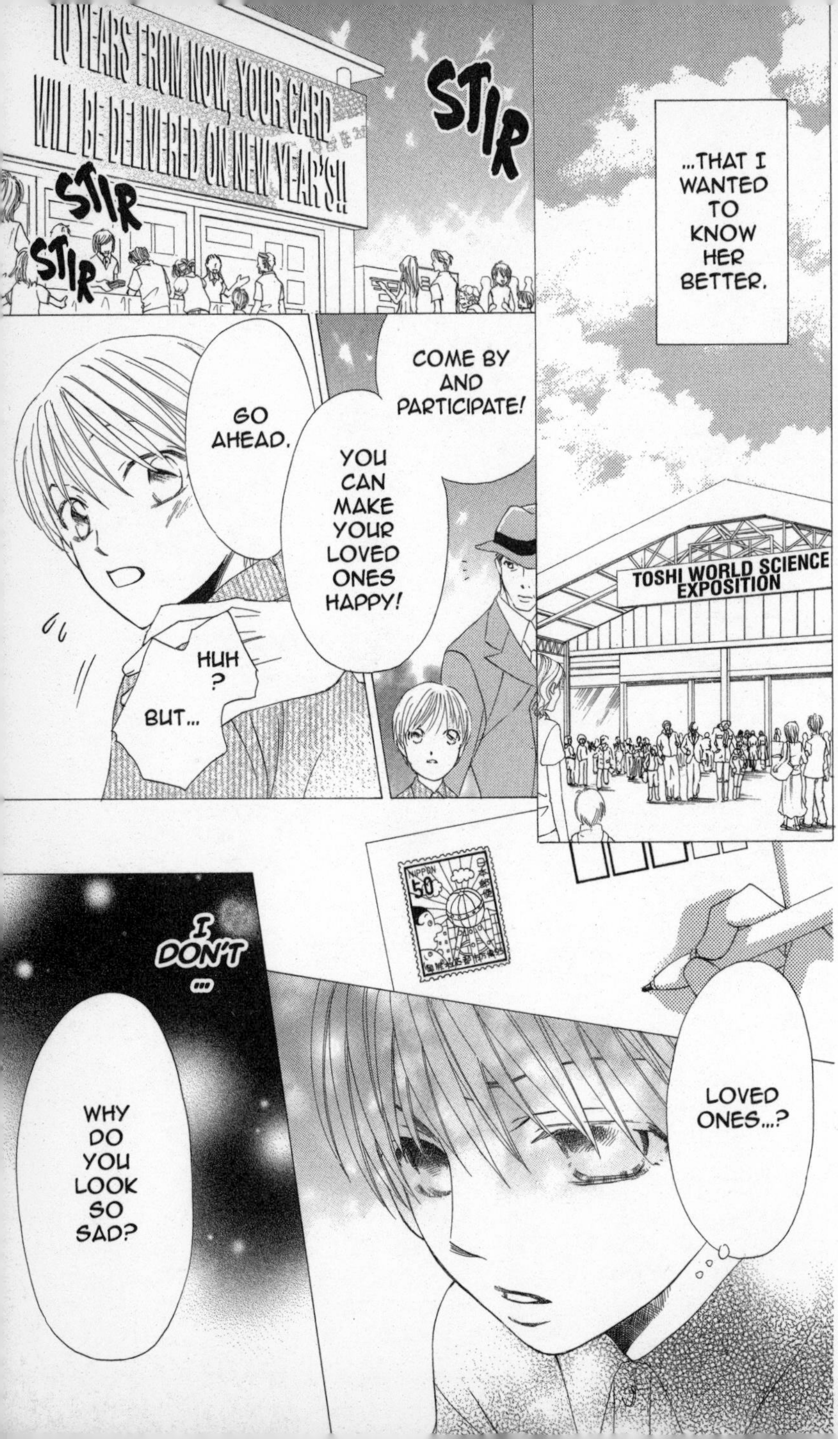
...THAT I WANTED TO KNOW HER BETTER.
TOSHI WORLD SCIENCE EXPOSITION
10 YEARS FROM NOW, YOUR CARD WILL BE DELIVERED ON NEW YEAR'S!!
STIR
STIR
STIR
COME BY AND PARTICIPATE!
YOU CAN MAKE YOUR LOVED ONES HAPPY!
GO AHEAD.
HUH?
BUT...
NIPPON
50
LOVED ONES...?
I DON'T ...
WHY DO YOU LOOK SO SAD?

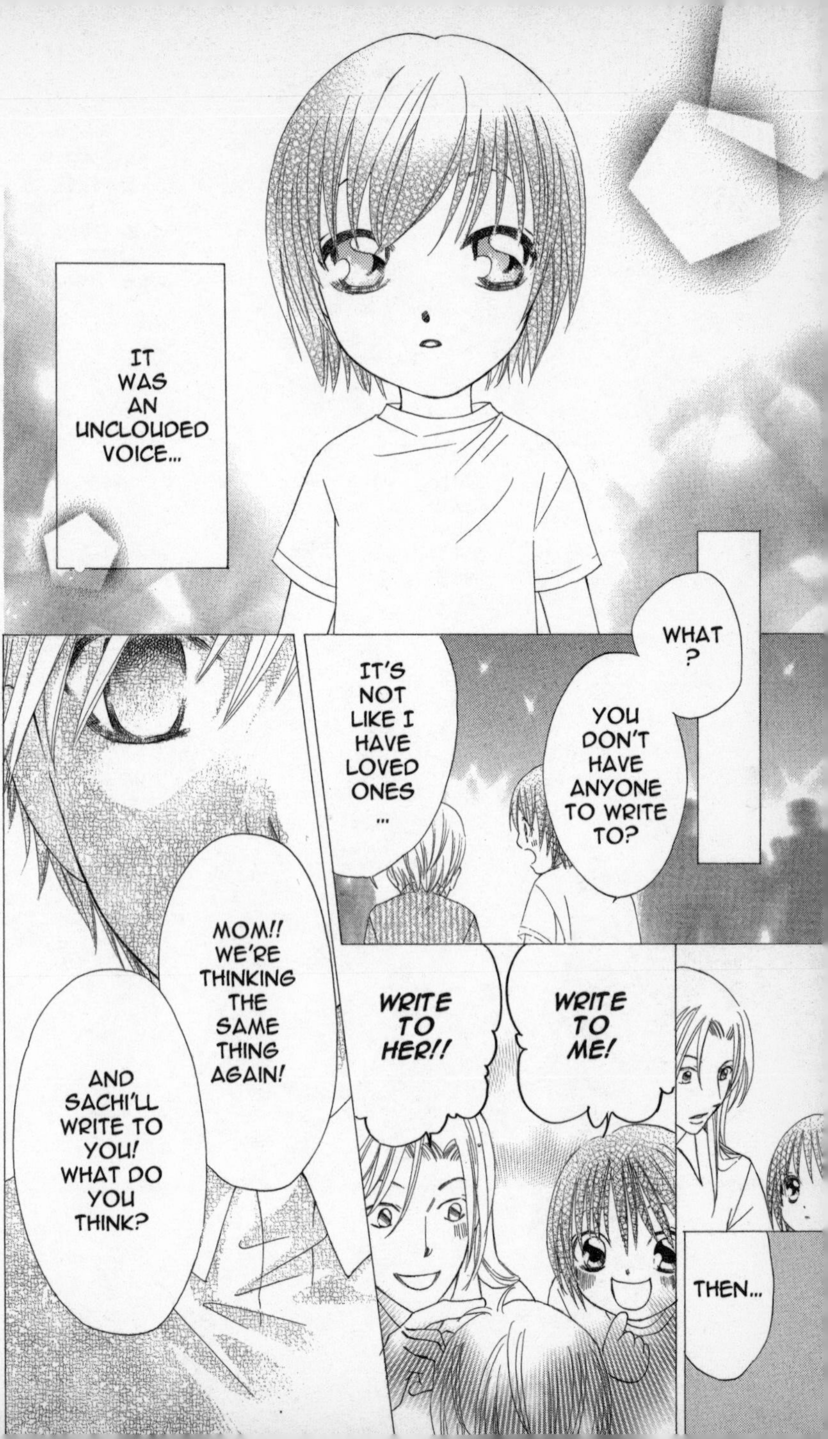
IT WAS AN UNCLOUDED VOICE...
WHAT?
YOU DON'T HAVE ANYONE TO WRITE TO?
IT'S NOT LIKE I HAVE LOVED ONES...
THEN...
WRITE TO ME!
WRITE TO HER!!
MOM!! WE'RE THINKING THE SAME THING AGAIN!
AND SACHI'LL WRITE TO YOU! WHAT DO YOU THINK?

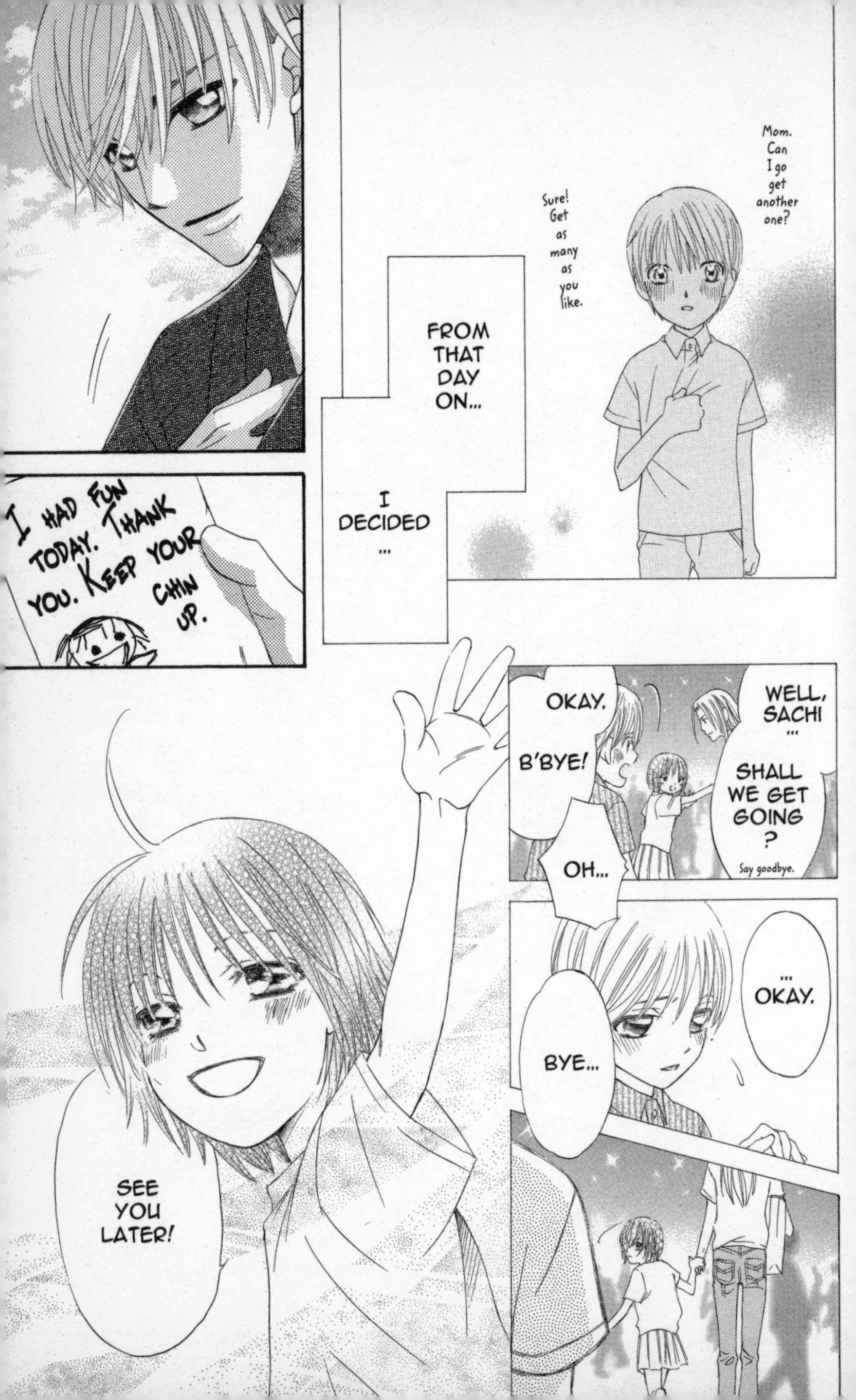
Mom. Can I go get another one?
Sure! Get as many as you like.
FROM THAT DAY ON...
I DECIDED ...
I HAD FUN TODAY. THANK YOU. KEEP YOUR CHIN UP.
WELL, SACHI ... SHALL WE GET GOING ?
Say goodbye.
OKAY.
B'BYE!
OH...
... OKAY.
BYE...
SEE YOU LATER!

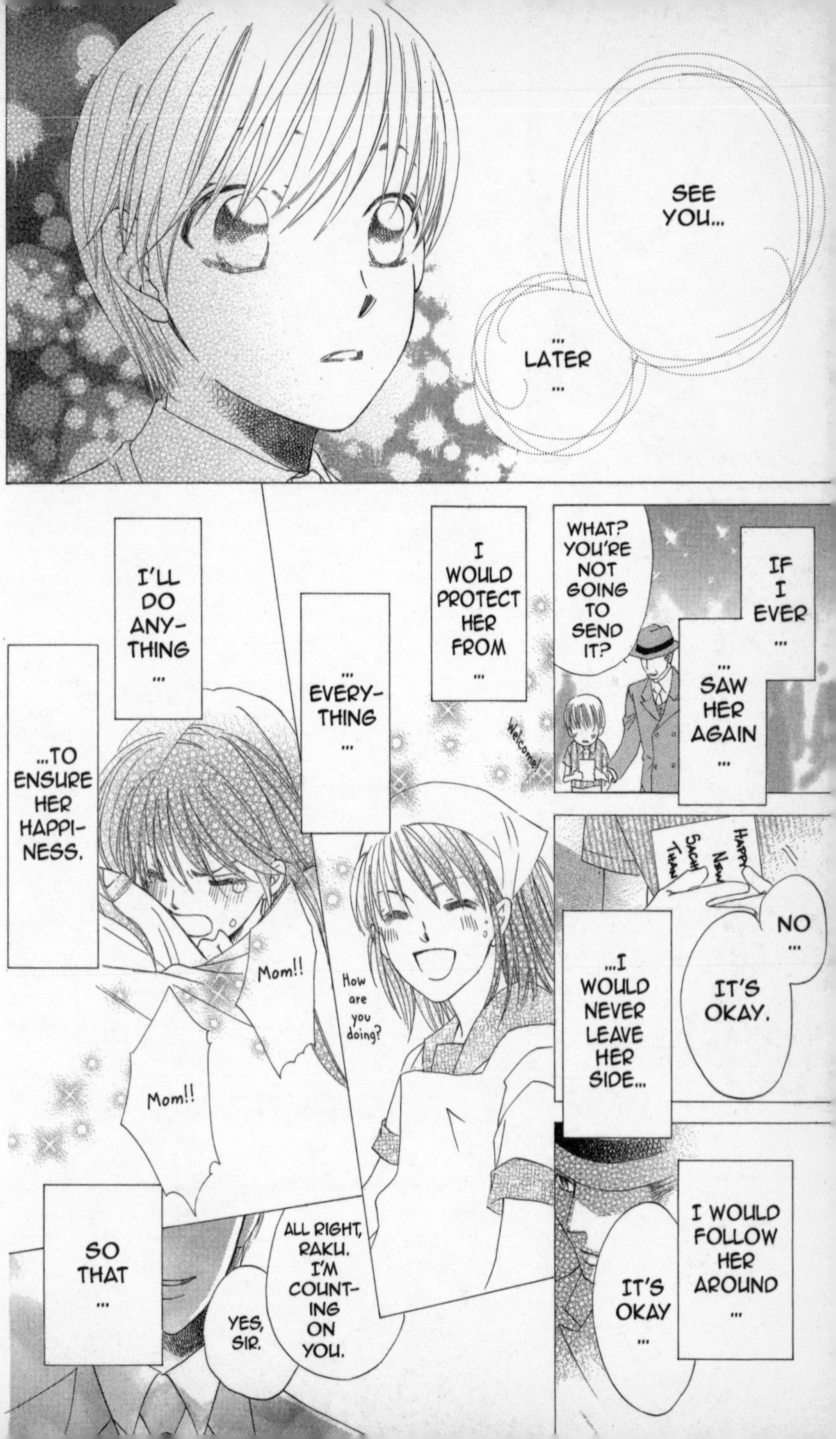
SEE YOU...
...LATER...
IF I EVER...
...SAW HER AGAIN...
WHAT? YOU'RE NOT GOING TO SEND IT?
I WOULD PROTECT HER FROM...
Welcome!
...EVERYTHING...
I'LL DO ANYTHING...
...TO ENSURE HER HAPPINESS.
NO... IT'S OKAY.
...I WOULD NEVER LEAVE HER SIDE...
How are you doing?
Mom!!
Mom!!
I WOULD FOLLOW HER AROUND...
IT'S OKAY...
ALL RIGHT, RAKU. I'M COUNTING ON YOU.
YES, SIR.
SO THAT...

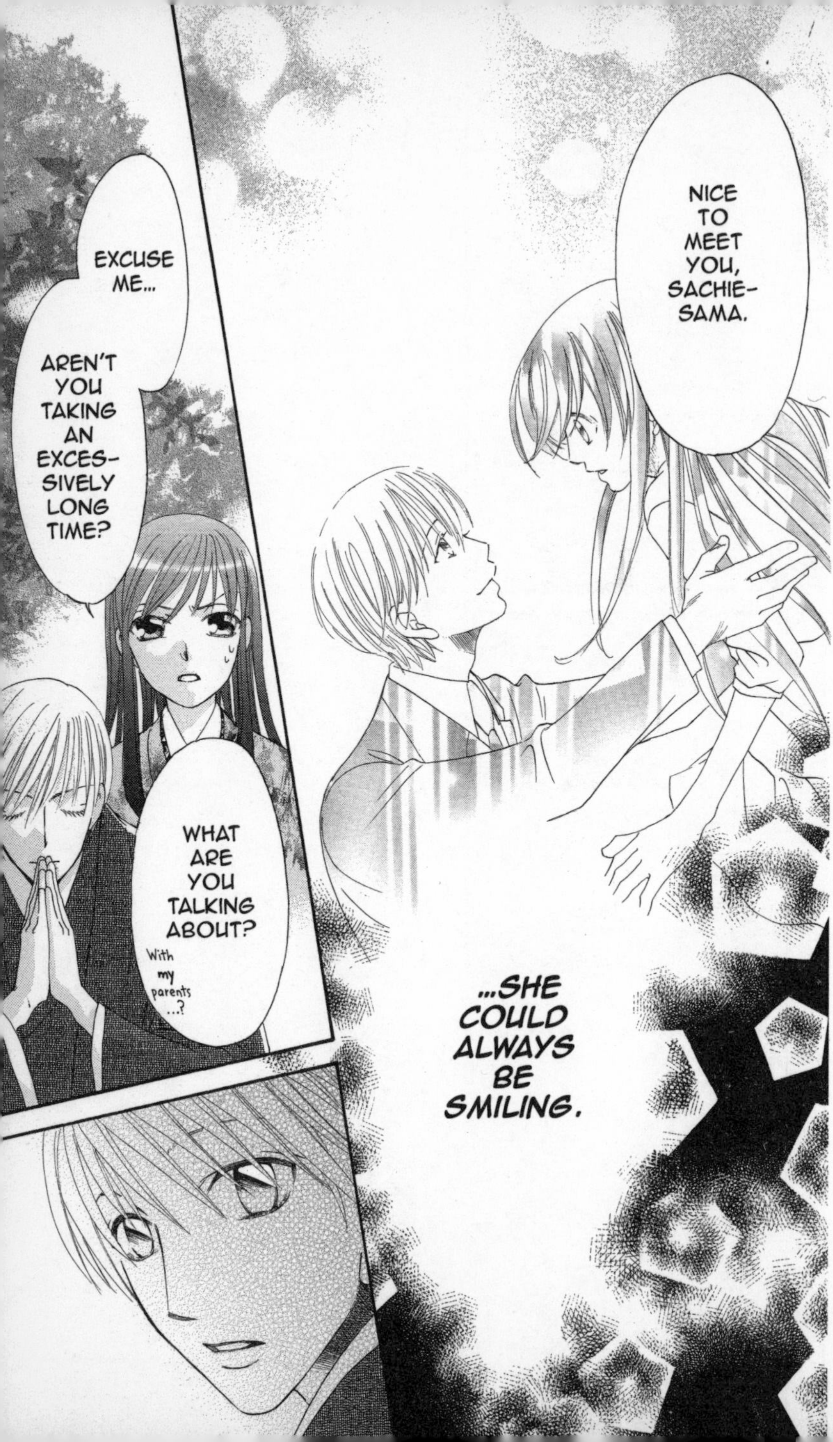
NICE TO MEET YOU, SACHIE-SAMA.
...SHE COULD ALWAYS BE SMILING.
EXCUSE ME... AREN'T YOU TAKING AN EXCES-SIVELY LONG TIME?
WHAT ARE YOU TALKING ABOUT?
With my parents ...?

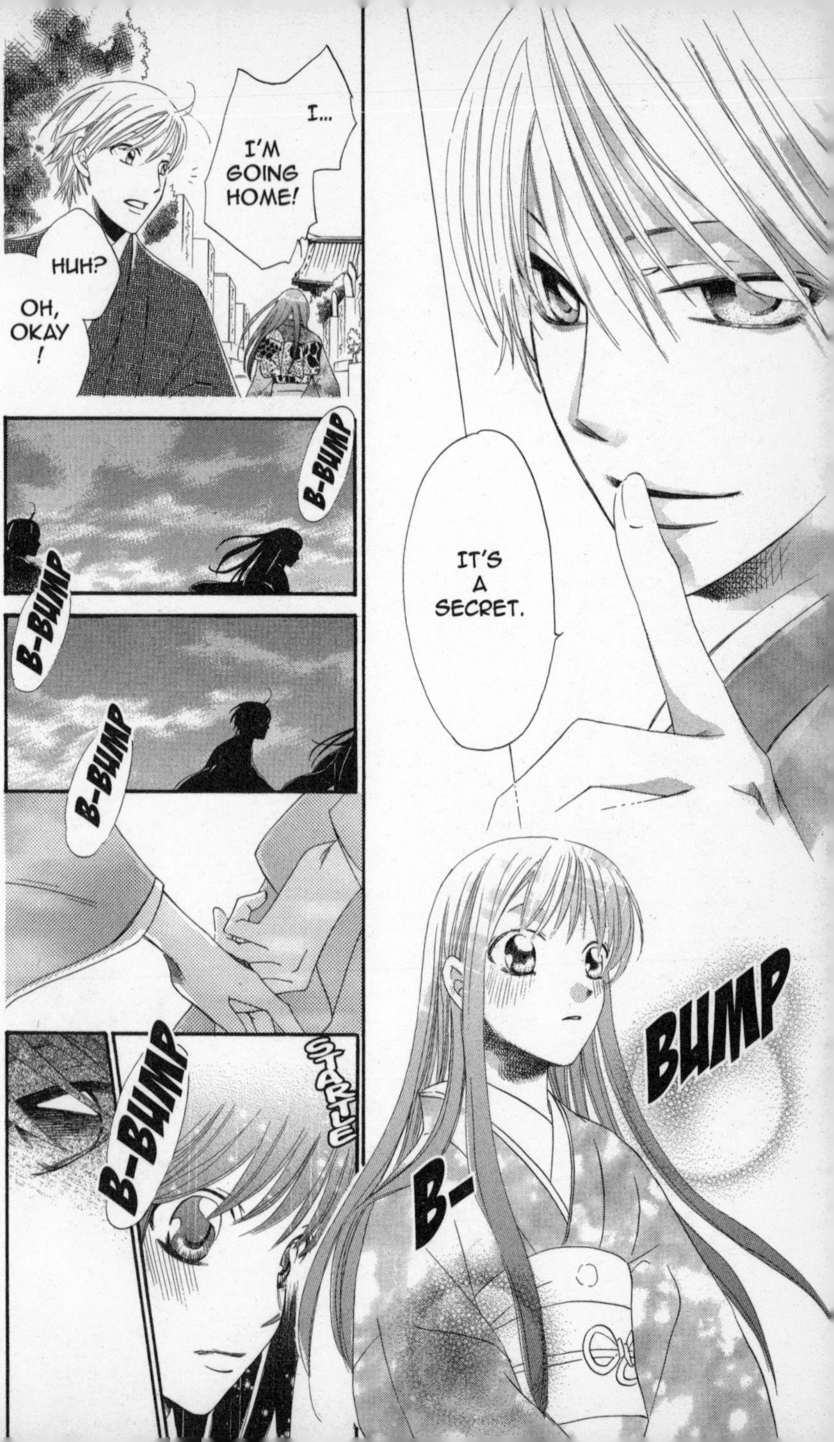
IT'S A SECRET.
B-
BUMP
I...
I'M GOING HOME!
HUH?
OH, OKAY!
B-BUMP
B-BUMP
B-BUMP
B-BUMP
STARTLE
B-BUMP

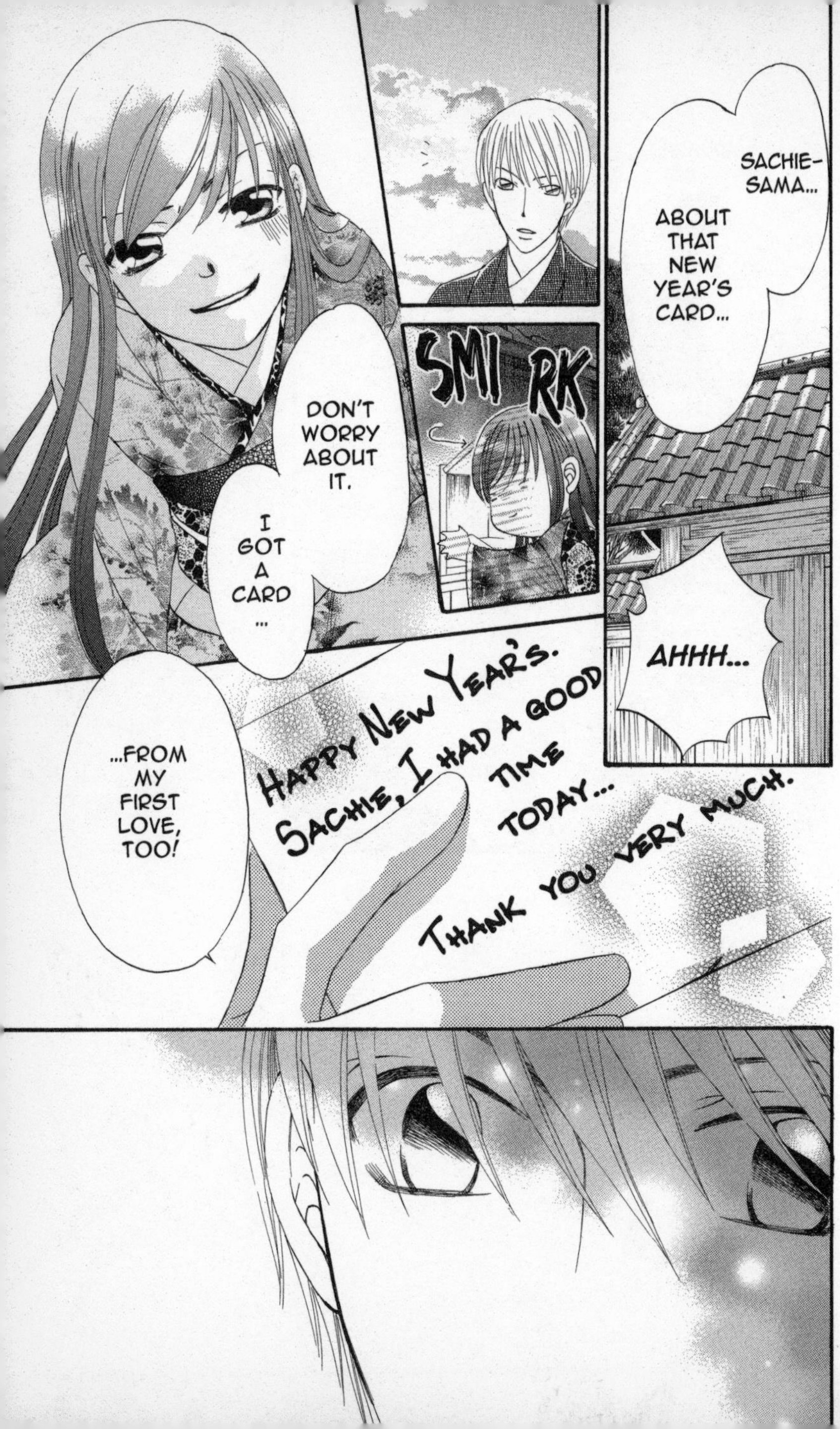
SACHIE-SAMA...
ABOUT THAT NEW YEAR'S CARD...
AHHH...
SMIRK
DON'T WORRY ABOUT IT.
I GOT A CARD...
HAPPY NEW YEAR'S.
SACHIE, I HAD A GOOD TIME TODAY...
THANK YOU VERY MUCH.
...FROM MY FIRST LOVE, TOO!

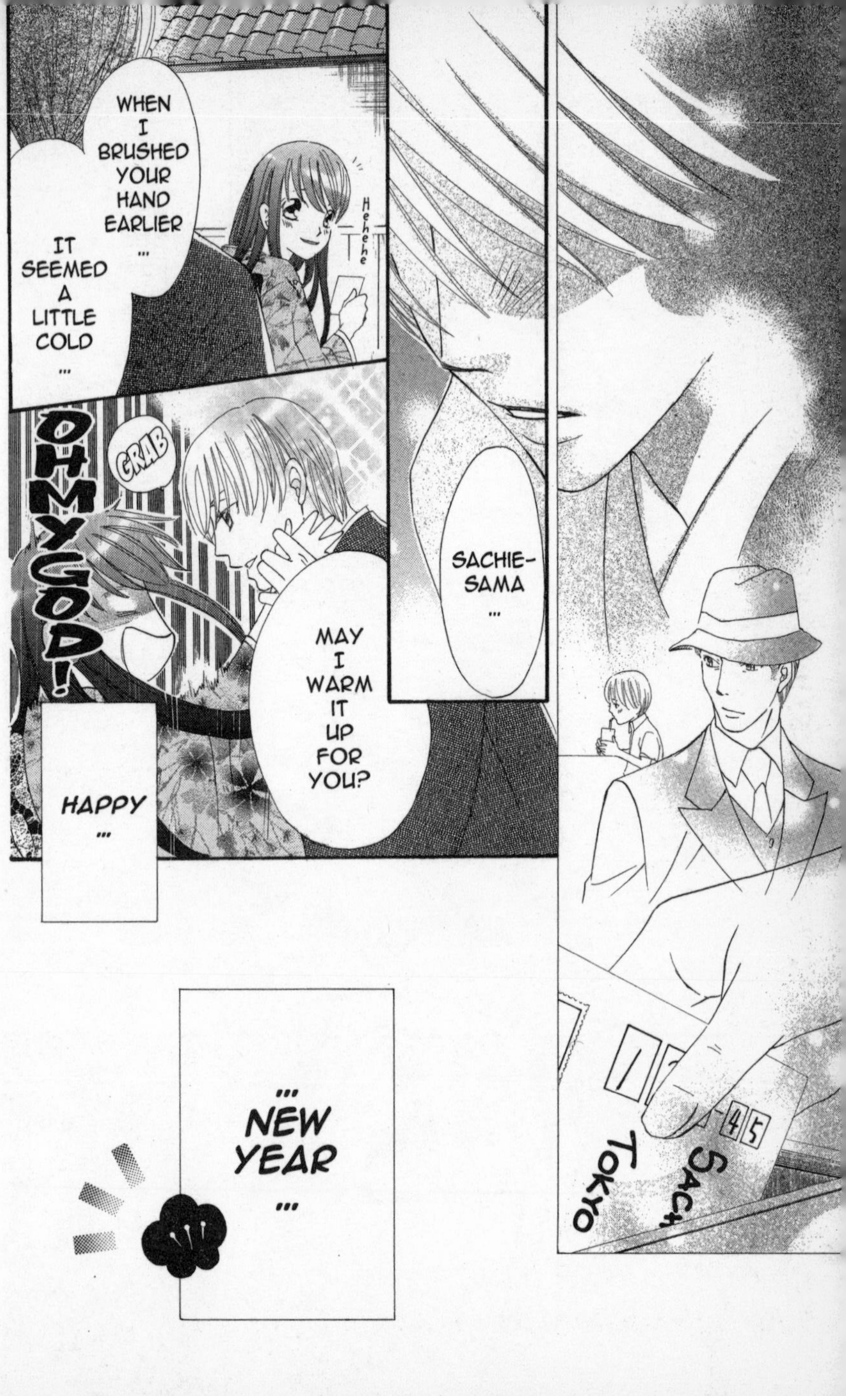

45
Tokyo
SACHIE-SAMA...
WHEN I BRUSHED YOUR HAND EARLIER...
IT SEEMED A LITTLE COLD...
Hehehe
GRAB
MAY I WARM IT UP FOR YOU?
OHMYGOD!
HAPPY...
...NEW YEAR...

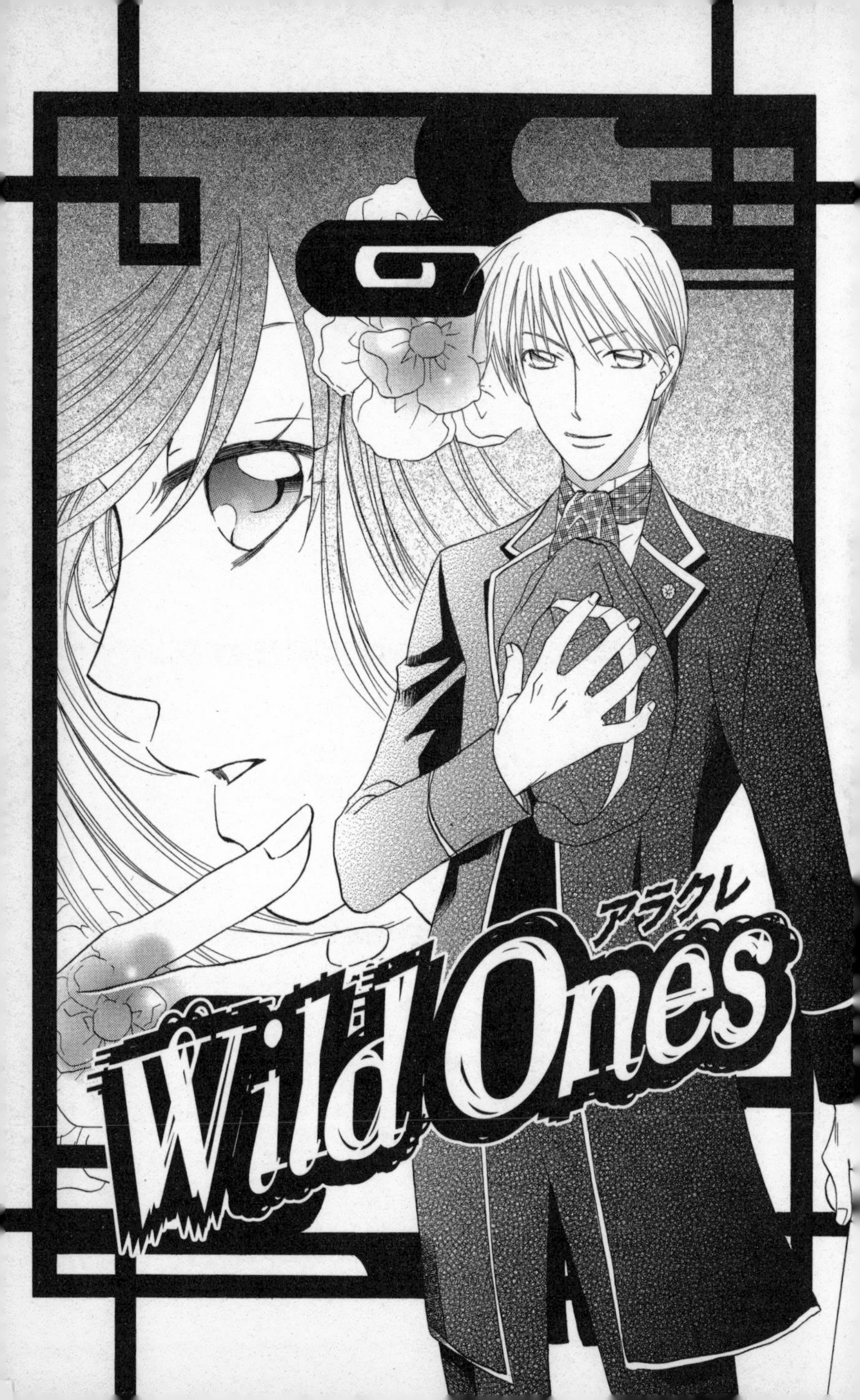

アラクレ
Wild Ones

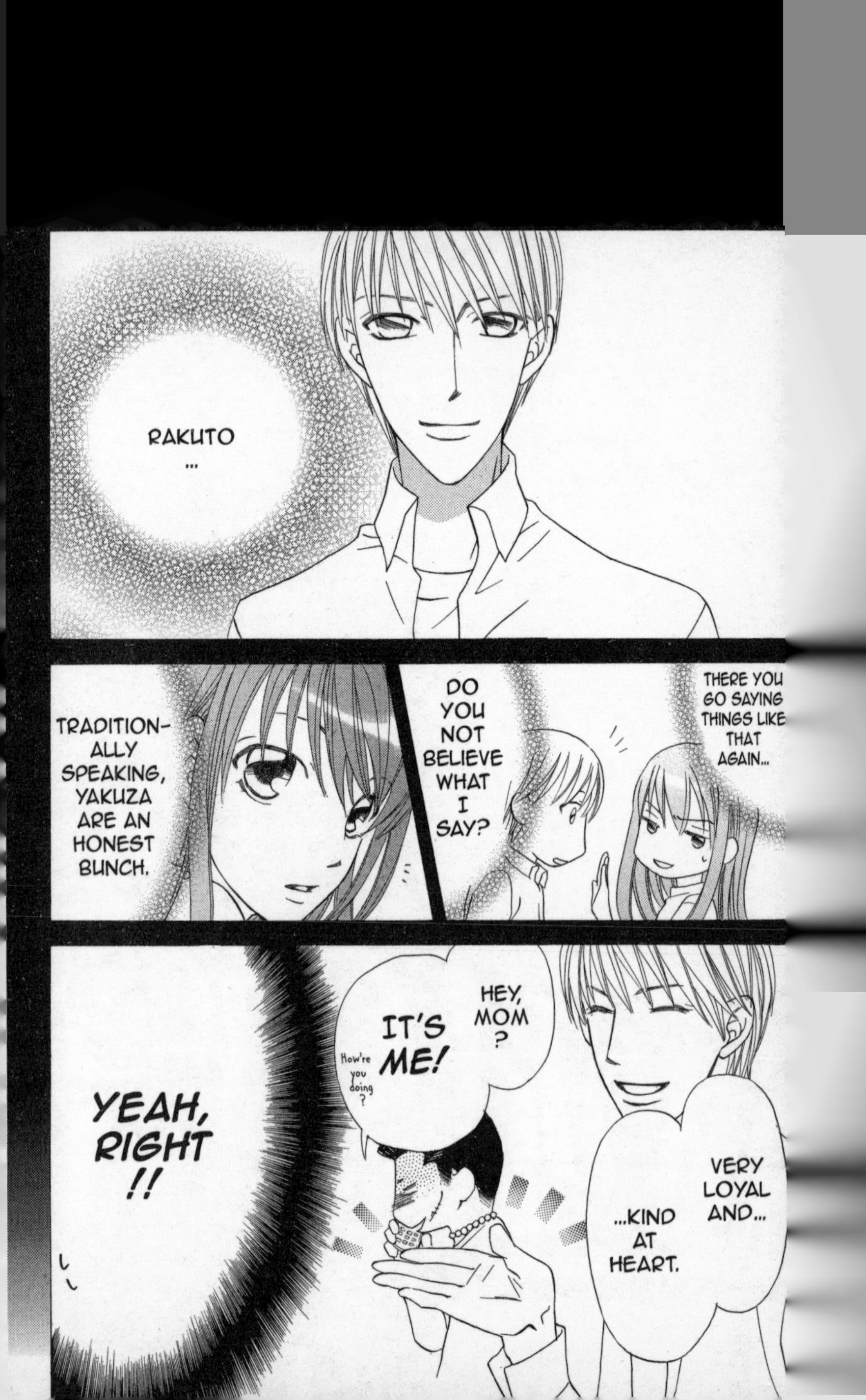
RAKUTO ...
THERE YOU GO SAYING THINGS LIKE THAT AGAIN...
DO YOU NOT BELIEVE WHAT I SAY?
TRADITION-ALLY SPEAKING, YAKUZA ARE AN HONEST BUNCH.
HEY, MOM?
IT'S ME!
How're you doing?
VERY LOYAL AND...
...KIND AT HEART.
YEAH, RIGHT!!

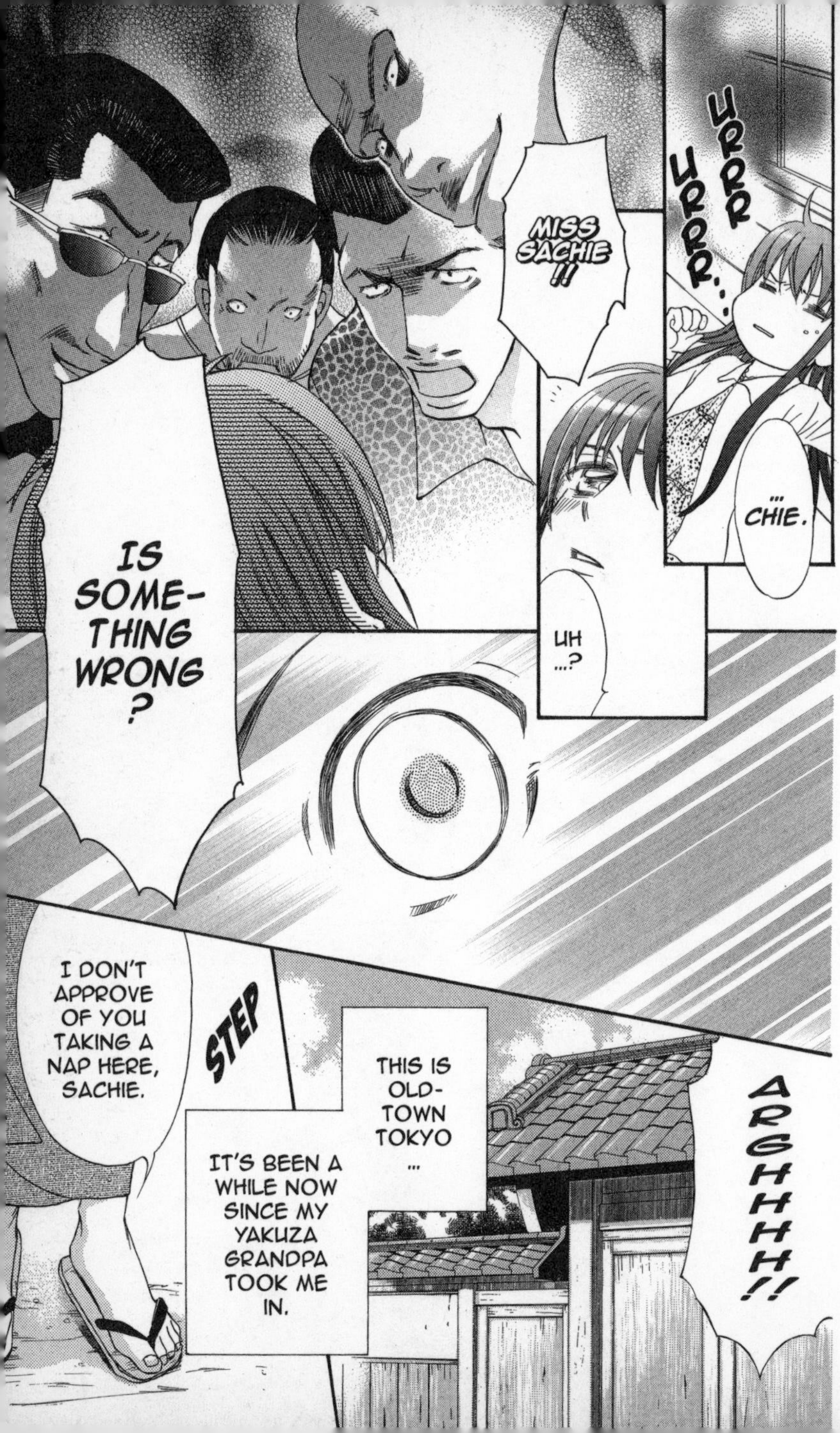
URRR URRR...
...CHIE.
UH ...?
MISS SACHIE !!
IS SOMETHING WRONG?
ARGHHHH!!
THIS IS OLD-TOWN TOKYO ...
IT'S BEEN A WHILE NOW SINCE MY YAKUZA GRANDPA TOOK ME IN.
STEP
I DON'T APPROVE OF YOU TAKING A NAP HERE, SACHIE.

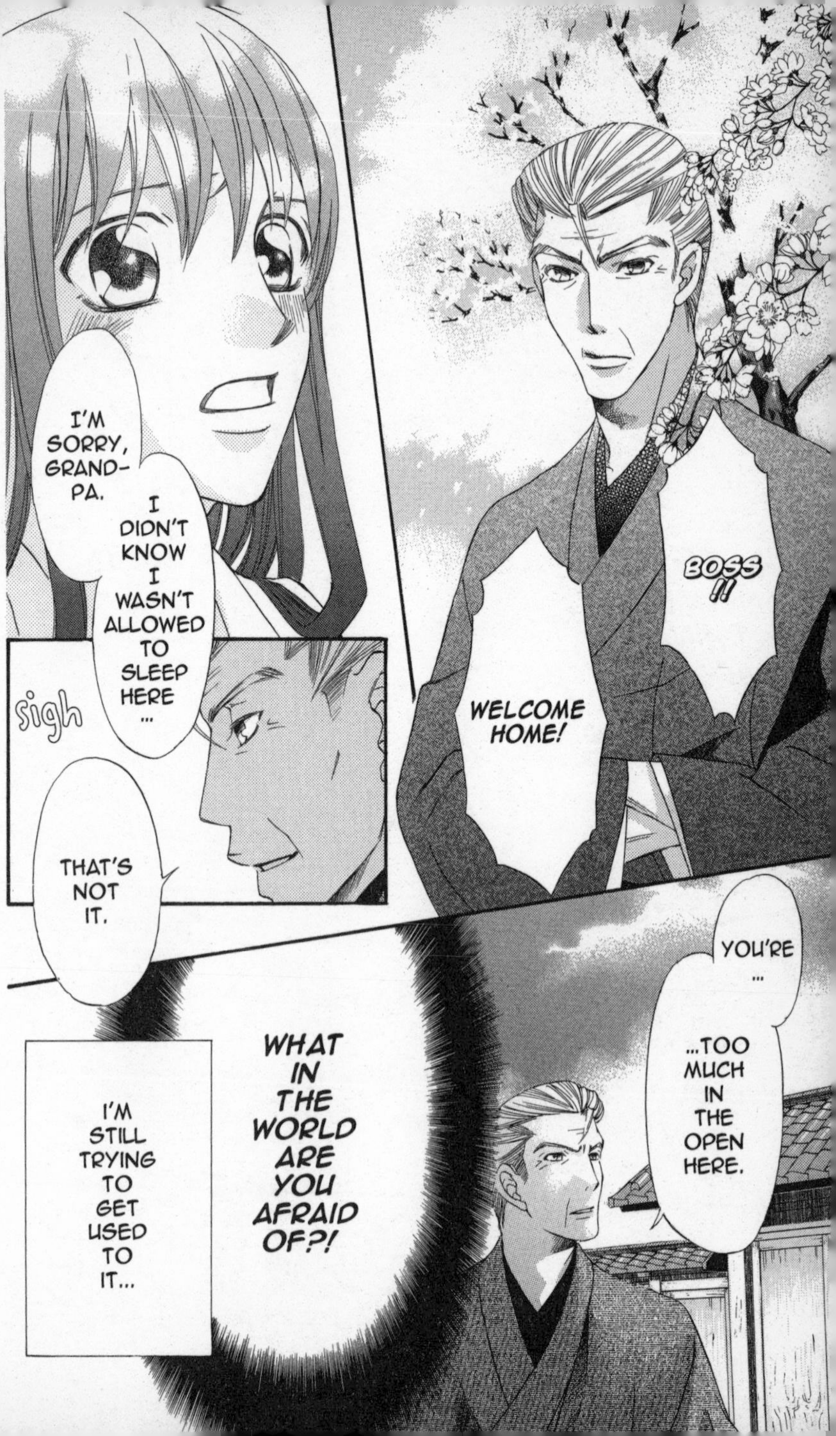
BOSS!!
WELCOME HOME!
I'M SORRY, GRAND-PA.
I DIDN'T KNOW I WASN'T ALLOWED TO SLEEP HERE...
sigh
THAT'S NOT IT.
YOU'RE...
...TOO MUCH IN THE OPEN HERE.
WHAT IN THE WORLD ARE YOU AFRAID OF?!
I'M STILL TRYING TO GET USED TO IT...

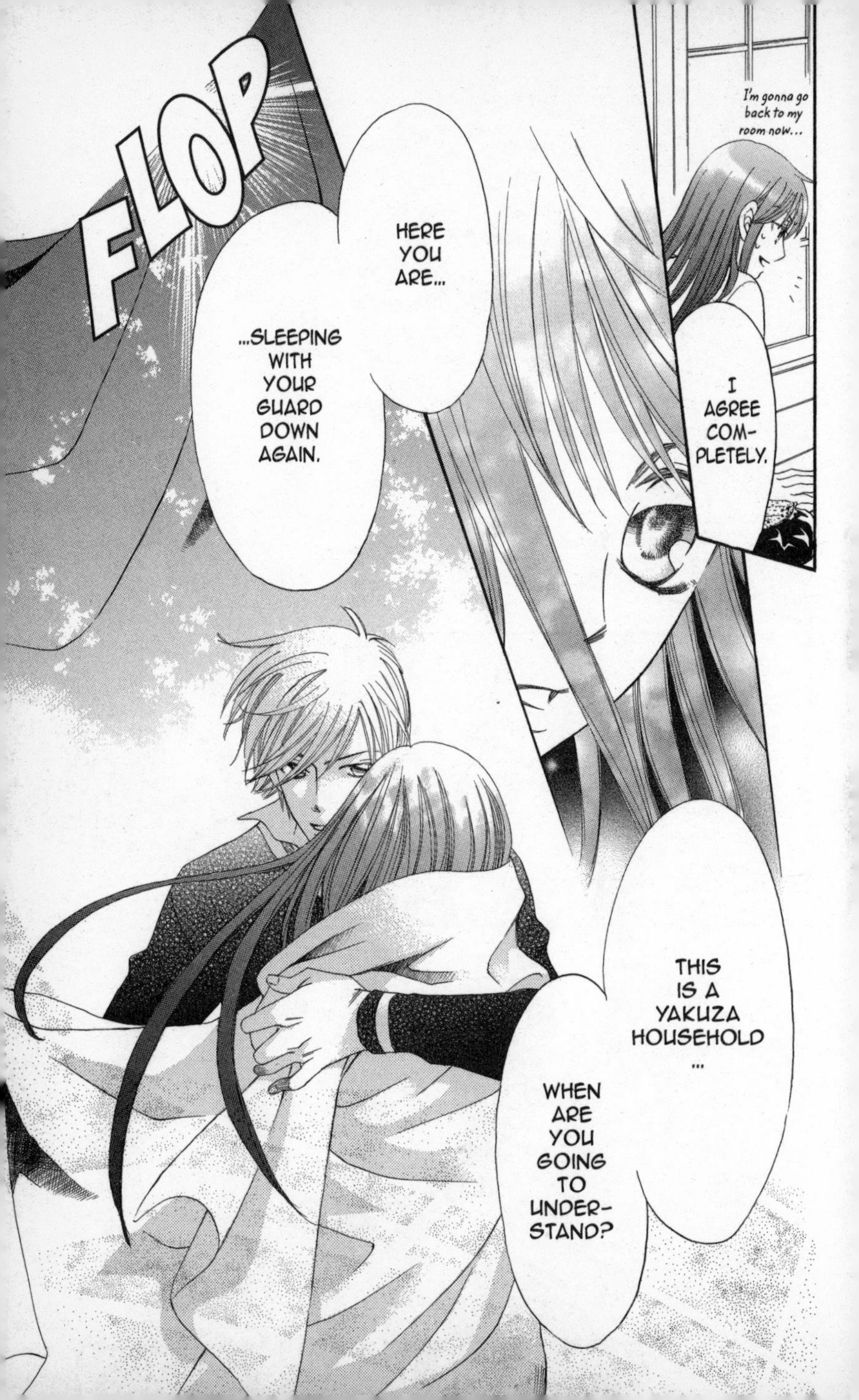
I'm gonna go back to my room now...
I AGREE COMPLETELY.
FLOP
HERE YOU ARE...
...SLEEPING WITH YOUR GUARD DOWN AGAIN.
THIS IS A YAKUZA HOUSEHOLD...
WHEN ARE YOU GOING TO UNDERSTAND?

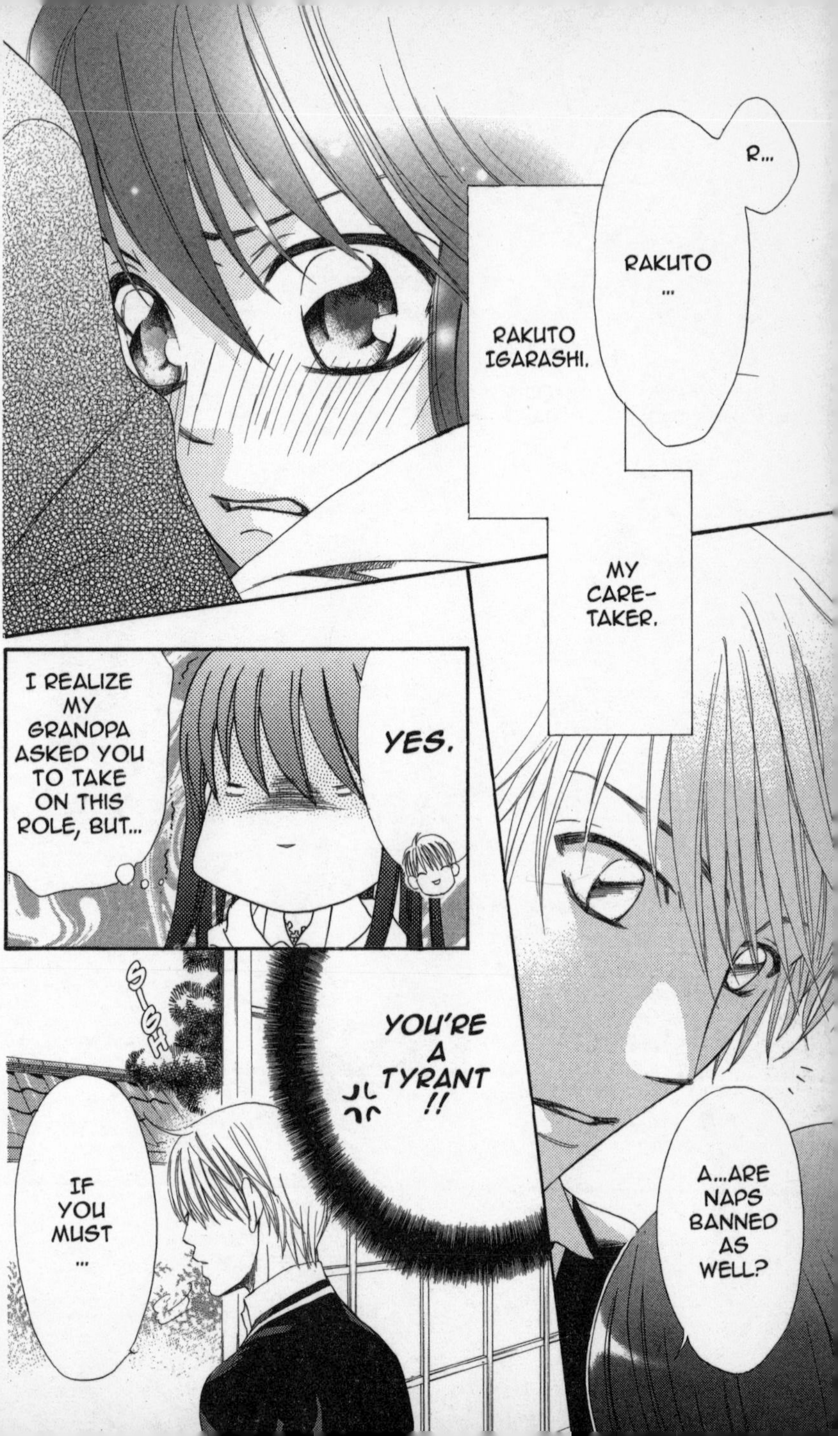
R...
RAKUTO ...
RAKUTO IGARASHI.
MY CARE-TAKER.
A...ARE NAPS BANNED AS WELL?
YES.
I REALIZE MY GRANDPA ASKED YOU TO TAKE ON THIS ROLE, BUT...
YOU'RE A TYRANT!!
SIGH
IF YOU MUST ...

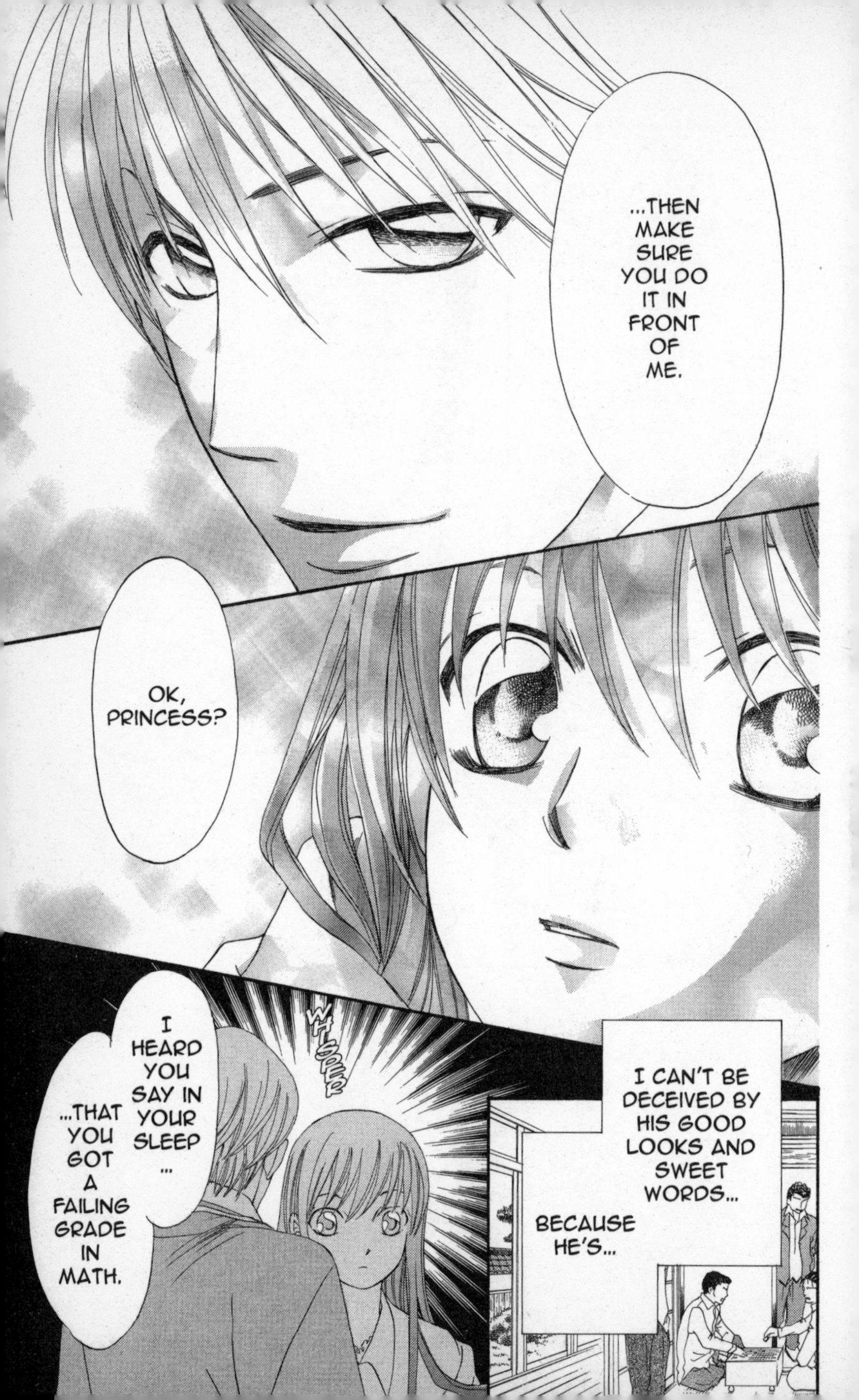
...THEN MAKE SURE YOU DO IT IN FRONT OF ME.
OK, PRINCESS?
I CAN'T BE DECEIVED BY HIS GOOD LOOKS AND SWEET WORDS...
BECAUSE HE'S...
WHISPER
I HEARD YOU SAY IN YOUR SLEEP ...
...THAT YOU GOT A FAILING GRADE IN MATH.

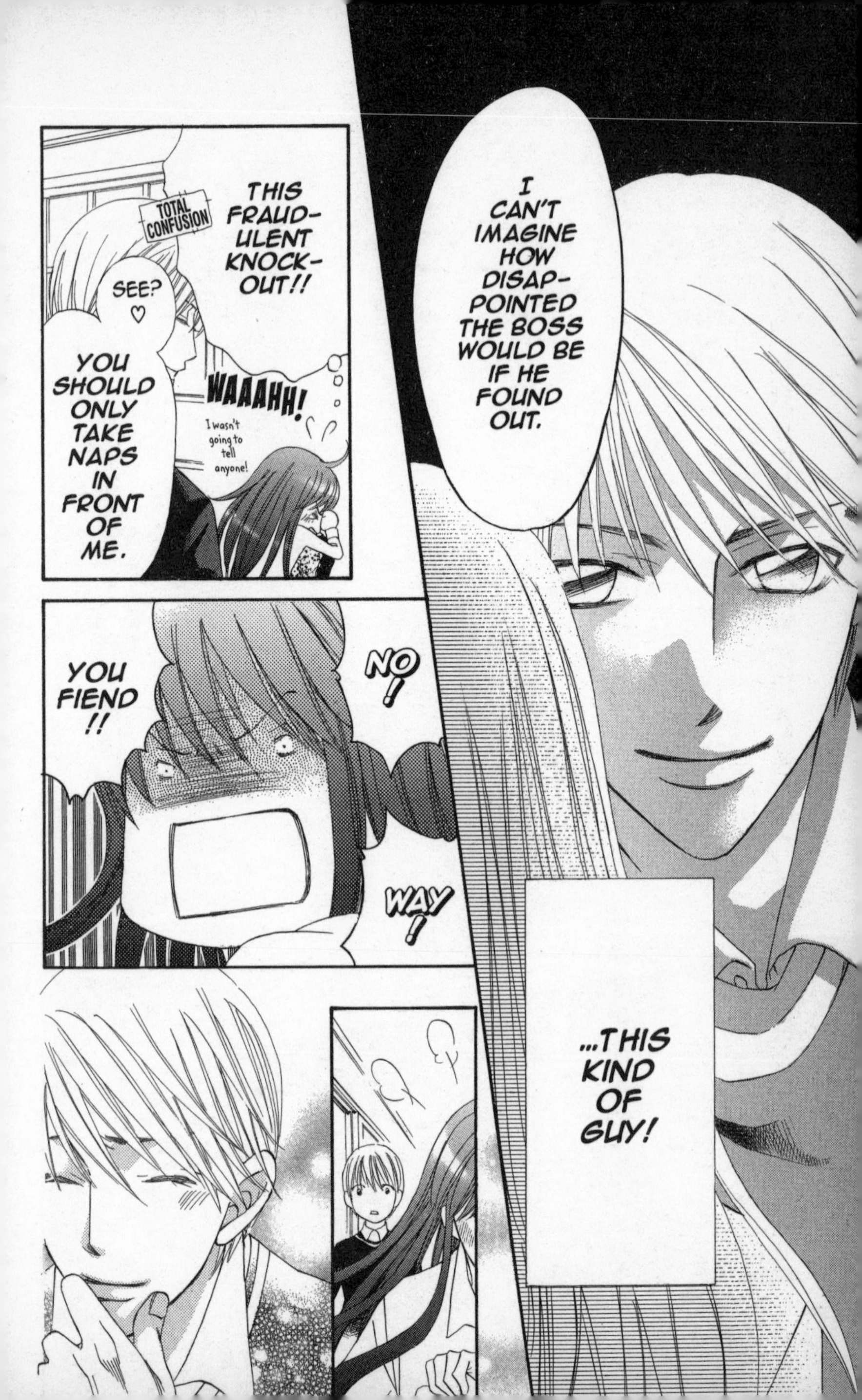
I CAN'T IMAGINE HOW DISAPPOINTED THE BOSS WOULD BE IF HE FOUND OUT.
...THIS KIND OF GUY!
THIS FRAUDULENT KNOCKOUT!!
TOTAL CONFUSION
SEE? ♡
WAAAHH!
I wasn't going to tell anyone!
YOU SHOULD ONLY TAKE NAPS IN FRONT OF ME.
NO WAY!
YOU FIEND!!

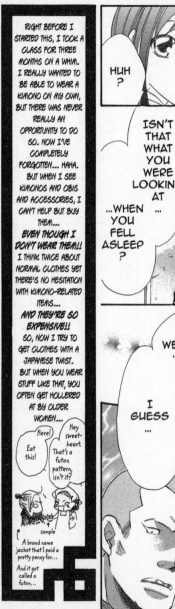

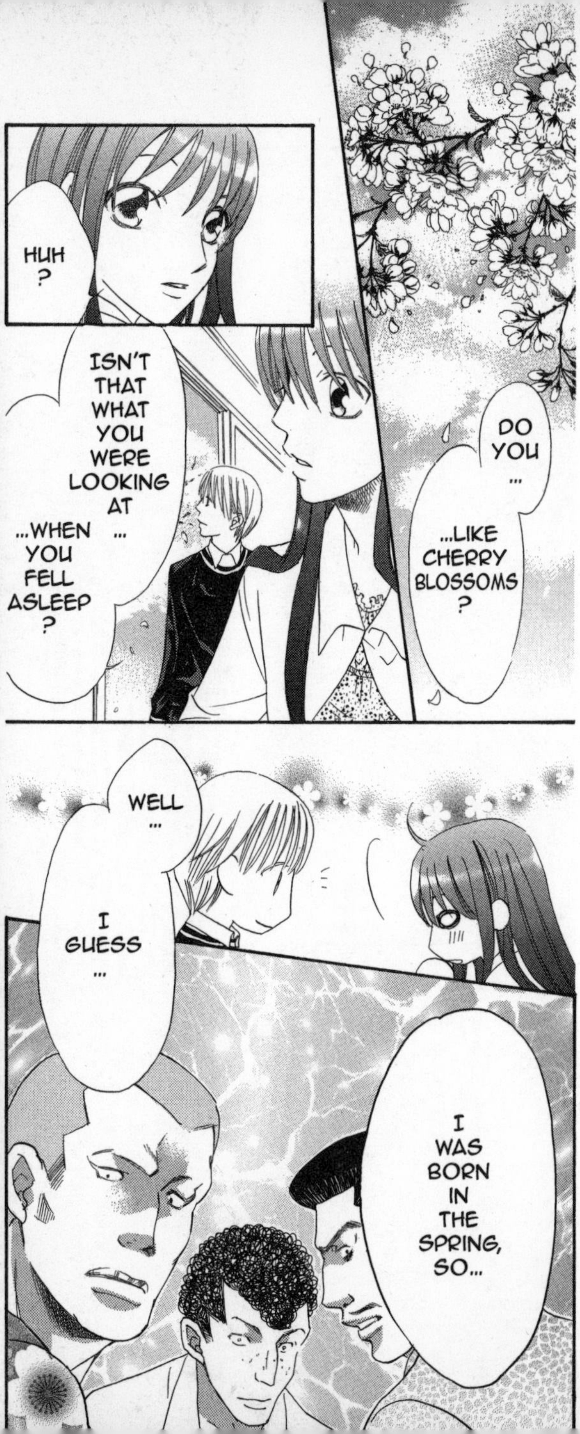
DO YOU ...
...LIKE CHERRY BLOSSOMS?
HUH?
ISN'T THAT WHAT YOU WERE LOOKING AT ...
...WHEN YOU FELL ASLEEP?
WELL ...
I GUESS ...
I WAS BORN IN THE SPRING, SO...

RIGHT BEFORE I STARTED THIS, I TOOK A CLASS FOR THREE MONTHS ON A WHIM. I REALLY WANTED TO BE ABLE TO WEAR A KIMONO ON MY OWN, BUT THERE WAS NEVER REALLY AN OPPORTUNITY TO DO SO. NOW I'VE COMPLETELY FORGOTTEN... HAHA. BUT WHEN I SEE KIMONOS AND OBIS AND ACCESSORIES, I CAN'T HELP BUT BUY THEM... ***EVEN THOUGH I DON'T WEAR THEM!!*** I THINK TWICE ABOUT NORMAL CLOTHES YET THERE'S NO HESITATION WITH KIMONO-RELATED ITEMS... ***AND THEY'RE SO EXPENSIVE!!*** SO, NOW I TRY TO GET CLOTHES WITH A JAPANESE TWIST. BUT WHEN YOU WEAR STUFF LIKE THAT, YOU OFTEN GET HOLLERED AT BY OLDER WOMEN...

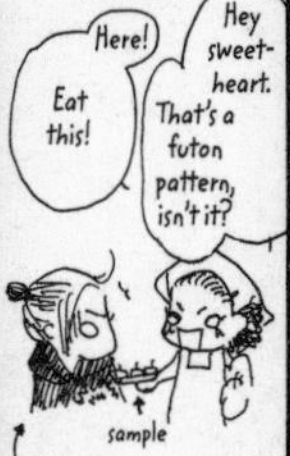
Hey sweetheart. That's a futon pattern, isn't it?
Here!
Eat this!
sample

A brand name jacket that I paid a pretty penny for...
And it got called a futon...

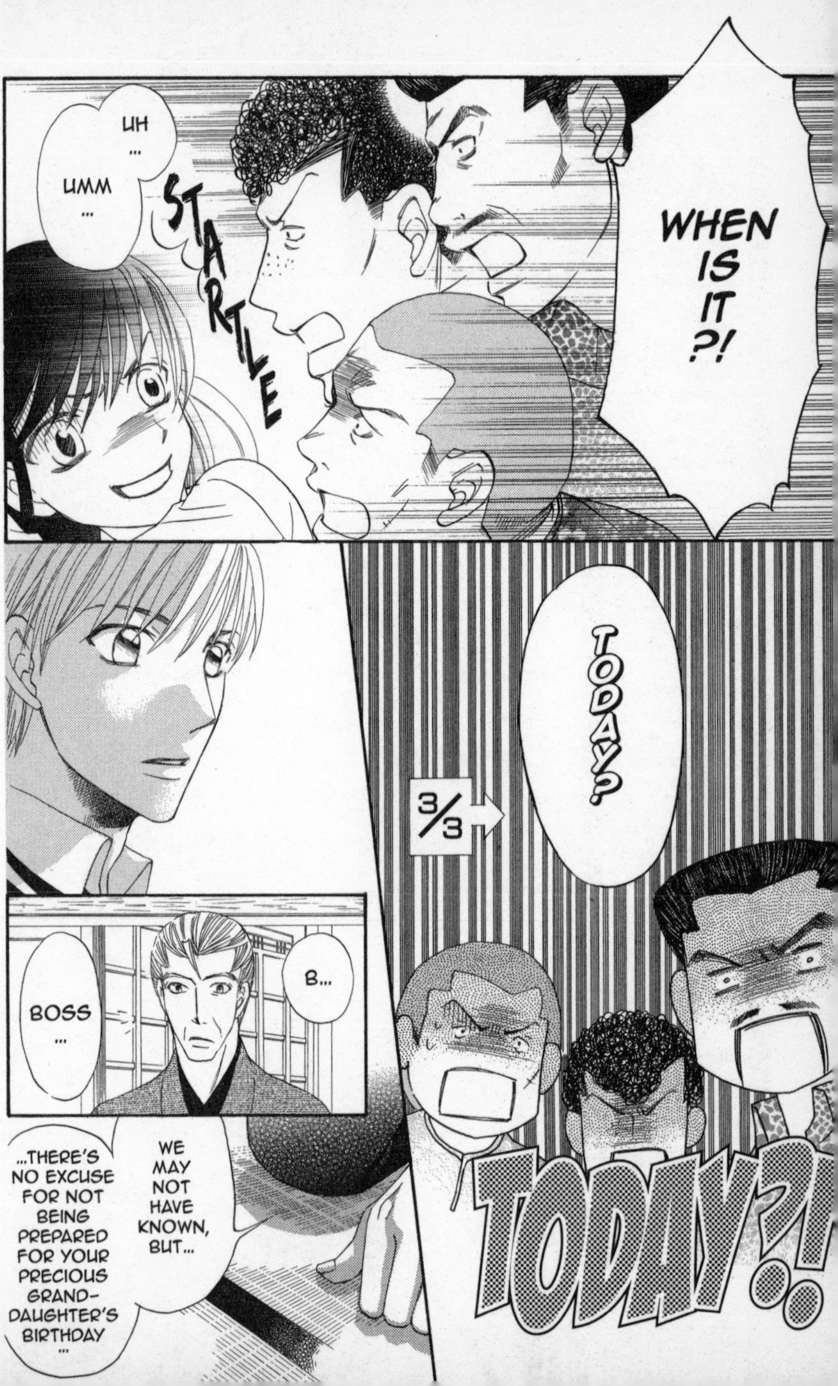
WHEN IS IT?!
UH ... UMM ...
STARTLE
TODAY?
3/3
TODAY?!
B... BOSS ...
WE MAY NOT HAVE KNOWN, BUT...
...THERE'S NO EXCUSE FOR NOT BEING PREPARED FOR YOUR PRECIOUS GRAND-DAUGHTER'S BIRTHDAY ...

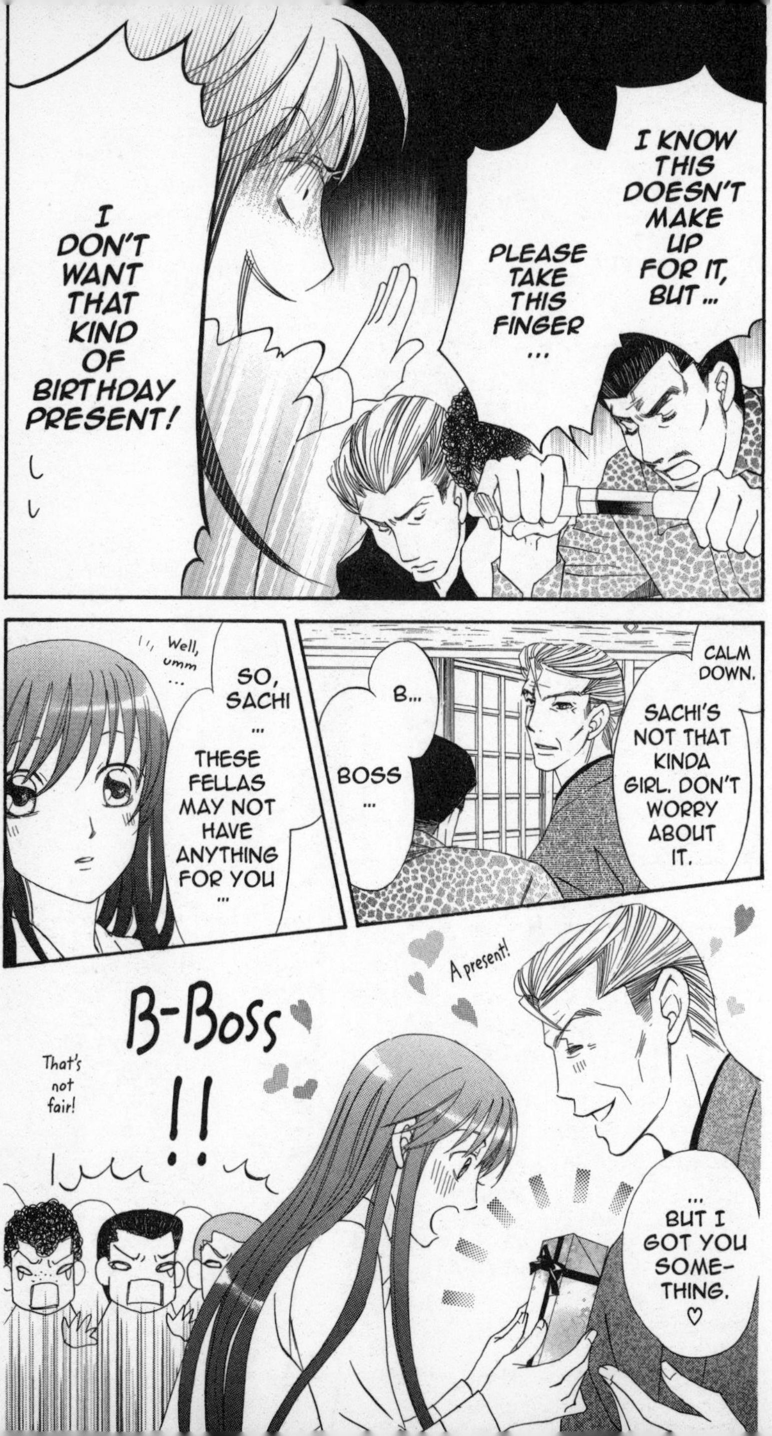
I KNOW THIS DOESN'T MAKE UP FOR IT, BUT ...
PLEASE TAKE THIS FINGER ...
I DON'T WANT THAT KIND OF BIRTHDAY PRESENT!
CALM DOWN.
SACHI'S NOT THAT KINDA GIRL. DON'T WORRY ABOUT IT.
B...
BOSS ...
Well, umm ...
SO, SACHI ... THESE FELLAS MAY NOT HAVE ANYTHING FOR YOU ...
A present!
... BUT I GOT YOU SOME-THING. ♡
B-Boss !!
That's not fair!

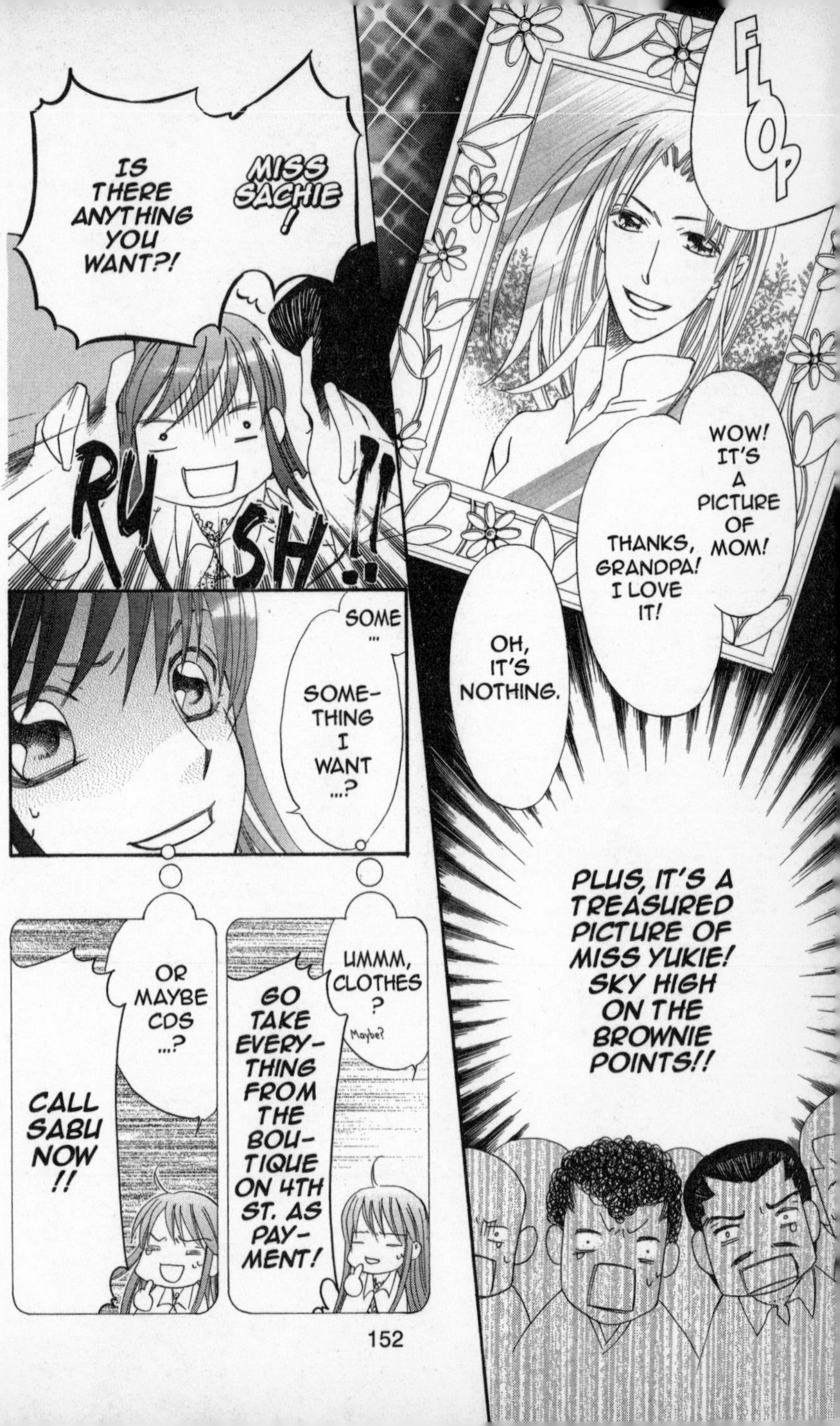
FLOP
WOW! IT'S A PICTURE OF MOM!
THANKS, GRANDPA! I LOVE IT!
OH, IT'S NOTHING.
PLUS, IT'S A TREASURED PICTURE OF MISS YUKIE! SKY HIGH ON THE BROWNIE POINTS!!
MISS SACHIE!
IS THERE ANYTHING YOU WANT?!
RUSH!!
SOME...
SOMETHING I WANT...?
UMMM, CLOTHES?
Maybe?
GO TAKE EVERYTHING FROM THE BOUTIQUE ON 4TH ST. AS PAYMENT!
OR MAYBE CDS...?
CALL SABU NOW!!

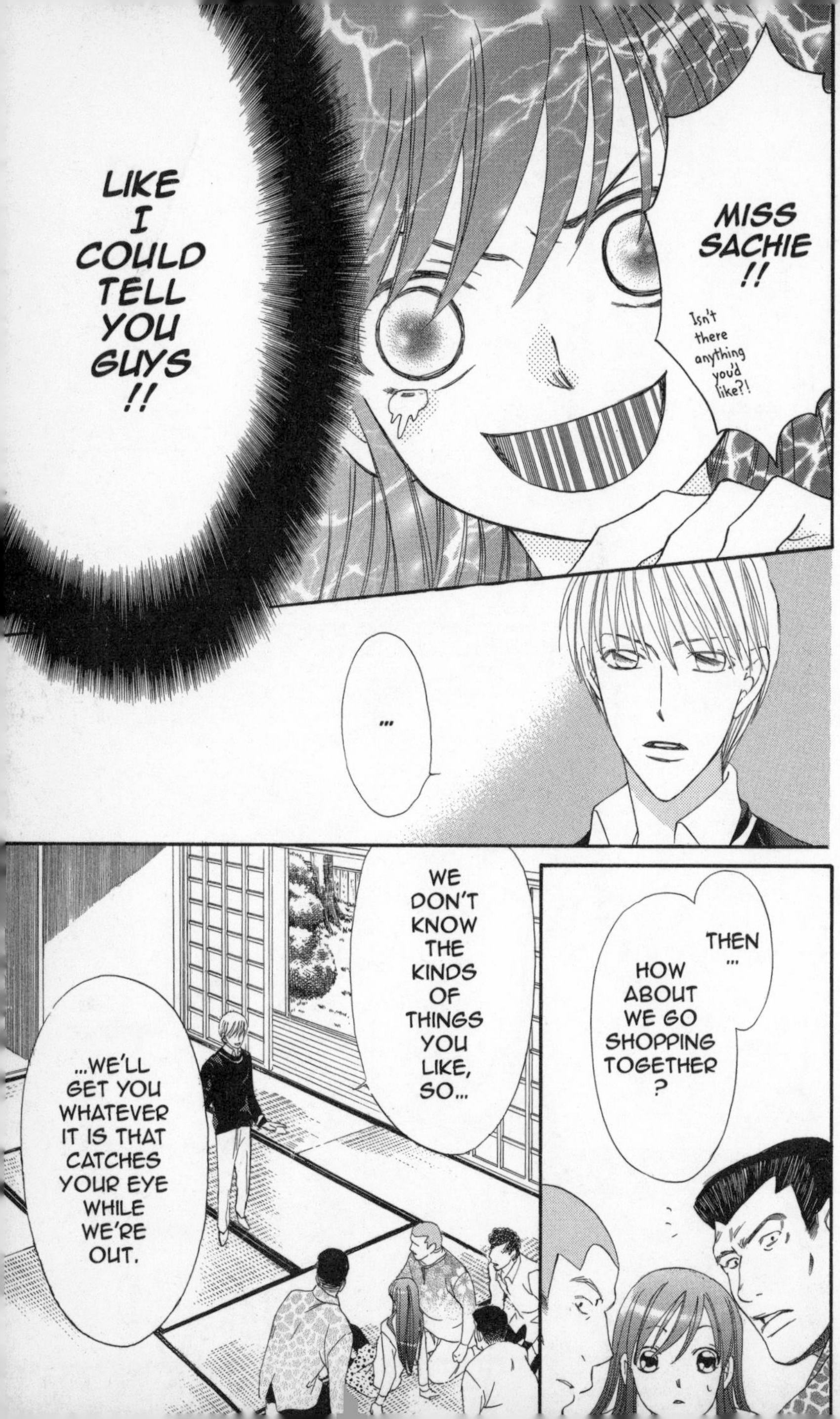
MISS SACHIE!!
Isn't there anything you'd like?!
LIKE I COULD TELL YOU GUYS!!
...
THEN... HOW ABOUT WE GO SHOPPING TOGETHER?
WE DON'T KNOW THE KINDS OF THINGS YOU LIKE, SO...
...WE'LL GET YOU WHATEVER IT IS THAT CATCHES YOUR EYE WHILE WE'RE OUT.

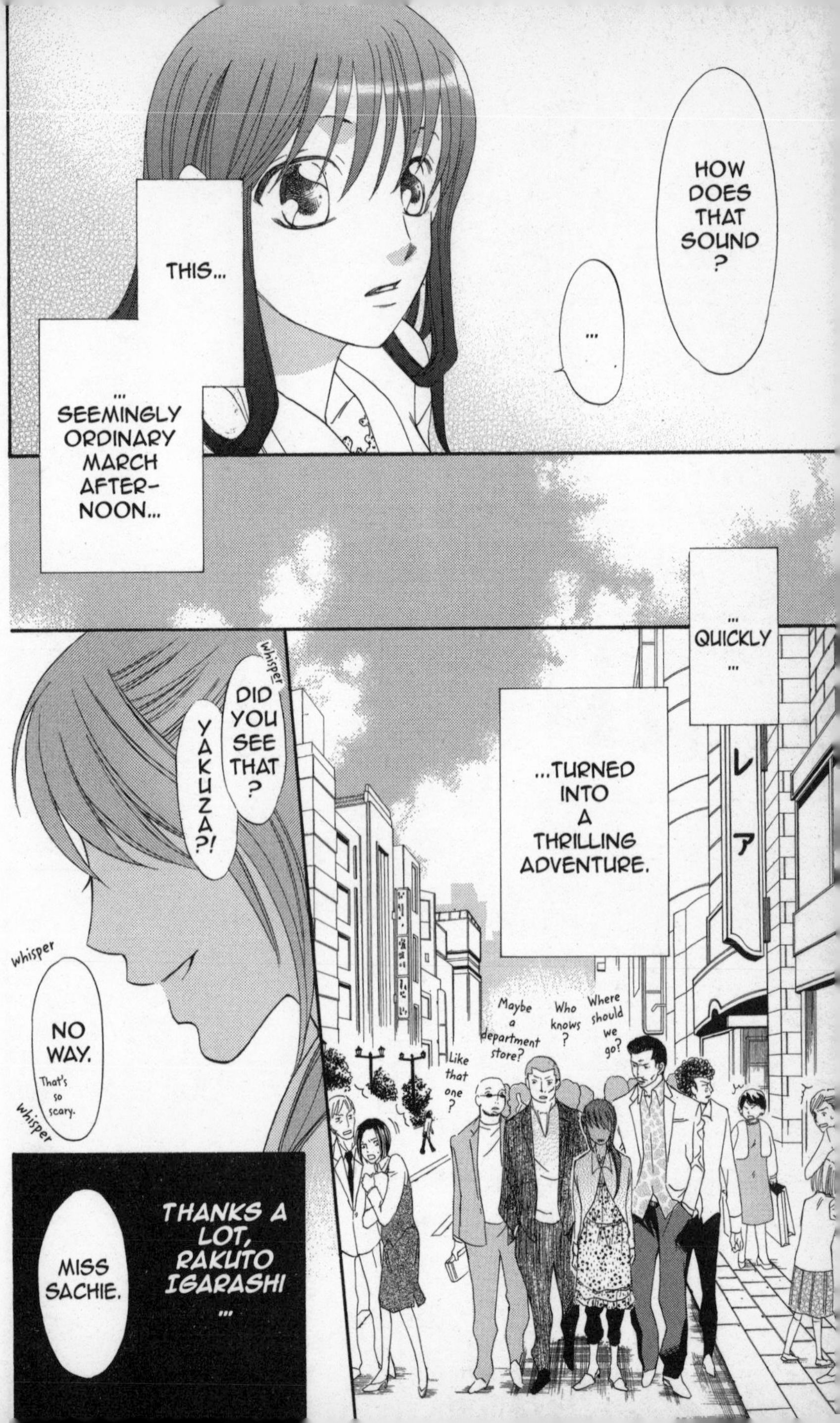
HOW DOES THAT SOUND?
...
THIS...
...SEEMINGLY ORDINARY MARCH AFTER-NOON...
...QUICKLY...
...TURNED INTO A THRILLING ADVENTURE.
レア
Where should we go?
Who knows?
Maybe a department store?
Like that one?
whisper
DID YOU SEE THAT?
YAKUZA?!
whisper
NO WAY.
That's so scary.
whisper
THANKS A LOT, RAKUTO IGARASHI...
MISS SACHIE.

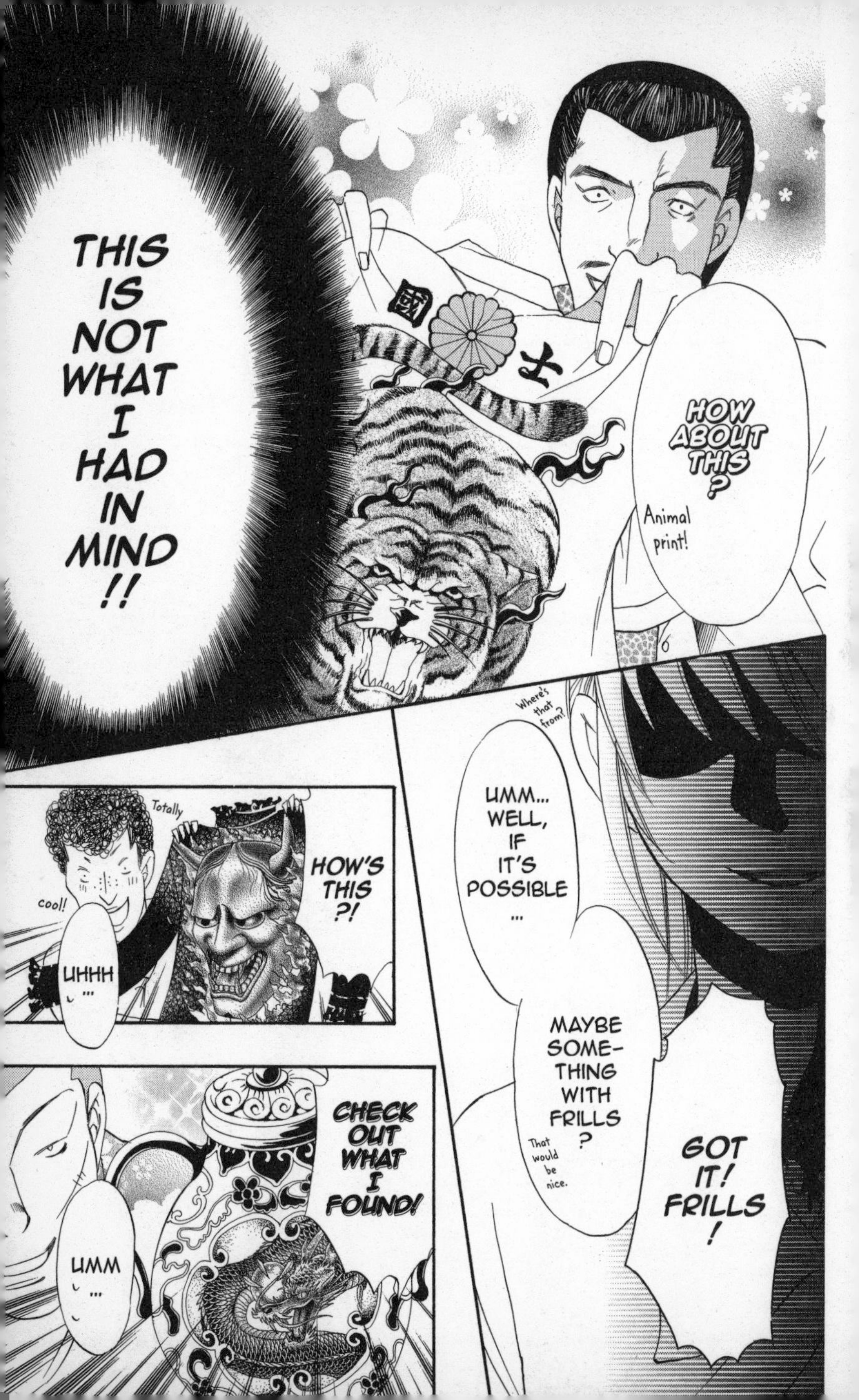
HOW ABOUT THIS?
Animal print!
THIS IS NOT WHAT I HAD IN MIND!!
Where's that from?
UMM... WELL, IF IT'S POSSIBLE...
MAYBE SOMETHING WITH FRILLS?
That would be nice.
GOT IT! FRILLS!
HOW'S THIS?!
Totally cool!
UHHH...
CHECK OUT WHAT I FOUND!
UMM...

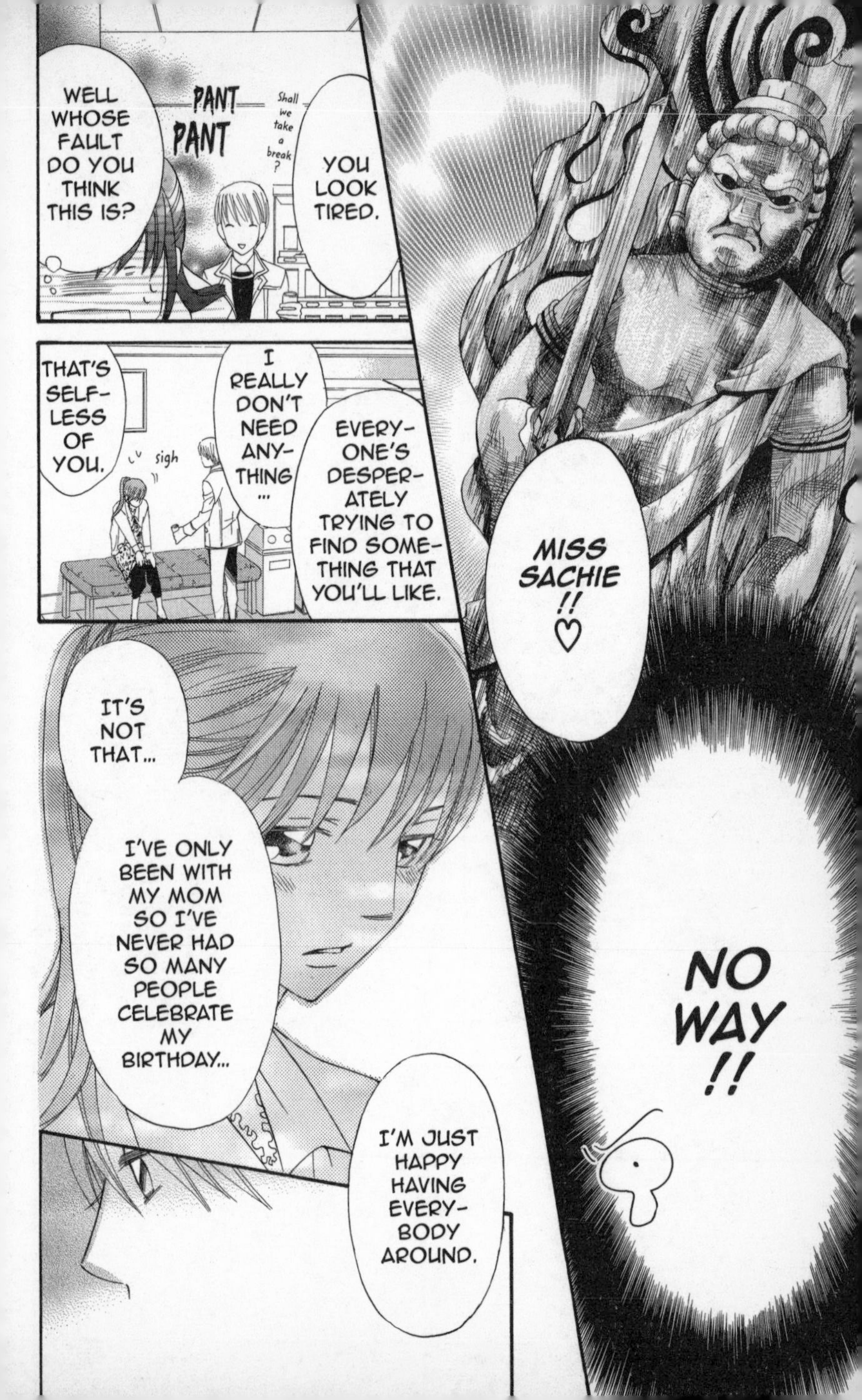
MISS SACHIE!! ♡
NO WAY!!
YOU LOOK TIRED.
Shall we take a break?
PANT PANT
WELL WHOSE FAULT DO YOU THINK THIS IS?
EVERYONE'S DESPERATELY TRYING TO FIND SOMETHING THAT YOU'LL LIKE.
I REALLY DON'T NEED ANYTHING...
sigh
THAT'S SELFLESS OF YOU.
IT'S NOT THAT...
I'VE ONLY BEEN WITH MY MOM SO I'VE NEVER HAD SO MANY PEOPLE CELEBRATE MY BIRTHDAY...
I'M JUST HAPPY HAVING EVERYBODY AROUND.

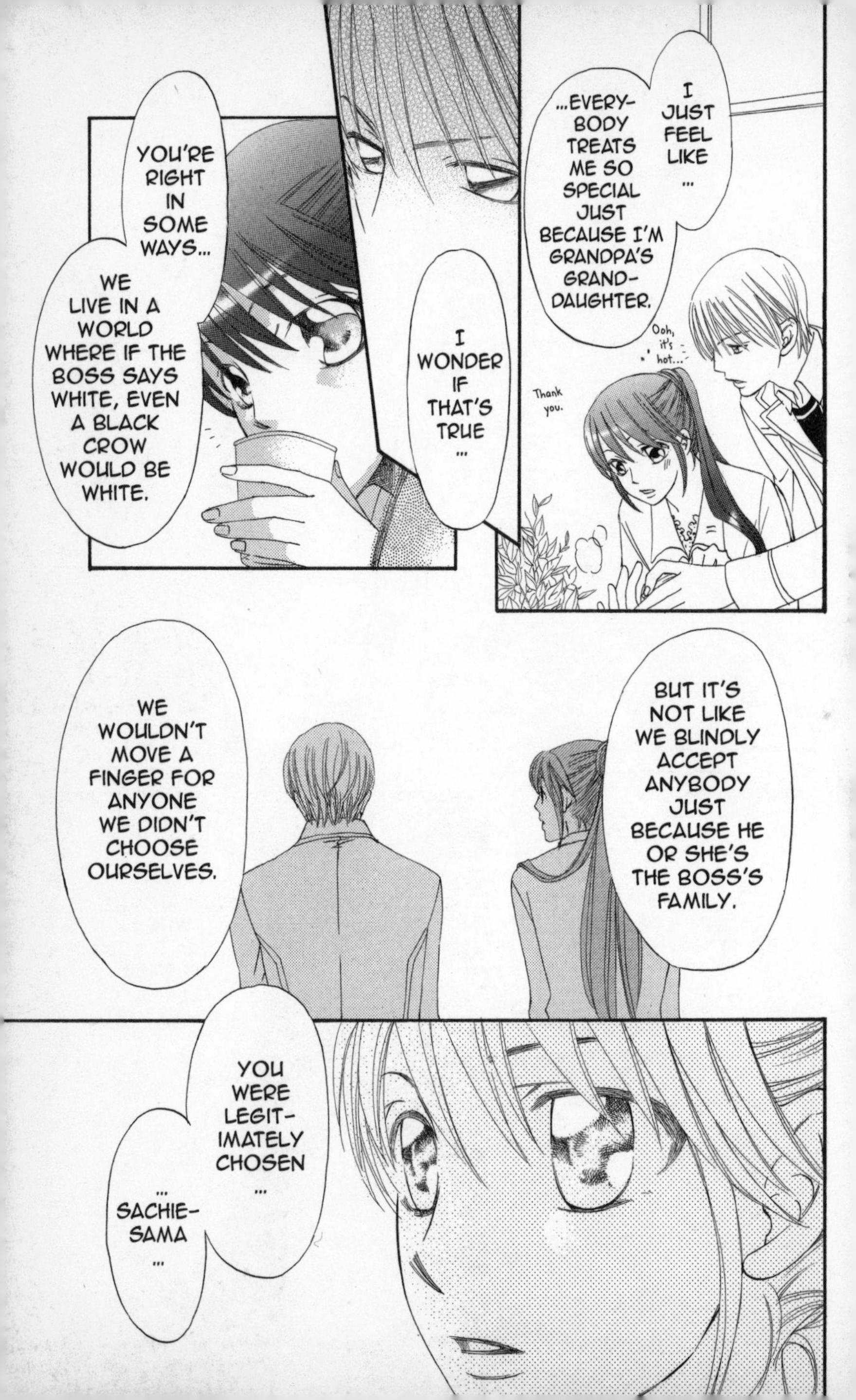
I JUST FEEL LIKE ...
...EVERY-BODY TREATS ME SO SPECIAL JUST BECAUSE I'M GRANDPA'S GRAND-DAUGHTER.
Ooh, it's hot...
Thank you.
I WONDER IF THAT'S TRUE ...
YOU'RE RIGHT IN SOME WAYS...
WE LIVE IN A WORLD WHERE IF THE BOSS SAYS WHITE, EVEN A BLACK CROW WOULD BE WHITE.
BUT IT'S NOT LIKE WE BLINDLY ACCEPT ANYBODY JUST BECAUSE HE OR SHE'S THE BOSS'S FAMILY.
WE WOULDN'T MOVE A FINGER FOR ANYONE WE DIDN'T CHOOSE OURSELVES.
YOU WERE LEGIT-IMATELY CHOSEN ...
... SACHIE-SAMA ...

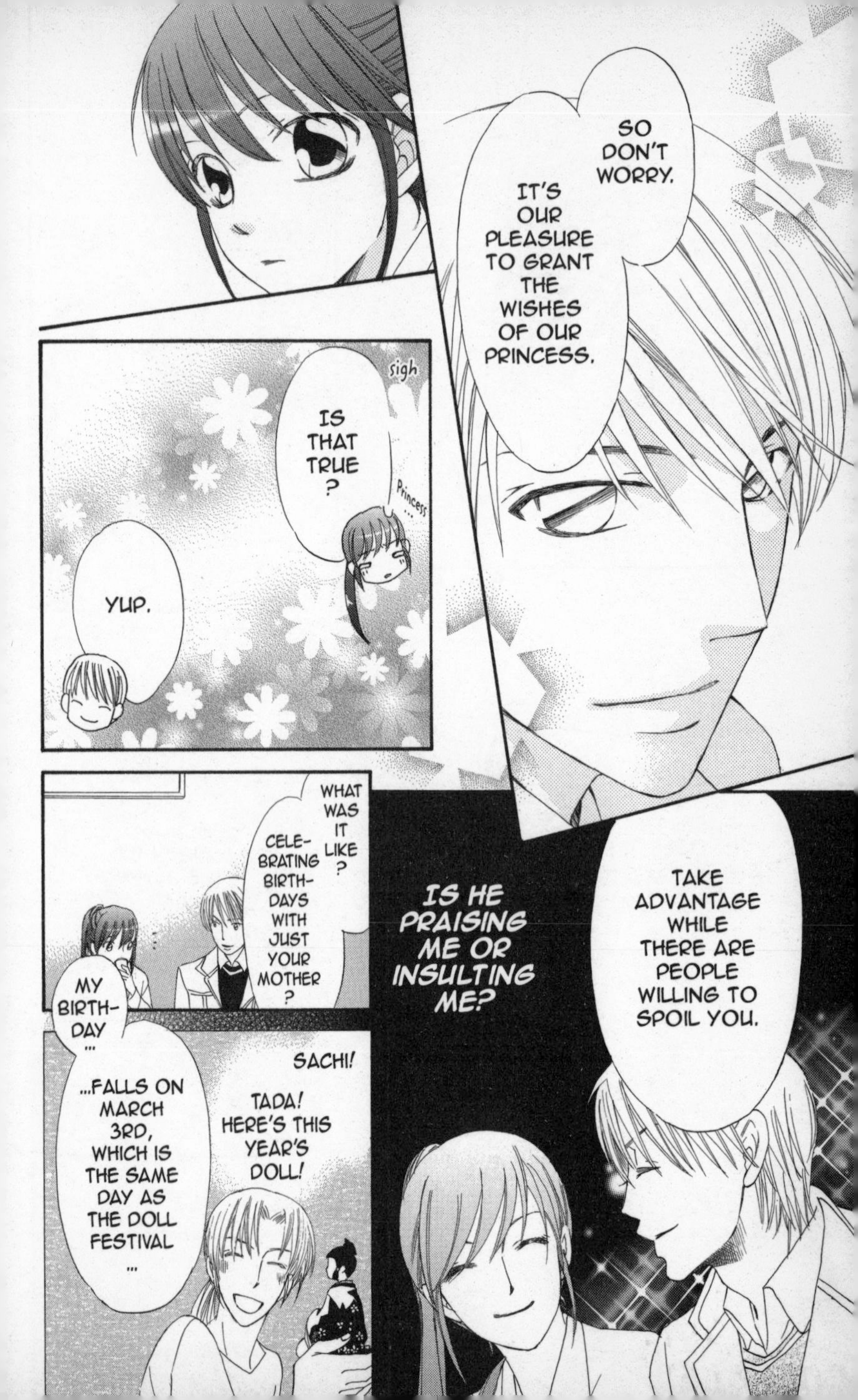
SO DON'T WORRY.
IT'S OUR PLEASURE TO GRANT THE WISHES OF OUR PRINCESS.
sigh
IS THAT TRUE?
Princess...
YUP.
TAKE ADVANTAGE WHILE THERE ARE PEOPLE WILLING TO SPOIL YOU.
IS HE PRAISING ME OR INSULTING ME?
WHAT WAS IT LIKE CELEBRATING BIRTHDAYS WITH JUST YOUR MOTHER?
MY BIRTHDAY...
SACHI!
TADA! HERE'S THIS YEAR'S DOLL!
...FALLS ON MARCH 3RD, WHICH IS THE SAME DAY AS THE DOLL FESTIVAL...

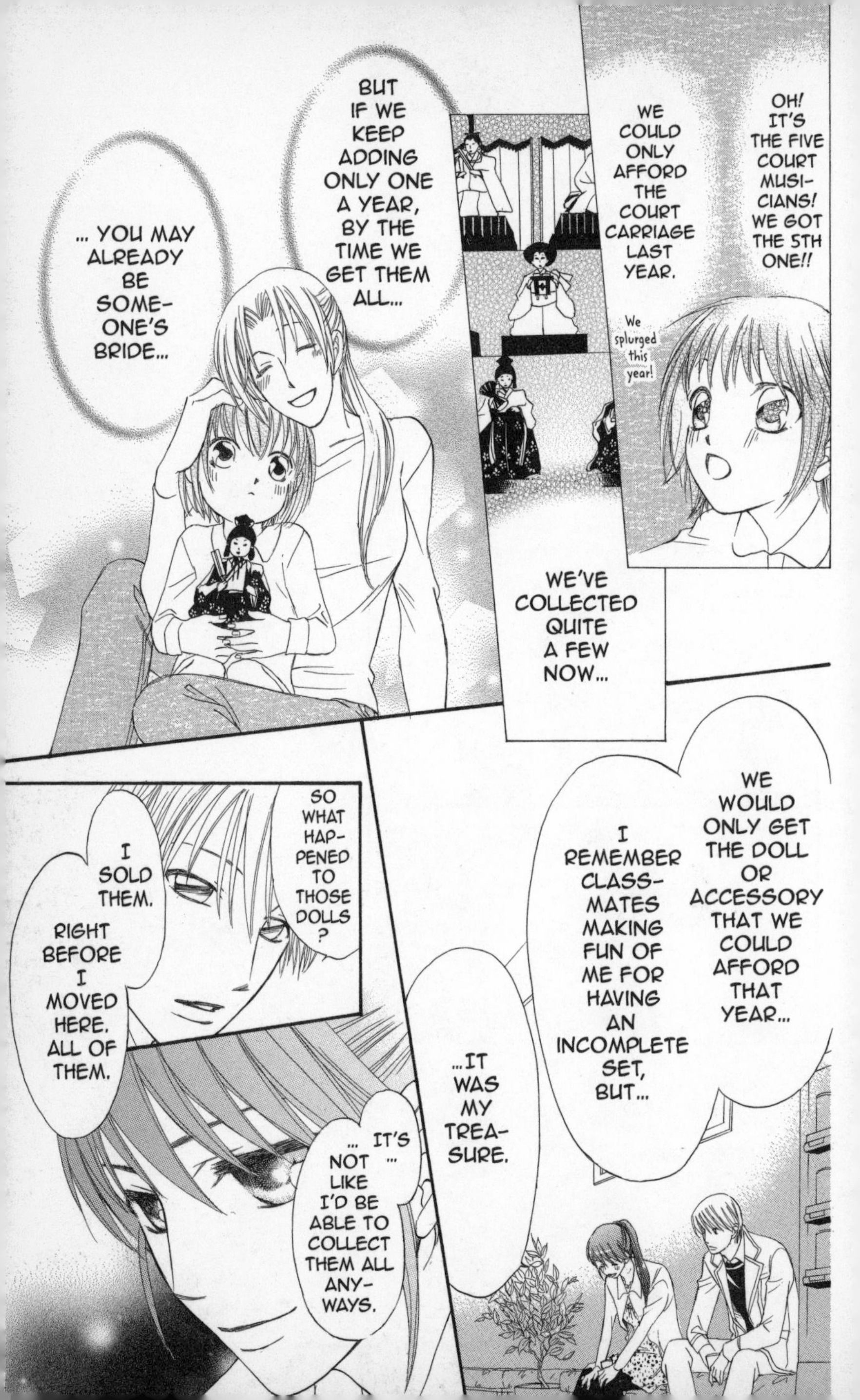
OH! IT'S THE FIVE COURT MUSICIANS! WE GOT THE 5TH ONE!!
WE COULD ONLY AFFORD THE COURT CARRIAGE LAST YEAR.
We splurged this year!
WE'VE COLLECTED QUITE A FEW NOW...
BUT IF WE KEEP ADDING ONLY ONE A YEAR, BY THE TIME WE GET THEM ALL...
... YOU MAY ALREADY BE SOMEONE'S BRIDE...
WE WOULD ONLY GET THE DOLL OR ACCESSORY THAT WE COULD AFFORD THAT YEAR...
I REMEMBER CLASSMATES MAKING FUN OF ME FOR HAVING AN INCOMPLETE SET, BUT...
...IT WAS MY TREASURE.
SO WHAT HAPPENED TO THOSE DOLLS?
I SOLD THEM.
RIGHT BEFORE I MOVED HERE. ALL OF THEM.
... IT'S ... NOT LIKE I'D BE ABLE TO COLLECT THEM ALL ANYWAYS.

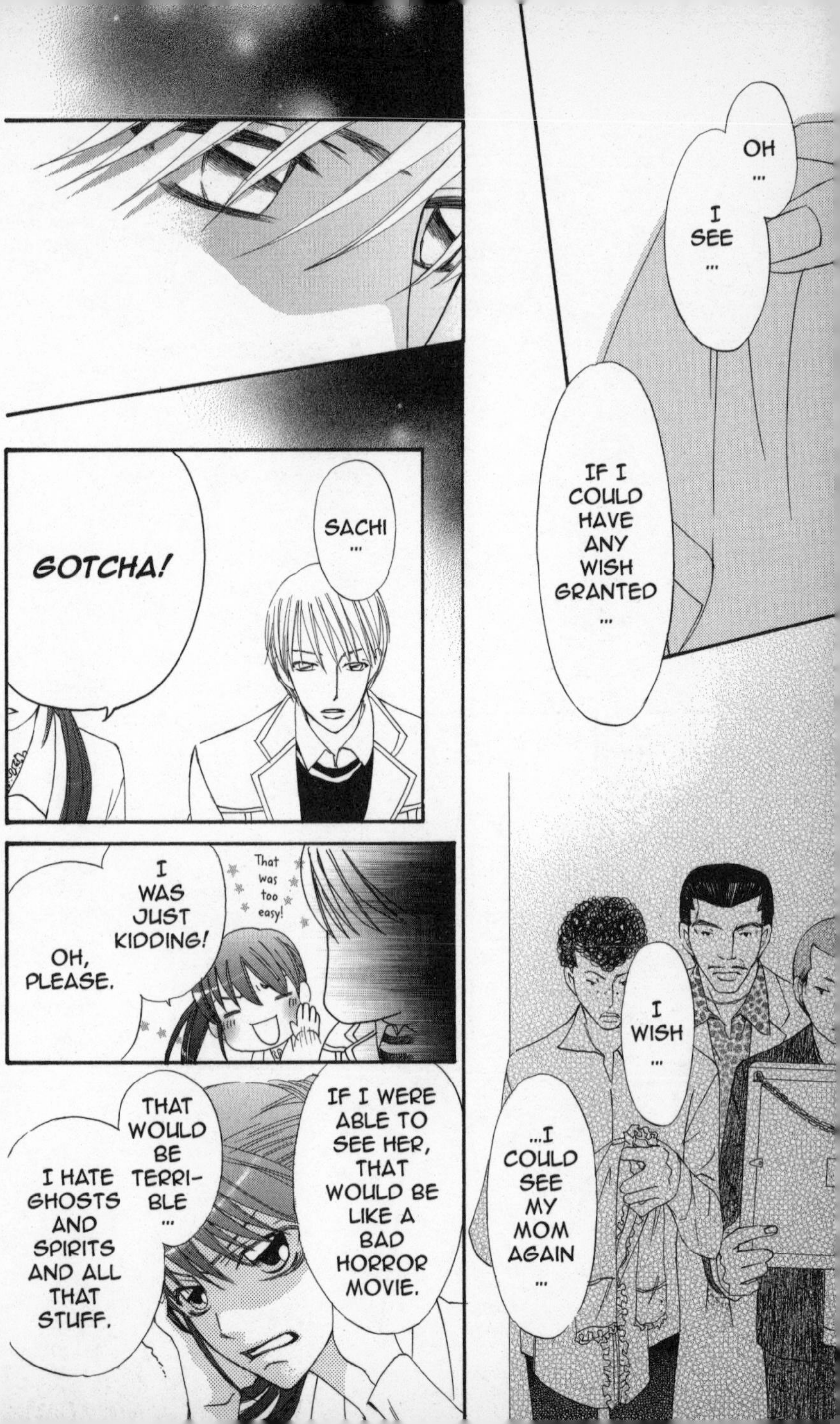
OH... I SEE...
IF I COULD HAVE ANY WISH GRANTED...
I WISH...
...I COULD SEE MY MOM AGAIN...
SACHI...
GOTCHA!
I WAS JUST KIDDING!
That was too easy!
OH, PLEASE.
IF I WERE ABLE TO SEE HER, THAT WOULD BE LIKE A BAD HORROR MOVIE.
THAT WOULD BE TERRI-BLE...
I HATE GHOSTS AND SPIRITS AND ALL THAT STUFF.

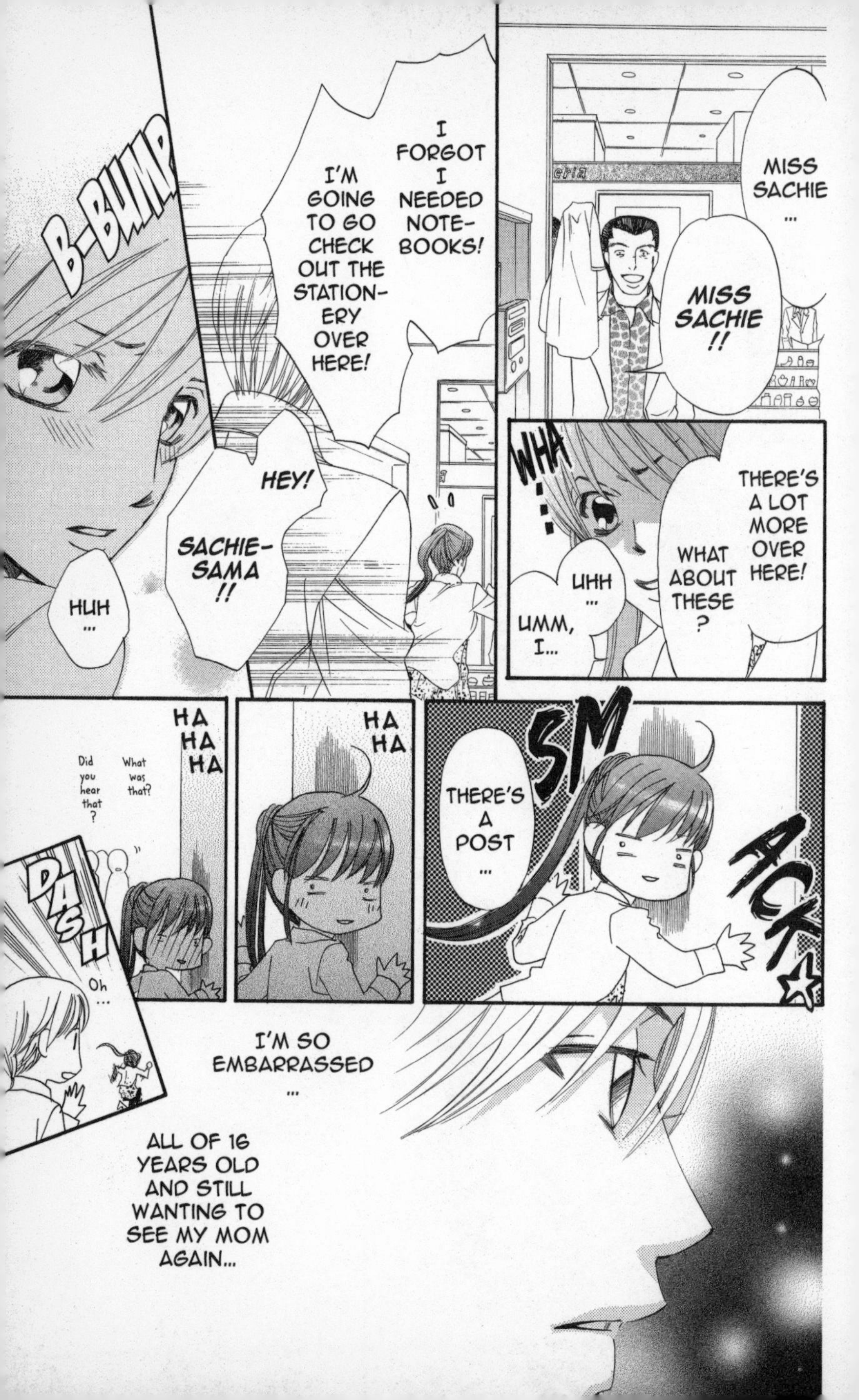
MISS SACHIE ...
MISS SACHIE !!
WHA ...
THERE'S A LOT MORE OVER HERE!
WHAT ABOUT THESE ?
UHH ... UMM, I...
I FORGOT I NEEDED NOTE-BOOKS!
I'M GOING TO GO CHECK OUT THE STATION-ERY OVER HERE!
HEY!
SACHIE-SAMA !!
B-BUMP
HUH ...
SMACK☆
THERE'S A POST ...
HA HA
HA HA HA
What was that?
Did you hear that ?
DASH
Oh ...
I'M SO EMBARRASSED ...
ALL OF 16 YEARS OLD AND STILL WANTING TO SEE MY MOM AGAIN...

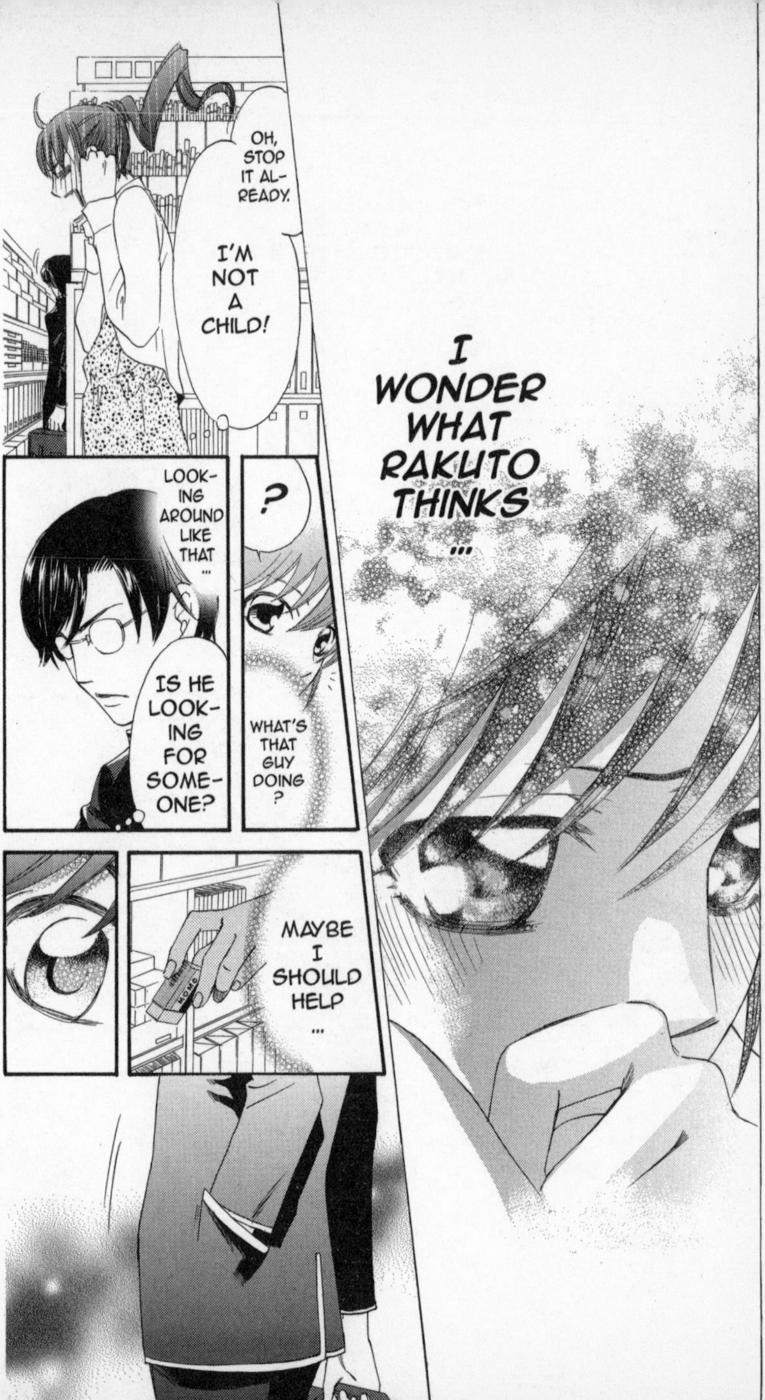
I WONDER WHAT RAKUTO THINKS ...
OH, STOP IT AL-READY.
I'M NOT A CHILD!
?
WHAT'S THAT GUY DOING ?
LOOK-ING AROUND LIKE THAT ...
IS HE LOOK-ING FOR SOME-ONE?
MAYBE I SHOULD HELP ...

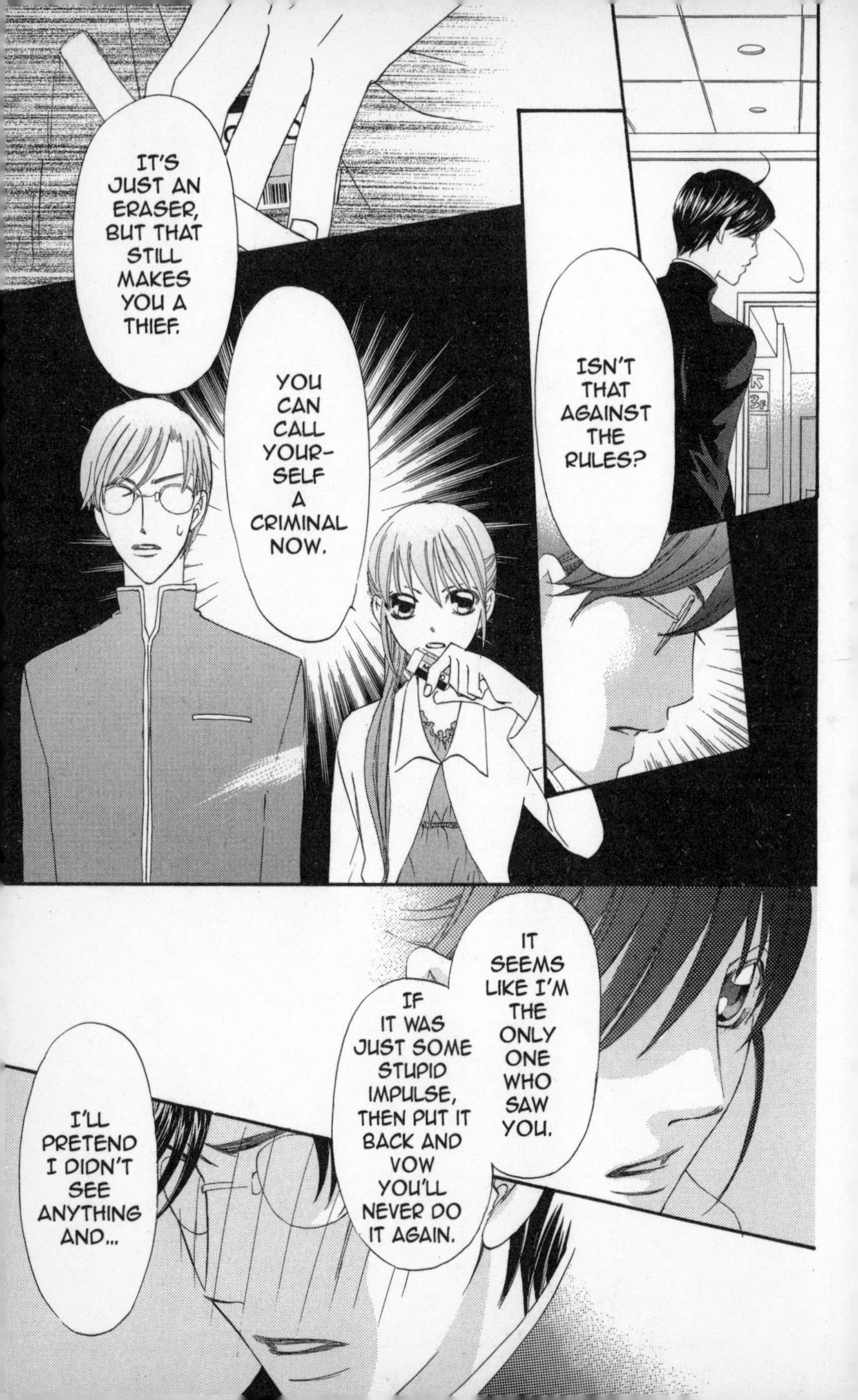
ISN'T THAT AGAINST THE RULES?
IT'S JUST AN ERASER, BUT THAT STILL MAKES YOU A THIEF.
YOU CAN CALL YOURSELF A CRIMINAL NOW.
IT SEEMS LIKE I'M THE ONLY ONE WHO SAW YOU.
IF IT WAS JUST SOME STUPID IMPULSE, THEN PUT IT BACK AND VOW YOU'LL NEVER DO IT AGAIN.
I'LL PRETEND I DIDN'T SEE ANYTHING AND...

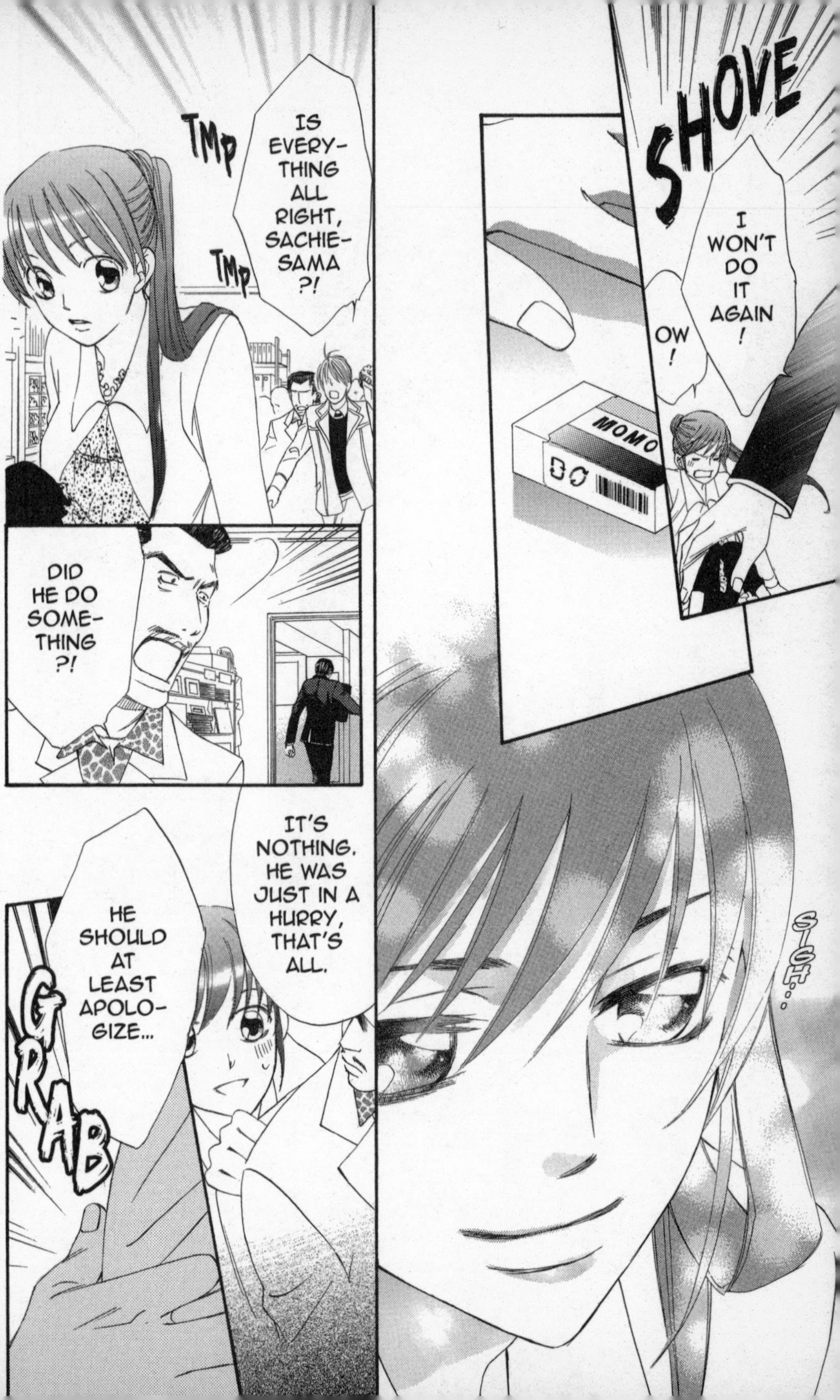
SHOVE
I WON'T DO IT AGAIN!
OW!
MOMO
SIGH...
TMP
TMP
IS EVERYTHING ALL RIGHT, SACHIE-SAMA?!
DID HE DO SOMETHING?!
IT'S NOTHING. HE WAS JUST IN A HURRY, THAT'S ALL.
HE SHOULD AT LEAST APOLOGIZE...
GRAB

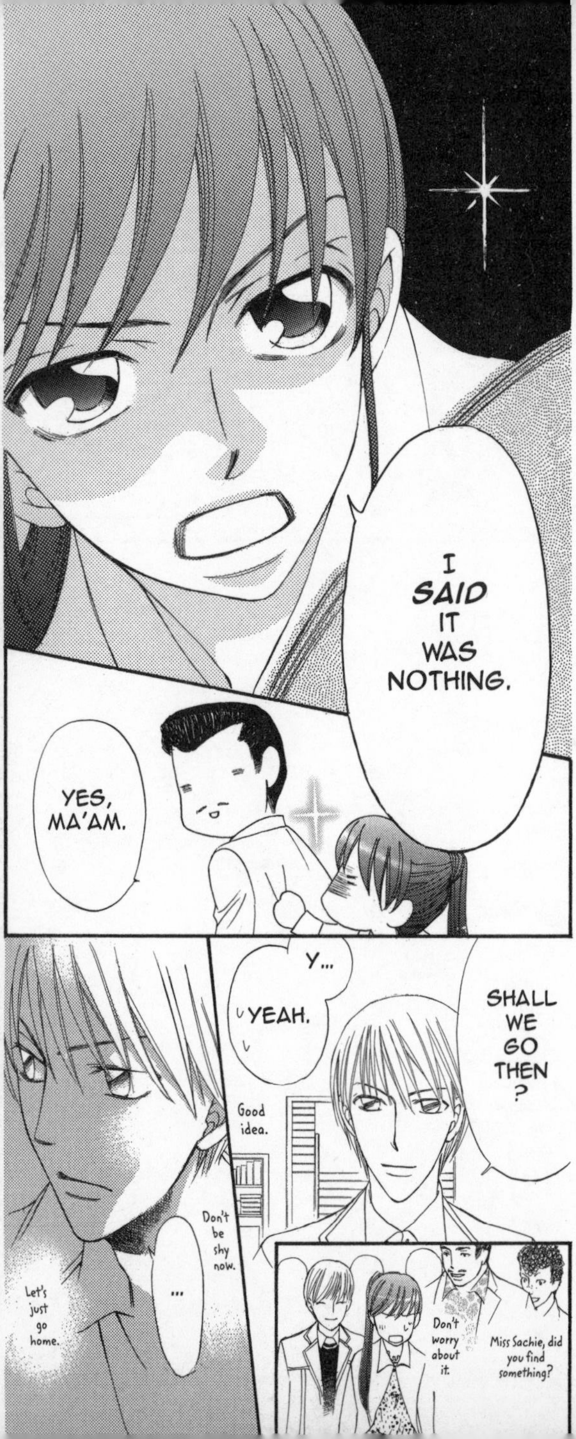
I SAID IT WAS NOTHING.
YES, MA'AM.
SHALL WE GO THEN?
Y... YEAH.
Good idea.
Miss Sachie, did you find something?
Don't worry about it.
Don't be shy now.
...
Let's just go home.

I'VE GOTTEN A LOT OF SUPPORT, AND THAT'S THE REASON I'VE BEEN ABLE TO CONTINUE.

THANK YOU!

MAESHIMA-SAN
SHI-CHAN
OUKOSHI-SAN
ITO-SAN
IGARI-SAN
ON-SAN
NECCHI
AND...
MO-CHAN!!

I REALIZE HOW BUSY YOU ALL ARE, SO THANK YOU FOR EVERYTHING! AND TO ALL MY READERS AS WELL!
I'M GOING TO CONTINUE DOING MY BEST, SO I HOPE YOU'LL CONTINUE SUPPORTING ME!

JUNE 2005
KIYO FUJIWARA

HTTP://WWW016.UPP.SO-NET.NE.JP/ROS/

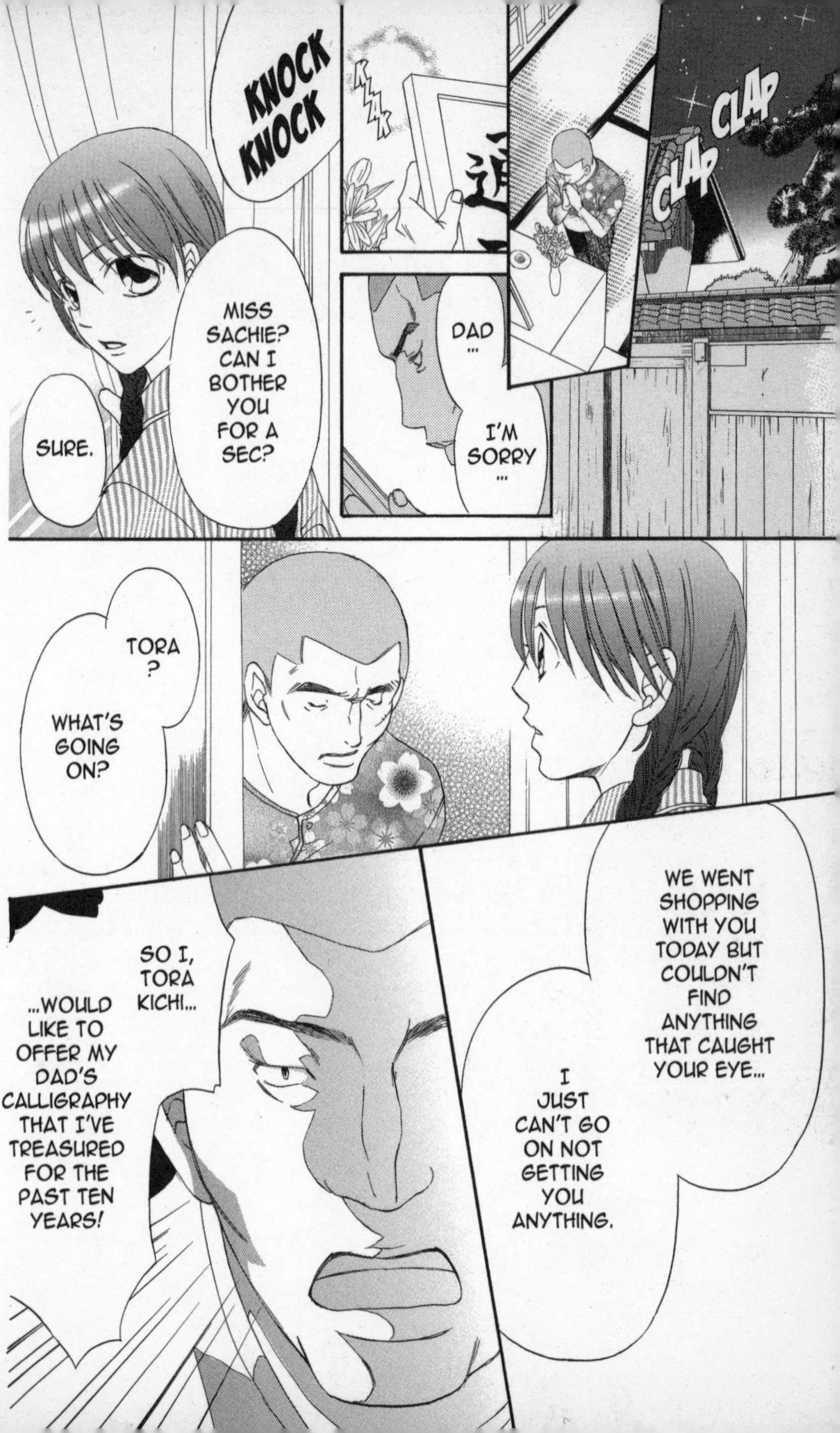
CLAP CLAP
KLAK
DAD ...
I'M SORRY ...
KNOCK KNOCK
MISS SACHIE? CAN I BOTHER YOU FOR A SEC?
SURE.
TORA ?
WHAT'S GOING ON?
WE WENT SHOPPING WITH YOU TODAY BUT COULDN'T FIND ANYTHING THAT CAUGHT YOUR EYE...
I JUST CAN'T GO ON NOT GETTING YOU ANYTHING.
SO I, TORA KICHI...
...WOULD LIKE TO OFFER MY DAD'S CALLIGRAPHY THAT I'VE TREASURED FOR THE PAST TEN YEARS!

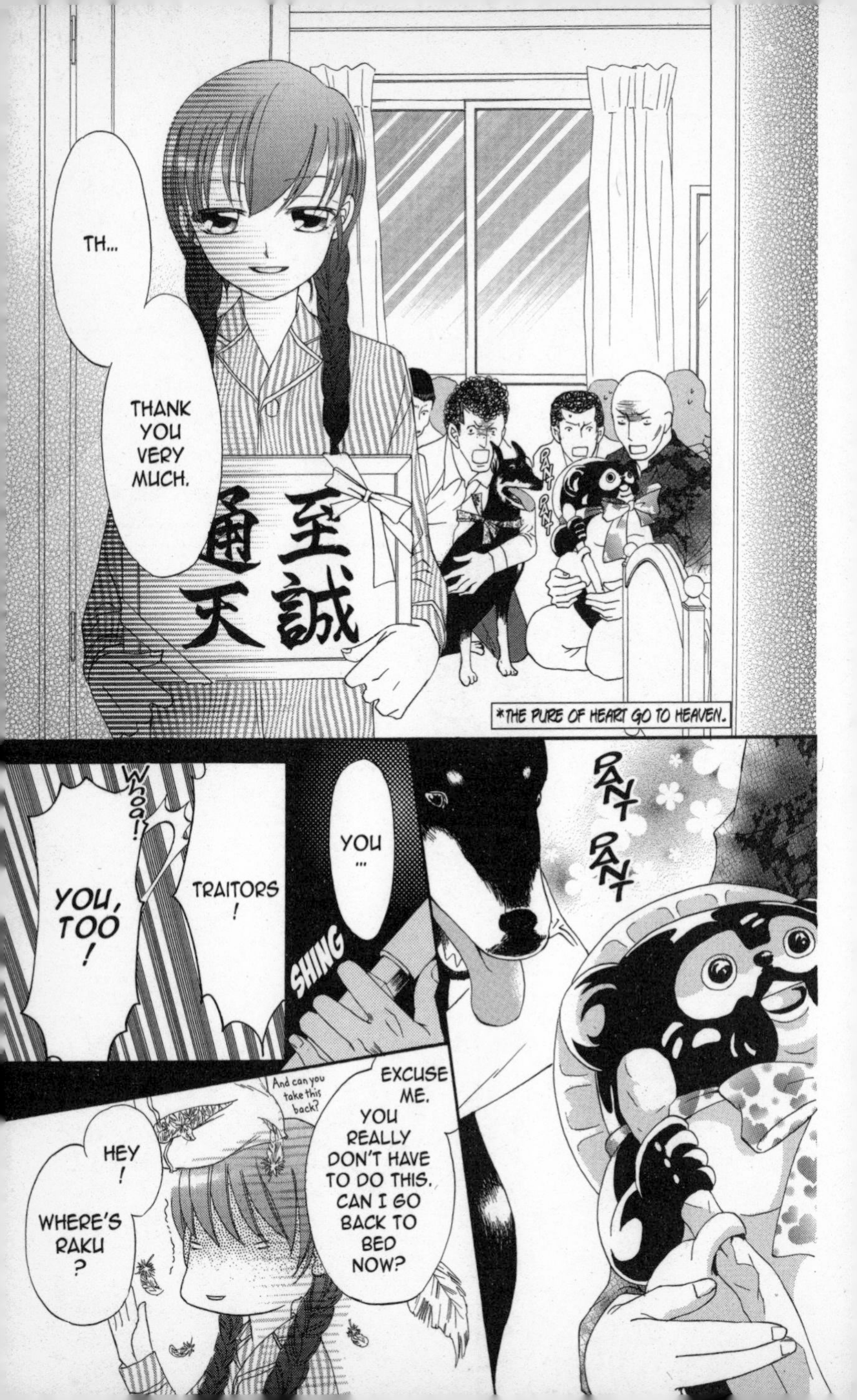
TH...
THANK YOU VERY MUCH.
至誠通天
PANT PANT
*THE PURE OF HEART GO TO HEAVEN.
PANT PANT
YOU ...
SHING
TRAITORS!
Whoa!
YOU, TOO!
EXCUSE ME. YOU REALLY DON'T HAVE TO DO THIS. CAN I GO BACK TO BED NOW?
And can you take this back?
HEY!
WHERE'S RAKU?

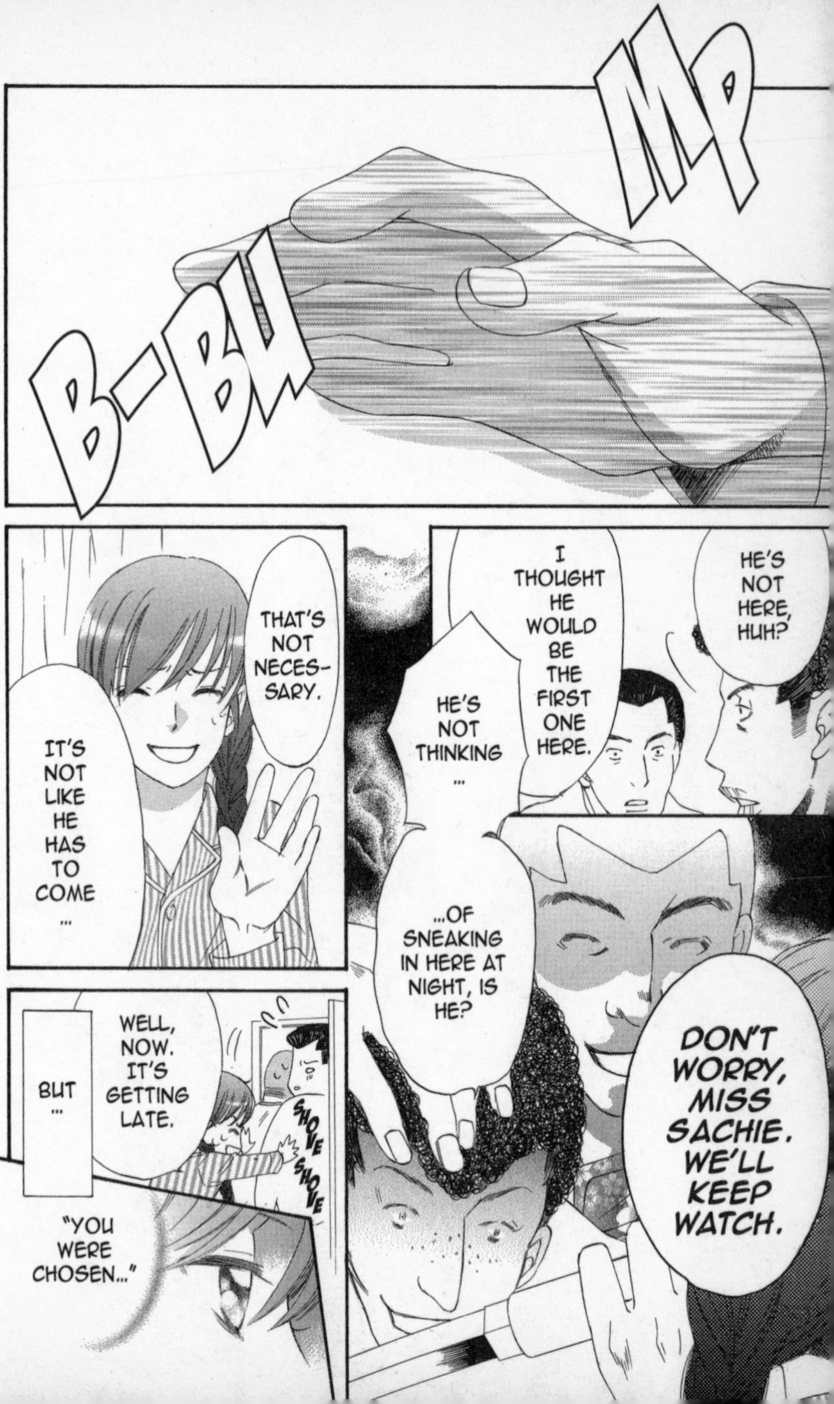
B-BUMP
HE'S NOT HERE, HUH?
I THOUGHT HE WOULD BE THE FIRST ONE HERE.
HE'S NOT THINKING...
...OF SNEAKING IN HERE AT NIGHT, IS HE?
THAT'S NOT NECES-SARY.
IT'S NOT LIKE HE HAS TO COME...
DON'T WORRY, MISS SACHIE. WE'LL KEEP WATCH.
WELL, NOW. IT'S GETTING LATE.
SHOVE SHOVE
BUT...
"YOU WERE CHOSEN..."

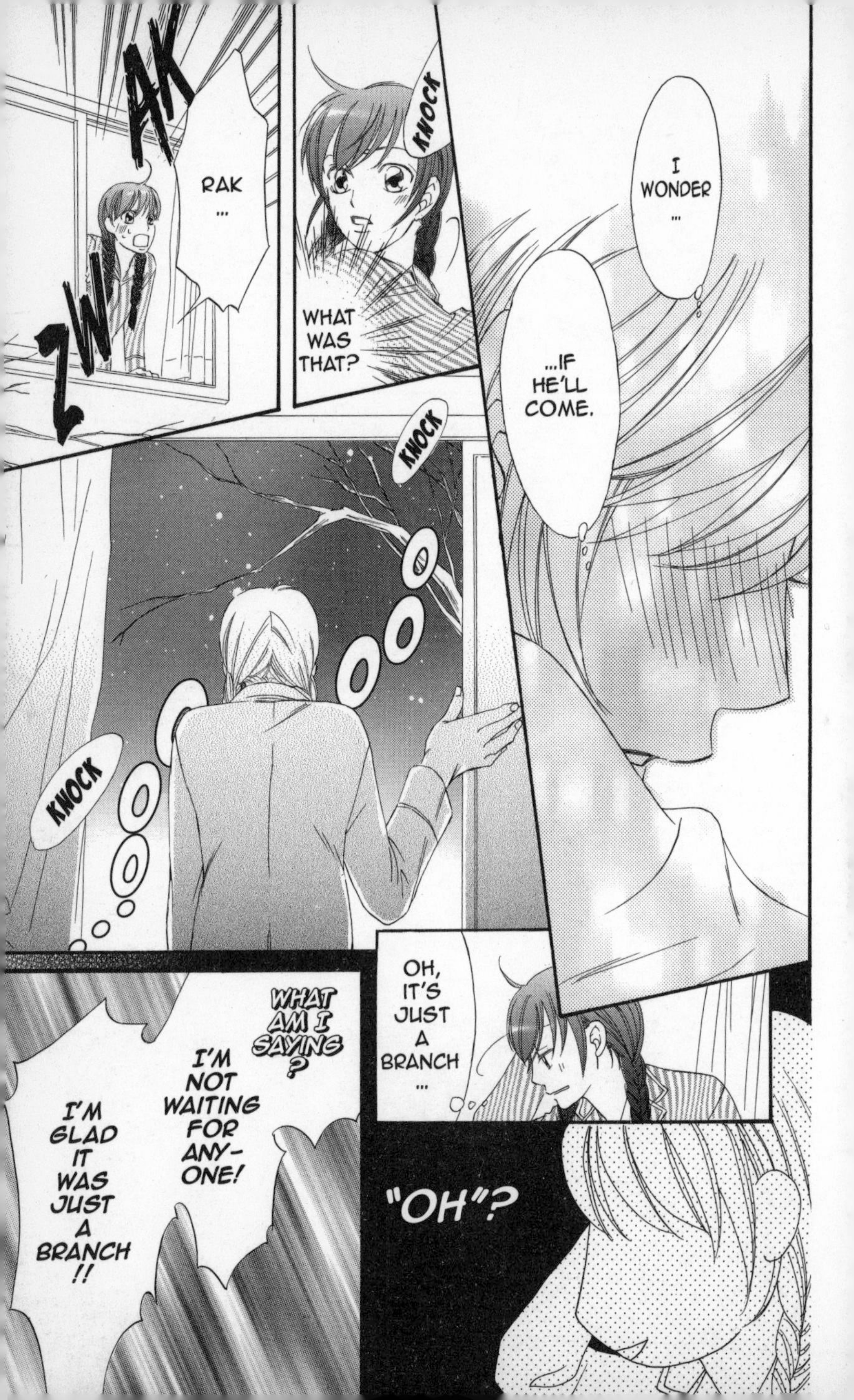
I WONDER ...
...IF HE'LL COME.
KNOCK
WHAT WAS THAT?
ZWAK
RAK ...
KNOCK
KNOCK
OH, IT'S JUST A BRANCH ...
"OH"?
WHAT AM I SAYING?
I'M NOT WAITING FOR ANY-ONE!
I'M GLAD IT WAS JUST A BRANCH!!

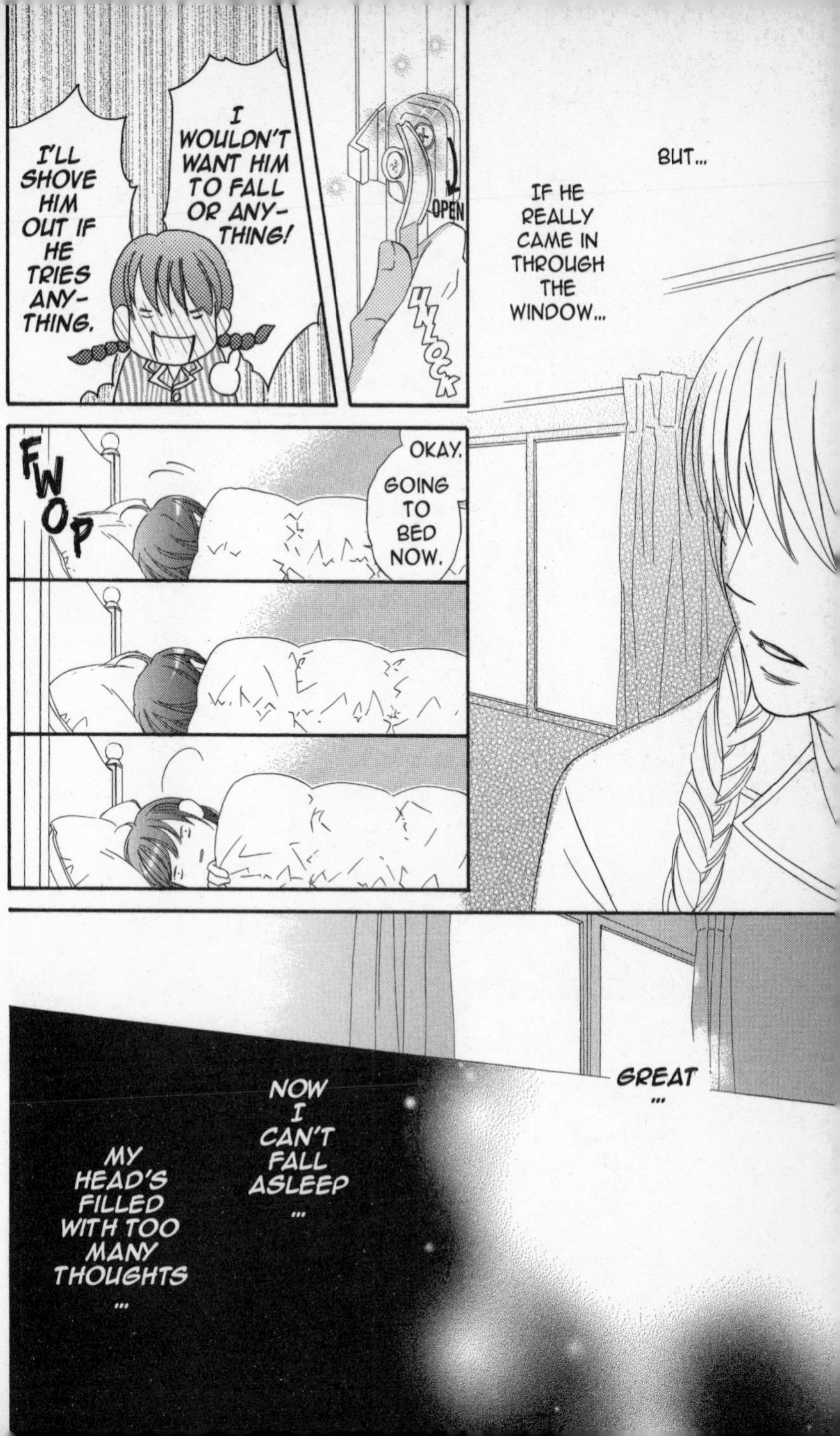
BUT...
IF HE REALLY CAME IN THROUGH THE WINDOW...
OPEN
UNLOCK
I WOULDN'T WANT HIM TO FALL OR ANYTHING!
I'LL SHOVE HIM OUT IF HE TRIES ANYTHING.
OKAY. GOING TO BED NOW.
FWOP
GREAT...
NOW I CAN'T FALL ASLEEP...
MY HEAD'S FILLED WITH TOO MANY THOUGHTS...

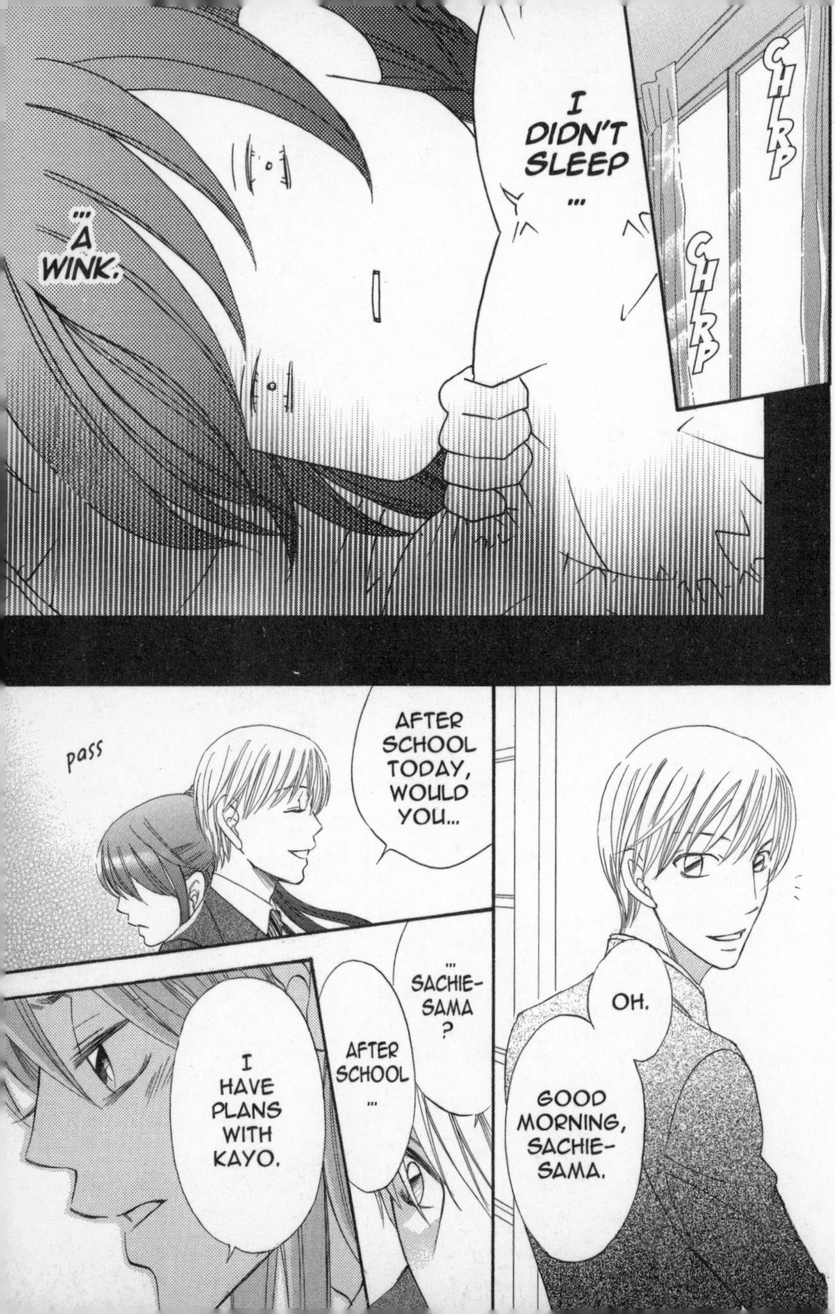
CHIRP
CHIRP
I DIDN'T SLEEP ...
... A WINK.
OH.
GOOD MORNING, SACHIE-SAMA.
AFTER SCHOOL TODAY, WOULD YOU...
pass
... SACHIE-SAMA ?
AFTER SCHOOL ...
I HAVE PLANS WITH KAYO.

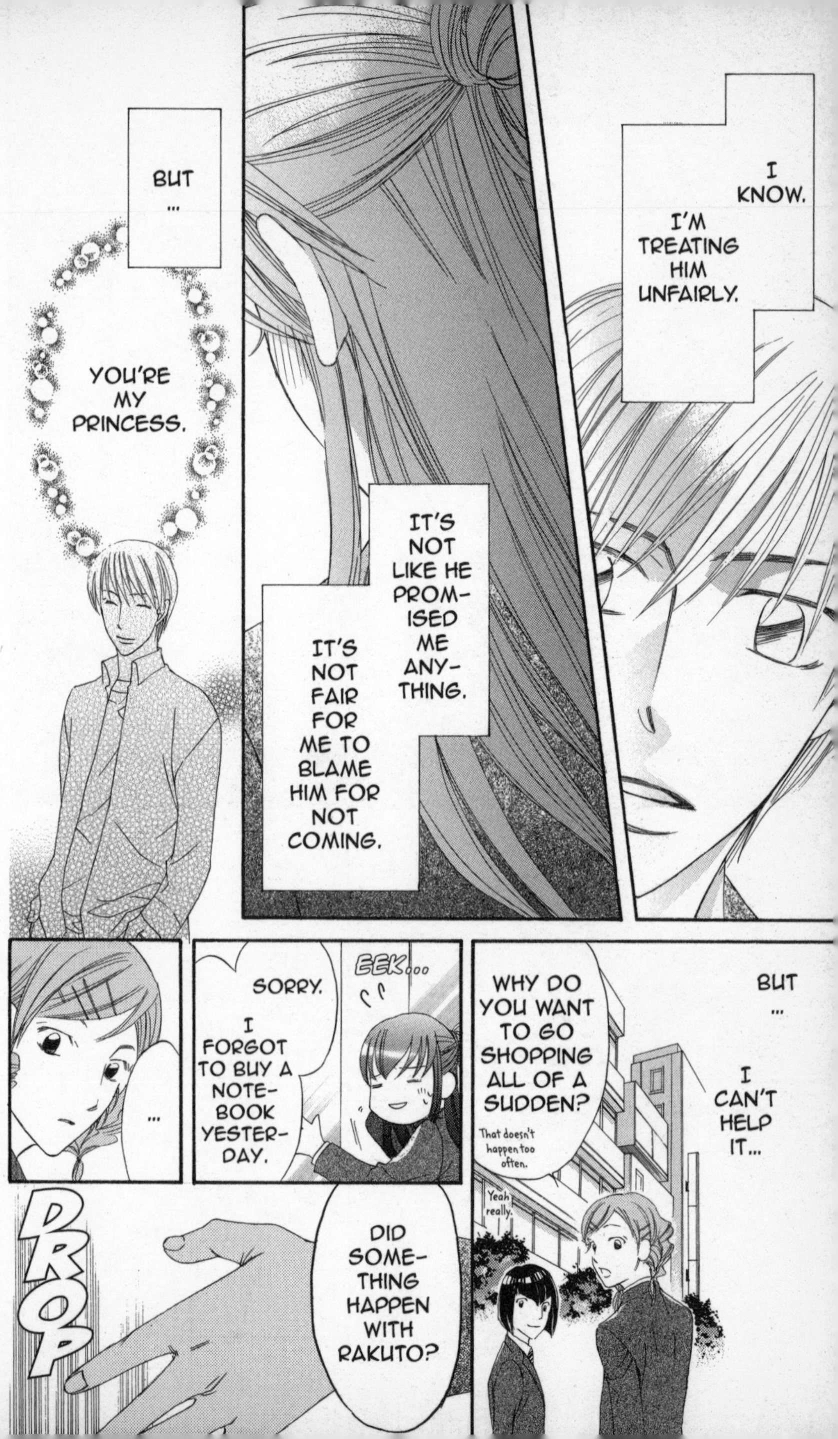
I KNOW.
I'M TREATING HIM UNFAIRLY.
IT'S NOT LIKE HE PROMISED ME ANYTHING.
IT'S NOT FAIR FOR ME TO BLAME HIM FOR NOT COMING.
BUT ...
YOU'RE MY PRINCESS.
BUT ...
I CAN'T HELP IT...
WHY DO YOU WANT TO GO SHOPPING ALL OF A SUDDEN?
That doesn't happen too often.
Yeah really.
EEK...
SORRY.
I FORGOT TO BUY A NOTE-BOOK YESTER-DAY.
...
DID SOME-THING HAPPEN WITH RAKUTO?
DROP

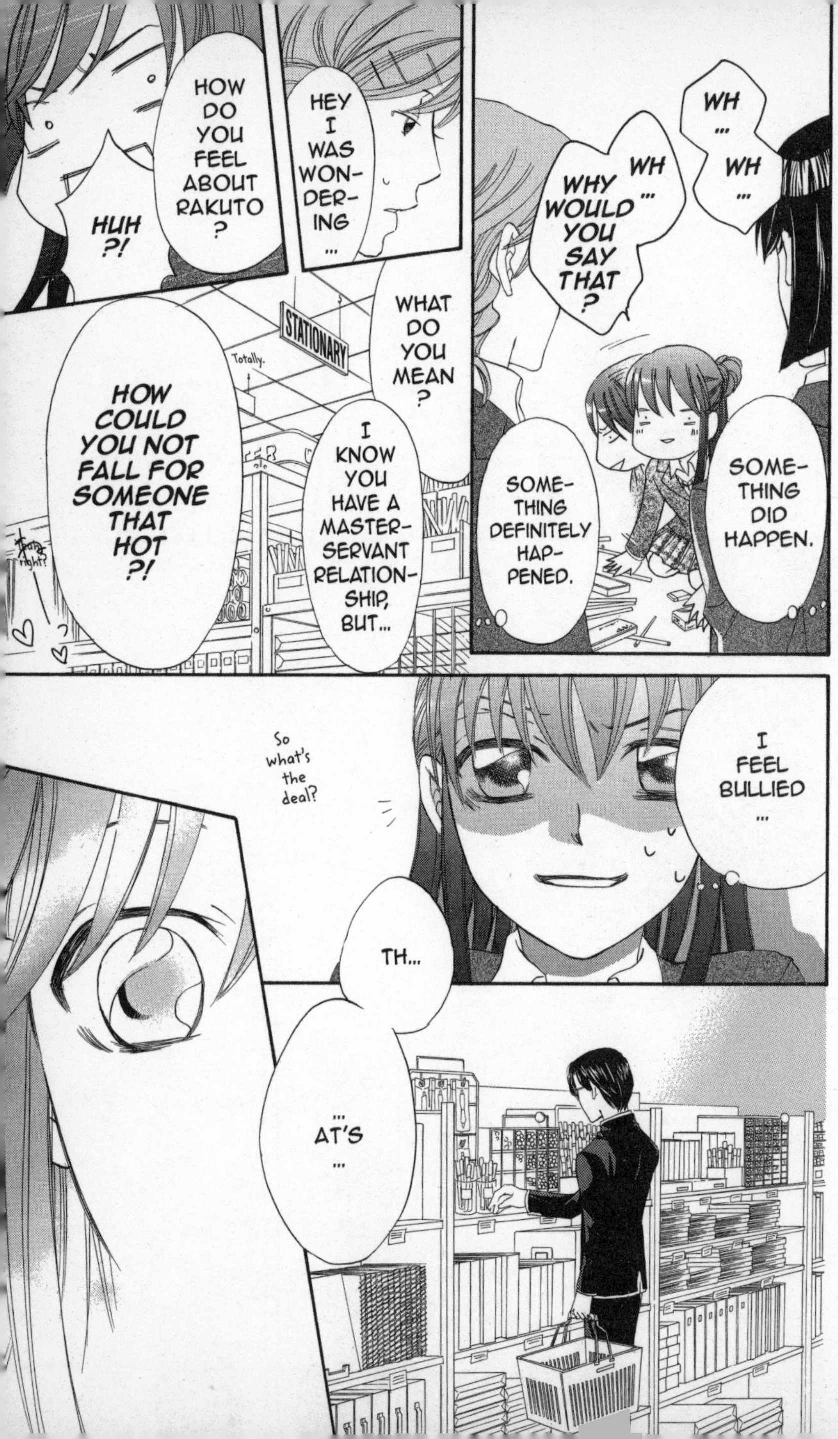
WH... WH...
WH...
WHY WOULD YOU SAY THAT?
SOMETHING DID HAPPEN.
SOMETHING DEFINITELY HAPPENED.
HEY I WAS WONDERING...
HOW DO YOU FEEL ABOUT RAKUTO?
HUH?!
STATIONARY
WHAT DO YOU MEAN?
I KNOW YOU HAVE A MASTER-SERVANT RELATIONSHIP, BUT...
Totally.
HOW COULD YOU NOT FALL FOR SOMEONE THAT HOT?!
right?
I FEEL BULLIED...
So what's the deal?
TH...
...AT'S...

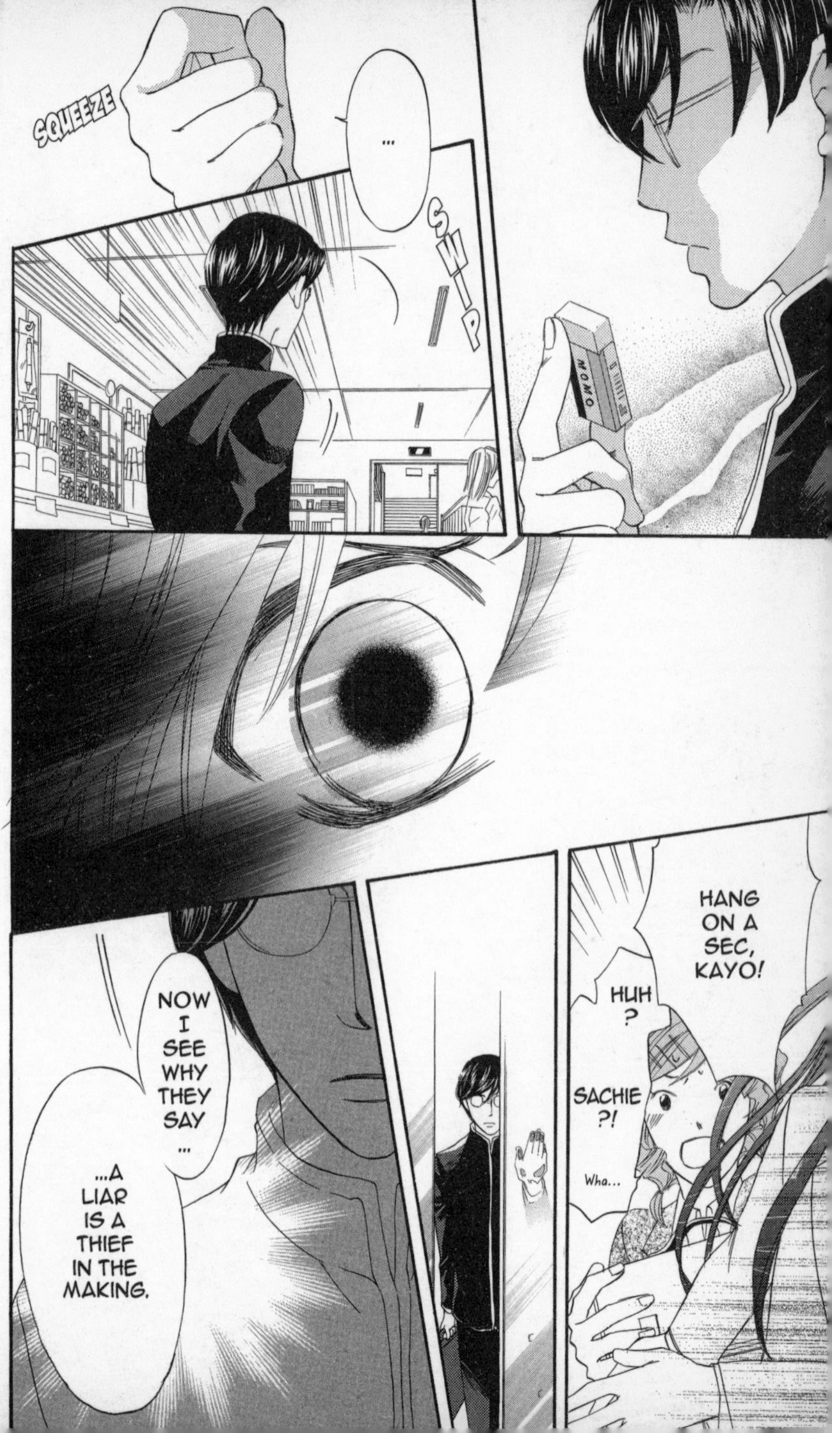
SQUEEZE
...
SWIP
MOMO
HANG ON A SEC, KAYO!
HUH?
SACHIE?!
Wha...
NOW I SEE WHY THEY SAY...
...A LIAR IS A THIEF IN THE MAKING.

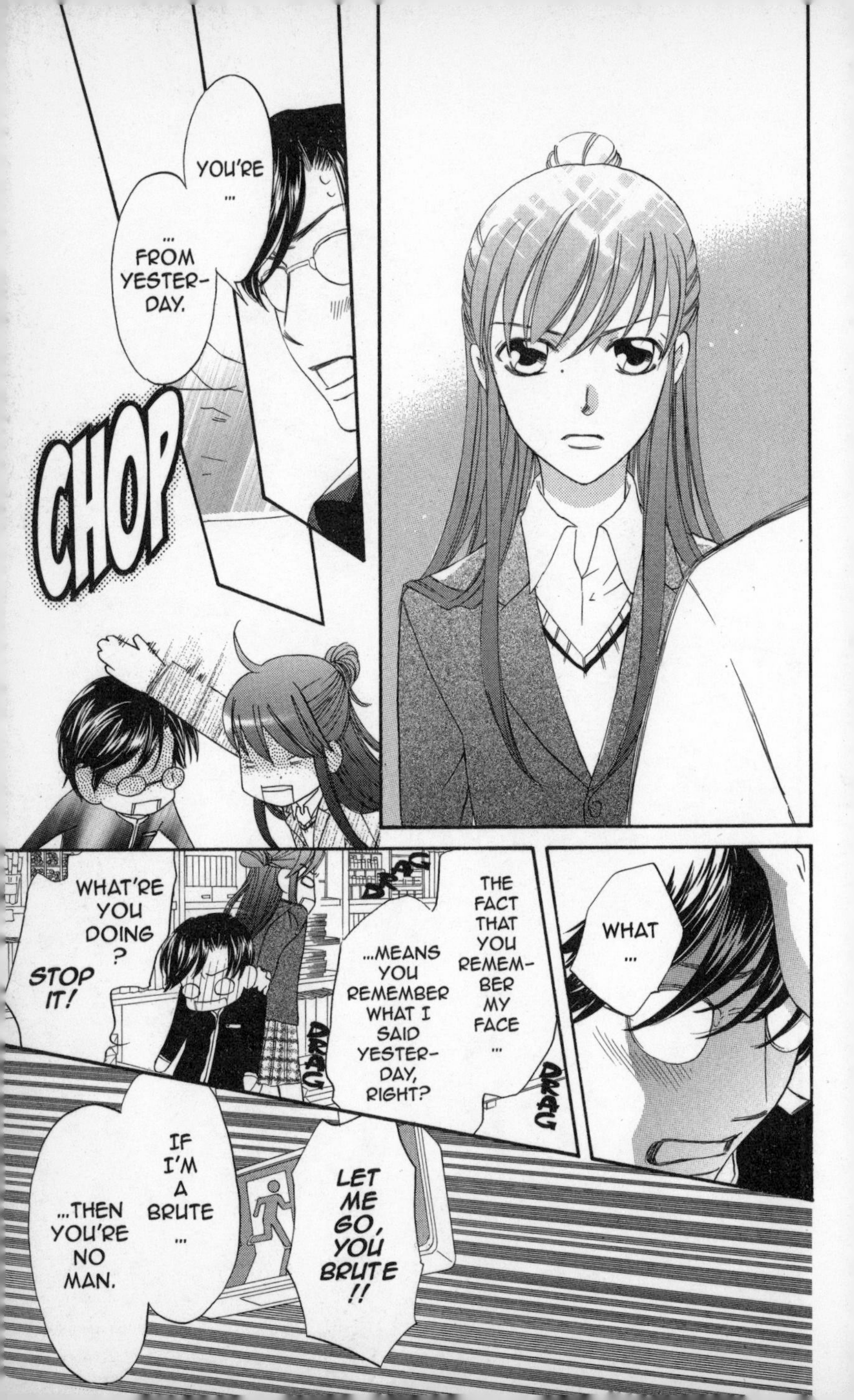
YOU'RE ...
... FROM YESTER-DAY.
CHOP
WHAT ...
DRAG
THE FACT THAT YOU REMEM-BER MY FACE ...
...MEANS YOU REMEMBER WHAT I SAID YESTER-DAY, RIGHT?
DRAG
DRAG
WHAT'RE YOU DOING?
STOP IT!
LET ME GO, YOU BRUTE!!
IF I'M A BRUTE ...
...THEN YOU'RE NO MAN.

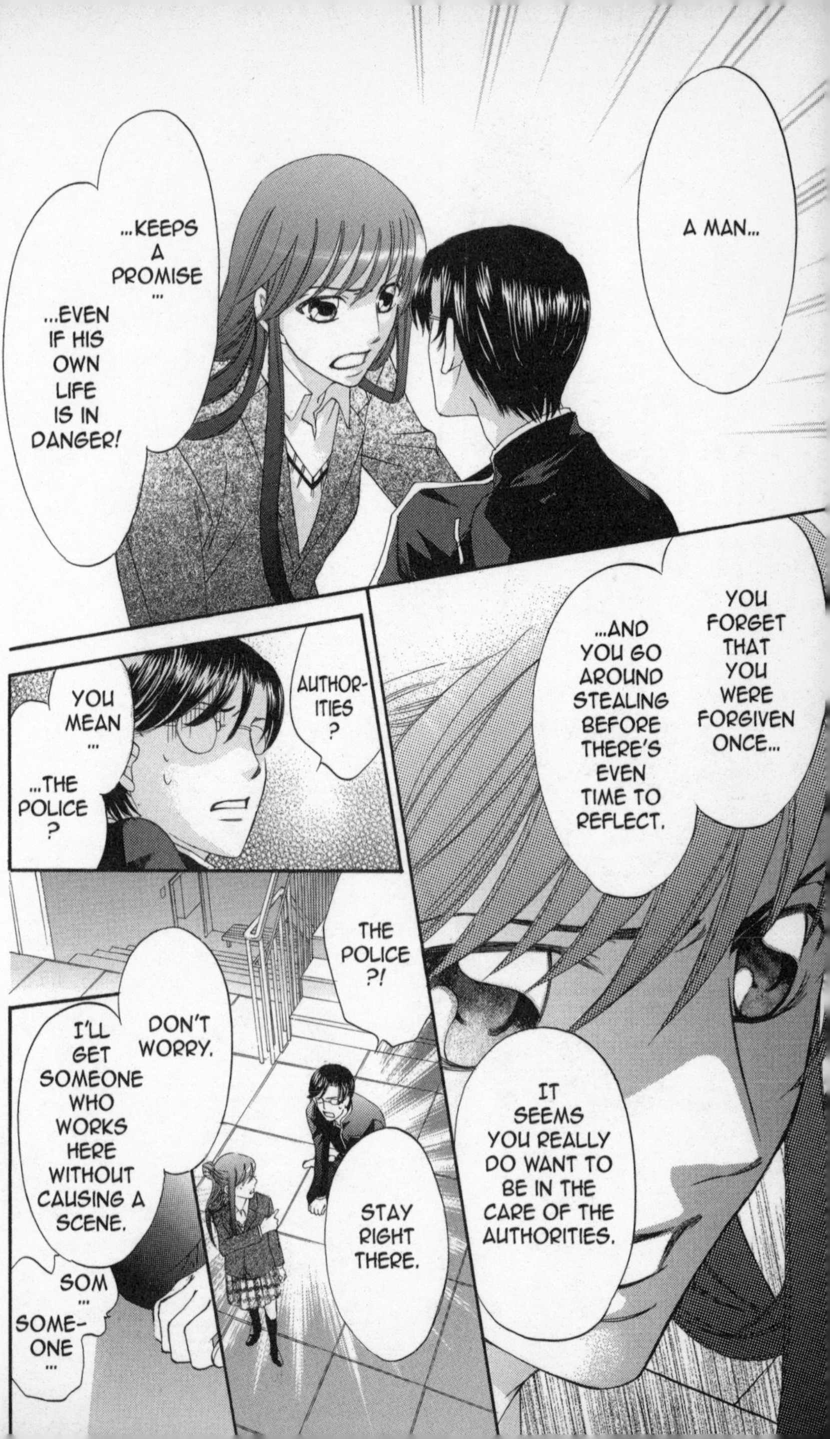
A MAN...
...KEEPS A PROMISE ...
...EVEN IF HIS OWN LIFE IS IN DANGER!
YOU FORGET THAT YOU WERE FORGIVEN ONCE...
...AND YOU GO AROUND STEALING BEFORE THERE'S EVEN TIME TO REFLECT.
IT SEEMS YOU REALLY DO WANT TO BE IN THE CARE OF THE AUTHORITIES.
AUTHOR-ITIES ?
YOU MEAN ...
...THE POLICE ?
THE POLICE ?!
DON'T WORRY.
I'LL GET SOMEONE WHO WORKS HERE WITHOUT CAUSING A SCENE.
STAY RIGHT THERE.
SOM ... SOME-ONE ...

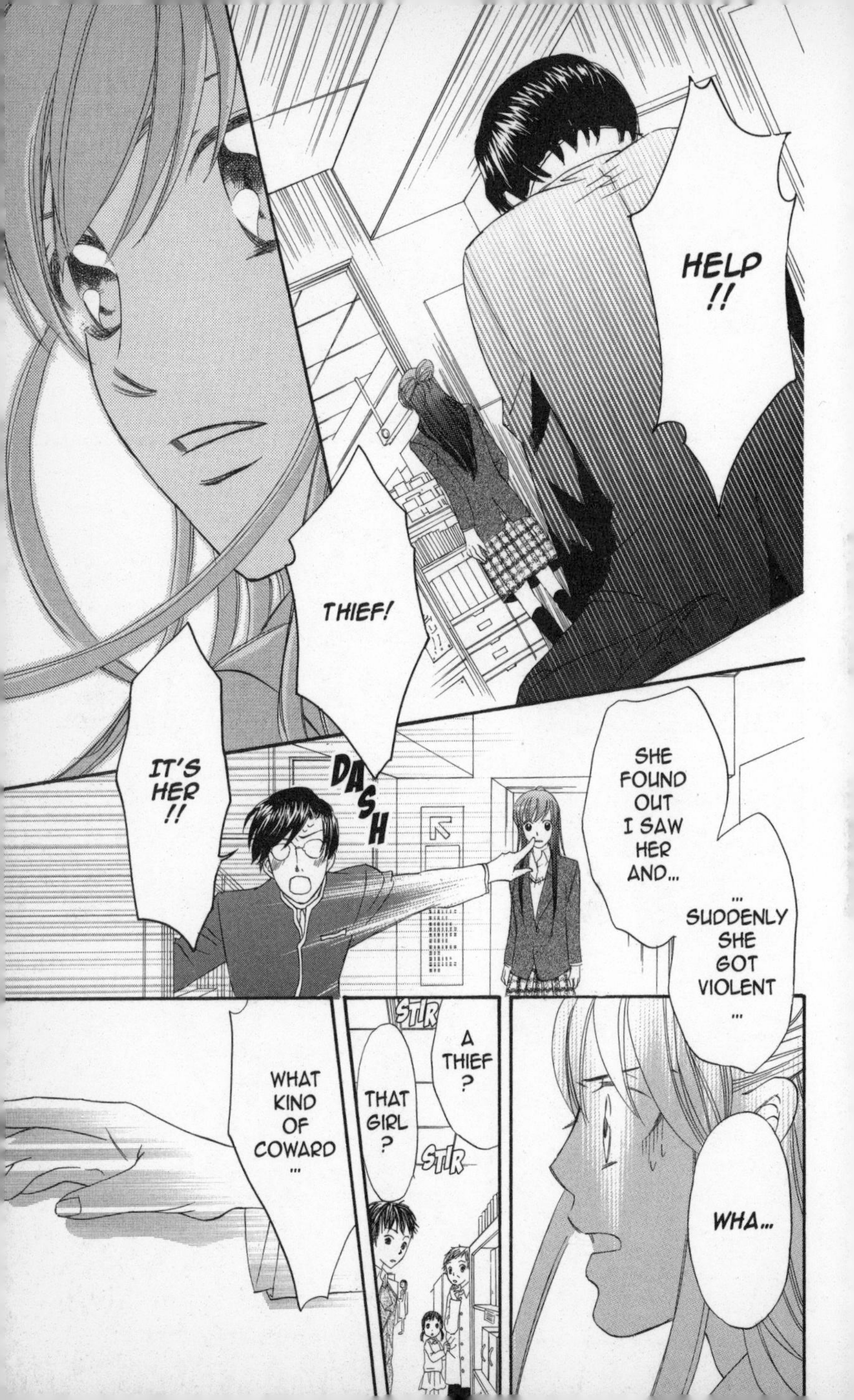
HELP!!
THIEF!
SHE FOUND OUT I SAW HER AND...
... SUDDENLY SHE GOT VIOLENT ...
DASH
IT'S HER!!
WHA...
STIR
A THIEF?
THAT GIRL?
STIR
WHAT KIND OF COWARD ...

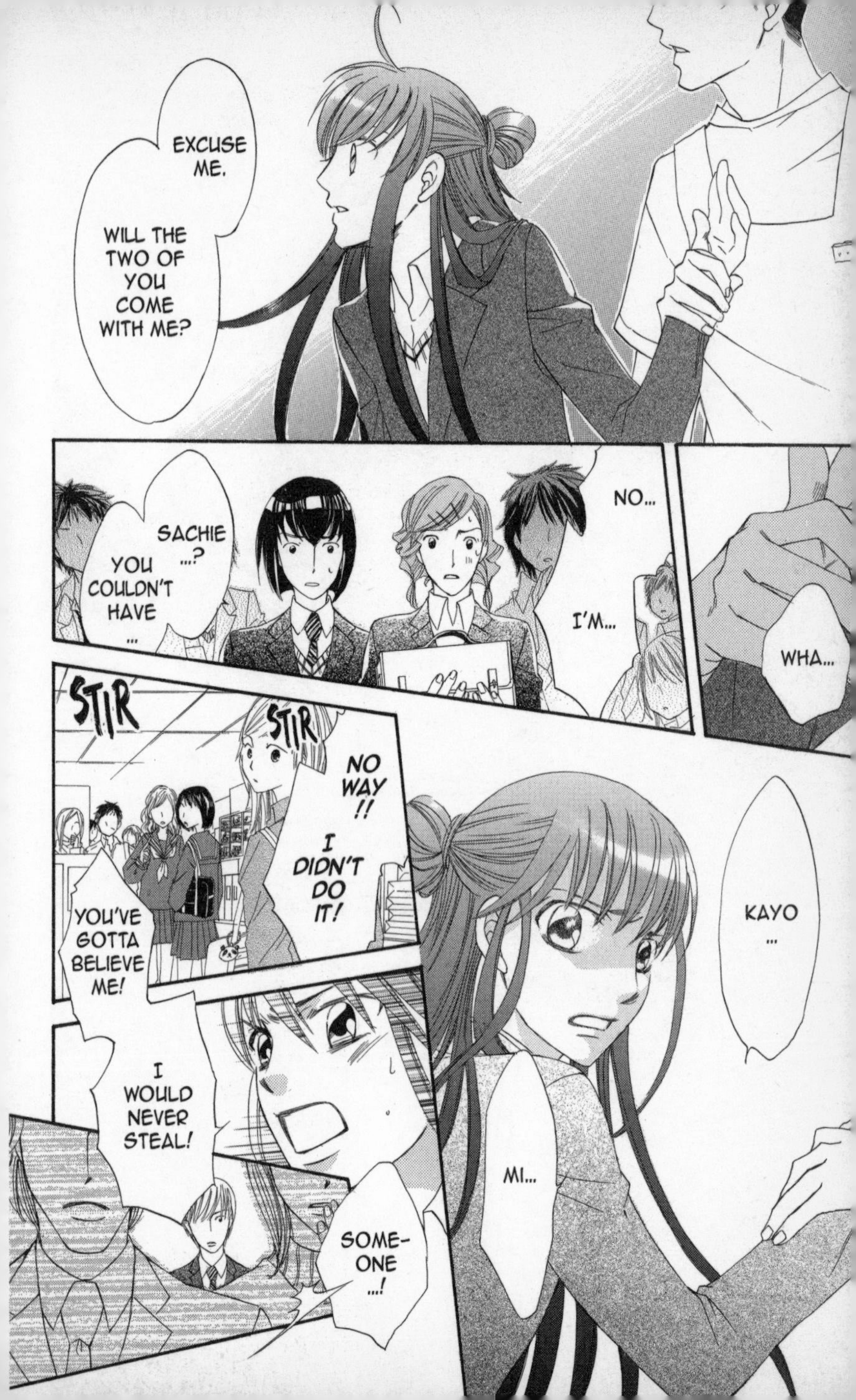
EXCUSE ME.
WILL THE TWO OF YOU COME WITH ME?
WHA...
NO...
I'M...
SACHIE ...?
YOU COULDN'T HAVE ...
STIR
STIR
NO WAY!!
I DIDN'T DO IT!
YOU'VE GOTTA BELIEVE ME!
KAYO ...
I WOULD NEVER STEAL!
MI...
SOME-ONE ...!

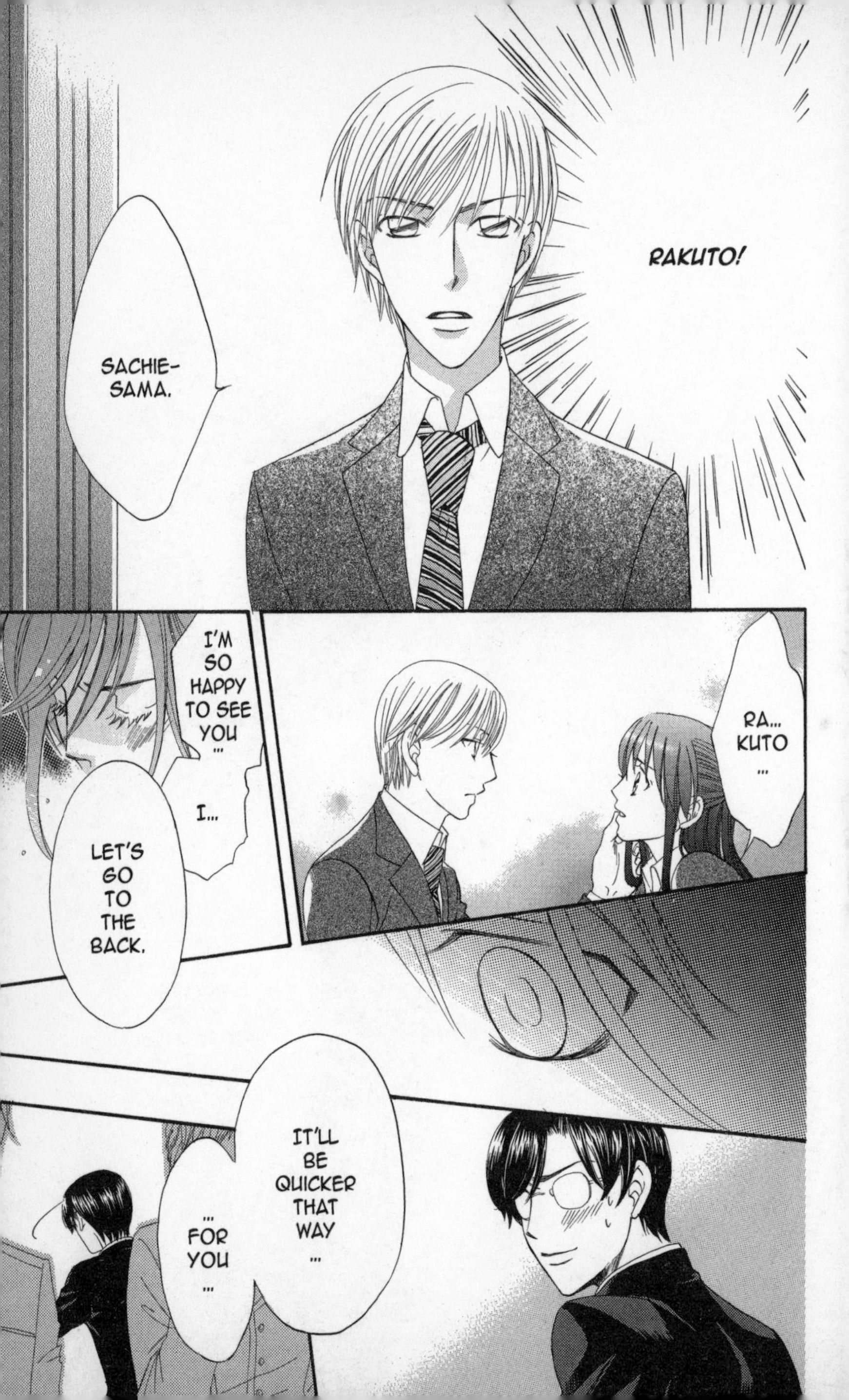
RAKUTO!
SACHIE-SAMA.
RA... KUTO ...
I'M SO HAPPY TO SEE YOU ...
I...
LET'S GO TO THE BACK.
IT'LL BE QUICKER THAT WAY ...
... FOR YOU ...

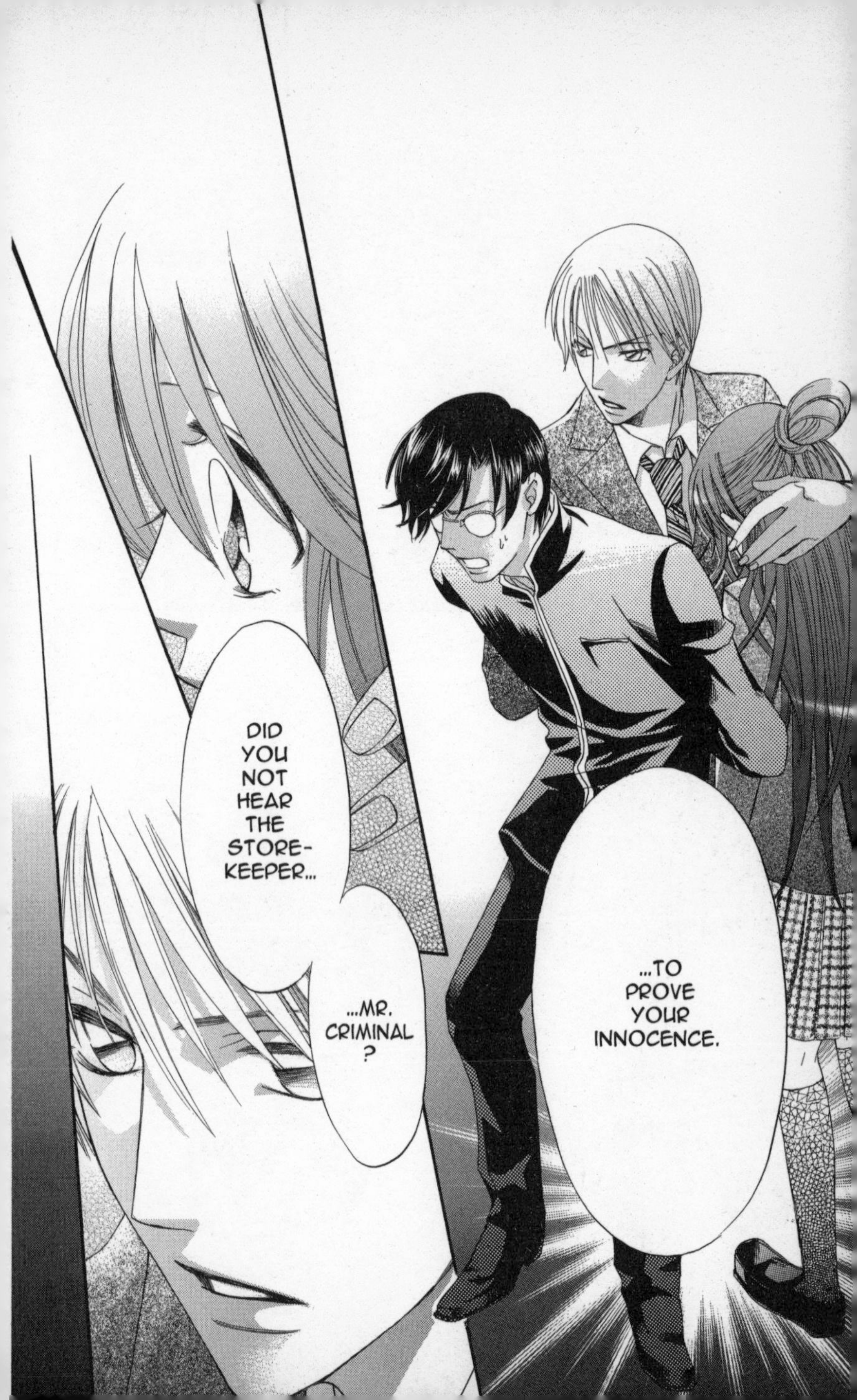
DID YOU NOT HEAR THE STORE-KEEPER...
...MR. CRIMINAL?
...TO PROVE YOUR INNOCENCE.

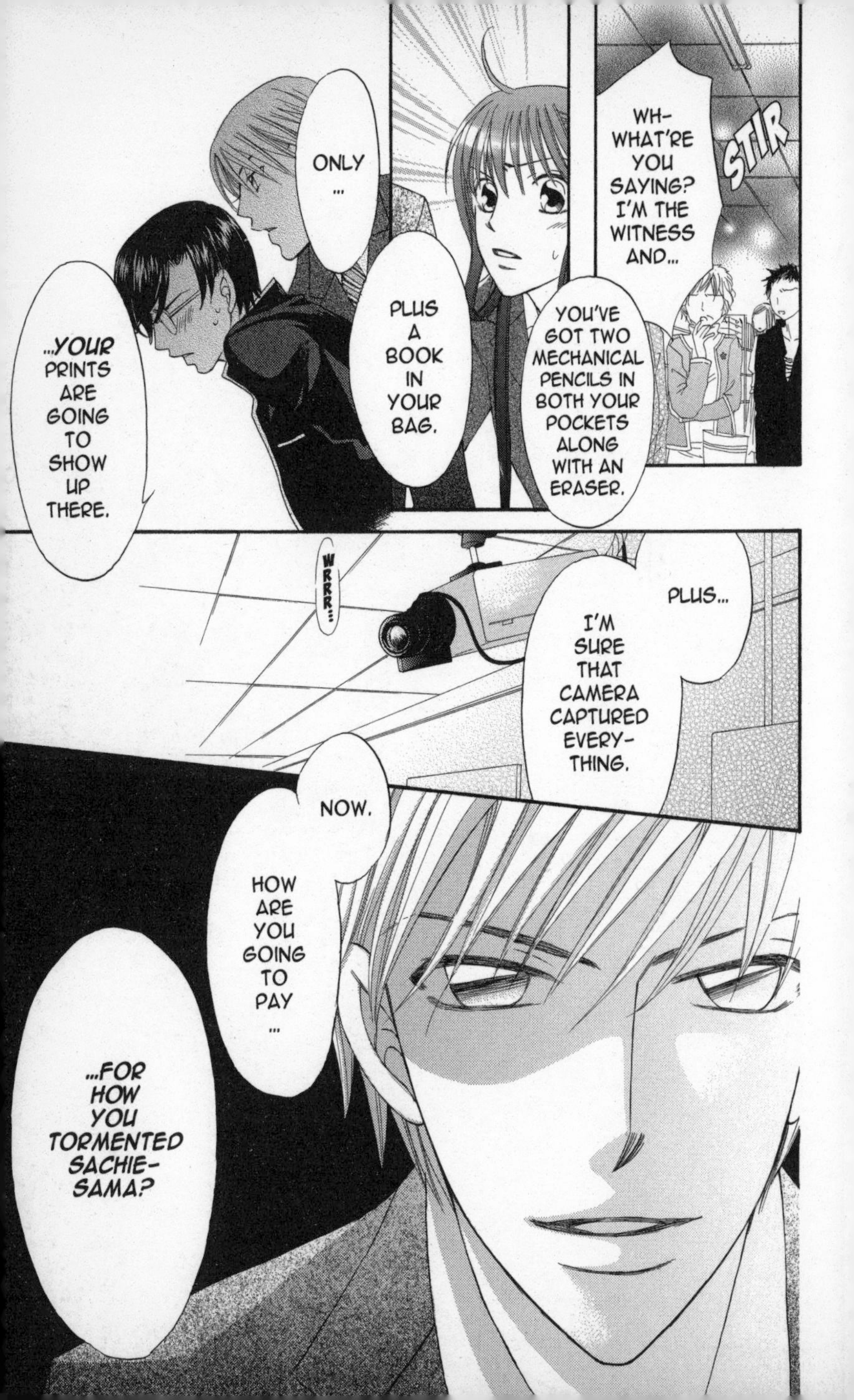
WH- WHAT'RE YOU SAYING? I'M THE WITNESS AND...
STIR
YOU'VE GOT TWO MECHANICAL PENCILS IN BOTH YOUR POCKETS ALONG WITH AN ERASER.
PLUS A BOOK IN YOUR BAG.
ONLY ...
...YOUR PRINTS ARE GOING TO SHOW UP THERE.
PLUS...
I'M SURE THAT CAMERA CAPTURED EVERY-THING.
WRRR...
NOW.
HOW ARE YOU GOING TO PAY ...
...FOR HOW YOU TORMENTED SACHIE-SAMA?

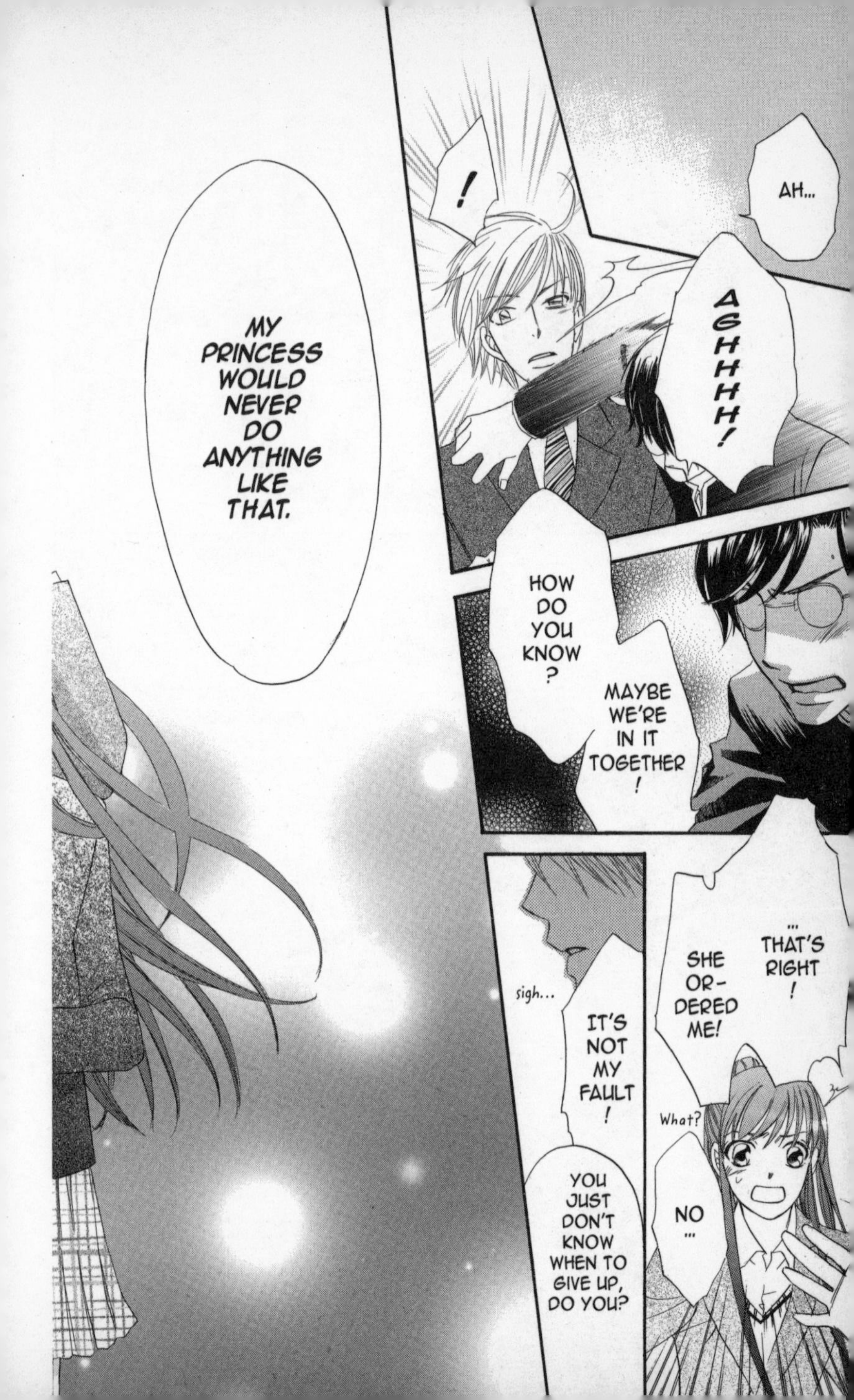
AH...
AGHHHH!
!
HOW DO YOU KNOW?
MAYBE WE'RE IN IT TOGETHER!
...THAT'S RIGHT!
SHE OR-DERED ME!
sigh...
IT'S NOT MY FAULT!
What?
NO...
YOU JUST DON'T KNOW WHEN TO GIVE UP, DO YOU?
MY PRINCESS WOULD NEVER DO ANYTHING LIKE THAT.

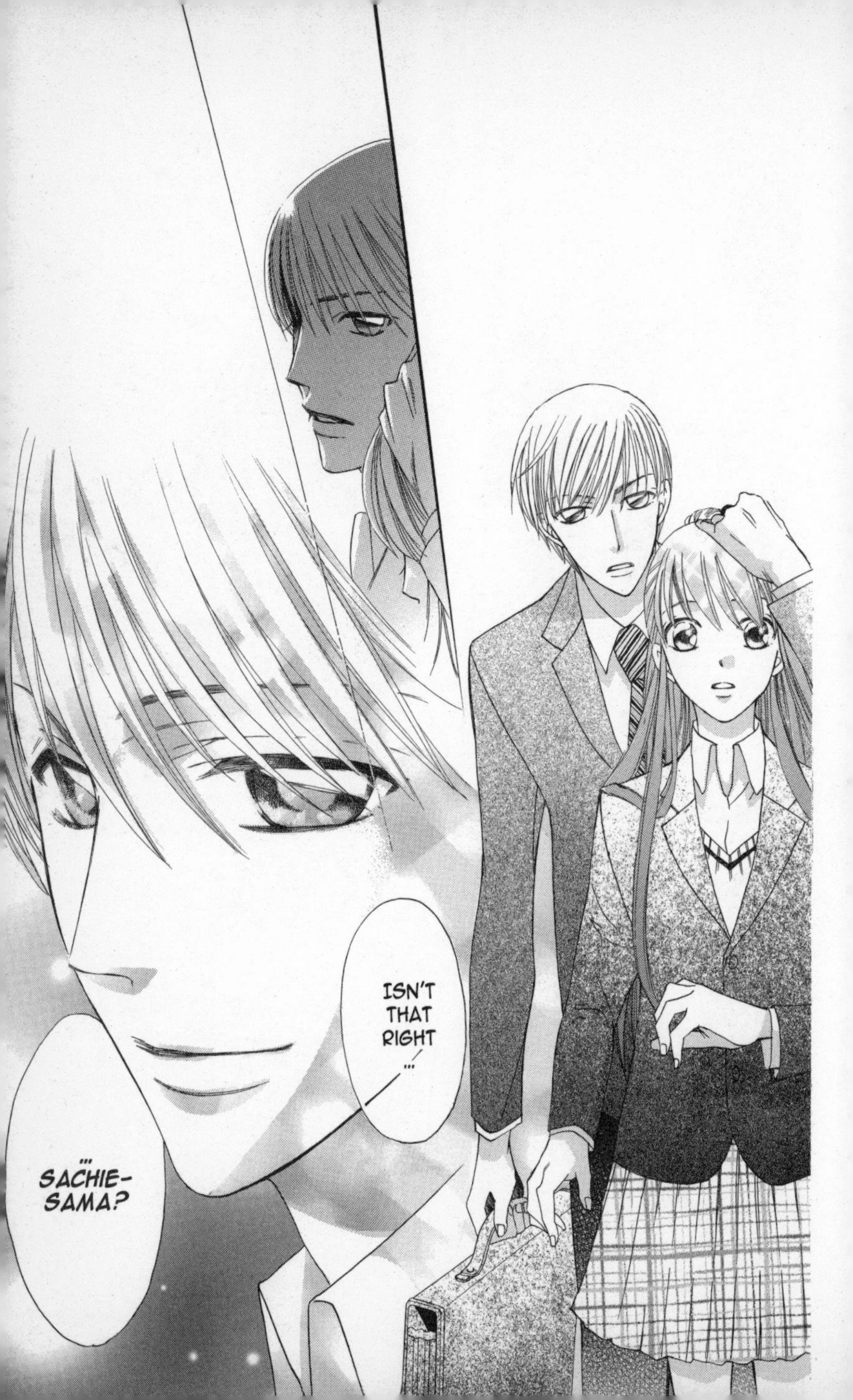
ISN'T THAT RIGHT...
...SACHIE-SAMA?

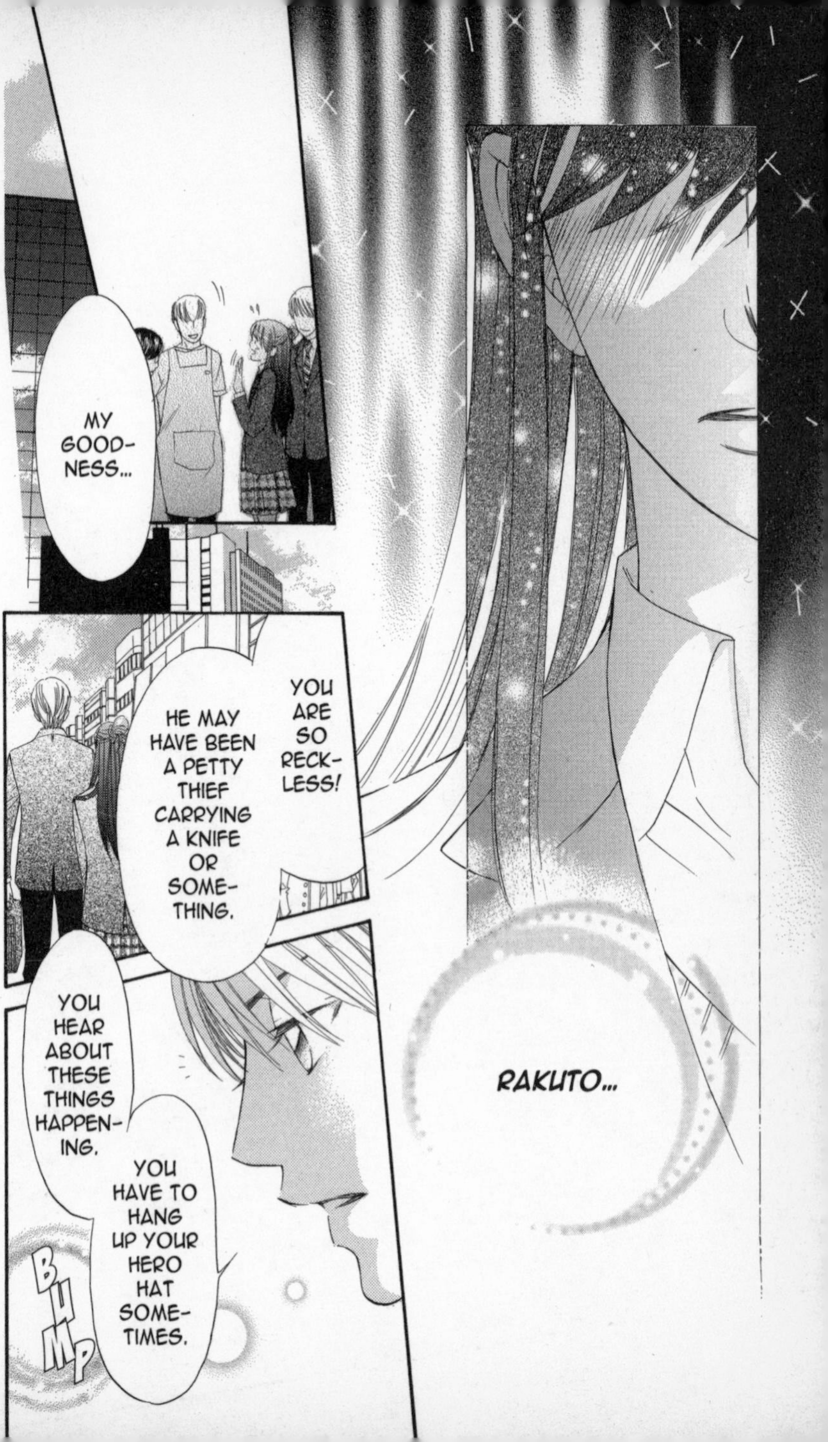
RAKUTO...
MY GOODNESS...
YOU ARE SO RECKLESS!
HE MAY HAVE BEEN A PETTY THIEF CARRYING A KNIFE OR SOMETHING.
YOU HEAR ABOUT THESE THINGS HAPPENING.
YOU HAVE TO HANG UP YOUR HERO HAT SOMETIMES.
BUMP

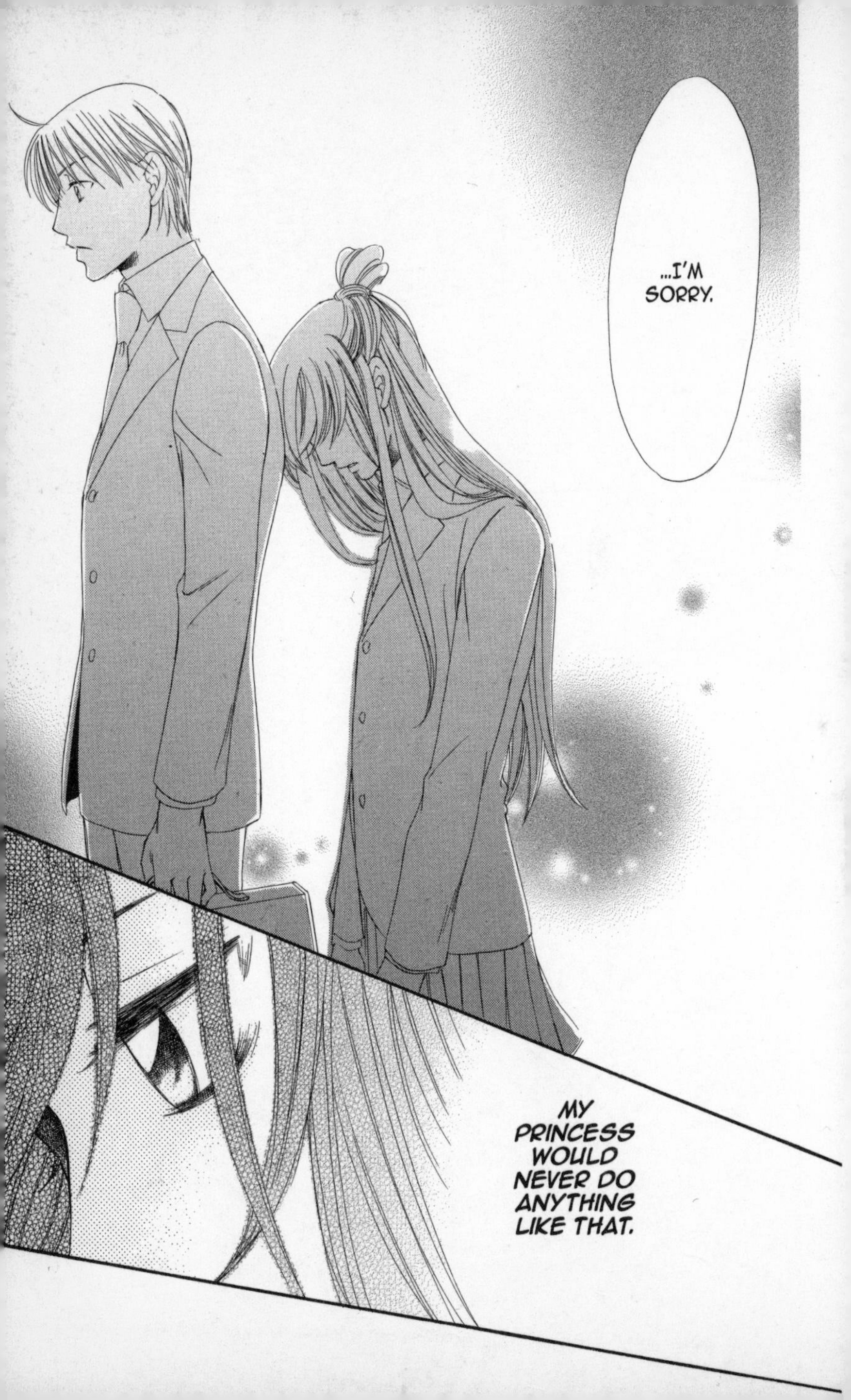
...I'M SORRY.
MY PRINCESS WOULD NEVER DO ANYTHING LIKE THAT.

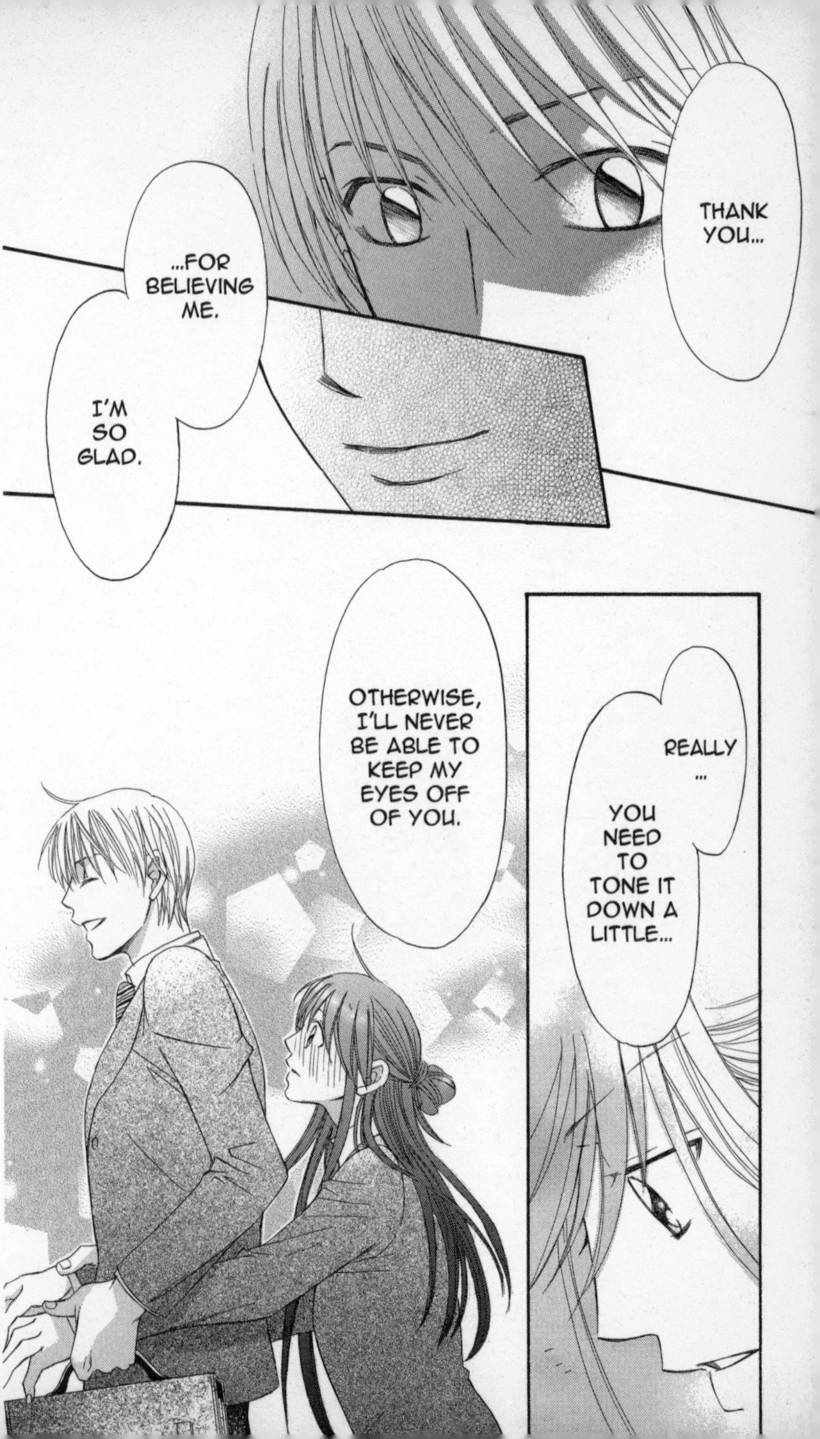
THANK YOU...
...FOR BELIEVING ME.
I'M SO GLAD.
REALLY... YOU NEED TO TONE IT DOWN A LITTLE...
OTHERWISE, I'LL NEVER BE ABLE TO KEEP MY EYES OFF OF YOU.

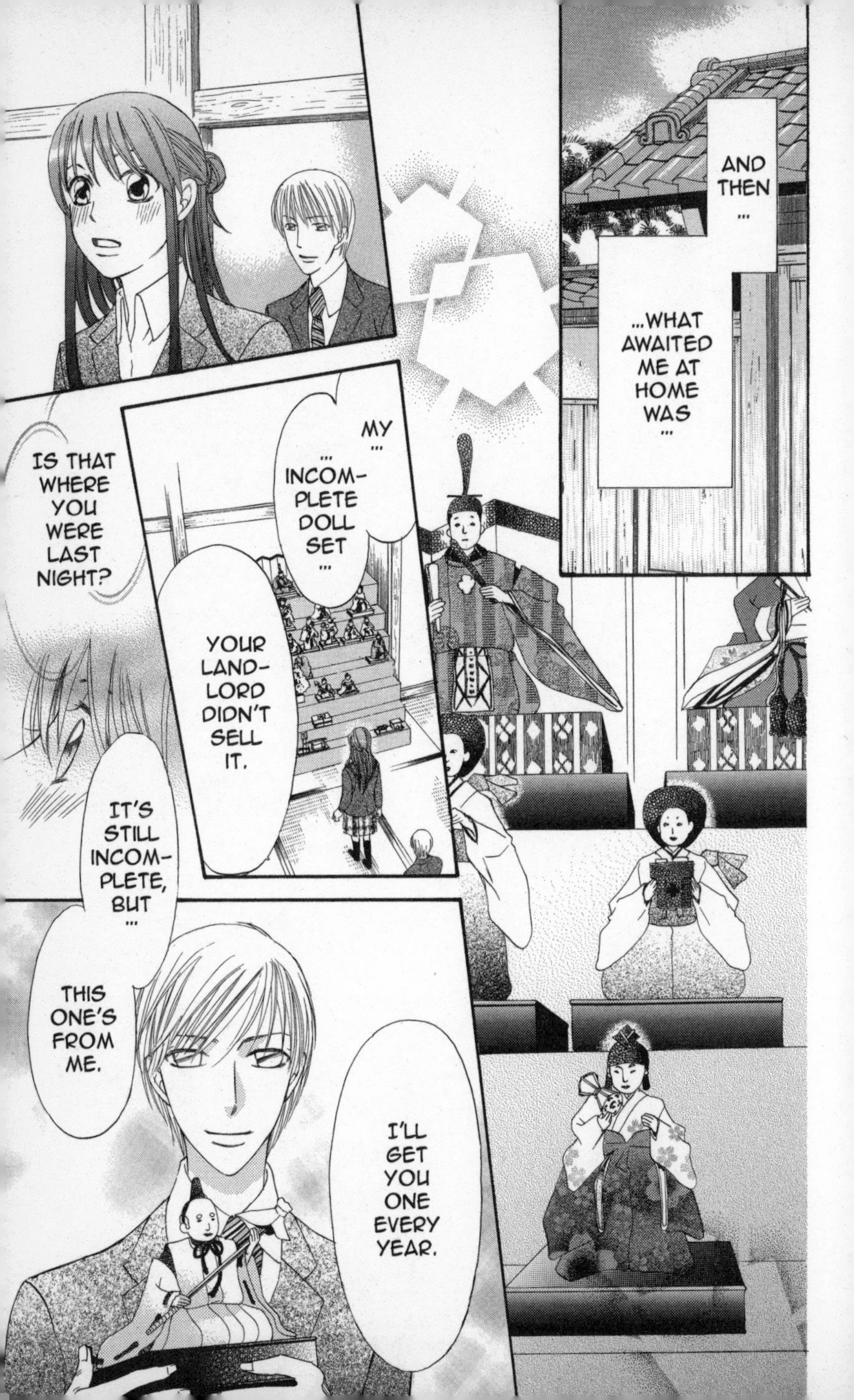
AND THEN ...
...WHAT AWAITED ME AT HOME WAS ...
MY ... INCOMPLETE DOLL SET ...
YOUR LANDLORD DIDN'T SELL IT.
IS THAT WHERE YOU WERE LAST NIGHT?
IT'S STILL INCOMPLETE, BUT ...
THIS ONE'S FROM ME.
I'LL GET YOU ONE EVERY YEAR.

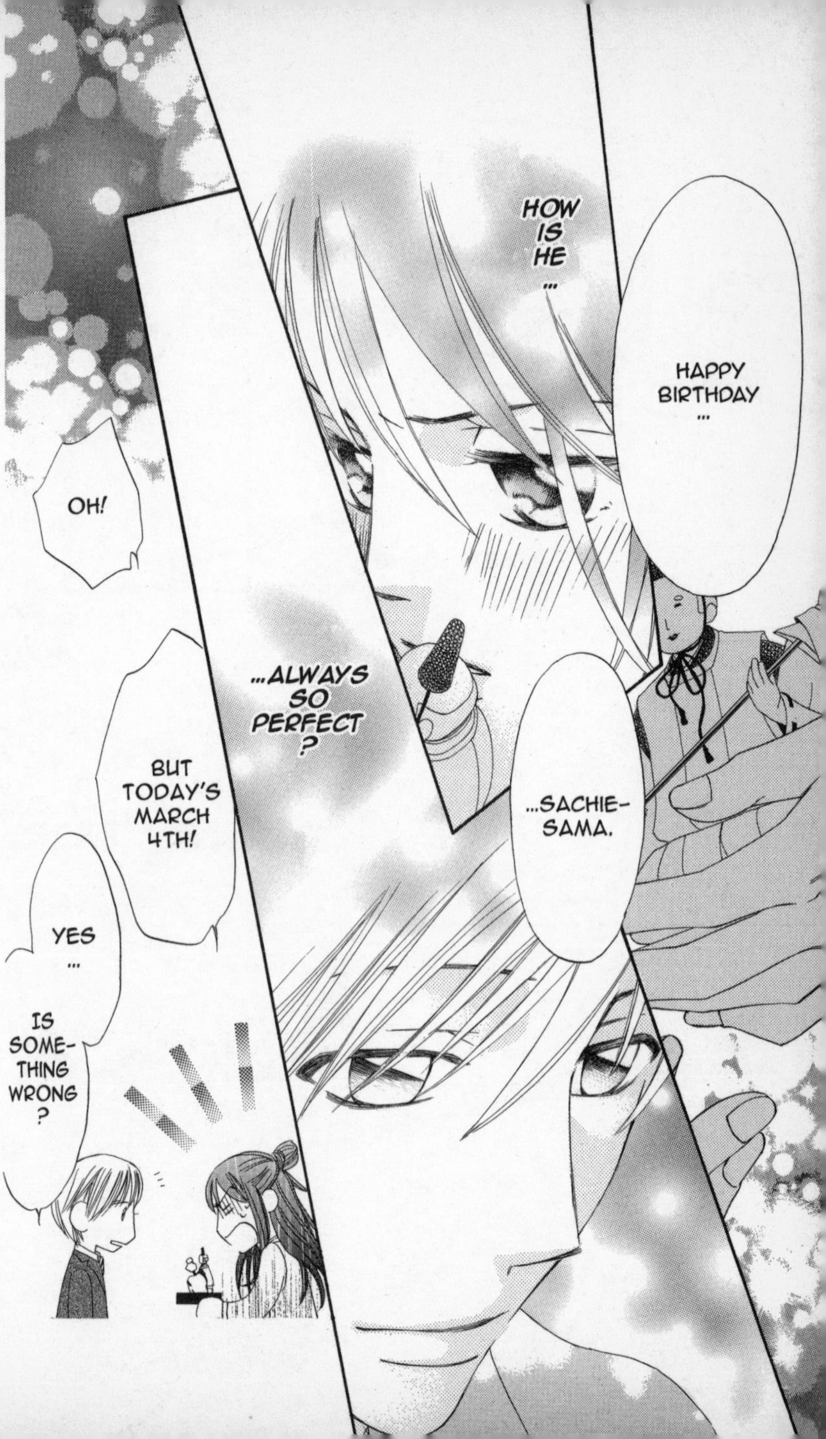
HAPPY BIRTHDAY ...
...SACHIE-SAMA.
HOW IS HE ...
...ALWAYS SO PERFECT?
OH!
BUT TODAY'S MARCH 4TH!
YES ...
IS SOMETHING WRONG?

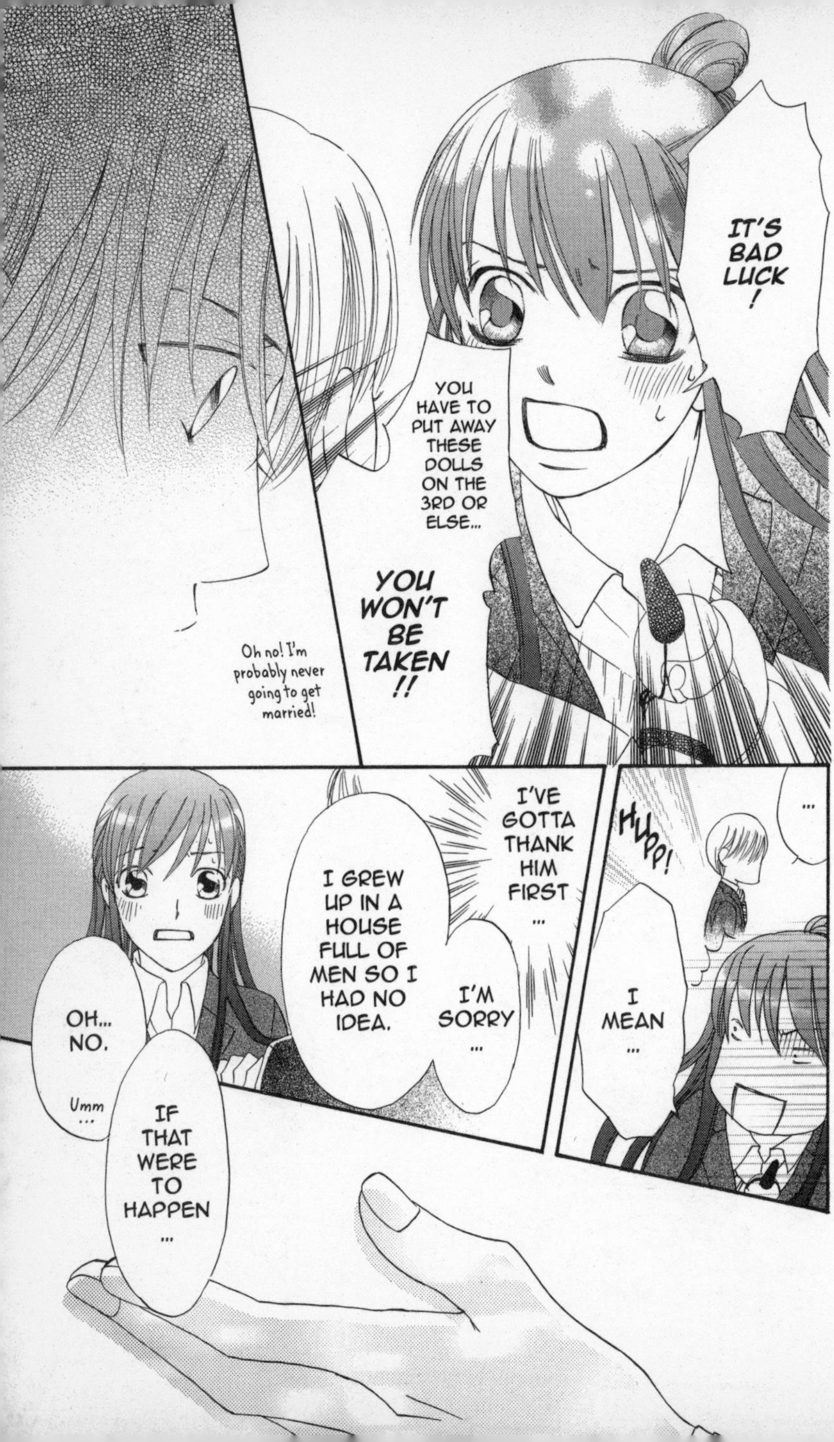
IT'S BAD LUCK!
YOU HAVE TO PUT AWAY THESE DOLLS ON THE 3RD OR ELSE...
YOU WON'T BE TAKEN!!
Oh no! I'm probably never going to get married!
...
HUPP!
I MEAN...
I'VE GOTTA THANK HIM FIRST...
I GREW UP IN A HOUSE FULL OF MEN SO I HAD NO IDEA.
I'M SORRY...
OH... NO.
Umm...
IF THAT WERE TO HAPPEN...

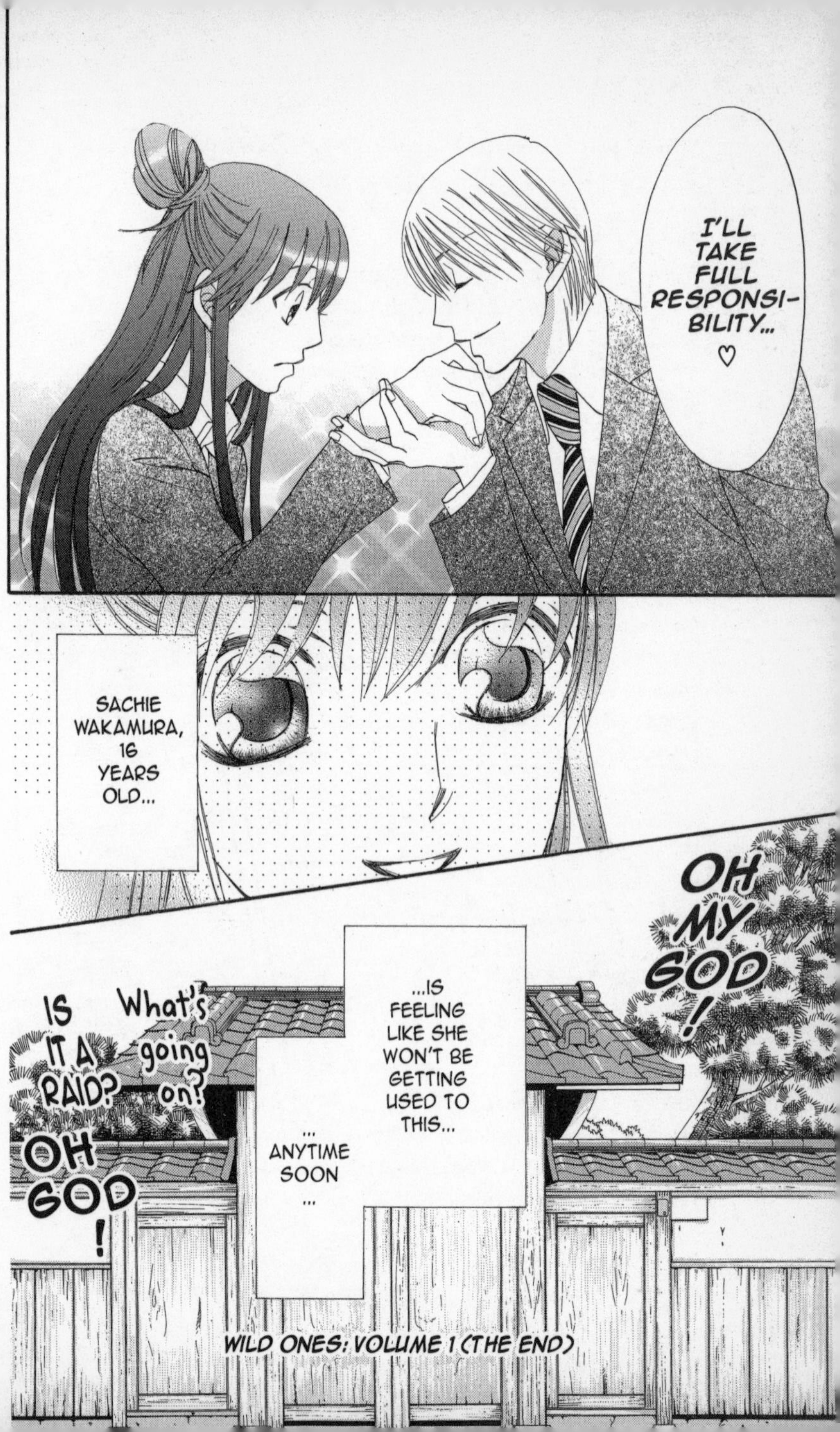
I'LL TAKE FULL RESPONSIBILITY... ♡
SACHIE WAKAMURA, 16 YEARS OLD...
OH MY GOD!
...IS FEELING LIKE SHE WON'T BE GETTING USED TO THIS...
... ANYTIME SOON ...
What's going on?
IS IT A RAID?
OH GOD!
WILD ONES: VOLUME 1 (THE END)

Wanna be part of the *Wild Ones* gang? Then you gotta learn the lingo! Here are some cultural notes to help you out!

HONORIFICS

San – the most common honorific title; it is used to address people outside one's immediate family and close circle of friends. (On page 29, one of the yakuza members asks Sachie to stop referring to her grandfather as "Asagi-san" because it makes their relationship seem formal and distant for family members.)

Chan – an informal version of "san" used to address children and females. "Chan" can be used as a term of endearment between women who are good friends. (On page 16, Yoshiko asks Sachie if she may call her "Sachie-chan" because she wants to be considered a close friend.)

Sama – the formal version of "san"; this honorific title is used primarily in addressing persons much higher in rank than oneself. "Sama" is also used when the speaker wants to show great respect or deference. (On page 10–and for pretty much the rest of the series–Rakuto calls Sachie "Sachie-sama" in addition to "princess.")

NOTES

Page 6, panel 5 - **Missing Pinky**
A missing pinky refers to *yubitsume*, or finger-cutting. Among the yakuza, the cutting of one's pinky is a form of penance or apology.

Page 21, panel 3 – **Yakuza**
Yakuza refers to Japanese organized crime in general or more specifically to its gang members.

Page 28, panel 2 - **Yukata**
The *yukata* is a garment that is worn in the summertime in Japan, especially to outdoor festivals and events. Though it resembles the more formal kimono, yukata are made out of cotton rather than silk.

Page 34, panel 5 – **Rai**
The kanji character for "Rai" in Raizo means thunder in Japanese.

Page 41, panel 3 – Takoyaki
Fried dough balls with pieces of octopus in it. This snack originated in Osaka and is often sold by street vendors.

Page 59, panel 2: Fudo
Fudo is a Buddhist deity who is often called upon for protection during dangerous times. He is frequently depicted with two protruding fangs that have one tooth pointing down (to represent his compassion to the world) and one tooth pointing up (to represent his passion for truth).

Page 101, panel 4: Osechi
Traditional Japanese New Year's foods. The dishes that make up *osechi* each have a special meaning for celebrating New Year's. For example, *kobu*, a type of seaweed, is associated with the word *yorokobu*, which means "joy."

Page 105, author's note: Karuta and Hyakunin Isshu
The poem game, otherwise known as *Hyakunin Isshu*, is a famous game using poems that is often played on New Year's. The beginning of a poem is read and the object of the game is to find the card with the correct ending quicker than your opponents.

Page 109, panel 2: New Year's Cards
It is customary in Japan to send postcards with New Year's greetings. They are delivered on New Year's Day.

Page 142, panel 5: "It's me!"
There's a common type of fraud in Japan where the caller cons the person he/she is calling by saying, "It's me!" The caller then asks for money after posing as a relative who needs help.

Page 155, panel 1: Animal Print
Yakuza are often associated with bright colors and loud animal prints such as tigers and dragons (also often depicted in their infamous tattoos).

Page 158, panel 6: Japanese Doll Festival
The Japanese Doll Festival (*Hina-matsuri*), or Girls' Day, takes place on March 3rd and involves the custom of displaying a set of ornamental dolls representing the Emperor, Empress, attendants, and musicians in traditional court dress of the Heian period.

Kiyo Fujiwara made her manga debut in 2000 in *Hana to Yume* magazine with *Bokuwane*. Her other works include *Hard Romantic-ker*, *Help!!* and *Gold Rush 21*. She comes from Akashi-shi in Hyogo Prefecture but currently lives in Tokyo. Her hobbies include playing drums and bass guitar and wearing kimono.

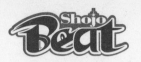

WILD ONES
VOL. 1
The Shojo Beat Manga Edition

This manga volume contains material that was originally published in English in *Shojo Beat* magazine, November 2007 issue. Artwork in the magazine may have been altered slightly from what is presented in this volume.

STORY AND ART BY
KIYO FUJIWARA

Translation & Adaptation/Mai Ihara
Touch-up Art & Lettering/Mark McMurray
Design/Hidemi Dunn
Editor/Amy Yu

Editor in Chief, Books/Alvin Lu
Editor in Chief, Magazines/Marc Weidenbaum
VP of Publishing Licensing/Rika Inouye
VP of Sales/Gonzalo Ferreyra
Sr. VP of Marketing/Liza Coppola
Publisher/Hyoe Narita

Printed in Canada

Published by VIZ Media, LLC
P.O. Box 77010
San Francisco, CA 94107

Shojo Beat Manga Edition
10 9 8 7 6 5 4 3 2 1
First printing, December 2007

www.viz.com

store.viz.com

PARENTAL ADVISORY
WILD ONES is rated T for Teen and is recommended for ages 13 and up. This volume contains suggestive themes.
RATED T FOR TEEN
ratings.viz.com

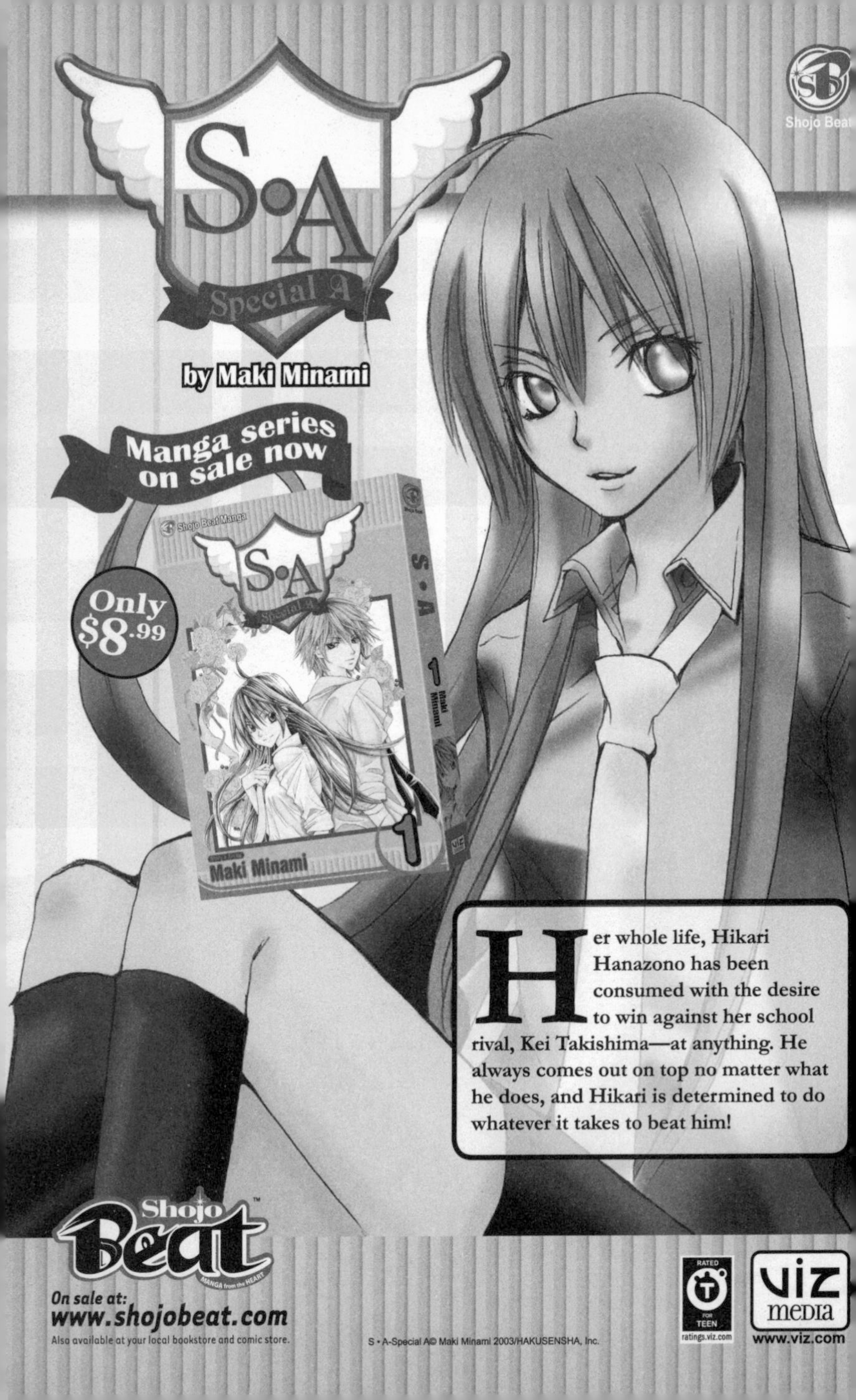
Shojo Beat
S•A
Special A
by Maki Minami
Manga series on sale now
Only $8.99
Shojo Beat Manga
S•A Special A
Maki Minami
1
Her whole life, Hikari Hanazono has been consumed with the desire to win against her school rival, Kei Takishima—at anything. He always comes out on top no matter what he does, and Hikari is determined to do whatever it takes to beat him!
Shojo Beat
MANGA from the HEART
On sale at:
www.shojobeat.com
Also available at your local bookstore and comic store.
S • A-Special A© Maki Minami 2003/HAKUSENSHA, Inc.
RATED T FOR TEEN
ratings.viz.com
VIZ media
www.viz.com

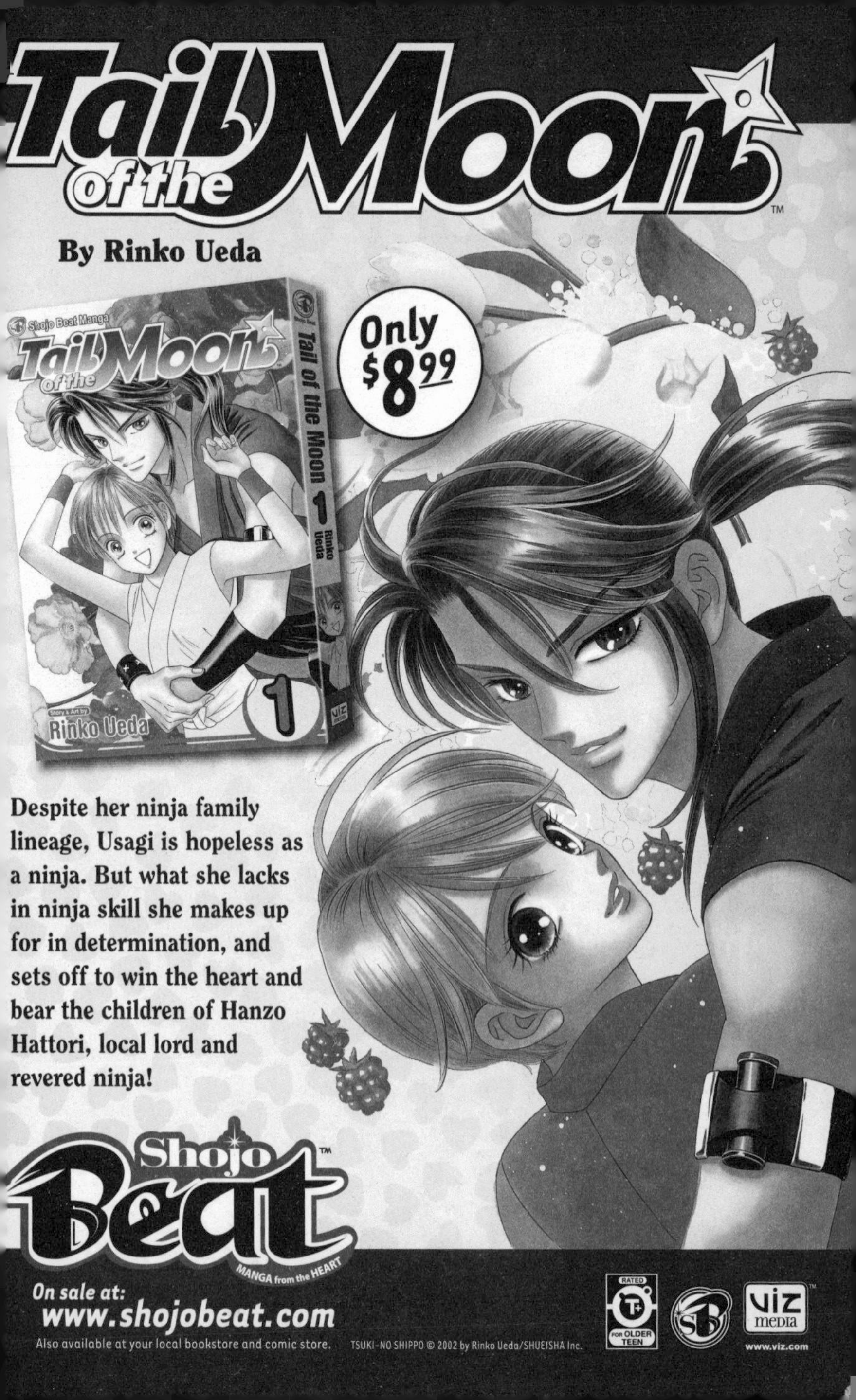
Tail of the Moon™
By Rinko Ueda
Shojo Beat Manga
Tail of the Moon
1
Rinko Ueda
Story & Art by
Rinko Ueda
Only $8.99
Despite her ninja family lineage, Usagi is hopeless as a ninja. But what she lacks in ninja skill she makes up for in determination, and sets off to win the heart and bear the children of Hanzo Hattori, local lord and revered ninja!
Shojo Beat™
MANGA from the HEART
On sale at:
www.shojobeat.com
Also available at your local bookstore and comic store.
TSUKI-NO SHIPPO © 2002 by Rinko Ueda/SHUEISHA Inc.
RATED T+ FOR OLDER TEEN
VIZ media
www.viz.com

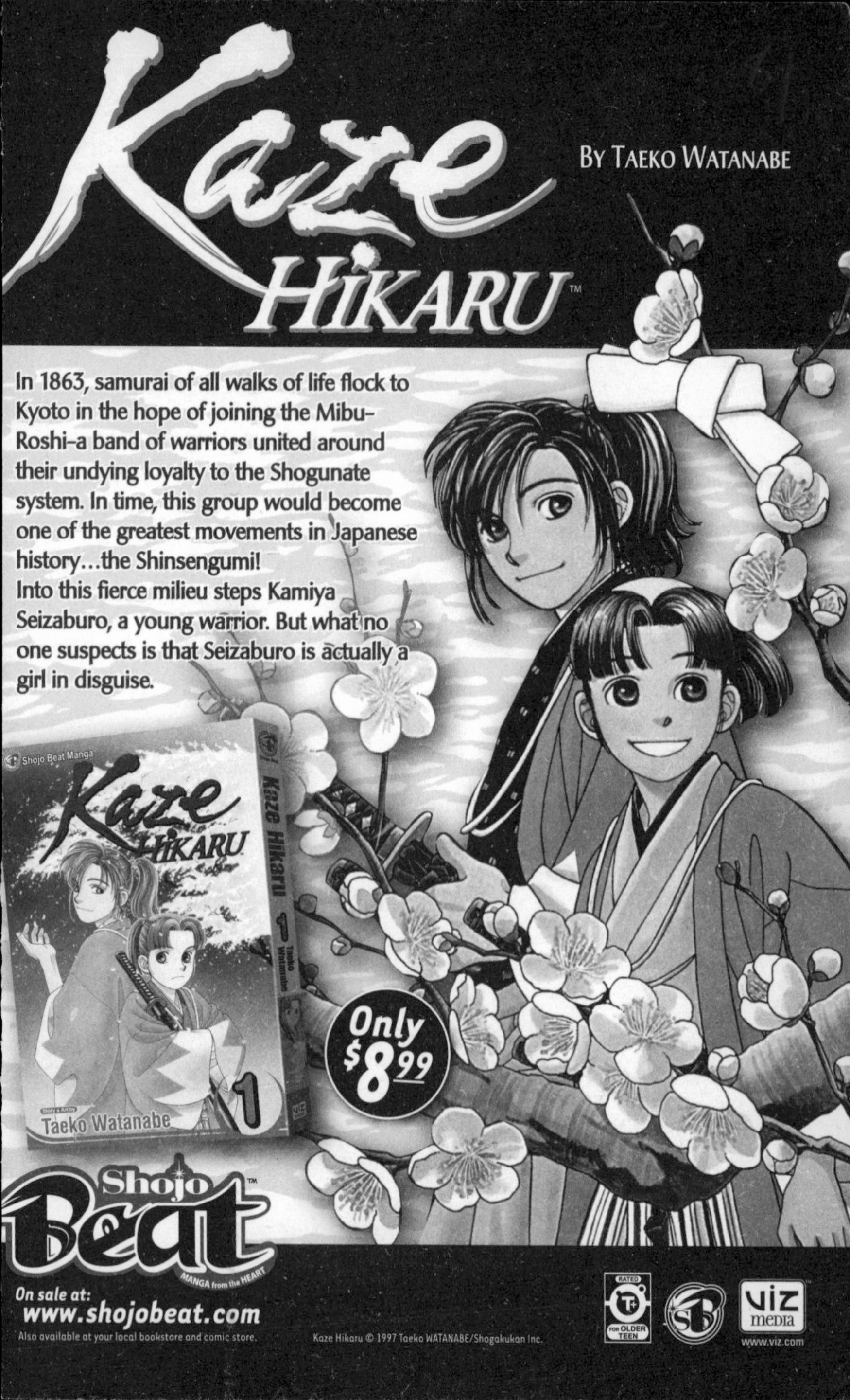

Kaze Hikaru™
By Taeko Watanabe
In 1863, samurai of all walks of life flock to Kyoto in the hope of joining the Mibu-Roshi–a band of warriors united around their undying loyalty to the Shogunate system. In time, this group would become one of the greatest movements in Japanese history…the Shinsengumi!
Into this fierce milieu steps Kamiya Seizaburo, a young warrior. But what no one suspects is that Seizaburo is actually a girl in disguise.
Shojo Beat Manga
Kaze Hikaru
Taeko Watanabe
Kaze Hikaru 1 Taeko Watanabe
Only $8.99
Shojo Beat™
MANGA from the HEART
On sale at:
www.shojobeat.com
Also available at your local bookstore and comic store.
Kaze Hikaru © 1997 Taeko WATANABE/Shogakukan Inc.
RATED T+ FOR OLDER TEEN
viz media
www.viz.com